BUDDHISM IN CENTRAL ASIA

BUDDHIST TRADITION SERIES

VOLUME 4

Buddhism in Central Asia

B.N. Puri

MOTILAL BANARSIDASS PUBLISHERS
PRIVATE LIMITED • DELHI

5th Reprint : Delhi, 2015
First Edition: Delhi, 1987

ISBN: 978-81-208-0372-5

MOTILAL BANARSIDASS
41 U.A. Bungalow Road, Jawahar Nagar, Delhi 110 007
8 Mahalaxmi Chamber, 22 Bhulabhai Desai Road, Mumbai 400 026
203 Royapettah High Road, Mylapore, Chennai 600 004
236, 9th Main III Block, Jayanagar, Bangaluru 560 011
8 Camac Street, Kolkata 700 017
Ashok Rajpath, Patna 800 004
Chowk, Varanasi 221 001

Printed in India
by RP Jain at New Age Books Printing Unit,
A-44, Naraina Industrial Area, Phase I, New Delhi–110028
and published by JP Jain for Motilal Banarsidass Publishers (P) Ltd,
41 U.A. Bungalow Road, Jawahar Nagar, Delhi-110007

FOREWORD

Central Asia is still an enormously important area of the world in a political sense, its vitality unabated. Buddhist texts were certainly disseminated into the Khotan area during the time of the 'Old Silk Road' (100 B.C. – A.D. 200). This road went from China to the Oriental Roman empire through Central Asia and had a branch extending down into Northwest India. A variety of dialects and dialect mixtures were current in Central Asia. Buddhism spread from India by way of the trade routes, in China starting with Tunhuang at the Western gateway. After the downfall of the Han in A.D. 220 Buddhism rapidly advanced and from about A.D. 300 had penetrated the high gentry clans in Northern China. When the Tibetan king Sroṅ-btsan sgam-po (b. A.D. 569) was converted to Buddhism by two Buddhist princesses, one Nepalese, the other Chinese, whom he married, he sent a mission to India (possibly Kashmir) to create a Tibetan alphabet. Then translations were begun in the seventh century, at first from both Sanskrit and Chinese, by end of that century just from Sanskrit.

B. N. Puri's work on Buddhism in Central Asia recounts these fascinating events. He has spared no inspection of previous scholarly work for his coverage of the main facts. Whether it be the history, the literature, realities of life, or the art, Puri maintains a firm control of the relevant supporting treatises. Students of Central Asia should welcome this addition to the topic and the bibliographical introduction. There are of course many specialized works on particular aspects of Central Asia but Puri's broad coverage is probably unique. Sixteen tastefully chosen plates add an artistic touch to this valuable addition for the Buddhist Traditions series.

ALEX WAYMAN

PREFACE

The study of Buddhism in Central Asia cannot be carried out in isolation, since it is related to several factors. Its introduction there was the result of religious missions as also of peaceful international relations. Traditional accounts, no doubt, suggest that Indian colonists settled in Khotan during the reign of Aśoka. This may not be accepted as final since no precise date can be fixed for the introduction of Buddhism in the Tarim basin. It is, however, evident that the religion of the Tathāgata was flourishing in Central Asia about the time of the Christian era. It was from there that Buddhism spread to China not later than the middle of the first century A.D. The enormous breadth of the landscape provided by Buddhism and Buddhist savants in Central Asia from China to the frontiers of Persia, during the course of a long period of nearly a millennium or more, with various races contributing to its growth from the Yuehchi and the Kuṣāṇas to the Uighurs, therefore, demands its comprehensive study. This study is to be undertaken against the background of the geographical area—its configuration and peoples—nomadic and sedentary, as also its location as the meeting ground of the Orient and the Occident. It was a two-way traffic with the role of Central Asian peoples in other countries, and that of others in different parts of this region.

The political history of Central Asia has to be studied in details since royal patronage to the creed of the Buddha was always forthcoming, as recorded by the Chinese pilgrims who passed through their kingdoms. Those lying on the Northern Route—Badakshan, Kashgar and Kucha—were great centres of the Sarvāstivādin school, while Mahāyānism dominated in Khotan and Yarkand. This demarcation of distinct representation symbolised two religious currents passing over these areas. The spread of the Sarvāstivādin school of Buddhism is no doubt connected with the growth of the Kuṣāṇa empire, maybe preceding the conversion of Kaniṣka as supposed by some scholars. Mahāyānism subsequently became more popular. The two schools were like coaches provided for travelling the same road to salvation, gradually absorbing the traffic awaiting the final journey. Names of Hindu rulers in the north and a long list of Vijaya monarchs of Khotan, available from the Kharoṣṭhī records which also mention purely Indian as also mixed names of donors and administrators, suggest the Indian way of life being adopted in the countries of the Tarim basin.

Those contributing towards the expansion of Buddhism in Central Asia, as also providing new dimensions included savants of different nationalities, besides the Indian ones. These comprised Tokharian, Parthian, Sogdian and Yuehchi scholars, some of whom were from royal families. The names of Dharmagupta from Kashghar, Sūryabhadra and Sūryasena from Chokkuka—Karghalik-Yarkand, Dharmskṣema, Śikṣānanda from Khotan, and, above all, Kumārajīva of Kucha and his contemporaries—Dharmamitra, Buddhayaśa, Buddhabhadra and many others, are notable for translating Buddhist texts into Chinese. The Buddhist literature discovered in Central Asia is equally abundant and, like its architecture, represents several periods, catering to the needs of both the schools. The fragments of the Sanskrit Āgamas from Turfan, Tun-huang, and in the Khotan district those of the dramas and Kāvyas of Aśvaghoṣa from Turfan, the *Prātimokṣa* of the Sarvāstivādins from Kucha and numerous versions of the anthology called Dharmapada or Udāna, with extracts in Tokharian and Sanskrit, may be noted in this context. The newer stratum of literature consists of Mahāyānist sūtras and includes *Prajñāpāramitā*, 'the Lotus of True Law'—*Saddharmapuṇḍarīka* and *Suvarṇaprabhāsa Sūtra* —translated into Uighur and Iranian oriental, and to a still later period the *dhāraṇīs* or magical formulae which have been found in great numbers. Turkish sūtras discovered at Turfan contain a discourse of the Buddha to the merchants Trapuṣa and Bhallika. Buddhist texts in Kuchean, Tokharian, Sogdian and Bactrian Greek have also been traced. A survey of the Buddhist literature and the contribution of the Buddhist savants have been made separately. The relation of Buddhism to other religions, especially Manichaeism and Nestorian Christianity was in tune with the eclectic and tolerant spirit of the peoples of Central Asia. Tibetan Lamaism and its acceptance in Mongolia suggests that Buddhism provided a creed acceptable in different forms to superstitious, emotional and metaphysical minds.

The study of material culture in Central Asia provides an insight into cultural integration and people's life, manifested through different facets—with joint family ties, position of women, items of food and food habits, dress and ornaments, pastime and recreations, agricultural and pastoral economy, trade and transport and several other items related to the socio-economic life. It is interesting to find Buddhist monks owning land and slaves, and participating in the material life of the time. Buddhism, thus, provided a living and a changing stream of thought adaptable to men of different emotional backgrounds. New forms of Buddhism providing a moral ideal and not personal perfection or individual salvation were evolved with Buddhas and Bodhisattvas serving as angels of mercy, peace and knowledge. These are manifest in Central Asian art. These Bodhisattvas are supposed to have indefinitely postponed their nirvāṇa process for the sake of alleviating the sufferings of mankind, while faith in a Buddha, especially in Amitābha could secure rebirth in his paradise.

Factors accounting for this change in the gospel of Buddhism were both internal or Indian, and external. The Indian factor, involving development of both Brahmanism and Buddhism in a parallel way with more areas of similarities in thought and action, seems to have emanated from Taxila—Takṣaśilā, the great centre of learning, as also from Kashmir which provided the largest number of Buddhist savants to Central Asia, and from thence to China. Foreign influence was the product of all those who contributed to Buddhism after accepting it in their way of life. Greeks, Parthians, Śakas and Kuṣāṇas were greatly responsible for stimulation to Buddhist mythology and imagery. When Buddhism passed into the hands of those foreigners, especially Greeks, who were accustomed to Greek statuary, the desire to venerate Buddhist personalities, especially the figures of Buddha and the Bodhisattvas, took a definite shape on the western model without alienating Indian characteristic features.

The Central Asian artists—some being imported from the region of Gandhāra and including Greeks, like Titus at Miran, were inspired by Greek tradition as modified in Rome. Native tradition, however, accepted and adopted these artistic influences with discrimination. With the expansion of Buddhism in Central Asia and setting up of stūpas and free-standing shrines, the demand for artists and sculptors shot up. Commercial enterprise on the trade routes with the patronage and contribution of traders and merchants provided incentives for artists who received handsome payments for their service. Well-defined styles of Central Asian paintings are the result of contributions and impacts of different art traditions—Indian, Persian and Chinese. The common factor, however, is the Buddha and his legend. Diversities in design and treatment did not rule out an identical mannerism in the same composition at different places. A study of the Central Asian Centres of art with particular reference to paintings at Buddhist Cave Shrines, lying on the Northern as well as the Southern routes, would not fail to reveal, in a way, the competitive spirit of the votaries of the Buddha in venerating their lord. They displayed their artistic talents in projecting new forms of Buddhist ideals for the masses.

A comprehensive study of Buddhism in Central Asia is, thus, attempted in this work, taking into account all the factors and forces responsible for its introduction, prosperity, and eventual decay and decline. Nature no doubt provided complete shelter to Buddhist art treasures and polyglot libraries which were sealed off to protect them from vandalists and marauders. These lay enveloped till the spade of explorers and archaeologists could reveal the mysterious past of Buddhism in this vast area of the Tarim basin studded with sites and spots which are separated by considerable distances, and which were once humming with the spiritual and temporal activities of the people wedded to the religion of the Buddha.

The present study fulfils the demand of the Indian Council of Historical Research, New Delhi, which provided me a fellowship as also contingency expenses towards its successful completion. I am grateful to the Council.

This work is dedicated to the memory of my younger daughter Taruna, who left us over seven years back in a road accident. Her memory is ever fresn and green and is a source of constant incentive for me to work with dedication.

B. N. Puri

CONTENTS

PLATES (after p. 352)

CHAPTER I

INTRODUCTION

The term Central Asia is supposed to connote the Tarim Basin, with the inclusion of neighbouring regions such as the Oxus region and Badakshan. This basin is a depression, surrounded on three sides by high mountains. On the north it is bounded by the Tien-Shan 'the Celestial Mountain', while the snowy Kiun-Lun on the south separates it from the Tibetan part of Central Asia. To the west, the Pamirs, the 'Imaos' of the ancients, join the Tien-Shan to the Hindu Kush, giving rise to the head-waters of the Oxus on its western flank. On the east, the barrier dividing it from China is relatively low. The water of the entire area is discharged through the many branched Tarim river into Lake Lob-Nor—only a flooded morass. The basin is a desert with occasional oases lying chiefly near its edges. There might have been more fertile portions in the past, but this remote and lonely region has only provided interest for exploration among archaeologists and explorers of different nationalities within the last hundred years or more. Its complete isolation from oceanic influences as also its geographical insularity have no doubt contributed to evolving its own cultural pattern with the contribution of warring tribes of this as well as the neighbouring areas in the past. While in the north the *taiga,* the Siberian forest zone serves as a barrier for any communication, in the south an almost unbroken chain of mountain ranges, nearly four thousand miles or six thousand four hundred kilometres long running from China to the Black Sea restricts any access in the direction of the South-East Asia, the Indian Sub-continent and the Middle East. Only certain sections of this long chain of mountain ranges—the Hindu Kush, the Paropamisus and the Elburz have never restricted the movements of peoples in either direction. The two plateaux—Tibet on the south, enclosed by the Himalayas, and Iran, flanked on the south-east by the Kirthar and Sulaiman ranges, and on the south-west by the Zagros, have provided historical links with Central Asia proper.

The eastern and western limits of Central Asia are not properly defined. In the east, the Great Wall of China could provide an approximate line, while in the west the grasslands of the Ukraine extending as far as Rumania and Hungary supposedly provide both a geographical and historical extension of the Central Asian steppe zone.[1] This might be an exaggerated concept of Central Asian western limit, but it is now accepted that the vast region in its geographical and political aspects need not extend beyond Iran, especially its eastern part. The physical features of Central Asia with its predominant steppe and desert area, include some of the highest mountain ranges in the world as also depressions like those around Turfan in Sinkiang and the area north-east of the Caspian with extreme rise of temperature. This last region of Central Asia lying approximately between latitude 35°N and 55°N could be divided in a convenient manner into a northern and a southern zone separated by a line along the Syr Darya and the Tien-Shan. The northern zone with its sufficient moisture, provided extensive grazing ground for pastoral peoples, while the southern one was primarily an urban area and oasis society with extensive cultivation of land through skilful application of irrigational techniques for agricultural purposes. Shortage of water no doubt required hard and laborious efforts in storage of rain water into reservoirs. The clash between the northern nomads and the settled and domesticated peoples of the southern region was natural. The nomadic peoples north of the Tien-Shan from time to time plundered and occupied the oases of the

1. G. Hambly. *Central Asia* (London, 1969)—henceforth Hambly, p. 2. In contemporary Soviet usage the geographical term 'Central Asia' has rather different connotation from the term as it is normally used in western Europe. It includes the territory of the Uzbek, Tadzhik, Turkmenian and Kirghiz Republics and the southern part of the Kazakh Republic, but excludes eastern Turkestan, Mongolia and Tibet which are covered by the western European term (Aleksandr Belenitsky : *Central Asia* translated by James Hogarth—London (date not mentioned)—henceforth *Belenitsky*, p. 15.

Tarim Basin without making their occupation a permanent feature.

The configuration of the mountain ranges has no doubt exercised control over the movements of peoples of Central Asia from one region to the other. So also the influence of the deserts has been profound in this direction. Geographical factors, thus, tended to segregate civilizations bordering on its peripheries—Indian, Iranian and Chinese in the past. The ancient caravan routes provided not only mutual information but also established some sort of limited but important contact between the two extreme ends—China and Iran and the western world. Of course, in terms of commerce and cultural achievements there have been only some important parts of Central Asia, as for instance the one between the Amu-Darya (Oxus) and the Syr-Darya (Jaxartes), and the area known as Khurasan to the Arabs, which lay to the south of the Amu-Darya and extended south-west as far as the Iranian Dasht-i-Kavir. Between the middle reaches of the Amu-Darya and the Syr-Darya lay the country known to the Greeks as Transoxania, and to the Arabs as Mawarannahr, with Bukhara and Samarkand as its most important urban centres in the medieval period. The latter has no doubt an old history of its own, tracing its antiquity to the period of Alexander's invasion, or even earlier. There were many other centres of importance—political and cultural—in the medieval period. Khwarazm on the lower reaches of the Amu-Darya, Shash, north-east from Mawarannahr beyond the Syr-Darya comprising the country round Tashkent, were other areas of importance in the medieval period. For the earlier period one has to follow the ancient caravan routes linking China with the west, which passed through many centres. These caravan trade routes are also described as 'Silk Routes' or 'Silk Roads', transgressing the Central Asian forbidden no-man's land. While geographical factors provided insularity and security to the Central Asian peoples, with the Lop and Gobi deserts in the east, the long chains of the Tien-Shan and the Kun-Luns to the north and south respectively and the Pamirs to the west linked to the Kun-Luns by the Karakoram ranges, man triumphed over natural barriers and successfully crossed the hurdles lying in his way.

Silk, one of China's chief mercantile commodities became the key word along the general trade and transport routes. It was along these routes that not only traders and merchants moved from one direction to the other, but Chinese pilgrims and Indian Buddhist savants covered long distances to satisfy their intellectual curiosity as also to convey the message of the Tathāgata in the language of the peoples of those areas where these scholars were invited or where they finally settled down. The expansion of Buddhism in Central Asia is closely linked with the silk trade routes and the centres associated with these communication lines as also the settlements and the sylvain retreats nearby for meeting the seclusive requirements of the Buddhist monks. The finds of monuments associated with Buddhism no doubt confirm this affirmation. A study of Buddhism in Central Asia would demand fuller reference to the land and its peoples, as also to its physical and political geography in depth, and also to the nature of migratory movements of these peoples and its impact on the areas lying with the peripheries of Central Asia.

This interior portion of Asia is at present divided politically into three parts : a Soviet one, a Chinese one and Mongolia. The Soviet part of Central Asia was called Turan, now referred to as Russian or Western Turkestan. It includes the present territory of Uzbek, Tadzhik, Turkmanian and Kirghiz Republics and the southern part of the Kazakh Republic. The Chinese part, historically known as Chinese Turkestan, is now represented by Sinkiang-Uighur Autonomous Region. It is bordered on the north-east by the Mongolian Peoples' Republic, on the south-west by Kashmir and a narrow strip of Afghanistan, and on the west and north by the Central Asian Republics of the Soviet Union. Sinkiang, physiographically, consists of two mountain-ringed basins from the east-west treading Tien-Shan. The Dzungarian basin in the north, with an elevation of 600 to 1500 ft., receiving summer rainfall, makes it an ideal grazing land, while the Tarim basin with an elevation of 2500 to 3000 ft., more arid than Dzungaria, has the sandy Takla Makan desert in the centre and the salt lake and marsh land of Lop Nor, at the eastern end. Thus, Central Asia, as a whole, is a land of sharp geographical contrasts with the greater part of the area occupied by high mountain systems or great deserts, unfavourable for human settlement. Many of its river valleys, however, with their fertile loess soil, have been occupied by settled population from very early times.

It has, no doubt, been established by archaeological investigations and explorations that man appeared in Central Asia as early as the Palaeolithic period and continues to be in occupation of some part or the other since then, and has been in communication with peoples of the Orient and the Occident. The continental forces have never been lull and the role of the peoples of Central Asia has always been significant in the history of other countries as also in the export of tribal culture in those areas. It is proposed[2] that the wild horse was first domesticated on the steppes of Central Asia and that it was from this region that the horse-culture—the use of the horse for driving and later on for riding—gradually spread to other parts of the world. Many objects associated with horses, the saddle and the stirrup of the later times, had their origin in Central Asia. As horse riding became very common, so also the custom of wearing trousers spread from Central Asia to other parts of Asia and Europe. Another product closely associated with horse riding, namely boots, gradually replaced the slippers and sandals, which were universally worn. At a later time the Central Asian people also initiated the custom of putting heels on boots and shoes. As such, the contribution of Central Asia to the diffusion of culture has been significant and the role of this region is considered still more important in the transmission of cultural traits from one part of the world to another.

The exchange of cultural traits between East and West also took place by way of Central Asia. New inventions, ideas,

2. McGovern : *Early Empires of Central Asia*, Chapel Hill, 1939 —henceforth—*McGovern*, p. 2. Horses are known to have existed sporadically at a very early time in different parts of the old world. They were certainly known to the vase-painters of Anau, of Tripolye, and of North-Western China, but among these peoples horses remained relatively unimportant adjuncts. With the northern nomads, on the other hand, the horse played an all important role, and the spread of these Nomads into other regions is always associated with the spread of horses and horsemanship (*op. cit*, p. 36). For the close association of the horse with the Aryans, see Childe : *The Aryans*, p. 83.

manners and customs were transmitted from one region to another transgressing political boundaries. Constant exchanges between East and West were provided through this region of the world—from Europe or the Near East to the East, India and China, as also in the reverse direction. These exchanges of cultural traits started long before the period of written history. Excavations at Anau[3] in Central Asia suggest that the ancient civilization here provided a link between the early Near Eastern and Far Eastern civilization. In historical times, too, Alexander's invasion provided cultural stimulus to the Far East through the peoples of Central Asia. The emergence of the well-known Greek school of art, also called Greco-Buddhist Art, exerted a widespread influence in different parts of Turkestan and eventually reached China where it revolutionised the indigenous school of painting and sculpture.[4] It is proposed that the importation of Greco-Roman glass through Central Asia into the celestial Empire of China had a profound influence on local workmanship, and indirectly contributed to the invention of Chinese porcelain. It was also through Central Asia that China imported from Iran alfalfa and grape vine, and that country also contributed towards the development of Chinese armour as also its military strategy. Manicheanism, a third century Persian religion and for a long time a rival of Christianity in Central Asia, could also secure a foothold in China. Central Asia also estab-

3. For the excavations at Anau, see R. Pumpley : *Explorations in Turkestan* (Washington, 1903-04) and also his *Pre-historic Anau* (Washington, 1905-08).

4. Bachhofer in his work '*A Short History of Chinese Art*' (London, 1944)—henceforth—Bachhofer=*Chinese Art* refers to the existence of Buddhist sculpture of the Khotanese type in northern China. According to him, rarely in the history of sculpture can the origin of certain forms be so exactly located as in the case of the large standing Maitreya in bronze, now in the Metropolitan Museum, New York. They had been taken over lock, stock and barrel from the clay and mud statues of Kucha in Central Asia. This particular style of representing a garment had developed there as an imitation of the mature stucco sculpture of the Kushāṇas in north-western India and Afghanistan. Chinese Buddhists and sculptors in the second half of the fifth century looked upon them as Buddhist statutory par excellence; they took them as models and endeavoured to copy them as faithfully as possible. (*Op. cit*, pp. 65-66). See also Waldschmidt, E; *Gandhāra, Kutscha, Turfan* (Leipzig, 1925).

lished communication between India and China, and it was from here that Buddhism spread to China.[5] Many of the early missionaries carrying the message of the Buddha to the land of Confucius were not from India but native scholars of Central Asia.

China, in return, also transmitted cultural traits of its own to the Near and Middle East.[6] Many features of her civilization were passed on the same channel. Peach and apricot, as also ginger and tea and several other items were indigenous Chinese products which were introduced into the western world through Central Asia. It was in the time of Augustus that Chinese silk reached Rome, and for several centuries the import of silk from China was a regular feature of the commercial activity of the Roman Empire. The Great Silk Road from China to Rome passed through Central Asia, and the control of this Road, occasionally became a subject of dispute leading to important political changes. It is also suggested that the art of paper making discovered by the Chinese in the second century A.D. was carried through Central Asia to the Arabs in the eighth century, and the European method of paper making is merely a copy of the old Chinese craftsmanship. The issue of paper currency, well-known in China, was taken to Persia during the thirteenth century by the Mongols, a Central Asian people, whose extensive empire covered both China and Persia. Several other instances could be quoted like the art of printing of books, known in China as early as the beginning of the tenth century, which were taken from the Chinese and then developed in the West.

Role of Central Asian Peoples

While Central Asia provided cultural stimuli and also served as a transmitting centre in communication between the Far East

5. The story of the first contact between India and China is mixed up with legend. It is proposed by Bagchi that Buddhist missionaries from India made their first appearance in the Chinese capital as early as 217 B.C. under the Tsin dynasty. This story has no historical confirmation. It is, however, known through an undisputed authority that in the year 2 B.C. Buddhist texts and images were first presented to the Chinese court by the Yueh-chi rulers. Buddhist missionaries certainly did not arrive in China before the year A.D. 65. (Bagchi : *India and China*, Greenwood Press, West Port, Connecticut, 1975, p. 6).

6. For a fuller account—see McGovern : *Op. cit.*

Oriental and the Occidental world, the role of the peoples of this region in the history of Asia and Europe also deserves consideration. In fact, this participation has been the result of a long series of migrations and invasions carried out by the warring tribes claiming Central Asia as their homeland through the ages. From earliest times Central Asia had at least two distinct and separate racial and linguistic groups, called the Scythians and the Huns. The former are supposed to belong to the 'Great White race', speaking an Aryan or Indo-European language. The Huns, however, belonged to the 'Great Yellow race' with a good deal of Mongoloid blood, and speaking a language different from the former and generally termed as Turanian or Ural-Altaic. The Scythian or Indo-European element in the population of Central Asia was dominant in the region now called Turkestan and it was here that the members of this group, pressed by political as well as economic forces, spread outward in all directions.[7] The Scythian migrations had greater impact upon the regions to the south of Turkestan, sweeping over the Persian Plateau and into North-Western India where they settled down permanently, shaking off their nomadic norms and habits. Those Scythians left in Turkestan, however, retained their nomadic habits and were not slow to invade their kinsmen to the south, leading to permanent conquest and occupation. The Scythian group in Parthia ruled there for nearly five centuries, establishing political control over the agricultural population of the Persian Plateau. The position in North-West India (now Pakistan) was, however, different with several Scythian groups ruling one after another.

The Hunnish group, consisting of various tribes generally spoken of as Hiung-nu, a term given by the Chinese to their adversaries, dominated that region of Central Asia, called Mongolia. The unified Hunnish empire posed danger to the security of China. Earlier, the Great Wall of China was built in 214 B.C. to keep the Hunnish nomads out of bounds from the fertile plains of the Yellow River. The Chinese no doubt managed to prevent the Huns from securing a permanent footing in China till the close of the third century A.D. The centuries

7. McGovern : *Op. cit*, pp. 6ff.

following, however, witnessed the turn of fortunes[8] with the Huns becoming masters of all Northern China. The Hiung-nu or Huns also moved westward and dislodged the Yueh-chi from their homeland who, in turn, clashed with the Wu-Suns and overpowered them. The latter with the support of the Hiung-nu had another clash with the Yueh-chi, compelling them to leave westwards, and occupy the territory of the Sakas, called Ta-hia. After settling down, they were no longer nomads and had divided their territory into five principalities, of which the Kuei-Shuang was the most important. The capital of the kingdom of Ta-Yueh-chi was Kien-chi (Lan-chu) with Ki-pin lying on its southern frontier. In the *Annals of the Later Han Dynasty*, the Yueh-chi capital is Lan-shi, the old capital in Badakshan, and it also refers to the integration of five principalities by the Kuei-shuang prince Kieou-Stsieou-Kio (Kujula Kadphises) who styled himself as king.

The movements of these wild tribes and their occupation of Bactria is also noticed by classical Greek and Latin writers. Strabo mentions a Saka conquest of Bactria[9] where the Greek kings were ousted by Scythian nomads, and some of these nomadic tribes are mentioned by him, notably the Asioi, Pasianoi, Tocharoi and Sakarauloi. Trogus also provides an account in the 41st Book, while dealing with the establishment of an empire in Bactria by Diodotus about the middle of the 3rd century B.C., of the way the Scythian tribes, the Saraucae and the Asiani took possession of Bactria and Sogdiana. In this connection, according

8. While Turkestan was ruled by the Scythians, Mongolia in this period was dominated by various Hunnish tribes, generally spoken of as Hiung-nu, a term given by the Chinese. The Great Wall of China was built in 214 B.C. to keep the Hunnish nomads out of the fertile plains of the yellow river. Shortly afterwards the Hunnish inhabitants of Mongolia integrated themselves to form a single empire which in one form or another lasted for over three hundred years (B.C. 209—A.D. 160). McGovern : *Op. cit*, p. 18.

9. The references to the Yueh-chi and their relations with the Kuei-shuang-Kuṣāṇas, as recorded in the classical Greek and Latin sources, are recorded in full and considered in detail in my work *India under the Kuṣāṇas*, pp. 5ff. and note pp. 10ff.—henceforth Puri—*Kuṣāṇas* with comprehensive bibliographical details. The political history of this Central Asian dynasty in India is discussed in detail in this work.

to Justin, the Bactrians lost both their empire and their freedom being harassed by the Sogdians, the Drangae and the Arii, and were finally oppressed by the Parthians. Further information relating to the Asiani becoming kings of the Tocharians and of the annihilation of the Saraucae is provided by Trogus in the 'Prologus' of the 42nd book. The Asiani are identified by Sten Konow with the Yueh-chi of the Chinese Annals. According to the late Norwegian Professor, the Tocharians were well-settled in and to the east of Bactria, when the Yueh-chi became their masters. The relations of the Kuṣāṇas with the Yueh-chi, either as one of the five Yab-gou or tribe of the big pastoral race, or as one of those five clans or kingdoms which became dependent on the Ta-Yueh-chi after their conquest of the Ta-hia is evident from the Chinese annals. The capital of the Yueh-chi became the old Ta-hia capital Lan-shi in Badakshan which remained their stronghold down to the fifth century A.D. The Yueh-chi occupied the whole of Ta-hia country in the period of the Hou-Han-Shu. According to Chavannes, henceforth they are Ta-hia.

The Kuṣāṇas supposed to be an important branch of the Yueh-chi finally succeeded in consolidating their hold and established a vast empire from the southern parts of Central Asia, including Afghanistan to Bihar in India, and from Kashmir to Sind (now in Pakistan) in the south-west. It was in fact the Kuṣāṇas who were instrumental in bringing out an integration of peoples of different nationalities into a single political fabric. A detailed study of the Kuṣāṇa history in the context of political unification as also their contribution to Buddhism, would, however, be made later on. In this context of the role of the Central Asian people, it may be pointed out that the Huns who had pushed out or absorbed the Scythians or Indo-European peoples, slowly moved westward. By the fifth century A.D. they had complete control over all parts of Turkistan, and in a clash with their immediate neighbours the Sassanids, they defeated them and forced them to pay tribute. The Huns moved further west and set up their kingdom in the middle Danube basin[10] and

10. McGovern : *Op. cit*, p. 385. The centre of the Hunnish kingdom in this period was the middle Danube basin, corresponding to the Austro-Hungarian domain of the nineteenth century.

extended their tentacles in different directions, dominating over other tribes.

References might as well be made of the Hephthalite Huns, also called the White Huns[11] who originally lived in the Altai region and are mentioned by the Persian historians as Hayathelite and the Chinese as Ye-ta or Hephtha, and in Indian records as Huna. In the beginning of the 5th century they were an important people who owed allegiance to another nomadic tribe of Turkish origin called Juan-Juans in Mongolia. In the second quarter of the same century they started spreading westwards and conquered the entire steppe area upto the Aral. Their territory included the valley of the Ili up to the Balkash, the valley of the Issiq-kul. The steppes of Chu and Chao, and the valley of the Jaxartes upto Aral, they occupied Sogdiana and Tokharestan by A.D. 440, and probably Balkh followed suit about the same time. Akhsunwar of the White Huns invaded Khorasan in 484 and killed king Peroz. In the South they clashed with a branch of the Kuṣāṇas, known as Kidāra Kuṣāṇas, named after their king Kidāra, ruling in Tokharestan. The latter crossed the Hindu Kush and settled down in the Kabul valley, after ousting the later Kuṣāṇas from that region. The Hephthalites, in the meantime, consolidated their position in Tokharestan and with their conquest of Talekhar, Mervard, Herat and later on of Gandhāra extended their dominion further South-east. Subsequently they crossed the Indus and invaded India. At that time the Hun empire had reached its zenith, including the entire steppe from the upper Yulduz (north of Karasahr) to the Aral and Sogdiana, Merv, Eastern Iran, Afghanistan and the Punjab.

The role of the Central Asian peoples in the centuries following is equally notable. In the sixth century, the Huns were succeeded by the Turks as overlords of Turkestan. The Turks, closely affiliated to the Huns, both in race and language, proved more dangerous to their neighbours than their predecessors. For some time they made occasional inroads into Persian territory, but finally the Seljuk Turks overran the whole of Persia and were soon masters of all the countries in the Near East. The

11. For a succinct account of the Hephthalite Huns, see—Bagchi : *India and Central Asia*, Calcutta, 1955, pp. 9ff—henceforth—Bagchi—*Central Asia*.

Turks are mentioned in the Chinese accounts as Tu-Kiu i.e. Turkut, meaning 'strong', and according to Bagchi,[12] they are known in Indian literature as Turuṣka. They were descendants of the ancient Hiung-nu race and were living towards the beginning of the sixth century A.D. in the region of Altai mountains as dependents of the Juan-Juans. The internecine struggle among the ruling class chieftains paved the way for the emergence of the Turks to absolute power and alienation with the former overlords. The Turks too were divided into Eastern and Western groups.

Reference might as well be made to the Parthians and Sogdians and their interest in Buddhism and its expansion. While Parthian relations with India could be traced to the Achaemenian times, and Parthian satrapies were established in North-West India (now Pakistan) before the Christian era, these did not result in the inflow of Buddhist culture to Iran—the region occupied by the Parthians. It was the Tokharians who seem to have transmitted Buddhism in that region and attracted Parthians to the religion of the Tathāgata. The Parthian monks studied Buddhism and the original Buddhist texts in the Buddhist centres of Tokharestan, like Balkh before proceeding to China, where these monks are distinguished by the prefix An (Ngan), named after their country An-She (Arsak). A Parthian prince is said to have appeared in the western country of China with a load of Buddhist texts in the year 148 A.D.—the date of the commencement of the war and the downfall of the Arsacidan dynasty. The contribution of the Parthian monks towards Buddhist textual translations need not be assessed here, though the flow of such monks from Parthia to China could be traced in the 3rd and 4th centuries A.D.[13]

12. The role of the Turks is also assessed by Bagchi in the chapter on 'Nomadic Movements in Central Asia' in his book *India and Central Asia*, Op. cit, pp. 10ff).

13. A reference to the contributions by Parthian scholars is made by Bagchi : *Op. cit*, pp. 36ff. The Parthian prince visiting China is known to the Chinese as Ngan She-Kao or Lokottama. He abdicated the throne in favour of his uncle and became a Buddhist monk at an early age. He left for China and reached Lo-yang in A.D. 144 where he settled down in the monastery of Po-ma-Sse or 'The White Horse Monastery' built for the first two Indian monks, Dharmaratna and Kāśyapa Mātaṅga.

Besides the Parthians, the Sogdians are also worth recording in this context. Ancient Sogdiana was situated to the north of Tokharestan with its centre at Samarkand. The earliest reference to the country and its people could be traced to the Achaemenian records and the Greek historian Herodotus. The Behistun inscription describes them as Suguda, while the Greek historian calls them Sogdoi with Xorasmioi, Areioi (Haraiva), Parthoi, Gandarioi and Dadixai as their neighbours. The Achaemenian inscriptions, however, mention Parthians, Arienas, Sogdians, Xorazmians, Bactrians, Zarankes, Sakas and Gandarians. Sogdians, primarily traders, had gone to different parts of Central Asia and established colonies, and they were in contact with Buddhism and its culture in other parts of Central Asia. Sogdian monks also played their part in the transmission of Buddhist culture to China,[14] and were noted by the prefix K'ang, after the ancient name of Sogdiana in Chinese Kang-Kiu.

The Tibetans and the Mongols are the two other important people who effectively contributed towards Buddhism and its expansion in Central Asia in the early and later medieval times respectively. The Tibetans, a Mongoloid people, inhabited the Tibetan plateau and lived in isolation for a long time, with nothing known about their history prior to the seventh century A.D. It is generally accepted that Buddhism was first preached in Tibet at the instance of King Srong-tsan-gam-po, who ascended the throne in A.D. 629. The Tibetans, like the Chinese, had heard something about it either from India or Khotan in Central Asia, before they invited Indian preachers to visit them. According to tradition the Tibetan ruler Thonmi Sambhoṭa was sent to India for evolving Tibetan script which was borrowed from the Indian Brāhmī script of the Gupta[15] period. The reign of this ruler esta-

14. Some Sogdian monks actually belonged to the school of Ngan-She-Kao. The earliest reference is that of the Sogdian collaborator with the Parthian Ngan She-Kao, named Yen-Fo-tiao (Buddhadeva). Sogdians were in close contact with India where they were known as Śūlika. The Sogdian monks equally contributed in the transmission of Buddhist culture to China. Their names are distinguished in Chinese by the prefix *Kang*, as the ancient name of Sogdiana in Chinese was Kang-kiu. (Bagchi : Op. cit, p. 39).

15. See Hoernle : *Manuscript Remains found in East Turkestan*, 1916, pp. xvii ff and Franke : *Epigraphica Indica* (EI XI. pp. 266ff) and on the other side Laufer in JAOS. 1918, pp. 34ff. According to Eliot, there is a

blished the foundations of a civilization conducive to the efflorescence of Buddhism as also the unification of Central Tibet. The monarchy also provided the necessary leadership during the period of expansionism, with the Tibetans coming into conflict with most of their neighbours, particularly China under the Tang dynasty (A.D. 618-907). The Mahāyāna Buddhism brought to Tibet during the seventh and eighth centuries, overladen with a growth of Tantric occultism, soon absorbed elements of Bon faith, resulting in a synthesis of the two with lofty metaphysical speculation flourishing alongside with gross superstition. Padmasambhava summoned from Nalanda—the main object of veneration of the Nying-ma-pa or Red Hat Sect—gave to Tibetan Buddhism its distinctly Tantric character. The later history of Tibetan Buddhism and the contribution of Tibetans in the political and cultural history of Central Asia need not be considered here, and could receive exhaustive and fuller treatment later on.

The Mongols—said to be members of one small tribe living south-east of Lake Baikal did not make any contribution to the political and cultural history of Central Asia before the time of Chingiz Khan in the twelfth century A.D. At the beginning of this century three important tribes dominated the region, now called Mongolia—the Tatars, the Karaits and the Naimans. Living in close proximity to the Chinese frontier, they were most affected by Chinese culture.[16] Most of the inhabitants of Mongolia were

---

considerable difference between the printed and cursive forms of the Tibetan alphabet. Is it possible that they have different origins and that the former came from Bengal, the latter from Khotan. A number of Papers contributed by Sarat Chandra Das in the 'Journal of the Asiatic Society of Bengal' between 1881-82 provide comprehensive information as also the role of Indian scholars who were invited there for the propagation of Buddhism in that country. (See Das : *Indian Pandits in the Land of Snow*, Calcutta, 2nd edition, 1965).

16. According to Hambly, the influence of China on these tribes whether direct or indirect, depended partly upon their respective military strength at a particular time and partly upon the receptivity of different tribes to the blandishments of Chinese civilization. It is suggested by him that the Mongolian tribes probably acquired more knowledge of Chinese civilization from the dynasties of nomadic origin—the Khitans or Liao (947-1125) and the Jurchids or Kin (1122-1234) ruling over northern China, than from the Chinese direct. In general, it was the tribes in closest proxi-

Shamanists, with the Shaman (boge) exercising a dominant role. Tribal chieftains were called Khans and the ruler of a tribal confederacy had the title of Khagan. It is also suggested[17] that a new pattern of social relationship was emerging—a sort of nomadic feudalism in the twelfth century which provided the social and military basis for Chingiz Khan's conquests. It was from Tibet that Buddhism reached Mongolia in the thirteenth century under the Chingiz Khanids[18] who were eclectic in religious matters. Chingiz Khan is said to have corresponded with the famous Sākya Paṇḍita (1182-1251), the abbot of the Sākya monastery, which had been founded in the second half of the eleventh century and was a great centre of learning. Tibetan-Mongolian relations were established on the political and religious fronts with the nomination of Sākya Paṇḍita as viceroy of Tibet by the Mongol prince Godan, an authority which was passed on to his nephew Phagwa who exercised great influence over Qublai. It was during this period that the Mongols first became familiar with Tibetan Buddhism. Phagwa also provided the Mongols with an alternative script to the Uighur earlier adopted by Chingiz Khan.

The role of the peoples of Central Asia in the history and culture of that region as also in that of the neighbouring ones has been very conspicuous and effective. The Sakas and the Huns, followed by the Turks closely affiliated with the latter in race and language more or less shaped the destiny of the countries conquered by them. The Turks proved more dangerous than their

---

mity to the Chinese frontier who were most affected by Chinese culture, their chieftains proudly accepting such Chinese titles as *Wang* and *Tai-tsi*, (*Op. cit*, pp. 86-87).

17. *ibid.* p. 88. The origin of this body of feudal lords seems to have been the personal following of Chingiz Khan at the outset of his career, who helped him in asserting his supremacy over neighbouring rivals. The Mongol word for retinue—*nokod*—plural of *nokor* (a companion) is supposed to carry distinct feudal and heroic overtones.

18. Hambly : *Op. cit*, pp. 246-247. Similarity between Tibetan and Mongolian Lamaism is very close and there seems to be no difference between the two in deities, doctrines or observances. Mongolian Lamas imitate the usuages of Tibet, study these when they can, and recite their scriptures in Tibetan, though there are translations of these scriptures in their own language. (Eliot : *Op. cit*, p. 401).

predecessors. They made occasional inroads into Persian territory, but in 1040 the Seljuk Turks overran the whole of Persia and were soon masters of all the countries in the Near East. Later on, with the decay of their power, their place as overlords was taken by the Mongols early in the thirteenth century, to be followed later on by the Mongol-Turkish hordes led by Timur. The Huns who had created havoc in Europe, with Bleda and Attila noted for their empire as also their vandalism, like Toramāṇa and Mihirakula in Northern India more or less at the same time, were finally absorbed in the local population. The Turanian Turks, a few centuries later on their conversion to Islam, were not slow to invade India for booty and eventually for settlement. The Mughals—more conspicuous than the Mongols—were prominent among the foreign Muslim dynasties who ruled in India. It may, thus, be suggested that the Hunnish or Turanian invasions had permanent impacts on the historical development of the other peoples of Asia as also of Europe. According to Mc-Govern[19], among the most important factors in the shaping of the European world, the background of all the stupendous events—the fall of the Roman Empire, the pushing of the Germanic peoples into the west of Europe, the introduction of the Slavic people into Central and Southern Europe, the Renaissance and the revival of the ancient classics in Western Europe, and finally the voyages leading to the discovery of the New World, lurked the hordes of Central Asia. In case of each of these events it can be shown that one of the most, if not the most, important of the immediate conditioning causes was the invasion and conquest of some portion of Europe by peoples of Central Asiatic origin.

It must as well be understood that prior to the fall of Constantinople, there was an active trade between Europe on the one side and China and India on the other, and the fluctuations in this oriental trade had much to account for the rise and fall of several of the great European cities. The Europeans could secure fine silks from China, spices from the East and cotton prints and precious stones from India. While the Greeks in the old days had a virtual monopoly of the oriental trade, followed by the Romans through their cities of Venice and Genoa, in the thirteenth cen-

19. *Op. cit*, p. 11.

tury, Italian merchants including the famous Marco Polo, had made their way all over China and India, carrying tales about the great wealth of these countries. The Turkish conquest of Constantinople put a brake on the overland communication between Europe and the distant East, reducing movement of Asiatic merchandise, once a mighty stream, to a negligible trickle.

Ancient Routes :[20]

While the role of the geography and peoples of Central Asia in the political and cultural history of that region and the coun-

20. Detailed information about the routes is provided in Chinese accounts. From very early times important trade routes passed through the Tarim basin from the frontiers of China to the west. These are also known as the Silk-routes during the first few centuries of the Christian era. Two routes passed through the Tarim basin from the frontiers of China upto Balkh. These routes were also used by the Buddhist monks and savants for dissemination of Buddhist culture and thought to the States of Eastern Turkestan and to China. Tun-huang, like Puruṣapura(Peshawar), situated on the highway was a meeting place of foreigners, and had become a great centre of Buddhist art and culture. The southern route from here passed by the Gate of Yang-Kuan, and proceeding westward it reached the country of Shan-shan (to the south of Lob Nor). From there it went along the course of the river Tarim upto So-Kiu (Yarkand) and crossing the Pamir reached the country of Yueh-chi (Balkh) and Parthia (Ngan-si). The northern route passed by Kiue-she (Turfan), the ancient capital of the kingdom of Lou-lan. Following the Tarim right up to the west to Shu-lei (Kashgar), it continued across the Pamir (Kizil) upto Ta-wan (Fergana). Kang-Kiu(Sogdiana) and other countries in the valley of the Oxus. (Bagchi : *Op. cit*, p. 16).

Fa-hien notices in detail the route to India with the principal localities lying on it—from the province of Kanu-su westwards, Lan-chou, Leang-chou, Kan-chou, Su-chou—and Tun-huang and Shan-shan to the south of Lop-Nor. The outward journey lay through the countries of Yen-ki (Kara-sahr), Yu-tien (Khotan) and Kie-cha(Kashgar). Passing by To-li (Darel in Dardistan) and then crossing the mountains one reached the valley of Gilgit finally leading to the region of the Indus. Song-yun, however, followed the southern route upto the Pamir region—Tash-kurghan (Tsiu-mo) to Pa-ho (Wakhan) and passing by Po-che (the mountainous region to the north of Chitral to She-ni, directing southwards to Udyana in the valley of Swat and then to Gandhāra (Peshawar).

Hsuan-tsang taking the northern route from Kan-su to Kao-chang (Yark-hoto near Turfan), visited the countries of A-ki-ni (Karasahr), Kiu-che (Kucha), Po-lo-kia(Yaka-aryk), to the south of the Tien-shan. Crossing it by the Bedal pass, he passed by Sogdiana and crossing the 'Iron Gates', to the

tries in the periphery has been assessed rather summarily, it is necessary to take into account the routes and the regions lying on the international line or lines of communication connecting China with India and the Near East, and finally the western world. The ancient route started from the capital Chang-an (present Sian) in the province of Shensi and crossed the Gobi desert to the oasis of Tun-huang where, approaching the Taklamakan desert, it bifurcated into two : the northern route passed through Hami, Turfan, Karashahr, Kucha, Aksu, Tumshuk and Kashgar to Samarkand and the southern route traversed via Miran, Cherchen, Keriya, Khotan and Yarkand to Herat and Kabul. These overland routes opened since the Han times, passed through Central Asia—called the Innermost Heart of Asia, receiving the currents of life and civilization from different quarters, and also serving as an intermediary through which different cross currents passed. As pointed out earlier, the Tien-Shan or Celestial Mountains in the north and the Kun-lun ranges in the south, bounded by the Nan-Shan in the east and the Pamir in the west provided flow of the rivers—the Kashgaria and the Yarkand—powerful at the source and gradually diminishing in volume in the proximity of the desert of Taklamakan. It is along the basin of these rivers that flourishing colonies of peoples from different directions had been established. It was in the first century A.D. that Buddhism was taken to these countries, and peoples from Kashmir and North-West India proceeded to the region of Khotan and Kashgar and set up small colonies[21] with kings claiming descent from Indian

---

south of Kesch (Sahar-i-sabz) he reached the country of Tokharestan with its capital Huo (Kunduz) to the south of the Oxus. He descended by the pass of Bamiyan to the valley of Kāpiśa. On the return journey twenty years later, the pilgrim followed the southern route from Kāpiśa after crossing the Hindu Kush by the valley of Panjshir, reaching Kunduz, Balakshan (Pa-to-chuang-na), Yung-po-kien (Yamgan) and Hun-to-lo (Kandut). Crossing the Pamir, he visited the countries of Tash-Kurgan (Kie-pan-to), Ki-She (Kasghar), Che-Kiu-kia (Karghalik) and Kiu-sa-tan-na (Khotan) from where he followed the usual route by the south of Lop-nor to Chang-ngan, the capital. (Bagchi : *Op. cit*, p. 17).

21. The colonies that flourished in the southern part of this region were from west to east—Cokkuka in the region of modern Yarkand, Sailadesa in that of Kashgar, Khotamna—Godana in the region of Khotan and Calmadana in the region of Cherchen. The Kharoṣṭhī documents from

royal families. The routes starting from North-West India in those days passed by Hadda and Nagarahara (Jalalabad), and reached Bamiyan before crossing the Hindu Kush. It had grown into an important centre of Buddhist culture and was a halting place for the Indian monks proceeding to Central Asia and China, and also attracted traders and pilgrims from all quarters. Further to the north of this region beyond the hill was Bactriana (modern Balkh)—the Bahlika of the Indian and Fo-ho of the Chinese. Its local culture had blending of Hellenic and Indian influence with the Iranian one in its sub-stratum.

Buddhism is supposed to have been introduced in this region in the first century A.D. or even earlier in the time of Demetrius and Menander.[22] The political changes in the country from the Greeks to the Sakas, from the latter to the Yueh-chi-Kusanas, and finally to the Hephthalite Huns, in no way affected the allegiance of the people of this region towards Buddhism. In the time of Hsuan-tsang, in the seventh century A.D., the great Buddhist establishment of Balkh, known as the Nava-Samghārāma, was a great centre of Buddhist learning with a continuing chain of commentators of the Buddhist canon. Bactria was, in fact, the meeting place of two different roads leading to Central Asia and China. The northern one passed through ancient Sogdiana, crossing the Jaxartes, reaching Tashkent and then through the passes of Tien-Shan reached Uch-Turfan. The southern route, rather the shorter one, and used mostly by the travellers proceeding to China, passed through the country of the

---

Niya, Endere and Lou-lan mention Indian names with rulers assuming Indian titles *devaputra* and the official documents commencing with the formula : *mahāniava mahāraya lihati*. A comprehensive study of Indian culture in Central Asia, based on these inscriptions is made in my book in Hindi entitled *Madhya Asia me Bhāratiya Sanskriti* (Lucknow, 1981). For the study of the original documents, see Boyer, Rapson and Senart : *Kharoṣṭhī Inscriptions discovered by Sir Aurel Stein in Chinese Turkestan*—Text and Translation, Oxford, 1928.

22. See Bagchi paper on *Krimiśa and Demetrius* published in Indian Historical Quarterly; XXII, pp. 81 ff, in which he refers to this Indo-Greek ruler's interest in Buddhism. As regards Menander, his general-successor, the *Milindapañho*—discourse with Nāgasena, the famous Buddhist scholar is a conclusive proof of it. See Lamotte: *Histoire du Bouddhisme Indien*—Louvain, 1958, pp. 461-469.

Tokharians, the Tu-ho-lo of the Chinese, near Badakshan, and over the difficult passes of the Pamirs reached the plains at Kashgar. Here it was joined with a still shorter route passing through the Gilgit and the Yasin valleys upto Tashkurgan.

The importance of Kashgar both from the point of view of commercial activity and that of Buddhist expansion was great. The place, because of its geographical location, provided relief and hospitality to the travallers after an arduous journey through the hills. Numerous monasteries had also come up, and by the middle of the seventh century A.D. the Chinese pilgrim Hsuen-tsang could count these by the hundreds. From this place again two routes extended upto the borders of China—one known as the southern route went along the fringes of the Tarim basin with a number of prosperous states growing up along this passage. These included, beyond Kashgar, Yarkand, Khotan. Niya and also a number of other sites like Dandanulik, Endere and Miran. These centres played an important role in the development of cultural relations between China and the western countries, and were equally notable for Buddhist monasteries as centres of learning, revealing deep Buddhist influence on local culture. This whole region primarily constituted an Iranian zone, as the documents found by the explorers and archaeologists in this area are in Kharoṣṭhī. Khotan figures prominently in ancient records[23] and was known to the Chinese writers as Yu-tien, colonised in the time of Aśoka with the blinded prince Kuṇāla being set up as the ruler of this newly founded kingdom. The Gomatī vihāra here—the premier Buddhist establishment—was noted for its learned savants who also wrote canonical texts, thus contributing to the development of Buddhist literature.

23. Khotan (Sanskrit and Prakrit *Kustana* or *Kustanaka*; *Khotamina*, Khodana or Khotana; Chinese Chien-tun, Chu-sa-tan-na, Chu-tan, *Ho-tien*, *Huan-na*, *Huo-tan*, *Yo-tien* and *Yu-tun*, Manchu—*Ho-thian*, Mongol—*Hu-t'an*, *O-duan*, *Wa-duan*, *Wu-duan*; Tibetan *Li-yul*, *U-then* [*Ho-then*]) has a long history. The information from the Chinese Annals on the history of this place confirms the Tibetan account. A local dynasty which used the title of Vijaya had been ruling in Khotan since very early times. This dynasty was of Indian origin, as is evident from the names of its members. Buddhism was introduced in Khotan during the reign of king Vijaya Saṁbhava, grandson of Kustana, its founder. (For a comprehensive account of Khotan—in all aspects—see Stein : *Ancient Khotan*, Oxford, 1907.)

The countries along the northern route from Kashgar to the Chinese frontier were equally important from the commercial as well as the cultural viewpoints. These centres disseminated India culture and Buddhism in Central Asia as well as in China. The notable ones were Bharuka—Chinese Po-lu-Kia near Uch-Turfan, Kuchi or Kucha—Chinese Kiu-tse, modern Kuchar, Agnideśa, Chinese Yen-ki, modern Karasahr and Turfan—Chinese Kao-chang. The people and language of the countries or centres on the northern routes were different from those of the south; but both had common affinities in the form of Buddhist religion and culture. Kucha or Kuchi like its counterpart Khotan on the southern route was the most important[24] kingdom and its ancient rulers had Indian names like Suvarṇapuṣpa, Haradeva, Suvarṇadeva etc. The Buddhist monks of this place were well-conversant with Sanskrit, as is confirmed by the finds of manuscripts in Sanskrit and bilingual documents in Kuchean Sanskrit. In the words of the Chinese pilgrim, it was not only a centre of Buddhist studies but it also catered towards the expansion of Buddhism in China through its famous teachers and savants, who translated Buddhist texts as also gave discourses. The noted Buddhist scholar Kumārajīva[25] belonged to this place.

24. Kucha has all along been one of the most important territories in the Tarim basin, in many ways, according to Stein, 'a worthy pendant of Khotan owing to its geographical position and the role it has played in Buddhist art and civilization'. The Chinese annals provide exhaustive information about this place which was utilized by S. Levi in connection with his paper entitled *Le Tokharian B. Langue de Kouteha*, J.A. 1913, Sept. Oct., pp. 323-80. See Stein : *Serindia* (Oxford, 1921, p. 1238). The name of Kuchean king of the Tang period had been Sanskritised. According to Bagchi, from the old Kuchean documents we get the name of king Suarnage (Suvarṇadatta), that of his father So-fa-pu-kiue (Svarṇa), and brother Ho-li-pu-she-pi (Haripuṣpa). The Chinese pilgrim mentions a former ruler of Kucha named 'Gold Flower' (Suvarṇa-puṣpa)—(Bagchi : *Op. cit*, p. 79).

25. Kumārajīva's life history is important in several respects. His father came from India and he himself went as a youth to study in Kipin (Kashmir) and then returned to Kucha, his mother Jīvā's home. Living in this remote corner of Central Asia he was recognised as an encyclopaedia of Indian learning including a knowledge of the Vedas and 'heretical Śāstras'. After his return to Kucha he was converted to Mahāyānism. It was from Kucha that he was taken to China where he had a distinguished career as a translator, and brought China into intellectual touch with India. (For an account of Kumārajīva see Hastings : *Encyclopaedia of Religion and Ethics*, Edinburgh,

The grottos in the hills in the neighbourhood of Kuchar met the requirements of Buddhist monks for meditation and quiet stay, like those at Bamiyan in Afghanistan, and the ones in the western Ghats in India. Agnideśa[26]—in the region of Karasahr—the next place on the northern route was linked with Kuchi-Kucha in culture, race and language, and common Buddhist religion. The finds of literary texts and art objects in this region testify to the active role of this place and its scholars in the propagation of Buddhism. Turfan, the next stage on the northern route further towards the east, was a centre of Central Asian as well as of Chinese cultural impacts. It has preserved relics of Buddhist civilization and contributed in full towards the propagation of Buddhism in China.

The Northern as well as the Southern routes met on the Chinese frontier at a place called Yu-men-Kuan or the 'Jade Gate'[27], close to the famous Tun-huang—noted for its thousand grottos—one of the famous centres of Buddhist learning. In the hills nearby were the caves carved out between the fifth and the eighth centuries A.D. for the use of Buddhist monks proceeding to China; and these also served as the meeting place of Buddhist scholars coming from various countries—Persia, Bactria, India, Sogdiana, Khotan, Kucha and other places—for holding discussions and translating sacred text into Chinese. Situated on the cross road of the two main highways, Tun-huang had also its strategic importance, besides cultural and commercial one. From the first century of the Christian era

---

1926, Vol. VII, p. 701a; Eliot : *Hinduism and Buddhism*, III, p. 203ff; S.C. Das : *Indian Pandits in the Land of Snow* : Op. cit, pp. 33 ff.)

26. Agnideśa or Karasahr, according to Bagchi, was closely connected with Kucha. The Chinese accounts contain some references to the political condition of Karasahr from the Han times to the end of the Tang period. Its political history and relations with China are traced by Bagchi (*Op. cit*, pp. 75 ff).

27. The location of the Jade Gate barrier is discussed by Aurel Stein in Chapter XIX of his *Serindia*. Its history is also traced. It is said to have been established in c. 96 B.C. With a rapid increase in the diplomatic relations of China with the west and in trade also, it was necessary to safeguard the passage of envoys and of caravans, and to assure supplies for them en route. 'It is stated that military posts were established from place to place from Tun-huang westwards to the Salt Marsh' (*Serindia*, p. 728).

onwards, its importance[28] increased and it also attracted foreigners. While the Buddhist pilgrims from the second century onwards sought shelter here on their way to China, some Indian families settled down here in the third century A.D. and the place hubbed with activities—secular and religious. The finds of a large number of manuscripts by the archaeologists testify to the importance of Tun-huang as an active centre of learning. These manuscripts are in several languages—Chinese, Sanskrit, Tibetan, Syriac, Khotanese etc. suggesting that it was a meeting place of Buddhist scholars from China, India and the Near East.

The trade routes in Central Asia and the peoples living at important centres were equally instrumental in carrying cultural traits from one end to another. The Tarim basin people were in touch with Bactria and the regions conquered by Alexander and through them with western art and thought. Its inhabitants included not only Iranian tribes but also speakers of a language which is classed as Indo-Aryan. From the dawn of history down to the middle ages, warlike nomads were continually passing through this region of Central Asia. The Sakas, Yueh-chi and the Huns of the ancient period and the Turks and Mongols of the Medieval one had the same peculiarity. They communicated and transported ideas and cultural features from one region to the other. The peoples receiving these were equally interested and receptive. The finds of numerous manuscripts in different languages suggest the cosmopolitan nature of the peoples of different parts of Central Asia. It might be interesting to note that 20,000 manuscripts were discovered in Tun-huang[29] alone, where they had been walled up for 900 years for protection against invaders. These are in Brāhmī. Kharoṣṭhī, Persian, Tibetan, Turki, Uighur and Tokharian scripts and languages,

28. Tun-huang was famous among the four commands of *Ho-hsi* or western Kansu, side by side with Liang-chou, Kan-chou and Su-chou. It derived its importance from the great advantages which its geographical position and resources offered, and which, according to Stein, are easy to recognize even now when the line of the great Central-Asian route finally shifted northward. The Chinese realized the value which Tun-huang possessed for them at the time of their first advance into the Tarim basin. (*Serindia*, p. 581.)

29. Eliot. III. op. cit, p. 189.

and point to the cosmopolitan community of peoples that lived in these Central Asian kingdoms. The art of Central Asia, as depicted in the frescoes at Tun-huang and other places of Central Asia is expressive of the unique synthesis of religions and cultures of peoples. The languages recorded in the manuscripts and inscriptions are numerous, pointing to the number of tongues simultaneously in use for popular or learned discourses. Besides the great polyglot libraries like Tun-huang, even a small one at Toyug[30] contained Indian, Manichaean, Syriac, Sogdian, Uighur and Chinese books. The writing materials include imported palm leaves, leather and paper, the last one being in use from the first century A.D. onwards. These survived through the ages because of the dry atmosphere.

Buddhist Finds—Literary Texts and Monuments[31]

Besides numerous Sanskrit writings dealing with religious or quasi-religious subjects like medicine and grammar, comparatively modern Mahāyānist literature is traced in abundance. Portions of lost Sanskrit canons, corresponding to the Pāli ones, provide the original text for translation into Chinese. Portions of a Sanskrit grammar have also been found near Turfan, thereby suggesting that Sanskrit was probably understood in polite and learned society. According to the testimony of Fa-hien, the monks of Central Asia were all students of the language of India, and the same point was recorded about the Buddhist monks of Kucha by Hsuang-tsang. Some palm leaves from Mingoi contain fragments of two Buddhist religious dramas, one being the *Sāriputraprakaraṇa*[32] of Aśvaghoṣa, written in

30. Eliot : *Op. cit*, III. p. 189. At Toyuk Stein picked up a considerable number of torn fragments from Chinese Buddhist Sūtra rolls in a debris-strewn ravine where they had been thrown out from shrines above in the course of some previous exploration. (*Serindia*, 1167n).

31. A comprehensive study of the manuscript remains from Central Asian sites as also remnants of Buddhist monuments in this region is reserved for separate treatment in two to three chapters in this work. Here only a casual reference might be made in the context of importance of such from religious and literary viewpoints and the achievements of different missions in this vast region.

32. Remains of the works of the two great Buddhist poets Aśvaghoṣa and Mātriceta were discovered amongst the Central Asian finds. Fragments

the script of the time of Kaniṣka. It is the oldest known Sanskrit manuscript as well as the oldest specimen of Indian dramatic art. Besides these, the Prākrit version of the Dhammapada in Kharoṣṭhī characters discovered by Dutreuil de Rhines mission near Khotan[33] with numerous documents in this language and alphabet are more or less of the same time as the period of the Kuṣāṇas in India.

Central Asia is also supposed to provide two new languages written in a special variety of the Brāhmī script called Nordarisch, probably the language of the Śakas or of the Kuṣāṇas. Its basis is Iranian but it is strongly influenced by Indian idioms.[34] It is supposed to have been spoken principally in the southern part of the Tarim basin, and many translations of Mahāyānist works such as the *Suvarṇaprabhāsa*, *Vajracchedikā* and *Aparimitāyus-Sūtras* were made into it[35]. The other new language was that of the Tokharas or Indo-Scythians, spoken primarily on its northern edge, and was called the language of the Kucha or Kuchanese. It is supposed to exist in two different dialects whose geographical distribution is uncertain, but numerous official documents dated in the first half of the seventh century show that it was the spoken language of Kucha and Turfan. It was also a literary language and the translations discovered in this one include those of the Dhammapada and Vinaya. This language spoken by the early and perhaps original people of Kucha is supposed to belong to the Aryan family, closely related to the western than the eastern branches. It is classed in the Indo-Iranian group.

Besides the Nordarish language mentioned above, written in Brāhmī, remnants of three other Iranian languages are traced

---

of the works of the former were brought by the German mission from the Turfan region. This drama—not traceable elsewhere—was discovered in the Turfan region only in fragments. The work is in Sanskrit but there are dialogues in Prākrit, older than those used in Sanskrit dramas. (See Keith : *Sanskrit Drama*, Oxford, 1924, pp. 80 ff.)

33. Eliot : *Op. cit*, p. 190. The Central Asian finds include the *Dhammapada* in Prakrit and the *Udānavarga* in Sanskrit, the former from the region of Khotan and written in Kharoṣṭhī script of about the 3rd century. See Senart : *Les ms Kharoṣṭhī du Dhammapada* JA. 1898 II, p. 193.

34. Eliot : *Op. cit*, p. 190. See Luders : '*Die Śakas und Die Nordarische Sprache*'—quoted by Eliot; see also Bagchi : *Op. cit*, pp. 98 ff.

35. Hoernle : JRAS, 1910, pp. 837 ff and 1283 ff.

in Central Asia. These are written in an alphabet of Aramaic origin.[36] Two of them apparently represent the speech of the south-western Persia under the Sassanids, and of north-western Persia under the same rulers. Manichaean texts are preserved in both these languages. Sogdian—the third language—has a more varied literary content offering Buddhist, Manichaean and Christian texts. Originally the language of the region round Samarkand, it acquired an international character being used by the merchants throughout the Tarim basin, and it spread even to China.

Buddhist literature from Central Asia is not confined to languages and scripts noticed above. It is available in other alphabets and dialects as well. A Turkish dialect written in the Uighur alphabet, derived from the Syrian, was, like Sogdian, extensively used for Buddhist, Manichaean and Christian literature. Uighur[37] represented the literary form of the various Turkish idioms spoken north and south of the Tien-Shan. It was used considerably for Buddhist literature when the Uighur supplanted the Tibetan power in the Tarim basin about A.D. 860 and founded a kingdom which extended upto China and lasted for quite some time. It is suggested by Eliot that Sūtras in Uighur were printed at Peking in 1330, and Uighur manuscripts of the time of Kang-Hsi (1662-1723) were reported from a monastery near Suchow.

Besides these languages, the Tibetans who ruled in Central Asia in the Tarim basin from the middle of the eighth until the middle of the ninth century, also enriched Buddhist literature with their language. A large number of Tibetan manuscripts were found in the region of Khotan, Miran and Tun-huang. The Tibetan influence, however, seems less conspicuous in Turfan to the north. The documents discovered comprise many official and business papers as also Buddhist translations.[38] They are considerably important for the history of the Tibetan language

36. Eliot : *Op. cit*, p. 191.

37. Eliot : *Op. cit*, p. 192.

38. *Ibid*, p. 193. The list of manuscripts in Sanskrit, Khotanese and Kuchean prepared by A.F. Rudof Hoernle, and a note on Stein's collection of Tibetan documents from Chinese Turkestan figure as Appendix F and G in *Serindia*, pp. 1432-1459.

as well as Buddhism. There have not been any Tibetan translations of Manichaean or Christian texts.

The role of Central Asia and its intercourse with China is also evident from a large number of Chinese texts—both religious and secular. Some documents of the Tang dynasty are Manichaean with an admixture of Buddhist and Taoist ideas. A series of dated documents ranging from 98 B.C. –A.D. 133 have also been recovered from the old military frontier near Tun-huang. The Buddhist monuments of Central Asia comprising of stūpas, caves and covered buildings used as temples or vihāras point to the propagation and prosperity of the religion of the Tathāgata in this area. Representations of Hindu deities no doubt have been found, but Hinduism is not supposed to have existed there as an independent separate religious unit but only as a part of or rather a contributory factor to the religious ethos. The general scheme and style of the caves in the Tarim basin as also at Tun-huang on the frontier of China are similar to those in India. The ornamented figures, as sculptural pieces, add to the beauty and grandeur of the caves. These are in stucco. The walls at Tun-huang and Tarim have also fresco paintings reminding one of Ajanta frescoes. Temples and caves were sometimes combined, as for instance at Bazaklik many edifices were erected on a terrace in front of a series of caves in a mountain corner. The commonest type of temples was a hall with a cellar at its further end, with a passage behind for circumambulation. Occasionally side rooms were added to the halls.

Some buildings had also stūpas nearby, either in combination or independently, the best preserved being the stūpa of Rawak.[39] It is set in a quadrangle bounded by a wall which was ornamented on both its inner and outer face by a series of gigantic statues in coloured stucco. A rectangular base provides the setting of the dome. It is disposed of in three stories and is said to characterize all the stūpas of Turkestan as well as those of the Kabul valley and the nearby regions. In its architectural setting, the dome provides a synthesis of Indian (Gandhāra) and Persian elements. There are, however, some innovations

39. Stein : *Ancient Khotan. Op. cit*, p. 483 ff.

here, as for instance, some of the caves at Ming-oi have dome-like roofs ornamented with a pattern composed of squares within squares, set at an angle with each other.[40]

The frescoes on the walls of caves and buildings and paintings on silk paper provide evidence of other antiquities related to Buddhism in Central Asia. The influence of Gandhāra is noticeable in architecture, sculpture as well as painting. The oldest works are described simply as Gandhāran, but later on there is some development both in technique and in mythology, representing Indian Buddhist art as modified by local painters and sculptors. Thus, the frescoes in Turfan are Indian in drapery and composition, but the faces are eastern Asiatic, sometimes representing people with red hair and blue eyes. These testify to the influence of Eastern art on the ideas and designs of Indian Buddhism.[41] Persian influence is also noticed in many paintings. Aurel Stein refers to the Bodhisattva figures from Khotan—one being of the familiar Indian type, and the other suggesting at first sight a miniature of some Persian prince, black bearded and putting on high boots. Currents of art and civilization flowing from neighbouring and distant regions seem to have met and mingled here, providing a cosmopolitan nature of Buddhist art in Central Asia.[42] The Iranian link in the chain connecting the Greco-Buddhist art of the extreme North-West India with the Buddhist art of Central Asia and the Far East, is recorded by Stein on the basis of the finds of a Buddhist monastery in the terminal marshes of the Persian province of Seistan. The Indian Buddhist element dominates everywhere.

This introduction should provide a background for a proper study of Buddhism in Central Asia. The geographical factors with the nature of the peoples of different regions—nomadic as

40. Eliot : Op. cit, p. 194, quoting Grunwedel : *Buddh Kulstatten*, pp. 129-130 and plate and Foucher : *L'Art Greco-Bouddhique*, p. 145.

41. Eliot : *Op. cit*, p. 195. According to Bussagli, in the first stylistic phase of painting at Turfan, there was a slow decline of the classical Iranian and Indian characteristics which had penetrated into the region and been re-elaborated in the Kuchean manner. These gave way before Chinese influence, which sometimes managed to modify even the common motifs of Buddhist iconography. (*Paintings of Central Asia*, Geneva, 1963)

42. Eliot : Op. cit, p. 195, quoting *Ancient Khotan—Op. cit*, Vol. II plates lx and lxi.

well as pastoral—receptive to external influences but equally dominating and aggressive—present a picture of external challenges and internal responses. In this context, the international trade and its routes facilitated the movement of ideas from one part to another. In the process of cultural communication between the Orient and the Occident, the role of Central Asia was significant and equally substantial. The process of introduction of Buddhism in Central Asia was the work of missionaries, savants, merchants and traders and banished princes. The Chinese sources, however, point to royal invitations extended to Indian Buddhist scholars to visit their country and propagate the message of the Tathāgata. These people were from the Buddhist religious establishments in Central Asia itself, or from the country of the Śākyamuni and passed through Central Asia. Tradition, no doubt, connects Buddhism in Khotan with Kuṇāla, the banished Mauryan prince from Taxila in the last years of Aśoka, or might be even a little earlier. A number of Indian colonies had come up in Central Asia as recorded by the Chinese pilgrims. While the earlier picture of Buddhism and expansion of Indian culture in Central Asia might not be very distinct and sharp, that of the later times is more pronounced, vivid and clear, as is evident from the finds of Buddhist manuscripts as also monuments and sculptures. Patronage to the Buddhist scholars was extended by the local rulers whose historical account no doubt demands some study.

CHAPTER II

EARLY HISTORY OF CENTRAL ASIA

The early history of Central Asia is closely related to the movement of its peoples sharply divided and concentrated in two regions, named after their traits—the nomadic and the sedentary. The former comprises North Steppes from South Russia to Manchuria, while the region to the south includes the oases of Turkestan occupied by the sedentary peoples. The nomadic region itself is further divided into two : one from South Russia to the valley of the Yenisei occupied in the past by the nomadic hordes of Aryan stock called Scythians, the other one in the east including outer and Inner Mongolia, Manchuria and further east occupied by Turco-Mongol hordes. In the south the land between the Jaxartes (Syr) and the Oxus (Amu) was occupied by the peoples of Iranian origin, while the Eastern Turkestan from the Pamirs up to the frontiers of China was occupied by the Aryan speaking people of different affiliations. The movements of the nomads of the steppes either on the west or the east affected the sedentary life in the south through the centuries. It is really the history of this southern region with the movements of different peoples affected by the onslaught of foreigners or the nomads of Central Asian origin that needs to be told on the basis of the available evidence, however scanty, whether archaeological or accounts of travellers or second-hand source material.

It is in the seventh century B.C. that history opens in the steppes of the Caspian sea, with a large-scale nomad migration in progress. The powerful Massagatae Confederacy had pushed westwards across the Volga the peoples who became later famous as the Scythians—a term given to various tribes of Indo-European origin, speaking either Iranian or other Indo-European dialects. They are supposed to be the nomadic section of the Iranians and others left behind in the north steppes who had refused to adopt the culture of the sedentary conquerors. They are known in Persia as Saka and in India as Saka.[1] The Śakas in old Persian inscription[2] include three different tribes of the Scythians: the *Śaka Haumvarka*—the Śakas of Persian and Indian literature settled in the region of Fergana and extended up to Kashgar; the *Śaka Tigrakhaude*—or Śakas with pointed caps who spread towards the Aral and occupied the lower valley of the Jaxartes, and *Śaka Taradraya* or Scythians who lived beyond the sea in south Russia. Besides the Śakas, other tribes noticed in old Achaemenian inscriptions and/or in Herodotus' *Historica* are Sarmatians, probably, neighbours of the Scythians of South Russia, Massagetes from Mausyagata—fishermen speaking Ira-

1. The Śakas are frequently mentioned in Indian literature. They are spoken of as belonging to the barbarous peoples who will rule in the Kaliyuga, or as degraded Kṣatriyas. They are mentioned together along with other north-western peoples, such as Kambojas and Yavanas. The word Saka is the same name which is handed down in Iranian and classical sources as Saka 7 *Sai* or *Sak* of Chinese annals. There is a general consensus of opinion to the effect that the Śakas were foreigners and Iranians. The history of the Śakas can be reconstructed on the basis of classical, Iranian and Chinese sources. The stray references found in classical literature give us some idea about the homeland of the *Sakai*. Herodotus mentions them together with the Bactrians, (I.153; VII·64; IX.113) and with India (VII.9; III.93) as forming the fifteenth nomos of the Persian empire together with the Kaspioi. Arrian connects them with Bactrians and Sogdians (*Anabasis*, III.8.3; VII·10.5) while Strabo (XI.8.2) and Pliny locate them beyond the Jaxartes. Strabo further states that the ancient historiographers of the Hellenes called the tribes beyond the Caspian Sea partly Sakai, partly Massagetai. They were mostly nomads and had spread over a large territory. Sten Konow suggests that the old home of the Sakai was in the Pamir country to the north of the Hindu Kush and east of Bactria, and that Śaka tribes were further considered to exist to the east of the Caspian Sea and beyond the Jaxarte. (*Corpus Inscriptionum Indicarum*—henceforth CII.II(1) Calcutta, 1929, pp. xvi ff.)

2. In the Behistun inscription 1.6 Darius mentions the countries which he inherited, and Śaka here comes between Bactria, Sogdiana and Gandhāra on one side, and Thatagush, Arachosia and the Makas on the other. In ii.2 Śaka is mentioned among the provinces which revolted while Darius was in Babylon, after Parthia, Margiana and the Thatagush. They are also mentioned in the Persepolis Inscription, as also in the Naksh-i-Rustam one, which mentions some individual Śaka tribes : the Tigra Khauḍa, the Haumvarka and those beyond the sea (*taradrayā* or *paradrayā*) (ibid, p.xviii). In Darius's Suez inscription the hieroglyphic text renders the first as 'Sacae of the marshes' (presumably those on the shore of the Aral sea) and the second as 'Sacae of the plains' (G. Posener, *La premiere domination perse en Egypte*, Cairo, 1936, p. 183, quoted by Hambly : *Central Asia*, p. 25 and note).

nian language who lived near the Aral, Arinaspes and Issidones —who lived in the east in the northern steppes—the former probably Iranian and lover of horses, and the latter of a different race.

The old Persian inscriptions provide information relating to the Achaemenian domination over Central Asia and its states, while Herodotus notices their annual assessments of tribute to the Persian treasury.[3] The Achaemenian control over these provinces was no doubt fully effective during the reign of Darius I. His Susa building inscription records that gold for the work on the palace was obtained from Bactria, lapis-lazuli and carnelian from Sogdiana, and turquoise from Chorasmia. Ivory came from India and Ethiopia and also from the province of Arachosia. The Achaemenians are said to be the intermediaries who transmitted the irrigation techniques of Babylonian civilization to Central Asia. During the reign of Xerxes (486-465 B.C.) the Central Asian contingent formed part of the Persian army invading Greece in 480 B.C. The Bactrians and Assyrian Sacae (old Persian Haumvarga) were under the command of Hystaspes, son of king Darius and Queen Atossa.[4] There is probably no evidence regarding the nomadic tribe living beyond the Achaemenian northern frontiers.

A significant role of Central Asia and its peoples, however, comes in view from 330 B.C. when Alexander passing through the Caspian Gates expanded Greek rule across the Trans-Oxus region in the province of Sogdiana and Bactria. There was not much of resistance and the Macadonian ruler founded a number of cities named after him[5] in this region, which remained key-

3. Herodotus (III.91 ff) quotes the annual assessments of tributes to the Persian treasury which varied between 170 and 600 talents. That to be paid by the Sacae was 250. The tribute was paid in Silver bullion. (Hambly : *Op. cit*, p. 22; 317 n. 15)

4. Herodotus. VII.66. There are references to other provinces and the contingents provided by them, as also their commanders. (Quoted by Hambly: *Op. cit*, p. 24)

5. The compaign of Alexander is also noted for the foundation of cities which became famous later on in history. These were named after him and include Alexandria in Ariana, modern Herat; Alexandria Prophthasia in Drangiana (location uncertain); Alexandria in Arachosia (placed by Tarn in Ghazni-*Greeks in Bactria and India*—henceforth *Tarn*, Cambridge, 1938,

points in Asia for centuries. These were strongly garrisoned for keeping a firm hold on the land routes. Internal dissentions, army revolts and finally Alexander's death left his eastern empire in a state of dissipation. Seleucus, however, attempted the reunification of his Master's eastern provinces with Bactria and Prathia forming part of his empire, only to become independent later on in the time of Antiochos III, under Diodotus and Arsaces respectively.[6] There is, however, no ancient narrative about the tale of this Greek kingdom of Bactria—that of Euthydemus and his successors, Demetrius and Menander, and later on of Eucratides and his family, subsequently followed by the emergence of Antialkidas whose ambassador Heliocles recorded his dedication to the Indian god Viṣṇu at Besnagar (Vidisā) in Madhya Pradesh, India.

While the Bactrians and Indo-Parthians were involved in struggles, storm clouds, gathering along the Central Asian frontier of Jaxartes, posed threats to these political kingdoms. New pressures in this river's steppe were the outcome of fast eastern nomadic unrests along the frontiers of China consequent to the pressure from the warring tribe of Hiung-nu. They had reached the height of their power in Mongolia in the third century B.C. and posed great threat to the rulers of northern China. The great Wall[7] was constructed to ward off their attacks.

---

p. 470); Alexandria of the Caucasus probably located on the site of the medieval city of Parvan, at Jebel Suraj on the Salang; and the short-lived Alexandria on the Jaxartes (Hambly: *Op. cit*, pp. 207-29).

6. Bactria was the rich country between the Hindu Kush and the Oxus, corresponding in large measure to Northern Afghanistan. Beyond it, between the Oxus and the Jaxartes (Syr Darya) lay Sogdiana (Bukhara). Parthia, an ancient land, corresponding roughly to the modern province of Khurasan in Iran, became independent under Arsaces. (For a detailed history of these two kingdoms—see *Cambridge History of India*—CHI, Vol. I, Chapter XVII, pp. 427 ff.)

7. In 214 B.C. the Emperor Shih Huang-ti of the Chin dynasty linked up the defensive lines by which the feudal kingdoms of the North had endeavoured to protect themselves against the inroads of the Hiung-nu or Huns and thereby first created the famous 'Great Wall'. At first it extended from Shan-hai Kuan, on the Gulf of Liao-tung, westwards as far as Lin-tas, corresponding to the present prefecture of Min, in the extreme south of Kan-su and about 110 miles south of Lan-chou. It was not until a century later that the 'Great Wall'

The clash between the Hiung-nu and the Yueh-chi, pastoral nomads led to the movement of the latter down westwards, clashing with the Wu-sun, another nomadic tribe. In the final confrontation between the Yueh-chi and Wu-sun, aided and supported by the traditional warring Hiung-nu, the former lost ground and were driven further west on the heels of the Sacae (Śakas) whom they had earlier dislodged from their home near Issyk-kul. These two powerful hordes—the Sacae and the Yueh-chi were poised against the Greco-Bactrian frontier of the Jaxartes. According to Strabo,[8] the nomads who became the most famous were those who took away Bactria from the Greeks—the Asii or Asiani, the Tochari, and the Sacaraucae, who set out from the far bank of the Jaxartes, adjoining the Sacae and the Sogdiani which the Sacae had occupied. The *Prolugues*[9] of Pompeius Trogus also refers to the seizure of Bactria and Sogdiana by the Scythian tribes of the Saraucae. The Asiani, according to the next Prologue, became kings of the Tochari and the Saraucae (Sacaraucas) were destroyed. The displaced nomad groups soon afterwards overran the Greco-Bactrian kingdoms. The invasion, according to Tarn[10], took place after 141 B.C. A wave of nomad invaders is said to have burst into Parthia in 129 B.C. It is also proposed that the region of the Helmand Lake (now called Hamun) ceased to be known as Drangiana and came to be called Sakastan (Seistan).

---

was extended to the north-west, while earlier this wall catered for consolidated defence; later on its purpose was offensive aiming at expansion into Central Asia (Stein : *Serindia*, Vol. II, pp. 722-23).

8. Strabo mentions a Śaka conquest of Bactria (XI·8, 4) where the Greek kings were ousted by Scythian nomads, and some of these nomadic tribes are enumerated by him, notably, the Asioi, Pasianoi, Tocharoi and Sakarauloi (cf. XI.8.2). Śakas were thus instrumental in overthrowing the Greek empire in Bactria and some of these seem to be called Sakarauloi (cf. Ptolemy Sagaraukai, VI.14.14) who could be identified with the Sai-wang. According to F.W. Thomas, the Saraucae or Sacaraucae started from the country north of Parthia and between the Caspian and the Aral Sea (JRAS, 1906, p. 186).

9. Trogus deals with the establishment of an empire in Bactria by Diodotus in the 41st book, and this event took place about the middle of the third century B.C. (Sten Konow : *Op. cit*, p. xxi).

10. *Greco-Bactrian Rule in India*, 2nd Edition, Op. cit, p. 280. See also Puri : *India under the Kushāṇas*, Bombay, 1965, pp. 5 ff and notes pp. 10 ff.

It is concluded that the Śakas during the first century B.C. passing through the Herat gap, established themselves in the former Drangiana and, continuing north-eastwards into Arachosia and reaching Indus, followed upstream until they reached Taxila on the one hand, and Saurāṣṭra and Ujjain on the other hand.

The first century B.C. is regarded as the epoch of the Śaka empire in India and Arachosia. The extreme mobility of the Śaka forces seems to have been an important factor in their overrunning such a wide region. The history of the Śakas in the North-west seems to have begun with Maues,[11] figuring at Taxila as the sovereign ruler at the expense of the Indo-Greeks. An analysis of the coins and other finds, no doubt, suggests fluctuating Śaka-Indo-Greek fortunes with the former under Maues being ousted; and the Indo-Greeks finally settled in the Kabul valley and Gandhāra region. Later on, Azes I seems to have put an end to the Greek dynasties and asserted his paramountcy; and probably started an era of his own. The Śakas in North-West India and Western India seem to have played an important role in political history and also made their contributions in the cultural ethos of the country of their adoption.

The other participants of the great migratory movement in Central Asia were the Tochari and the Asiani who were living on the north bank of the Oxus, and to the east of the Śaka advance line. The advance of the Tochari is suggested by the association of their name with the area called Tukharistan centring round Qunduz and Baghlan, close to the upper Oxus. Ptolemy in his *Geography* calls them a 'great tribe' with their advance guards pushing southwards towards the Hindukush passes. The identification of Asiani has been a matter of dispute

11. It is proposed by A.K. Narain that Maues led a separate Śaka group directly to Taxila from the north, passing from Khotan over the Pamirs and Indus Kohistan—an arduous route called that of the 'Hanging Pass' by Chinese chronicles (*The Indo-Greeks*, Oxford, p. 136). Hambly considers this suggestion fantastic. He proposes that Maues began his career as a commander of Saca mercenaries in the service of the late Indo-Greek kings. With the Indo-Greek princes divided and Saca invaders at the gates, such a personage would be well placed to assume sovereign power (*Op. cit*, p. 41). According to Sten-Konow, he was not the 'first Śaka emperor in India, (*Op. cit*, p. xj).

amongst scholars.[12] The Tocharians—Sanskrit, Tuṣāras—are equated with the Kuṣāṇas who consolidated their hold over the Kabul valley under their leader Kujula Kadphises.[13] The early history of the Kuṣāṇas or Kwei-shuang, a yabqou of the Yueh-chi, is recorded in the well-known passage of the *Hou-Han-shu* or 'Annals of the Later Han Dynasty'. A reference to the relations between the Kuṣāṇas and the Yueh-chi and the later history of the former has already been made, but the historical aspect demands fuller consideration in the context of their contribution to political integration of Northern India, including present Pakistan with South-west Central Asian territories. Their empire extended in the east probably as far as Khotan and certainly Bactria, their earlier hold according to the Chinese Annals. The first ruler Kiu-tsiu-kio who had attacked the other four hi-hou, styling himself as king of his kingdom called Kwei-Shuang, later on invaded An-si (Parthia) and seized the territory of Kao-fu (Kabul). He triumphed over Pu-ta and Ki-pin and possessed these kingdoms. He died as an octogenarian and was succeeded by his son Yen-kao-chin, who, in turn, conquered India (Tien-Shu).

Kujula Kadphises is mentioned as a prince in the Takht-i-

12. The identity of Asiani, according to Hambly, presents some problems, though their historical role is, however, clear. They were the group who became king of the Tochari. Though the identity of the names is unlikely, their activity coincides with that of a clan-group later on famous as the Kushanas. They were regarded as historically equivalent by Tarn (*Op. cit*, 287, 533); lately endorsed by Sinor (*Introduction a l'etude del' Eurasie Centrale*, 233) that the Asiani were identical with the Wu-Sun (Hambly: *Op. cit*, p. 42).

13. The advance of Tochari is suggested by the attachemnt of their name to the district of Tokharistan, which centres round Qunduz and Baghlan close to the Upper Oxus. Ptolemy calls them a great tribe in his *Geography* (VI, 11, 6). Early in the first century B.C. their advance guards seem to have pressed southwards towards the passes of the Hindu Kush. But it was not until the opening decades of the Christian era that they achieved final unity under the leadership of the Kushan clan, and secured the Kabul valley. The history of the Kushana rulers Kujula Kadphises and his son Vima Kadphise (Yen-Kao-chen) is mentioned in the Chinese annals of the Later Han Dynasty (*Hau-Han-Shu*)—(Hambly : *Op. cit*, pp. 42-43). The Chinese account is noticed by Sten Konow (*Op. cit*, lvi, lxii) and is discussed in detail in my *Kushāṇas*—Op. cit, Chapter II, pp. 12 ff).

Bahi inscription[14] of Gondophernes. About two decades later this Kuṣāṇa is a full-fledged monarch (mahārāja) and in another fourteen years in the year 136 of the old era he is great king, king of kings and son of God'.[15] The Kuṣāṇa empire founded by this ruler expanded on both sides of the Hindukush and became the most influential civilizing force in Central Asia. The Kuṣāṇas also provided the means and resources to stimulate Chinese trade and to form a bridge between the civilizations of India and China. The political unification of peoples and tribes with a different ethnic background, language, culture and religion was the significant contribution of this period. This mighty Kuṣāṇa empire stretched from the Aral Sea to the Arabian Sea and heralded an era of political stability and unity.

While Bactria was the original nucleus and centre of the Kuṣāṇa kingdom, the vast empire of these Central Asian peoples included Northern India as far as Bihar in the east, and Sind and Baluchistan, now in Pakistan in the south-west. In the north and north-east it included Kashmir and extended upto Khotan, while in the north-west Bactria and Parthia were parts of it. The Greek traditions in Bactrian culture were preserved and further assimilated under the Kuṣāṇas who also looked to Hellenic, Iranian and Indian ideas and icons to form a totality of ethnic-cultural and socio-political phenomena. This is evident from the portrayal of divinities drawn from different pantheons[16] and portrayed on their coins. Buddhism was patronised by the great Kuṣāṇa ruler Kaniṣka in whose time the fourth Buddhist Council was held at Kālakavana, either in Kashmir or in Jalandhar.[17] The Great Silk Route, the first transcendental trade and diplomatic road in the history of mankind was laid along the kingdom of the Kuṣāṇas from China to the Mediterranean Roman empire.[18] The entire eastern Section of the Great Silk

14. Sten Konow : CII. II(1), pp. 57 ff.

15. Ref. Panjtar inscription (122) ibid, pp. 67 ff; and Taxila Silver Scroll inscription (136) ibid pp. 70 ff.

16. Ref. Puri : *Kushāṇas,* pp. 218 ff.

17. Kern : *Manual of Buddhism,* Reprint, Delhi, 1968, pp. 121 ff.

18. See '*Along the Ancient Silk Routes*—Introduction by Herbert Hertel, New York, 1982, p. 18. See also Gafurov : 'Kushan Civilisation and World Culture' in *Central Asia in the Kushan Period,* p. 76.

Route was plied by the Sogdian merchants who founded their colonies and settlements in Central Asia and established trade and cultural relations with peoples of different nationalities.

The co-existence of various ethnic-cultural traditions and different religious systems and creeds was remarkably significant in this period. It was noted for the spirit of tolerance and understanding involving the spirit of peaceful co-existence. As has been suggested, images of divinities associated with Indian, Iranian and Hellenistic pantheons were portrayed on the coins of Kaniṣka and Huviṣka.[19] These included Mithra embodying justice, the goddess Ordokhsh signifying fertility, Vertragna, the mighty God of War, Śiva, Buddha, Helios, Selena and Sarapis and many others. The syncretism of the Kuṣāṇa pantheon on their coins reflects the ethnic and cultural heterogeneity of the vast empire's population, its close association, reciprocal influences and mutual enrichment of peoples of different backgrounds—social and religious—who constituted the Kuṣāṇa state.

Despite the eclectic approach of Kaniṣka and his successors, the great Kuṣāṇa monarch was kind towards Buddhism. His patronage of the fourth Buddhist Council is already recorded. A Kharoṣṭhī record[20], probably of the year 1, from Shah-ji-Kidheri (near Peshawar) records his association with the foundation of the great stupa at the site where the famous casket was also found. This was the gift of the emperor Kaniṣka to the monastery in Kaniṣkapura. The Buddhist Council held in the time of this ruler prepared commentaries on canonical texts. One of these—the *Mahāvibhāsa*—was jointly compiled by Pārśva and Vasumitra. Buddhism seems to have made considerable progress not only in India but also in Central Asia in this period. Spreading across the Hindukush along the trade route to China, its contributions in this period were tremendous in the form of great Buddhist monuments at Bamiyan, Surkh-Kotal and Adjina-Tepe in Tajikistan. The knowledge of Indian Kharoṣṭhī script is revealed from the documents from Niya not far from

19. Rosenfield, J.M. : *The Dynastic Arts of the Kushāṇas*, California, 1967, pp. 69 ff; Puri : *Op. cit*, pp. 218ff.

20. CII.II(1) pp. 135 ff.

Khotan, and such Buddhist scriptures as the *Gandhārī Dharmapada.*[21]

The period of the Kuṣāṇas, corresponding with that of Hadrian and his successors in Rome, was one of great prosperity in the ancient world. In fact, this could be due to the great commercial activity for the overland silk trade between China and Rome in the first two centuries of the Christian era, and the Kuṣāṇas and the people under their rule seem to have participated in it. At the time of Parthian hostility, the Kuṣāṇas could divert the caravans southwards from Balkh to the Indus Delta for export of commercial goods by sea. Items of export from China included primarily silk, with Indians supplying spices, exquisite ivory etc; and, in return, Rome sent manufactured things like woollen tapestries, engraved gems, figurines, metal ware and magnificent glassware. A long list of items of export and import from and to Indian ports on the western coast is provided by Ptolemy, as is also furnished by the *Periplus.*[22] Excavations at Begram in Afghanistan have also revealed valuable information in this direction, and many other sites are equally helpful in supplying minor finds.

The Kuṣāṇa period in Central Asian history is equally notable for artistic activity. Mahāyāna Buddhism became wide spread in this area and with it grew great religious awakening, as also literary and artistic contributions of the people having faith in the religion of the Tathāgata. The spread of Buddhism did not mean the annihilation or assimilation of local creeds

21. Hambly : *Op. cit*, p. 48.

22. Sec. 41, 59. Majumdar : *Classical Accounts of India*, Calcutta, p. 290 ff. The material from these classical works has been utilised by several authors. See Warmington : *The Commerce between the Roman World and India*, Cambridge 1928; K.A. Nilakantha Sastri : *A Comprehensive History of India*, Calcutta, 1957, Chapter XV, p. 430; Puri : *Op. cit*, pp. 116 ff. Sewell on the basis of the study of Roman coins found in Southern India came to the conclusion that the culmination of trade between India and Rome had reached during the time of Augustus, and it continued upto A.D. 65, the time of Nero. He points out that the paucity of funds of Roman coins in Southern India was the consequence of the change of the social conditions of Rome itself rather than to any political reason. This contention of Sewell is challenged by Warrington who denies loss of trade (*Op. cit*, p. 89). For the *Gandhārī Dharmpada* see J. Brough's book under this name, London 1962.

and traditions. It was an intricate process of mutual influence, a creative adoption of the new doctrine with such modifications as were found necessary under the impact of local traditions. The creative approach to Buddhism was reflected in Buddhist temple architecture. Its layout and arrangement did not as a rule mean copying the Buddhist prototype of the pre-Kuṣāṇa or early Kuṣāṇa Indian counterpart, but it resembles the temples typical of the Near and Middle East, with their enclosed sanctuary surrounded by narrow processional corridors, as revealed from excavations at Kara-Tepe. This local strain in Central Asian Buddhism is said to have survived until a later period, as is evident from the excavations at Adjina Tepe, a Buddhist monastery in southern Tajikistan.

It is proposed by Gafurov[23] that the Bactrian-Tukharian school which became mature on the local central Asian traditions of Kuṣāṇa art, contributed in no less a manner to the Buddhist art of Central Asia. It was from this region that Buddhism, its art and literature was carried to China, Japan and Korea. The Chinese writings provide names of Buddhist savants from Bactria, Sogdia and Parthia contributing in terms of theological treatises and translations of original Buddhist texts into Chinese. Regular contacts were established between Asia and China in the Kuṣāṇa period.

The Kuṣāṇas in Central Asia were in turn supplanted by the Sassanians from Persia. The founder of this dynasty was Ardashir I who defeated and slew the Parthian emperor Artavan V and declared himself paramount ruler of Persia—modern Iran. According to Al-Tabari, he waged a war in the east of Iran, occupied Sistan, Abar Shab (modern Nishapur), Meru, Balkh and Khwarzim and received the homage of the Kuṣāṇas in A.D. 227. The Sassanian conquest is recorded in the inscription of Shapur I (A.D. 240-72) at Naqsh-i-Rustam, near Persepolis. This record, drafted in three languages—Pahlavi, Parthian and Greek—mentions the lists of provinces of the Sassanian empire in about A.D. 260. The victorious Persian army is said to have seized Peshawar, occupied the Indus country and pushing north, crossed the Hindukush, conquered Bactria,

23. *Central Asia in the Kushan Period*, Vol. I, Moscow, 1974, pp. 71 ff.

crossed over the Oxus and entered Samarkand and Tashkent. The Kuṣāṇa dynasty founded by the great Kaniṣka was deposed and replaced by another line of princes who recognized the suzerainty of the Persians and ruled over a considerably reduced area.[24] The Sassanian-Kuṣāṇa political relations were, however, disturbed when the latter helped the king's brother, who held the important post of viceroy of Seistan, in trying to seize the throne in the time of Babram II (A.D. 276-93). The feudal aristocracy was always a threat to the Sassanian monarchy. Bactria, Sogdiana and Gandhāra, however, remained under governors of the Sassanian royal house.[25]

At the other end in Central Asia, by the fourth century A.D., the nomad empire of the Hiung-nu in Mongolia had long been divided in two—the northern and southern portions—with incessant clash between the two groups. In A.D. 311 the southern section of the Hiung-nu captured and burnt Lo-yang,[26] the capital of the northern portion, where they set up a dynasty which survived for about four decades till its destruction by a renegade of the same race in A.D. 350. The northern section had to face another catastrophe in being driven away from the vicinity of Lake Baikal by their rivals, the Hsien-pi. They finally emerged upon the Jaxartes steppe to the north of Sogdiana. The various sections of the Hiung-nu from A.D. 350 onwards invaded the eastern provinces of the Sassanian empire where they came to be known as the Chionites.[27] The first clash bet-

24. Ghirshman, R. : *Iran* (Pelicans). (Reprint 1978, p. 292.)

25. Hambly : *Op. cit*, p. 51. Their coins have been described by Herzfeld —*The Kushans-Sassanian Coins*—(Memoirs of the Archaeological Survey of India, XXXVIII) Calcutta, 1930, and analysed by A.D.H. Bivar. 'The Kushans-Sassanian Coin Series, Journal Numismatic Society of India (JNSI) XVIII, 1956, 13-42.

26. McGovern : Op. cit, pp. 307 ff. Lo-yang was famous amongst the Romans as Sera Metropolis, the terminus of the overland Silk Route. The ensuing disturbances along the land routes further west are recorded in the Sogdian Ancient Letters. (W.B. Hennings, 'The date of the Sogdian ancient letters.' BSOAS.XII, 1948.603; Hambly : Op. cit, p. 53.)

27. According to Ghirshman, the Chionites (a term which he understood to include the Kidarites) were not distinct from the Hephthalites who play an important part in the history of the fifth century A.D. McGovern and Enoki consider the Hephthalites to be fresh arrivals who descended on Bactria early

ween Iran and the new power in the east, the kingdom of the Chionite—Hephthalites seems to have occurred under Yazdgard I. According to Ghirshman,[28] after they had been settled by Shapur II on Kuṣāṇa territory with the title of 'Confederates', the Hephthalites succeeded in evicting the Little Kuṣāṇas and formed a powerful kingdom which, towards the beginning of the fifth century, took advantage of Indian weakness to expand on both sides of the Hindukush, and also posed a threat to India.

The internal situation of the Sassanian empire further deteriorated under Peroz (A.D. 459-84). His wars against the Hephthalites brought the country to the verge of disaster; and in his ill-fated enterprise of attacking his adversaries, he paid with his life. During the reigns of the four successors of Peroz—a period of over half a century—the Hephthalite king not only exacted a heavy annual tribute in cash, but also intervened in Iranian domestic affairs.[29] The Hephthalites continued to pose threat to Iran and its security even after the restoration of their protege Qubad to the Sassanian throne in A.D. 488-89. It was only after A.D. 557 that with the help of the Turks called in western sources as Sinjibu or Silzibul, Khosrau Anoshirvan (A.D. 531-79) was able to crush the Hephthalites and their land was partitioned along the line of the Oxus.

It was during the predominance of these Hephthalites in Bactria in the fifth and early sixth centuries A.D. that they also undertook a series of incursions into the Punjab and shook the foundations of the Gupta empire. By A.D. 570 the Hūṇa chief Toramāṇa had set up his rule over a big chunk of land in Northern India from Kashmir to Madhya Pradesh (Malwa region). The Hūṇa rule beginning with Toramāṇa did not end with his son Mihirakula who in A.D. 525 was repulsed by a confederacy of Indian princes. Their hold in Kashmir lasted longer. Lakhana and Khingila in the second part of the sixth century A.D. are supposed to have ruled at Kabul or at Gardiz,

---

in the fifth century A.D. and drove the Kidarites southwards (quoted by Hambly : *Op. cit.* p. 55).

28. *Op. cit*, p. 298.

29. Ghirshman : *Op. cit*, p. 299; Hambly : *Op. cit*, p. 56.

the latter for at least eight years, as is evident from his record.[30] The Huns are mentioned as anti-Buddhists and were responsible for the destruction of Buddhist monasteries in India. Their rule in Bactria and other parts of Afghanistan as also in North-west India (now Pakistan) and Kashmir, had left their homeland open to other political forces. The Hsien-pi for a time dominated the steppes of Mongolia, but by the sixth century A.D. a group known as the Juan-juan, identified with the Avans of the later times in Europe, gained ascendancy. The rise of the Turks resulted in the expulsion of the Juan-juan dynasty from the Mongolian steppe and its final extinction by A.D. 552.

The founder of the Turkish empire was the chief called Tu-men (in Chinese sources) and Bumin in the Turkish inscriptions, with his residence at Aq-Dagh to the north of Kucha. Soon the Turkish realm extended westwards as far as Oxus and Caspian sea. Sinjibu (Silzibul), brother of Tu-men in alliance with Khosrau I Anoshirvan of Iran was responsible for the destruction of the Hephthalite kingdom, and after division set up a common frontier with Sassanian Iran.[31] Istemi, the brother of Tu-men, same as Sinjibu (Silzibul) died in A.D. 576 leaving strong Turkish influence in Sogdiana. The Turks were, however, divided into Eastern and Western; and both made nominal submission to the Tang dynasty of China in A.D. 630 and 659 respectively. In Mongolia a new empire of the Eastern (Blue) Turks was established[32] in A.D. 682. Qapghan of this dynasty subjugated the Kirghiz and Turgesh in the west and reached the Iron Gates in Sogdiana. Between A.D. 699 and 711, the Khanate of the Eastern Turks included that of the Western one as well. The Arab expansion with the conquest of Sogdiana, now named Mawarannahr, and their clash with the Iranian ruler which lead to the death of Yazdagird III (A.D. 632-51), finally poised the Arab armies on the banks of the Oxus against the Turks for the possession of the provinces to the north of the river.

30. EI. XXXV. pp. 45-7.

31. Hambly : *Op. cit*, p. 59.

32. Giraud : *L'Empire des Turcs Celestes*, and D. Sinor : *Introduction a l'etude de l'Eurasie Centrale*—quoted by Hambly : Op. cit, 323 notes.

At the eastern extremity of the Turkish world in Mongolia, a new state of the Uighurs[33] was formed at the expense of the Eastern Turks with its capital at Ordu-Balish in A.D. 744. The trilingual inscription of Qara Balgasun, the present name of the old capital records the conversion of the rulers of the Uighur Kaghanate to the Manichaean religion.[34] The text of this record is in Chinese, Sogdian and Turkish. Sogdian was originally the language round Samarkand, but acquired an international character as it was used by merchants through the Tarim basin and spread even to China. As a more varied literary content, this language has provided Buddhist, Manichaean and Christian texts. That explains its use in this record. The Turkish dialect written in the Uighur alphabet was extensively used for Buddhist and other literatures. It may be mentioned that the name Uighur is more correctly applied to the alphabet than to the language which appears to have been the literary form of the various Turkish idioms spoken north and south of the Tien-shan. The use of this dialect for Buddhist literature spread considerably when the Uighurs supplanted the rule of the Tibetans in the Tarim basin in about A.D. 860 and founded a kingdom themselves.[35] This might have been a later phase since the first Uighur empire lasted until A.D. 840 when a sudden rising of the Kirghiz tribes along the river Yenisei led to the destruction of its capital and the dispersal of its various tribes. Certain groups of survivors migrated south-westwards, and established themselves in the oases of the Tarim basin in Sinkiang.

33. A Turkic-speaking people of interior Asia are scattered for the most part in western China in the Sinkiang Uighur Autonomous Region, while a small number occupy Central Asian parts of the Soviet Union. These Uighurs located in various parts of Mongolia and western China during the 9th to 13th centuries, eventually moved westwards (*Encyclopedia Britannica*—Chicago 1972, Vol. 22 pp. 467-68). The earlier historical account is provided by Hambly (*Op. cit*, p. 60) based on Hamilton's study (*Les Ouighours a l'epoque des Cinq Dynasties*).

34. E. Chavannes and P. Pelliot—'Un traite Manicheen retrouve Chine'. *Journal Asiatique* J.A. 1913. 177. (Hambly : *Op. cit*, p. 324, n.32.)

35. Eliot : *Hinduism and Buddhism*—Vol. III, p. 192. This kingdom is said to extend into China and lasted long, for Sutras in Uighur were printed at Peking in 1330 and Uighur manuscripts copied in the reign of Kan-Hsi (1662-1723) are reported from a monastery near Suchow.

The Political States of Central Asia

Reference has no doubt been made to the different tribes playing an active role in the history of Central Asia as also in the carving out of big empires. The political condition of the country is clearly described by Hsuan-tsang in the middle of the seventh century A.D. The Chinese pilgrim divides the country into two zones—the western and the eastern. The western zone consisted of the sixteen states from Ta-mi (Termez) to Kien-chin (Gaz) covering the whole area from the Iron Pass (Derbent) to Gaz, the most fertile zone of the Oxus valley. The eastern zone consisted of the other states, beginning with An-ta-lo-Fo (Anderab), which were mostly mountainous and forming part of the ancient Tu-ho-lo (Tukhāra) country. These states were under Turkish domination, while the western ones were preserving some sort of autonomy. These might have been the original administrative divisions[36] of Tokharistan under the Yueh-chi. In a broader political perspective one need not enumerate these, but concentrate on the bigger states which had separate identity in the vast Tarim basin, and lacked political unity. These units centering round cities or groups of towns, divided by deserts lived their own civic life and had considerable independence under local rulers, although the Chinese, Turks or Tibetans stationed their troops there and appointed residents to supervise the collection of tribute. The chief of these cities or oases were Kashgar in the west; Kucha, Karashahr, Turfan and Hami successively to the north-east, and Yarkand Khotan and Miran

36. S. Beal : *Buddhist Records of the Western World,* London 1906, Vol. I, p. 37 ff. The pilgrim informs us that at that time the royal race had been extinct for many centuries, and in his time each of the 27 States, divided by natural boundaries, was under a chief who was ruling independently. The country as a whole was dependent on the Turks, and was divided into two zones—the western and the eastern. The former consisted of the sixteen states from Ta-mi (Termez) to Kie-Chin (Gaz), the most fertile zone of the Oxus valley. He visited these states on way to India. The eastern zone consisted of the other states, mostly mountainous, beginning with An-ta-lo-fo (Anderab) which he visited in the course of his return journey from India towards Kashghar. All these states are described by the pilgrim as 'the ancient Tu-ho-lo (Tukhāra) country—probably under the Turkish domination (See also Vol. II, pp. 286 ff). Bagchi enumerates these kingdoms and records their identification (*India and Central Asia,* Op. cit, pp. 25 ff).

to the south-east. Pelliot also notices[37] a Sogdian colony to the outh of Lob Nov, which according to him, might have had much to do with the transmission of Buddhism and Nestorianism to China. The historical account based on Chinese sources of these states might be traced with corroboration from archaeological evidence, with particular reference to Buddhism and its expansion in these areas.

Kashgar[38]

The earliest account of Kashgar could be traced in the 'Annals of the Former Han Dynasty'. The Chinese writers reproduce the name as Ch'ia-sha, Chich-cha, etc., but also call the region Su-le, Shu-le, or She-le. After the mission of Chang-Chien (c. 139-127 B.C.), there was expanding Chinese knowledge of the western Regions to the Oxus and the confines of Persia. Trade with Bactria and Sogdiana grew rapidly and Kashgar, which was a convenient emporium, became a Chinese protected state in the first century B.C. With the relaxation of the Chinese hold about the time of the Christian era, it was subdued by the neighbouring kingdom of Khotan. The conquests of Pan-ch'ao restored Chinese supremacy, but early in the second century A.D. the Yueh-chih interfered in the political affairs of this place and placed their protegé on the throne.[39] It is proposed that the interference of the Yueh-chih in the affairs of Kashgar in c. 120 A.D. resulted in the introduction of Buddhism into that territory.[40] This assumption, according to Stein, would

37. Eliot : *Op. cit*, 200 n; also J.A. January, 1916, pp. 111-123.

38. For a comprehensive account of Kashgar, see Aurel Stein : *Ancient Khotan* (Oxford, 1907) Chapter III, pp. 47 ff. Stein utilizes O. Franke's paper 'Kaschgar and die Kharosthi'; *Sitzungsber der Kon preuss. Akad der Wissenschaften*, Berlin 1903, pp. 184 ff for various Chinese designations of Kashgar.

39. Stein : *Khotan*, p. 55. For a summary of the Chinese records concerning the history of Eastern Turkestan during the first century of our era, see Richthofen : *China*, i, pp. 468 ff. See also Spect 'Etudes Sur L Asie Centrale ii in JA. 1897, p. 97.

40. Stein : *Op. cit*, p. 56 and note 23. Franke calls attention to a Tibetan text translated by Rockhill embodying traditions of Khotan or Li-Yul which mentions that a princess of Ga-hyag, who bacame the wife of king Vijayasimha of Khotan, helped to spread Buddhism in Shu-lik. (See Rockhill : *Life of the Buddha*, p. 240.)

agree with the tradition recorded by Hsuan-tsang which makes the princely hostage from the States east of the Tsung-ling, including Sha-la or Kashgar, reside in a Buddhist Convent,[41] and connects their allegiance with the reign of Kaniṣka, the great patron of Buddhism. He presumes that it is more probable that the Buddhist Church and its establishment, whatever its period, was the result of impact from Baktra and not Khotan, as Mahāyānism was the prevailing form of Buddhism in Khotan while Hīnayānism was prevalent in Kashgar.

The rapid decay of Chinese power in Central Asia commenced under Emperor An-Ti (A.D. 107-125) and for nearly five hundred years the Chinese sources provide only scanty information about the political conditions of Kashgar and eastern Turkestan. The revolt of the Uighur tribes in the region of Turfan and Hami threatened the Chinese domination in the Tarim basin at its north-eastern end about the same time that Kashgar fell under Chinese influence. Emperor Wu-Ti (A.D. 265-290) appears[42] to have made efforts to re-establish Chinese influence in the south of the Tarim basin, but the dynasties following in quick succession until the advent of the Tang (A.D. 618) were too weak to resume a policy of conquest beyond Sha-chou—the western-most part of Kan-su. There is no information about Kashgar during the subsequent centuries when probably it was part of the Khotanese kingdom. In the reign of Wen-Cheng-Ti[43] (A.D. 452-466) we hear of an envoy sent by the king of Su-le to the Imperial court to present a sacred relic, the reputed dress of Buddha which proved incombustible. Early in the following century, Kashgar figures among the numerous territories of Eastern Turkestan which, according to the Annals of the Liang Dynasty and the *Pei-Shih* (a work published about A.D. 644), was subject to the Yeh-ta or Hephthalites, who had founded a powerful empire in the Oxus Basin. They carried their conquests down to Gandhāra and beyond the Indus in the south, and as far as Khotan and Karasahr in the east.[44] The Hephthalites, in turn, succumbed to the attacks of

41. *Si-Yu-Ki* trans. Beal. i. p. 57.
42. Stein : *Op. cit*, p. 57.
43. ibid, p. 58.
44. The information about the Hephthalites and their conquests is avail-

the western Turks (called Tu-chuch by the Chinese) and all the territories north of the Oxus then passed under the domination of the western Turks, who exercised their sway from their encampments in the valleys of Tien-Shan north of Kucha and Kashgar. According to the Chinese accounts, the subject states were left in charge of their hereditary local rulers, each under the control of a Turkish Tudun who watched over the collection of the tribute.[45]

The reassertion of Chinese influence begins from A.D. 630 when they subjugated the Northern Turks while the western ones were dissipated by internal feuds after the murder of Tung Shin-hu Kagan who had accorded a grand reception to the Chinese pilgrim Hsuan-tsang in A.D. 630. The Imperial Chinese army in 640 had occupied Kao-chang or Turfan, and the Protectorate of An-hsi was established in that territory. The king of Karashahr, who in 632 sent an embassy to China, but later on had retracted, was vanquished and carried off as a prisoner. The Chinese conquest of the Tarim basin was complete with the defeat of the Western Turks in 658, and their suzerainty was re-established over Eastern Turkestan. The whole of this region was divided into four administrative divisions called Four Garrisons.[46] The Chinese conquest found Kashgar and other territories of Eastern Turkestan under the rule of the indigenous princes, and left them undisturbed after accepting their submission. The notice on Su-le contained in the Tang Annals mentions

---

able from the account of Sung-Yun who in A.D. 520 visited both the Yeh-ta seats in Badakshan and the king (Mihirakula) representing their power in Gandhāra, distinctly attests Khotan as the eastern limit of the vast dominion tributory to them. The Pei-Shih which derives its notices about the Hephthalites from Sung-Yun's missions, mentions Sha-li (Kashgar) along with Sogdiana, Khotan, Bokhara and over thirty smaller states as among the western countries, subject to them (Stein : *Op. cit*, p. 58, n. 5).

45. Stein : *Khotan*, p. 58 and n. 8.

46. According to the passage from the Tang Annals, the protectorate was intended to govern Yu-tien (Khotan), Suei-shin (Tokmak) and Su-le, the whole of these territories (including Kucha itself) being thenceforth known as 'Four Garrisons'. There can be no doubt that this term included all Eastern Turkestan, and not merely the territories enumerated as seats of the 'Four Garrisons (Stein : *Op. cit*, p. 60).

the despatch of the first embassy of the king of Kashgar in the year 635, and the second four years later as tokens of submission. The Chinese authority and its continuance depended upon their power to enforce it. The authority over Kashgar and the rest of the 'Four Garrisons' did not last long. In the year 662, a rebellion broke out among the western Turks and the Chinese army suffered humiliation at the hands of the Tibetans who, after their conquest of the Kuku-Nor region (663 A.D.), rapidly rose to be formidable rivals of the Chinese power in Central Asia. They made themselves masters of the 'Four Garrisons'. From 692 till the re-establishment of the Protectorate of An-hsi at Kucha and the reconquest of the 'Four Garrisons', the Chinese had to face two powerful enemies, the Arabs in the west and the Tibetans in the south. The struggle against both continued during the reign of Emperor Hsuan-tsung (713-762 A.D.), who had to adopt a purely defensive policy. In the year 714, the Chinese pursuing a more active foreign policy initiated by Emperor Hsuan-tsung recovered their supremacy over the western Turks, and were then face to face with the Arabs.[47] The Tibetan inroads were continuing into the southern portion of the Tarim basin, but Chinese diplomacy succeeded in checking them. The suzerainty of China was acknowledged by all the States threatened by the Arabs in the west from Kashmir to the Oxus and Jaxartes. Kao-Hsien-chih, a general of Korean origin specially appointed by Emperor Hsuan-tsung to take charge of the campaign against the Tibetans in the year 747 to wrest Little Po-lu (modern Gilsib) after marching over the Pamirs and Hindukush from Kashgar, suffered a crushing defeat in 751 from which the Chinese never recovered.[48]

A succession of disasters occurring about the same time were contributory factors to the decline of the Chinese prestige in Central Asia. The Tibetans who had a hand in fomenting internal troubles in China, availed of the opportunity, and between 758-59 they gradually overran the regions of Ho and Lung, corresponding to the present province of Kan-su and the extreme west of Shan-si, and all direct communication between China and the Protectorates of An-hsi and Pei-ting was inter-

47. Stein : *Op. cit*, p. 62.
48. ibid, p. 63.

rupted.[49] The Chinese governors, however, managed to maintain their authority as heads of the 'Four Garrisons' and of Pei-ting (near Guchen) over the territories under their charge, and succeeded in sending envoys to the Imperial Court through the friendly territory of the Uighurs. In A.D. 791, the Protectorate of Pei-ting was taken by the Tibetans, and from that time onwards nothing more is heard of An-hsi or the 'Four Garrisons'. The Eastern Turkestan disappears from the accounts of the Annalists of the Tang dynasty, and its history is shrouded under obscurity for more than a century. The Tibetans dominated over the Tarim basin, and posed as dangerous neighbours to their old friends and allies, the Arabs, in the region of the upper Oxus. Between 860 and 873 A.D. their supremacy was broken by the Uighurs who established a powerful kingdom comprising the region once ruled from Pei-ting and extending westward as far as Ak-su. Khotan apparently became independent. The rest of the territories once comprised in the 'Four Garrisons' became subject to Turkish princes of the Karluk tribe, residing at Bala Saghun, near Lake Issik-kul. Between A.D. 926-41 occasional missions were sent to the Chinese court. Very soon afterwards, the ruler holding the territories from the Issik-kul to Kashgar, was converted to Islam. As Satok Boghra Khan he established link with the west and the later history of Kashgar falls beyond the scope of this work.

The information relating to Buddhism in Kashgar, forming the subject of enquiry, is no doubt supplied by the Chinese pilgrims who visited Kashgar on their way to or from China.[50] The general description of Kashgar and of its people in the Tang Annals is substantially the same as found in Hsuen-tsang's[51]

49. Ibid; Bushell : *Early History of Tibet*, p. 41.

50. From the time of the Former Han Dynasty when the States of Central Asia were first opened upto the political interference of China, down to the Tang Period the region of the present Kashgar was generally known by the name of *Su-le* or *Shu-le*. The name Sha-le is given to Kashgar in the accounts of the journeys of the pilgrims Sun-Yun, Kumārajīva (400 A.D.), Fa-Yung (420 A.D.), Dharmagupta (c. 593-595 A.D.) and Wu-Kung; the latter's itinerary distinctly records the identical application of Sha-le and Sh-li (Stein : *Ancient Khotan*, p. 48).

51. Stein : Op. cit, p. 66 ff; Beal : Op. cit, Vol. I, p. 19. The notices of Kashgar during the Tang period are collected by Stein in his work on Ancient Khotan (pp. 65-70).

Hsi-Yu-chi. The name of the ruling family (Pei) is actually found in the imperial decree conferring in A.D. 728 the royal title on An-chih, chief of Su-le. The title A-mo-chih is attested by the royal decree and was also shared by the rulers of Khotan in the eighth century A.D. Chih-meng (A.D. 404) saw at Chi-sha (Kashgar), besides Buddha's alms bowl, also his spittoon, which he describes as being made of a stone of variegated colour. The biography of Kumārajīva records a visit of this savant to Sha-le or Kashgar about A.D. 400 and specially mentions that he placed on his head the alms bowl (*pātra*) of Buddha which was believed to possess the miraculous quality of changing its weight. The Chinese monk Chih-meng who proceeded to India via Lop-nor and Khotan in the year 404 witnessed the identical miracle when handling Buddha's alms-bowl which was shown to him in the kingdom of Chia-sha. Fa-hien (Fa-hsien) also describes his stay at Chien-cha (Kashgar), being invited there to participate in the great quinquennial assembly (*pañca-pariṣad*), and the royal hospitality accorded to him and other monks (*śramaṇas*) participating in it. The pilgrim mentions a spittoon which belonged to Buddha, made of stone, and in colour like his alms-bowl. This alms-bowl was seen by Fa-hien in Purushpur or Peshawar, where it was a chief object of pious worship, and is described by him 'as of various colours, black predominating, with the seams that show its four-fold composition distinctly marked.' Chi-sha, like so many other places, also boasted of a tooth of Buddha, for which the people, according to the pilgrim, had set up a stupa. Connected with the stupa were more than a thousand monks and their disciples, all students of the Hīnayāna.[52]

Hsuen-tsang, the next Chinese pilgrim, provides some details about Chi-sha or Kashgar, with the uncomplimentary character of the people, but praise for the textile productions of the place. The written characters in his time were an Indian type, in all probability a variety of the Brāhmī script, but the language and pronunciation were quite different from other countries. Buddhism was at that time in a flourishing condition, taking into consideration the number of its followers and their zeal for the religion of Buddha. He records several hundreds of Saṅghārāmas

52. Stein : *Op. cit*, p. 56.

with some ten thousand followers, studying the Little Vehicle and belonging to the Sarvāstivādin school. Further, without understanding the principles, the monks recite many religious chants wading through the three *Piṭakas* and the *Vibhāsa*. Two other pilgrims Dharmacandra of India and Wu-kung of China passed through Kashgar, the former on his way back from China and the latter on his way to Gandhāra. The former died at Khotan, while the latter has left valuable evidence relating to Chinese control over the territory of the 'Four Garrisons'. The extension of Chinese power westwards, thus, was helpful not only in fostering intercourse with India—the home of Buddhism, but also with its centres in Central Asia. It also simultaneously profited both Christianity[53] and Zoroastrianism for missionary activities in this part of Central Asia as also in China itself. Stein records[54] a number of stūpas close to Kashgar—the stūpas of Kurghan-Tim and Kizul-Debe, as also the ruins near Khan-vi, including ruins of Topa-Tim and Maurn-Tim stūpa, but antiquities found in these are scarce.

Khotan[55]

The early history of Khotan and its importance in Central Asia are not matters of conjecture. Chinese, Tibetan and Archaeological sources provide ample information on both these points. Yu-tien, Yu-tun, Kiu-tan, Huo-tan etc. are the Chinese transcription of the original name Godana or Khotana. Hsuan-

53. *Op. cit*, p. 71. Marco Polo when passing here on his way to China (c. 1273-1274) notes of 'Carcar' that 'there are in the country many Nestorian Christians who have churches of their own'. In Yarkand too he found Nestorian and Jacobite Christians. (Yule : *Marco Polo*.1. pp. 182, 187.)

54. *Op. cit*, pp. 73 ff.

55. For a detailed account of Khotan, its early history and archaeological finds, see A. Stein : *Ancient Khotan*—Op. cit, pp. 151 ff. He also quotes A Remusat : *Histoire de la Ville de Khotan*, Paris, 1820; Stein : *Sand-buried Ruins of Khotan, Personal Narrative of a Journey of archaeological and geographical exploration in Chinese Turkestan*, London, 1903. Extracts from Tibetan Accounts of Khotan based on Rockhill's *Life of the Buddha*, pp. 230 ff, and the works there quoted, as also Notes from the *Gośriṅga Vyākaraṇa*—also figure in the form of Appendix E, communicated and annotated by F.W. Thomas (Stein : Op. cit, pp. 581-85). The present account is based on Stein's work, of course, with proper references and scrutiny to the sources quoted by him, as could be available.

tsang mentions the name Chu-sa-tan-na corresponding to the Sanskrit *Kustana*—'breast of the earth'—which is also noticed in Kharoṣṭhī documents of the third century A.D. from Niya Site. These in their Prākrit queerly mixed with Sanskrit phrases, employ the form *Kustana* or *Kustanaka* along with the far more frequent one *Khotamna*. The pilgrim also mentions the name formerly used Yu-tien by which Khotan is invariably designated in all the Chinese dynastic histories from the period of the former Han down to that of the Mings. The Tibetan notices of Khotan history called 'The Annals of Li-yul' also provide information about the foundation of the Khotan kingdom, as also about the origin of various Buddhist sanctuaries. These also provide a long string of royal names with occasional reference to pious foundations and doctrinal matters. The regal names are all Indian and formed with Vijaya as the pre-fix. The Chinese Annals and Wu-kung (Chinese pilgrim c. 786 A.D.) mention Wei-chih as the family name, which might be a rendering of Vijaya. The identity of Li-yul and Khotan first correctly indicated by Wassilieff is not questioned. The foundation of Khotan is traced to the God Vaiśravaṇa (Pi-sha-men) or Kubera. The Tibetan Annals make an exiled son of Aśoka (Kustana) ultimately establishing his kingdom in Khotan, while it is not possible to fix any date for the supposed Indian immigration. Both Hsuan-tsang and the Tibetan 'Annals of Li-yul', however, agree that it could be roughly placed before the introduction of Buddhism into Khotan, which took place in the reign of Vijayasambhava, 170 years after the establishment of the kingdom.[56] According to the Chinese pilgrim, Arhat Vairocana from Kashmir is said to have first preached the Law in Khotan and had also set up the earliest Buddhist convent there. It is no doubt presumed[57] on the basis of the Kuṇāla legend that there must have been communication between Buddhist Khotan and the Taxila region, through Kashmir or Gandhāra. A settlement of immi-

56. Rockhill : *Life of the Buddha* Op. cit, p. 234. Stein : Op. cit, p. 160.

57. According to the account uniformly told in the Hsi-Yu-chi as well as in the 'Life', there stood to the south of the royal city at a distance of 10 li a large convent built by an ancient king in honour of the Arhat Vairocana (Pi-lu-che-na) to whom was attributed the introduction of Buddhism into Khotan. (Op. cit, p. 231).

grants from the extreme north-west of India, as assumed in the Khotan tradition, seems confirmed by Stein,[58] who was frequently struck by a certain curious resemblance in general appearance of features between the Khotanese and the Kashmiris.

According to the Annals of the First Han Dynasty, the first embassy from the Yu-tien was received in China in the reign of Emperor Wu-ti[59] (140-87 B.C.). Khotan in this period was a small state with a population of 19,300 consisting of 3,300 families, and included 2400 soldiers. The other small states in its neighbourhood were then independent. During the second quarter of the 1st century A.D., Yu-tien rose to political importance for the Chinese. However, towards the end of the reign of Emperor Kuang-Wu-ti (25-27 A.D.), king Yu-lin of Khotan had become subject to the powerful king of *So-che* in the territory of Yarkand but soon after during the period 58-73 A.D., a Khotanese general named Hsiu-mo-pa revolted and asserted his independence. His nephew and successor Kuang-te conquered Cokkuka and made Khotan so powerful that thirteen states to the north-west as far as Kashgar acknowledged his sovereignty. Khotan and Shan-shan (near about Lop nor) are described as the two territories controlling the southern routes leading to China. Khotan, however, submitted to Pan chao, the generalissimo of the Imperial Chinese force. The Chinese power in the Tarim basin, however, was steadily waning during the second century A.D. Events recorded for the years 151-152 A.D. provide a glimpse of the modest limits of Chinese control at Yu-tien. According to the Tibetan Annals,[60] the successor of Vijayasiṁha, 16th in descent from Kustana, allied himself with king Kanika

58. Stein : *Op. cit*, p. 165.

59. Remusat : *Ville de Khotan*, pp. 1 ff; Stein : *Op. cit*, p. 166.

60. According to Sten Konow, citing the annals of Li country (Thomas : *Tibetan Literary Texts* etc., Op. cit, London, 1935, p. 119) originally king Kaniṣka and the king of the Gu-zan and the Li ruler, king Vijayakīrti, and others led an army into India and captured a city named Soked (evidently Sāketa). Similarly the translation of Kumāralāta's *Kalpanāmaṇḍitikā* by Kumārajīva (c. 405 A.D.) states that Chen-tan old pronunciation, according to Karlgran No. 1194 and Tsien-de'an 967, Kaniṣka conquered Tung Tien-chu i.e. Eastern India (Levi J.A. IX. viii. 1896, p. 447; IA. XXXII, 1903, p. 385; Sten Konow : IHQ. XIV, p. 149).

of Guzan (Kaniṣka of Kuṣāṇa family) and helped him in his conquest of Eastern India as far as Soked (Sāketa).

Khotan's relations with China were not smooth during this period. There was a revolt under the leadership of the local governor Shu-po against the Chinese, resulting in the killing of the Chinese commander but there was no retaliation from the Chinese side. Khotan, however, sent embassies to China between 202 and 220. During the epoch of the three kingdoms (A.D. 220-264) Yo-tien (Khotan) appears to have been under a powerful ruler, and subjugated the neighbouring states of Yu-ni (Kerniya), Su-le (Kashgar) and Yung-lu, but it did send another embassy to China in 222. During the period of the Tsin dynasties (A.D. 265-419), the Chinese influence seems to have been only casual and superficial, if any. Fa-hien's reference[61] to Khotan, where he reached in A.D. 400 after a difficult journey from Kucha is no doubt reproduced in *Pien-i-tien* which furnishes an acccount of Khotan for the period of the Northern Wei Dynasty (A.D. 386-534). The Chinese pilgrim found Buddhism in Khotan in a very flourishing condition and describes the glories of its monastic establishments in some detail. The monks numbered several thousands, most of them being students of the Mahāyāna. There were hospitable arrangements in the Saṅghārāmas for the reception of travelling monks, and he notices the custom of erecting small stūpas in front of each dwelling family. The Gomatī monastery, the residence of the pilgrim and his companions, alone contained 3000 monks of the Mahāyāna school. He also refers to Buddhist celebrations with the taking out of the images of the fourteen great monasteries, more than thirty cubits high. The religious festival commencing in the fourth month lasted for fourteen days with the king and queen participating in it and offering their obeissance. The pilgrim closes his account with reference to another great shrine, known as 'the King's New Monastery'.

In 445 Khotan was invaded by Mu-li-yen, the chief of Tu-yuk-hun,[62] resulting in the death of the king and the ravaging of the

61. *Fahien's Travels* trans. Legge, pp. 16-20; Stein: Op. cit, p. 169.

62. This chief of the Tu-Yuk-hun, named Mu-liyen was driven from the Tangut country by a Chinese army, and he had to take refuge westwards. He

country. Relations with China were, however, maintained with the despatch of embassies in A.D. 457, 466, 467 and 468. Towards the close of the reign of Hsien-Wen-ti (c. 470) an envoy called Su-mu-chieh arrived from Khotan to seek help against Juan-juan which was, however, denied. During the reign of king Vijaya Saṅgrāma, Khotan was invaded by A-no-so, resulting in devastation and burning of monasteries. The Khotanese also retaliated later on, and seem to have recovered very soon. Normal embassies were sent to China a number of times between 509 and 541, and the presents included a Buddha statue of Jade carved in foreign lands. In 519 Sung-Yun reached Khotan from the direction of Shan-shan and refers to the first stūpa of Khotan—erected miraculously by Vairocana. Both Sung-Yun and the Pei-shih agree in enumerating Khotan among the numerous states of the Tarim and Oxus basins which at the time of the former's journey acknowledged the sovereignty of the White Huns. This dependence on the basis of the reference from the Annals of the Liang dynasty continued during the whole period of this dynasty (A.D. 502-556). The pilgrim Jinagupta from India, who in A.D. 555 passed through Yu-tien on his way to China, just records this fact.[63] During the epoch of the Sui (A.D. 581-618), the king of Khotan was Wang with his title Pei-She-pi-lien (Vijaya). According to the Tang Annals as well, the family of the ruling dynasty was called Wei-che (Vijaya), the title borne by members as well, some of whose names are also mentioned. Reference is made to some rulers who sent embassies to China, like Wu-mi in 632. Fu-tu-Sin of Khotan went to China to receive a mandate personally from the Emperor in 643-649, followed by another Fu-tu-hiong in 674-675 to pay homage along with his retinues. The names of several Khotanese rulers are also mentioned in Annals, like Fu-tu-king, Fu-tu-ta, Fu-tu-koei and Fu-tu-sheng, the last one dying in China in 757. At that time his brother Vijaya-Yao was ruling the

---

is said to have killed the king of Khotan and to have effected great carnage (Remusat : Op. cit, pp. 18, 21; Voyage : de Song Yun, p. 16n; Stein: Op. cit, p. 170).

63. Stein. *Op. cit*, p. 172. For the life history of this prince of Gandhāra who lived in the city of *Fou-lieou cha fou lo* (Puruṣapura) see Bagchi, *Le Canon Bouddhiane en Chine*—henceforth Bagchi, *Le Canon*—Paris, 1927, pp. 276 ff.

country. He ruled till 786 when Wu-kong visited the country.[64] The Chinese supremacy in Khotan ended about 791, although several missions were sent to China between 940-966.[65] Khotan resisted for long against the Arab invaders but ultimately lost the ground and by the year 1000 the Muslim rule was established in Khotan.[66]

While the political history of Khotan and its relations with China have been sketched, reference might be made to its importance as a Buddhist centre as also the archaeological finds in the neighbouring areas constituting the old kingdom of Khotan. The introduction of Buddhism during the reign of king Vijaya Sambhava, the grandson of Kustana, has already been recorded, as also the reference made to the monk Ārya Vairocana who was supposed to be an incarnation of Maitreya and for whom king Vijaya Sambhava built the great monastery of Bar-ma, the first in Khotan. Fuller information about this event is provided by Song-yun and Hsuan-tsang. The former mentions the name of the monastery as Tsan-mo, the Tsar-ma of the Tibetan sources, identified by Stein[67] with Chalma-kazan in the neighbourhood of Yotkan. Three Arhats from India—Buddhaduta, Khagata and

64. See Chavannes and S. Levi—*L'Itineraire d'Ou-kong*, p. 27, cited by Stein—Op. cit, p. 177.

65. See Stein—Op. cit, p. 178. Remusat- *Ville de Khotan*, pp. 74-81. The renewed diplomatic relations were revived, it seems, to secure help against the Tibetans. The Chang-Kuang-yeh mission to Khotan was a step in this direction. The renewed presentations of tribute which are recorded for the next few decades, however, limited the practical advantages which Khotan could derive from the distant empire (ibid, p. 179). In 969, the king Nan-tsung-chang is named as the sender of a mission conducted by Chih-mo-shan, and accompanied by one of the Buddhist monks who had previously visited the Imperial court. In 971 it was again a Buddhist priest (Chi-hsiang) who brought a letter from the king of Khotan, offering to send in tribute a dancing elephant which he had captured in a war against the kingdom of Kashgar (Remusat. *Op. cit*, p. 86; Stein. *Op. cit*, p. 180).

66. The Pien-i-tien's extracts notice an embassy from Khotan (Yi-tien) sent in the year 1009 and sent by the king or hei-han of that territory and that the ambassador bringing the tribute was a hui-hu i.e. probably a Muhammadan Turk, called Lo-ssu-wen. This title is a transcription of the Turkish title Khakan (Khan). The Mohammadan historians furnish one definite fact, viz. that in 1006 Khotan was held by Yusuf Qadr Khan (Stein—*Op. cit*, p. 180).

67. Op. cit, p. 232.

Khagadrod settled at Aryastana (Sthāna) of Hgeu-to-san, the vihāra built by king Vijayavīrya.[68] Three generations later, the Chinese princess Pu-nye-shar (Puṇeśvarā), who was the queen of king Vijayajaya and responsible for introducing seri-culture[69] in Khotan, built two monasteries for Kalyāṇamitra Ārya Saṁghaghoṣa who had gone from India. One of the king's three sons, Dharmānanda became a monk and came to India. He belonged to the Mahāsaṅghika school of Buddhism and built eight monasteries for it. The number of monastries kept on increasing and at the time of Hsuan-tsang's visit there were in the capital over 100 monasteries with 5000 monks who were all followers of Mahāyānism. The pilgrim also mentions[70] some of the important monasteries, besides the oldest one of Tsar-ma : Ti-ko-po-Fa-na, Sha-mo-no, Gośṛṅga and Mo-She. The first one probably Durgha bhavana, contained an image of Buddha, mysteriously brought to Khotan and is the same as Bha-va-na of the Tibetan Annals. The monastery of Sha-mo-no was an important convent with a stūpa nearly 100 feet high. This seems identical with Sum-na of the Tibetan text, built by king Vijayasiṁha for Ānandasena, the king of Kashgar after his defeat and subsequent conversion to Buddhism. Its ruins, according to Stein, are located at the village of Somiya in the neighbourhood of Yotkan.

68. Ibid, p. 186, 223.

69. A painted panel discovered by Aurel Stein from Dandan-Uilliq presents a spirited picture of the Chinese princess in this act of offering protection to a basketful of unpierced cocoons. An attendant pointing to the princess's head dress recalls her beneficent smuggling by which Khotan was supposed to have obtained its first silk worms, while another attendant engaged at a loom or silk weaving implement symbolizes the industry which was founded at the princess's initiative. A divine figure seated in the background is supposed to represent the genius presiding over the silk worms. (Stein. Op. cit, p. 230. See also Chapter IX, Section V in this work.) This may be compared with the version provided by the Annals of Li-yul (Rockhill. Op. cit, pp. 238 ff). It is connected with the legend of the So-mo-je Convent and Vijayajaya's association with it. It seems he was hostile to the raising of silk worms till the queen Princess Pu-nye-shar, the daughter of the ruler of China, could exhibit the utility of this industry. The king called from India the Bhikṣu Saṅghaghoṣa and made him his spiritual adviser, and to atone for his wickedness, he built the Po-tarya and Ma-dza caityas and a great vihāra or, the caitya and the great vihāra of Ma-dza. (Stein—*op. cit*, p. 230.)

70. Beal : *Op. cit.*, I, pp. 10 ff.

The monastery of Mo-she was built by the Chinese queen of a former ruler (Vijayajaya of the Tibetan text), and was the same as Maza, built in commemoration of the successful introduction of sericulture. Aurel Stein locates its ruins at Kum-i-shahidan. The famous Gośrṅga or Gośīrṣa monastery was built on the slopes of the Gośrṅga Hill. Its inmates were all Mahāyānists in the time of Hsuan-tsang. The monastery is also mentioned in the *Sūryagarbha-sūtra*,[71], a Buddhist canonical text which was translated into Chinese between 589 and 619 by Narendra Yaśas in a list of holy spots (*pīṭhas*) sanctified by the presence of a Bodhisattva. The site has been located in a two-storeyed cave in the Kohmali hill on the bank of the Kara-kash. A fragmentary manuscript of Prākrit *Dhammapada* in Kharoṣṭhī was procured here by Duttrevil de Rhins.[72] Reference to the Gomatī monastery, as described by Fa-hien, is already noticed. The pilgrim also refers to the regulated life of the monks in that monastery.

Khotan at the height of its power extended upto Ni-jang (present Niya site) in the east and to So-kiu (Cokkuka) in the west. It originally included four states Jong-lu-yu-mi, Kiu-le, Pi-shan and Yu-tien (Khotan) proper. Later on the number was raised to six—Ilchi or Khotan, Yuruna-kash, Kara-kash, Khira, Keriya and Lo-la-Sung.[73] Explorations and excavations have not only identified the ancient capital of the country, located at the village of Yotkan, but have also revealed several other sites in the periphery of Yotkan. The ancient capital before the Christian era continued to be so till the end of the Buddhist period

71. Stein. Op. cit, p. 186, 190. The Chinese translation of the Sūryagarbha-sūtra made by Narendrayaśas between the years 589 and 619 A.D. in a list of holy spots (pīṭha) sanctified by the presence of a Bodhisattva mentions the residence and caitya of the saint *Chu-mo-so-lo-hsiang* or Goma Śālagandha near Mount Niu-tou (Oxhead : Gośīrṣa) on the steeply-scarped bank of the river in Yu-tien (cf. Levi. "Notes Chinoises sur l'Inde." IV. pp. 31, 40 quoted by Stein. Op. cit, p. 186n. 10).

72. Stein. Op. cit, p. 188; cf. Grenard. *Mission de Rhins*, pp. 142 Sq.; Senart. *Les Fragments Dutrevil de Rhins*. J.A. 1898. Sept-Oct. cited by Stein.

73. The place *Lo-la-sung*, according to Stein, is of doubtful identity. The *Hsi-yu-tu-chih*, a modern Chinese account quoted by Chavannes gives *Thakkaga* as the name of the sixth place. The term 'six cities' of the documents might be compared with the references made in the Tang annals to the five districts or towns dependent on Yu-tien (Stein. *op. cit*. p. 268).

(beginning of the eleventh century). A number of earlier Buddhist sites excavated in the desert include Dandan Uiliq (the house with ivory), identified with Li-hsieh[74] which was probably the Chinese garrison headquarters till the end of the eighth century, when it was abandoned by the Chinese. The finds here include a large number of stucco images and relics from various sites, as also frescoes with Brāhmī inscriptions. The manuscripts and other records are mostly in Brāhmī and Chinese. The manuscripts include fragments of two canonical works of Mahāyāna school of Buddhism—*Prajñāpāramitā* and *Vajracchedikā*[75] in Sanskrit. Brāhmī records, in languages other than Sanskrit, are mostly in ancient Khotanese, an Eastern Iranian language. The Chinese records are largely official ones of the military officers of Li-hsie, besides deeds of private transactions. Buddhist finds, similar to those of Dandan-Uiliq, have also been discovered from ruins of two stūpas at Rawak, 7 miles to the north of Dandan-Uiliq. The Buddhist images found in these areas seem closely related to the Gandhāra school.

Pi-mo[76] and Ni-jang[77], identified by Stein with Uzun-tati and Niya respectively, were other Buddhist sites mentioned by Hsuan tsang. The pilgrim refers to a sandalwood image of Buddha supposed to have been made by king Udayana of Kośāmbī in the life time of the Tathāgata. Ruins of old Buddhist stūpas have been found at the old site. Niya was also an important Buddhist centre in the time of Hsuan-tsang, but its ancient parts were probably destroyed by the erosion of the desert in his time. Explorations in these old sites have secured a large number of

74. *Ibid*, p. 267.

75. Stein Op. cit, pp. 257, 258, 295. The fragments of the first work belong, according to Hoernle, to the eighteenth and nineteenth chapters of a Mahāyāna text, apparently some kind of *Prajñāpāramitā* written in Gupta characters of the seventh or eighth century on leaves of very large size, about 18 by 17 inches. The size of the second work is 14½ by 3 inches, with six lines on each side of Brāhmī characters of the upright Gupta type. *Vajracchedikā* is a famous treatise of the Mahāyāna school.

76. Stein identifies it with Marco Polo's Pein (op. cit, p. 285) and modern Uzan-Tati (ibid, p. 462).

77. Stein (op. cit, p. 311) identifies it with Niya which may well be said to have retained for long the character of a frontier station as noted by Huen-tsang.

Kharoṣṭhī documents, mostly tablets on wood. These documents are in Kharoṣṭhī and Prākrit dialect of North-Western India in the Kuṣāṇa period.[78] The kings in these documents bear the title *devaputra*, while the names of persons occurring in them are purely Indian like Bhīma, Bangusena, Nandasena, Sītaka, Upajīva, etc., as also local adaptations of Indian names, like Angaca, Cuvatylina, Phummasena, Piteya, Saṅghita etc. There are some non-Indian names as well—Lipeya, Opgeya, Limira etc. These records shed light on the material culture and life of the people in that region during the period of the records.[79]

Khotan became an active centre of Buddhist studies. In A.D. 259, a Chinese monk Chu-she-hing[80] came to Khotan for the study of Buddhism. He is a fairly well-known figure in the early history of Buddhism in China being the compiler of the first catalogues of Buddhist texts translated into Chinese. She-hing as a serious scholar collected 90 bundles of original Buddhist texts which he could send to China with his disciple Fu-ji-tan (Puṇyadhana). He stayed on in Khotan and died at the age of 80. These texts sent home by Chu-she-hing were partly translated by a Khotanese Buddhist scholar Mokṣala[81] who had gone there in 291. His assistant was an Indian monk, named Śukla-

78. The tablets, though written by many different hands, shared throughout the characteristic peculiarities of that type of Kharoṣṭhī writing which is exhibited by inscriptions of the extreme North-West of India during the Kuṣāṇa or Indo-Scythian rule, falling within the first three centuries of our era (Stein. *Op. cit*, p. 320).

79. These Kharoṣṭhī documents from Niya and other sites in Chinese Turkestan have been collected and published without translation by Boyer, Rapson and Senart (Oxford. 1921-29), and are translated by T. Burrow, Cambridge 1936. The information deduced from these records forms an interesting piece of separate study.

80. Bagchi, *India & Central Asia* (Calcutta. 1955) pp. 59fl. The name is transcribed as Ko-shu-lan, an upāsaka of Indian descent, who was born in China, and translated 2 works in 5 fasciculi, under the reign of Hwvi-ti A.D. 290-306. His translations were lost in A.D. 730. (Nanjio : *A Catalogue of the Chinese Buddhist Tripitaka*, Oxford, 1882, Japanese Reprint, p. 394. Appendix II, 27.

81. Wu-lo-kha or Wu-kha-lo i.e. Mokṣala was a śramaṇa of Yu-then i.e. Kusutana (Khotan), who together with Ku-sho-lan translated one sūtra in A.D. 291. (*Pañcaviṁśati-sāhasrikā prajñāpāramitā* (ibid. ii. 26).

ratna.[82] The texts translated were *Pañcaviṁśati-Sāhasrikā-Prajñāpāramitā*, *Vinayakīrtinirdeśa* and *Suraṅgama-sūtra*—all Mahāyānist canonical texts. In the beginning of the 5th century, Dharmakṣema,[83] a Mahāyānist Buddhist scholar from Magadha was working in Leang-chou. He had an incomplete manuscript of the *Mahāparinirvāṇa-sūtra* which he had brought from India. For the restoration of the text, he had to go to Khotan probably in 412 or 413 and on recovering the second part of it, he returned to China. The text in 33 chapters was finally translated between 414 and 421. A pupil of Dharmakṣema, Tsiu-Kiu-king-sheng, from a noble family of Leang-chou, also went to Khotan to study Mahāyāna Buddhism. This he did at the Gomatīvihāra under an Indian teacher Buddhasena,[84] known as 'the lion among the savants' in all countries of the west. He brought back with him Mahāyāna texts on 'Dhyāna'. References to subsequent visits of Chinese monks of Leang-chou to Khotan, for the collection of Buddhist manuscripts for translation are fairly well-known. Some visited in 439, while earlier Fa-ling had brought the famous manuscript *Avataṁśaka-sūtra* which was translated by Buddhabhadra[85] in 418, and that of *Saddharma-puṇḍarīka* was brought from Khotan by a monk named Fa-hien in 475 and translated by Dharmamati[86] in 490. Khotan also transmitted Buddhism through its savants to China. Śikṣānanda, one of the greatest among the Buddhist scholars of Khotan, reached China in 695 and worked there till his death in 710. His translations of 19 texts include his *magnum opus*, *Mahāvaipulya* or the *Avataṁśaka-sūtra*[87] in 80 chapters.

82. Bagchi, Op. cit, p. 60. For *Vimala-kīrti-nirdeśa* and translations, see Nanjio : Op. cit, Nos. 144, 145, 146, 147, 149, 181.

83. Bagchi, *ibid.* He belonged to Central India and was a follower of Mahāyāna Buddhism. He went to China through the Central Asian route reaching Leang-chou in the beginning of the 5th century. He translated 25 texts into Chinese. While attempting to go back to Khotan in 433 he was murdered in the way (Bagchi : *India and China*, New York 1951) p. 209.

84. Bagchi, *Le Canon Bouddhique*, p. 222. Known to the Chinese as Fo-to-se-na, Buddhasena was an enthusiastic Mahāyānist, and called the lion (siṁha—*Che-tseu*) among the learned.

85. Bagchi, *ibid*, pp. 341 ff. Transcribed in Chinese as *Fo-to-po-to-lo* translated as 'intelligent sage'.

86. Bagchi, *ibid*, p. 409—translated in Chinese as *Tan-mo-mo-ti*.

87. Bagchi, *India & China*, Op. cit, p. 140.

The southern route from Niya onwards passed through several important places which are mentioned by Hsuan-tsang for their political and cultural importance. According to the pilgrim, the country to the east of Niya was all desert. About 400 li (about 67 miles or 90 K.M.) to the east was the old Tu-ho-lo country which was an important territory in early times being situated in the deltaic region of the Tarim river. Its arable area was eroded by the desert and the city fell in ruins. It has been identified with the actual Endere site.[88] The extent of the area over which pottery debris could be traced suggest a relatively large settlement. Several fragments of *Śālistambha-sūtra* on paper written in upright Gupta characters of the 7th or 8th century were found in the ruins here.[89] This is probably a Buddhist canonical work of the *Dhāraṇī* class.

Stucco relief fragments, as well as fresco paintings on stucco, were also found on excavations in the Temple area. An interesting painted panel in chapel E. 11 shows seated Gaṇeśa[90] with a (yellow) arm, wrist and ankle, ornaments (yellow), tiger skin *dhotī* (yellow), tight *paijāmās* (dark brown), feet bare, rest of flesh pink with red outlines and rosary of white dots. The archaeological finds from Endere have brought to light Kharoṣṭhī tablets and manuscripts of the type found in Niya. Ruins of a Buddhist stūpa also suggest that Buddhism was established here and was prospering before its final abandonment.

Hsuan-tsang also mentions further to the east, Che-mo-to-na[91] and Tsiu-Umo, same as Chu-mo, at a distance of 600 li from Niya and 1000 li from Niya respectively. It is identified with Calmadana of the Kharoṣṭhī documents, and present Cherchen.[92] The petty records in Kharoṣṭhī provide information relating to material culture, as also to Buddhism. A rectangular tablet dated in the ninth year of king Jitroghavarman relates to a transaction by a certain Buddhaghoṣa, apparently the slave of

88. Stein, *Khotan*, Op. cit, p. 435.
89. *ibid*, p. 439.
90. *Ibid*, p. 442.
91. *Ibid*, p. 435.
92. Ibid, p. 311 n. 7. Stein surmises that by Calmadana is meant the same locality which Hsuan-tsang calls Chh-mo-fo-na and which, being placed ten marches to the east of Niya, manifestly corresponds to the present charchan.

the Śramaṇa Ānandasena, concerning some household goods, pawned or perhaps taken in pledge. The prosperity of Buddhism as the widely spread, if not actually the prevailing, religion in the territory is well brought out by frequent references to Śramaṇas, and enumeration of many sacred categories of Buddhist heaven.[93] In Song-Yun's time (beginning of the 6th century), there were a hundred families[94] in the city of Cherchen. In this town there were representations of a Buddha and Bodhisattva in pure Chinese style which had been brought by Lu-Kuang towards the end of the 4th century A.D. in the course of his expedition in the Tarim basin. In Hsuan-tsang's time the place was abandoned but soon afterwards it was re-occupied by the Chinese army under the Tang, and its name was changed from Tsiu-mo to Po-hsien about A.D. 674-676. Recent explorations have exposed the ruins of a Buddhist stūpa thus testifying its association with Buddhism.

Other important towns lay to the north-east of Cherchen. This, according to the Hsuan-tsang include Na-fo-po which in ancient times was called Lou-lan, called in the Han Annals Shan-shan with two cities—the old one called Yu-ni and the new one Yi-hsiun. The Tibetan documents found here give the names 'Great Nob' and 'Little Nob' respectively. The Chinese name Na-Fo-po seems identical with Nob of the Tibetan documents and Lop of modern times.[95] Shan-shan replaces the old name Lou-lan, a Chinese transcription of the original name Kroraina or Krorayina of the Kharoṣṭhī documents, The location of Lop on the oldest route between Tun-huang and the western countries (like Niya, Khotan etc) along the foot of the Kuruknag and the Lop desert, adds to its importance.[96] A fairly

93. Stein, Op. cit, pp. 363, 367.

94. Stein, Op. cit, p. 436 n. 5. Sun of Yun travelling in 519 A.D. describes Tso-mo which, according to Chavannes, is identical with Chu-mo (Tsiu-mo) of Hsuan-tsang and the Tang Annals as a town inhabited by a hundred families only.

95. Khotan, Op. cit, p. 435.

96. This route retained its importance for traffic even during those times when Chinese political power had ceased to assert itself in the western region. The Chinese general and diplomat Pei-Chu has provided important description of the three routes to the west compiled about A.D. 607. According to him,

detailed account of ancient Kroraina (Lou-lan, Shan-Shan) is provided by the Chinese Annals.[97] The name Lou-lan under the former Hans, was changed by the Chinese to Shan-Shan from 77 B.C. The neighbouring territories like Tsu-mo (Cherchen), Hsiao-yian (on the road to Kucha in the north) and Ching-chuch (Niya) were all dependencies of the state of Shan-Shan. A military colony was actually established here to control the road to Karasahr and Kucha in the north and to fortify Shan-Shan against the Hiung-nus. The kings of various western countries came to offer submission. Despite the change of the name to Shan-Shan, the easternmost part of the country continued to bear the old name of Lou-lan (Kroraina).

Kroraina was a stronghold of Buddhism and was visited by Fa-hien on way from the frontier territory of Tun-huang, covering the distance in seventeen days.[98] The ruler of this place professed Buddhism. There were 4000 monks, all followers of Hinayāna in the country in his time. The common people, however, were not so strict in the observance of Buddhist rules of conduct, despite their professing Buddhism. Archaeological evidence proves, according to Stein, that the old settlement north of the Lop-Nor marshes was by that time abandoned and Shan-Shan of Fa-hien is actually represented by the remains of Miran and Charkhlik. Besides remains of stūpas[99] and Buddhist shrines a large number of Kharoṣṭhī documents[100] were also found on wood and paper. The use of Kharoṣṭhī—the same Indian script found in the records of the Niya site—in the Lop region for administration and business purposes poses interesting problems. While at Khotan its use might have been the result of early immigration from India as an important element in the local population, its popularity so far away to the east at the very threshold of China, could be due to the spread of Buddhism. The missionaries might have carried with them the language and script prevalent in the extreme north-west of India for common use throughout

the southern route passed through Shan-Shan, south of Lop-nor, on to Yu-tien or Khotan (Richthofen, *China* I, p. 530, note. Stein, *Serindia*, p. 323).

97. Stein, *Serindia*, pp. 325 ff.

98. *Ibid*, p. 324.

99. *Ibid*, pp. 389 ff.

100. *Ibid*, Sec. IX, pp. 413 ff.

the Tarim basin. The other possibility, suggested by Aurel Stein, is the temporary extension of the Indo-Scythian power from across the Pamirs. Some light is shed on this point by the Buddhist traditions in China. These documents show the closest agreement with those from the Niya site in character, language, phraseology and other aspects. Style, phonetics and spellings suggest that identical standards were followed from Khotan to Lop during the period of the records. In both the documents there are numerous names of unmistakably Buddhist or Indian derivation,[101] such as Ānandasena, Bhatisame, Bhīmaya, Budhamitra, Dhamnapāla, Komudvali, Purṇadeva, Caraka, Sujada, Vāsudeva occurring side by side with those of local origin such as Cauleya, Cuvalayina, Kapgeya, Kalpisa, Kipsa, Kitsaitsa, Lampurta, Maldraya, Porbhaya, Pulkaya, Signaya, Tasuca, Tameca, Varpeya. The common official titles in Kharoṣṭhī records from both the sites are Cojhbo, Gusura, Kori and Vasu.

In this context reference might as well be made to notices in the Chinese historical records which shed light on the character of the ruined settlement of the Lou-lan site. The change of the name from Lou-lan to Shan-Shan from 77 B.C. onwards has already been mentioned, as also the later events relating to proposed military colony and subsequent history of Chinese occupation and submission of the kings of Kucha and other western territories recorded. The fuller history and references in later Chinese annals now need be told. The epoch of the three kingdoms (A.D. 221-65) coincides with the period of the extant documents and other remains of the Lou-lan site date. The Wei-lo, a work composed by Yu-huan between A.D. 239-65, furnishes information[102] relating to the ancient route through Lou-lan, starting from Tun-huang and Yu-men-kuan (Jade Gate barrier). A later Chinese text, the commentary on the *Shui-ching* composed by Li-lao-yuan before his death in A.D. 527, also mentions Lou-lan and the ancient geography of the Lop country, as also the kingdom of Mo-Shan same as Shan-Shan through which the river Ho (i.e. River of the North)—rivers of Kash-

101. *Ibid*, p. 414.
102. *Ibid*, p. 418.

ghar and Yarkand passed. This river in its course eastwards passed through the town of Chu-pin, identified by Aurel Stein with Ying-pan, where remains of Buddhist sites were found. There is no trace of any Chinese record relating to the military colony established at Lou-lan of a date later than the time to which Li-tao-yuan's notice refers. It is proposed[103] that the abandonment of the Chinese station at Lou-lan took place some time during the fourth century A.D.

The site of Miran, explored and excavated by Aurel Stein-points to its strategic importance and also as a centre of Buddhism. Situated to the south of Lop-nor, it was of great importance to the Tibetans who in all probability built the fort in the eighth century. The Tibetan domination in the Tarim basin extended from the downfall of Chinese power westwards.[104] The excavations did not reveal the slightest scrap of Chinese writing while the Tibetan documents were found in abundance. This little oasis formed the key to the direct routes which led from the southern oases of the Tarim basin to the easternmost part of this basin and from Central Tibet and Lhasa across the high plateaus and ranges of the Kun-lun to this point. The Tibetans tried to keep a firm hold upon Miran as long as their political and military ambition was focussed towards Eastern Turkestan.[105] With the disappearance of Tibetan power in this region, Miran sank into insignificance. Excavations have revealed ruins of ancient Buddhist shrines with damaged stucco sculptures showing good modelling and proportions, influenced by the Greco-Buddhist Art of Gandhāra. Several colossal heads, all displaying with equal clearness features of Greco-Buddhist style, suggest that the outer wall was lined by huge seated figures of Buddha or Bodhisattvas in niches of which these heads formed part. Stein discovered in front of and close to the base of one statue a fragment of a palm-leaf manuscript about six inches long written in Sanskrit with early Gupta Brāhmī characters. These frescoes of Miran form a class by themselves and are considered the earliest, and are also supposed to be a product of the

103. *Ibid*, p. 426.

104. Stein. *Ruins of Desert Cathay*, London, 1912, p. 449—henceforth *Ruins*.

105. Stein. *Serindia*, p. 476.

Gandhāra school.[106] In one of the paintings depicting a scene from the Visvantara Jātaka, the painter's name Tita—a Prākrit form of Titus—is written on the leg of an elephant. A detailed study of the theme and technique of Miran paintings as also of finds in excavations is reserved for later consideration.

Representations of winged angels as in early Christian art point to western influence. The silk banners discovered in Miran contain Kharoṣṭhī inscriptions, which reveal donation of such banners to the Buddhist shrine. Most of the donor's names appear to be Indian like Asaga, Caraka, Caroka (Caruka), Samanay (Śramaṇaka), though a few Iranian ones like Friyana, Firina and Mitraka are also mentioned. Miran seems to have formed part of Kroraina[107] (old Lou-lan, Shan-Shan) and the frescoes, banners and other antiquities bearing Kharoṣṭhī inscriptions belong to about the fourth century A.D. The Kharoṣṭhī documents mention five kings of a dynasty which reigned in Kroraina in the 3rd century A.D. These are : Pepiya, Tajaka, Amgoka, Mahiri and Vasmana—the third and fourth probably had a longer reign. The rulers also used titles borrowed from the Kuṣāṇas—Mahāraya, Rayātiraya, Devaputra (*Mahārāja, Rājādhirāja, Devaputra*) and Dharmiya, Mahamta etc.

Northern Route States

The States on the Northern Route were equally important for their strategic location as also for their political and cultural history. They were culturally integrated, and they actively participated in the diffusion and expansion of Buddhist culture. The Chinese pilgrim Hsuan-tsang mentions them according to their

106. See Busagli. *Painting of Central Asia*, p. 20. According to the Italian Professor, Miran represents the beginning of Painting in Central Asia. Although the date of these wall paintings cannot be fixed with any precision, some clues are provided by the writing of the Kharoṣṭhī inscriptions. (Ibid, p. 21)

107. According to Stein, if the site of Miran was known to the Tibetans as 'Great Nob', it appears very probable that by 'Little Nob' they meant Charklik. This distinction would closely correspond to that which the Han Annals indicate between the two main places of Shan-Shan or Lou-lan. Yu-ni, 'the old town' to the east, and I-hsun or 'the New Town', these two being now represented, I believe, by the sites of Miran and Charklik respectively. (*Ruins*. I. p. 449)

location from west to east : Po-lu-chia, Kiu-che, A-ki-ni and Kao-chang. Po-lu-chia in earlier Chinese texts is mentioned as Ki-me and Ku-me. Some Sanskrit documents of Central Asia mention it as Bharuka and it is identified with modern Aksu.[108] The former Han Annals place it correctly to the west of Kuei-tzu or Kucha at a distance of 670 li or 110 miles. The documents from Central Asia mention it as Kuchi. These two kingdoms had many things in common like customs, literature and language. The third kingdom A-ki-ni is mentioned in earlier Chinese accounts as Yen-ki, Wu-ki and Wu-yi—all connected with Sanskrit Agni or its derivatives. The Sanskrit documents mention it as Agni and its rulers as Agni Mahārāja. It is identified with modern Karasahr. These kingdoms had separate identity but seem to have common history, especially with regard to their relations with China—political and cultural, and in the context of Buddhism.

Ak-su—the Ku-mo of Han Annals, is equated with the little kingdom of Po-lu-chia by Hsuan-tsang, whose description is reproduced in the Tang Annals without adding more than the identity of the 'Little Kingdom' with Ku-mo or Chi-mo. The area of the kingdom is recorded as about 600 li from east to west and 300 li from north to south, and the size of its capital as 5 to 6 li in circuit. According to the pilgrim, in general characteristics this country and its people resembled Chiu-tzu (Kucha) and its people, but the spoken language differed a little. There were some tens of monasteries with above a thousand brethren.[109] The fine cloth and serge of the district were esteemed by the neighbouring countries. Despite the material advancement and its geographical location—as the meeting ground of trade route between Karasahr and Kashgar and that to the great fertile valley, north of Tien-Shan, connecting the Tarim basin with the Ili valley and the trade emporium of Kulja, Aksu was far less important than Kucha in resources as also as a centre of Buddhist activities.

Kucha has at all the times been one of the most important territories in the Tarim basin owing to its geographical position

108. Stein. *Serindia*, pp. 1297 ff.

109. Watters. *Op. cit*, I. p. 64.

and the role it has played in Buddhist art and civilization. It is supposed to be a worthy pendant of Khotan. Its language too has engaged the attention of scholars.[110] During the Han times Kiu-she was divided by the Tien-shan into two zones –one was called Kiu-she anterior or inner, and the other Kiu-she posterior or outer. The name of the country was changed into Kao-chang from the beginning of the fourth century. The anterior part of Kiu-she is identified with modern Turfan, and the other one with Guchen. The history of the four northern states—Aksu, Kucha, Karasahr and Turfan—can be traced from the Chinese sources, which no doubt speak in greater detail about Kucha. It was the most powerful of the four states and played the same great role in the North as Khotan did in the South in the diffusion of Indian culture and Buddhism. The Chineres sources record its political relations with China as also the activities of the Buddhist savants of this place and their contribution to Chinese Buddhist literature.

According to the Annals of the former Han dynasty, the capital of the king of Kucha is called the city of Yen. In the south the country borders on Tsing-tsiue, in the south-east, Tsiu-mo, in the south west, Yu-mi, in the north Wu-sun and in the west Ku-mo. It was brought into contact with China in the reign of Wu-ti (40-87 B.C.) and it became a place of considerable importance, because of its position at the junction of the western trade routes leaving Kashgar and Aulieata respectively. Kucha accepted the Chinese civilization but it had its periods of troubles as well involving conflict with Imperial China. It is not until the western Tsin dynasty that it figures as a seat of Buddhism. The Tsin annals (265-317 A.D.) point to its enclosure by a triple wall and its containing a thousand stūpas and Buddhist temples as well as a magnificent palace for the ruler.[111] This suggests that by that time Buddhism was already established, but there is no evidence regarding the date of its introduction. In 383, Emperor Fu-chien of the Tsin dynasty sent

110. Levi. JA. 1913, pp. 311 ff.

111. For an account of the political history of the Kingdom of Kieou-tseu (Koutcha), see Appendix A, Part ii of Chavannes article 'Les Documents sur Bois de Niya' in Stein's Ancient Khotan, p. 544.

Luk-uang to subdue Kucha.[112] The expedition resulted not only in political success but also in the loss of the famous Buddhist savant Kumārajīva who was taken as a captive to China. Lu-kuang subsequently became ruler of the State known as southern Liang with Kumārajīva acting as his adviser.

The Chinese relations with the States of the Tarim basin could be traced to the time of Emperor Wu-ti (140-87 B.C.) of the Han dynasty. Dated records beginning with the year 98 B.C. testify to the presence of a Chinese garrison near the modern Tun-huang.[113] Earlier, an envoy named Chang-chien was sent to the Yueh-chi soliciting their cooperation against of the warring and growing power of the Hiung-nu which, however, proved infructuous. It only helped in revealing the importance of the nations on the Oxus which were in touch with India on the one hand and the mysterious one on the other. The Chinese were, therefore, interested in keeping the international trade route leading westwards from the extremity of the modern Kansu province open. The main hinderance to this intercourse with the west was the hostility of the wild tribes pillaging caravans and blocking the route. The Chinese, therefore, aimed at creating a wedge between two tribes with their alliance with the one against the other.

The reign of Emperor Ming-ti is important as the traditional date for the introduction of Buddhism as also for the victorious compaigns of the famous general Pan-chao, whose career lasted from A.D. 73-102. The Chinese activity ceased for quite some time after him. The relations with Kucha in the centuries preceding and following the Christian era were at times hostile and at others friendly.[114] A Wu-sun princess, connected with the Chinese imperial family on the mother's side, was married to Kiang-pin, the king of Kucha who went in 65 B.C. to China to pay his homage, and this bond of kinship continued in the time of Chen-gi (32-1 B.C.), his son. After the fall of the Hans in A.D. 24,

112. Eliot. *Hinduism and Buddhism*. Op. cit, p. 203. The circumstances which provoked this expedition are not very clear. It was escorted by the king of Turfan and other small potentates who were the vassals of the Tsin and also on bad terms with Kucha. They probably asked Fo-chien for assistance in subduing their rival which he was delighted to give (ibid. n.3).

113. *Ibid*, p. 197.

114. See Bagchi—*India and Central Asia*. Op. cit, pp. 70 ff.

the Hiung-nu dominated the Tarim basin and the small states, excluding Kucha, became dependencies of the Hiung-nu, Interstate rivalries and confrontations only helped foreign powers—the Hiung-nu or the Chinese in keeping their control over this area and its political activities. In A.D. 73 Kien was made king of Kucha by Hiung-nu who attacked Su-le (Kashgar) and conquered it. He appointed Tou-li, a man of Kucha, as its king, only to be defeated and taken prisoner a year later by Pan-chao, the Chinese General, who set up Chong, the nephew of the last king as his protegé on the Kashgar throne. After the death of Ming in A.D. 75, Kucha and Aksu attacked Kashgar. This was followed by Pan-Chao's arrival and a joint force of Kashgar, Sogdiana, Khotan headed by him attacked Aksu and She-chang (Uch Turfan) and defeated them. Kucha was finally robbed of its independence after a decisive battle in A.D. 88[115], and a later attempt to regain it with the help of the Yueh-chi forces failed to retrieve the situation. Po-pa was set up as king of Kucha with a Chinese governor-general to look after the local affairs and maintain peace. Subsequent attempts against the Chinese proved abortive.

In A.D. 124 the Kucha king Po-ying along with rulers of Aksu and Uch-Turfan helped the Chinese against the Hiung-nus[116] who were finally defeated. Kucha continued to maintain friendly relations with China and in 224 sent an ambassador with presents to the Chinese court. At that time Aksu and Turfan were dependencies of Kucha. This process was followed by the despatch of a Kuchean prince in 285 to enter the imperial service,

115. The Chinese power in the Tarim basin under the great general Pan-Chao reasserted itself with the conquest of Khotan and Kashgar about A.D. 74, followed by extending influence over other territories. In A.D. 88 Pan-Chao succeeded in subjecting So-Che (Yarkand) in spite of the help of Kucha, which too was obliged to make its submission along with other territories on the northern ruin of the Tarim basin. (Stein. *Serindia*. I. p. 83)

116. Chavannes. Toung-pao, 1906, p. 252 quoted by Stein—Op. cit, p. 332. It is said that after Pan-yung's arrival at Lou-lan in February A.D. 124, the king Shan-Shan was awarded for his submission by new honours. The kings of Kucha, Aksu, and Uch-Turfan came to offer their allegiance. Taking the numerous force brought by them, Pan-Yung then moved upon Turfan and after inflicting a defeat on the Hsiung-nu or Hunus, established a military colony at Lukchun in the Turfan depression.

and by embassies in the first quarter of the 4th century. Enmity between Kucha and Karasahr resulting in the killing of Po-Shan the Kuchean king, and subjugation of his kingdom was followed some years later by the reverse process of murder of Long-Huei. The Karasahr ruler of the Tarim basin, finally involved China in the political embroil of the region. Reference has already been made to the mission under General Lu-kuang which invaded Kucha in 382 and subjugated it.

During the Wei period (386-534) Kucha-Chinese relations were again strained and another punitive expedition was sent in 448. After this, a long series of tribute bearing missions were sent first to the court of Wei, and afterwards to the Liang, Chou and Sui. King Su-fa Pu-Kiu and Su-fa sent missions to China, the latter in 630. It was about this time that Hsuan-tsang passed through Kucha and gave an account of the kingdom and its rulers who were of the Kiu-che (Kuchean) race. He refers[117] to the use of modified Indian alphabets, and dwells on the many monasteries and great images, the quinquennial assemblies and religious processions. There were more than 100 monasteries and upwards of 5000 brethern who all followed the Sarvāstivāda school and the 'gradual teaching', probably meaning Hīnayāna as opposed to the sudden illumination caused by the Mahāyānist revelation. The monasteries were centres of learning.

The Kuchean-Sino relations entered a phase of bitterness and hostility, once again, in 648 when an expedition was sent against Kucha because of its help in the revolt of Karasahr against the Chinese authority. The Kuchean army led by Kie-lie-tien was totally defeated, resulting in the capture of king Ho-li Pu-sho-pi, minister Na-li and the general. They were sent to China. In 658 Kucha was made the seat of government for the territory known as the 'Four Garrisons,'[118] but the Chinese protegé of the old house continued to rule. Su-ki, son of Ho-li-pu-She-pi, appointed king by an imperial mandate, sent an embassy to China in 674 while Yen-tien-tie personally came to China in 692 to pay personal homage to the emperor. It was about this time that the

117. Beal. Op. cit. I. pp. 19 ff.

118. By the term 'Four Garrisons', the territories of Kashgar, Khotan, Kucha and Karasahr, then occupied by the Chinese forces, are meant (Stein. *Khotan*. 7n.).

Tibetans drove away the Chinese from the southern part of the Tarim basin, and extended their conquests as as far as Karasahr. The Chinese headquarters were removed to Kucha from Turfan. During the next century Kucha sent several missions to the Imperial Chinese Court, and, about 788 was visited by Wu-Kung,[119] who found Buddhism and Music flourishing here. He mentions an Abbot who spoke with equal fluency the language of the country, Chinese and Sanskrit. At that time Po-Hoan was the king of Kucha. The following period is a blank in the history of this kingdom as also in its relations with China. It is only in the eleventh century that reference is made to the mission going to China from this place. These were under the Uighurs, but Buddhism was not extinct even at that time. In 1096 the envoy presented a jade Buddha to the Emperor. The new rulers of the Uighur stock took the title of 'Lion-king'.

Agnideśa or Karasahr

The kingdom of Karasahr was politically connected with Kucha and very often they joined hands in resisting the Chinese aggression for retaining their independence. A Chinese tablet[120] (N.XV.93) mentions Shan-Shan along with Karasahr, Kucha and Kashgar as subject to an unnamed native ruler. It seems to belong to the time of Wu-ti (A.D. 265-290), the first emperor of the western Chin dynasty. The tablet probably refers to Lung-Hui, king of Karasahr who about the close of that reign established his hegemony over the whole of the Tarim basin.[121] Some documents from the Lou-lan site also provide interesting information about the affairs of Yen-chi or Karasahr. One such document[122] (No. 934) reports political events in which Tsang, King of Yen-chi, was implicated. It also mentions Kucha. In another document (935) there is reference to a declaration of war. Karasahr offered easy access and was a convenient gate for Hun inroads into the Tarim basin.[123] The Huns also made an

119. Eliot. *Hinduism and Buddhism*, p. 205.

120. Stein. *Serindia*, Op. cit, p. 329.

121. Cf. Chavvannes note entitled *Les Documents sur Bois De* Niya—Ancient Khotan, pp. 537 ff; also Royaume : *De Yen Ki* (Karachar) pp. 542 ff.

122. *Serindia*, p. 413.

123. *ibid*, p. 338.

attempt in 104 B.C. to cut off the return of an expedition to Ta-yuan (Farghana) by a force of cavalry posted in Lou-lan.[124] The Chinese accounts contain some references to the political conditions of Karasahr from the Han times to the end of the Tang. During the first expansion of the Chinese supremacy under Emperor Wu-ti (140-87 B.C.), Karasahr recognised Chinese suzerainty by sending an ambassador to the Imperial Court. The relations with China, however, vacillated between friendship and hostility. Karasahr threw off the Chinese domination towards the end of the first century B.C., but later on submitted to China along with the other states. Trouble started again with Shuen, the king of Karasahr, who revolted against Chinese authority and killed the Chinese governor and his retinue in A.D. 75. The Pan-Chao expedition reduced these states, once again, to the Chinese vassalage with the imposition of Yuang-Mong,[125] an officer of Karasahr in the Chinese Court, being placed on the throne of his country in A.D. 94. He, in turn, also revolted and was defeated by the Chinese force in 127, He then sent his own son to the Chinese court with presents. Since then Karasahr maintained friendly relations with China for some time. An embassy was sent to China in 225, and later on in 285, king Long-An sent his son to be enrolled in the Imperial Guard. Another son of Long-An, Huei, was successful against various states of the Tarim basin and became master of Kucha for some time. His son Hi was defeated by the Chinese in 345, and several embassies were sent to China from Karasahr in 437, 439 and 448, but the Chinese sent an expeditionary force due to the vacillating policy of Karasahr. Its ruler Kiu-She-pei-na fled to Kucha. The history of the country is blank for want of evidence for a century or more. There are references to embassies sent to China from Karasahr in 564 and 606, the second time by Long-Tu-ki, the then ruler. The Chinese pilgrim Hsuan-tsang visiting this place in 629 provides good information about the religion and culture of this place, but says practically nothing about the political condition,[126] except referring to the king of the country, a native of the place. There were some ten or more Saṅghārāmas with two

124. *Ibid.*
125. Bagchi. *India and Central Asia*. Op. cit, p. 76.
126. Beal. *Buddhist Records*. Op. cit. I. p. 17 ff.

thousand priests or so, belonging the Little Vehicle of the school of the Sarvāstivādins[127] (Shwo-Yis-tsai-yu-po). According to the pilgrim, the doctrine of the Sūtras and the requirements of the *Vinaya* are in agreement with those of India, as also the written characters might be with a little difference. The professors of religion read their books and observed the rules and regulations with purity and strictness.

The Annals of the Tang dynasty[128] mention Karasahr several times. In 632 king Long-Tu-ki-chi sent an embassy to the Imperial Court. He was equally helpful in getting a shorter route to China opened through the desert by isolating Turfan which was gradually passing under the influence of the Uighurs, and was interfering in the normal relations between China and the Tarim desert. The king of Turfan was defeated by the Chinese army in 640 and was forced to release those inhabitants of Karasahr who were held as prisoners. Soon afterwards Karasahr fell under Uighur influence with a treaty of alliance with this tribe, and alienated its relations with China. The younger brothers of the king named Hie-pi, She-hu and Li-po-chun, however, entered, into league with the Chinese to defeat and dislodge Long-Tu-ki-che. The last one was appointed king of Karasahr replacing his elder brother who was taken as a captive to China. This position did not last long. The Uighurs invaded Karasahr once again, and deposed Li-op-chun. A ding-dong struggle for the throne continued with the Chinese and Kucha interfering in the

127. According to Fa-hien who visited Yen-chi or Wu-ti, as he calls it, about A.D. 400 from Shan-Shan, has little more to tell us than that there were four thousand monks, students of the Hīnayāna in the territory (Legge. *Travals of Fahien*, pp. 14 Sq.). For the name Wu-i (also written Wu-chi) in other Buddhist texts cf Watters. *Yuan Chwang*, i. p. 46; Chavannes—Toung-pao, 1905, p. 564 n. 2. Wu-king, who stayed at Karasahr about A.D. 788, also calls the town Wu-chi. (J.A. 1895, Sept.-Oct. p. 364).

128. In a very long notice which the Tang Annals devote to Yen-chi (Kara-shahr) and its affairs, it is specially pointed out that the territory has always been subject to the western Turks. The geographical position of Kara-shahr no doubt added to its strategic importance, and from A.D. 719, Yen-chi is reckoned as one of the 'Four Garrisons' assuring the Chinese hold over Eastern Turkestan. These Annals estimate the number of households at four thousand and the number of soldiers at two thousand. Reference is also made to brisk trade in fish and salt (Stein. *Serindia*, p. 1181). See also Bagchi, Op. cit, pp. 76-77, for the relations with China.

affairs of this kingdom. Tu-Ki-che who was a hostage in China was sent back to his kingdom in 648. Relations between Karasahr and China continued on a cordial and stable plane with the former sending embassies between 742-755 after which the Tibetans conquered Karasahr, thus snapping all relations with China.

Kao-chang or Turfan[129]

Turfan is an oasis containing the ruins of several cities and probably different sites represent the ruins of capitals at different periods. The name Turfan appears to be modern. The Ming Annals state that this city lies in the land of ancient Che-shih (or Ku-shih) called Kao-chang in the time of the Sui. This name was abolished by the Tang but restored by the Sung. The main city now known as Chotscho seems to be identical with Kao-Chang[130] and Idiqutshari. It is called by the Mohammadans Apsus or Ephesus, connected with an ancient sacred site renamed 'the cave of the seven sleepers'. Extensive remains found in the oasis include works in Sanskrit, Chinese and various Iranian and Turkish idioms and also in the two dialects of the Tokharian language. According to the Chinese sources,[131] in the Han period there was a kingdom, called Ku-Shih with two capitals. It was destroyed in 60 B.C. by the Chinese general Cheng-Chi and eight small principalities were formed in its place. Earlier in the time of Wu-ti (160-108 B.C.) the southern part of the territory, which is Turfan, had submitted to China, but the northern one, Guchen, was under the domination of the Hiung-nus, who were completely defeated by the Chinese in A.D. 89. This did not mean the end of hostility. War between the two was frequent and Turfan had to seek Chinese help in A.D. 96

129. The political history of Kao-Chang or Turfan is summarily described in Bagchi's *India and Central Asia* (Op. cit), pp. 77-79. Aurel Stein provides 'Glimpses of Turfan Ruins' in his earlier work, '*Ruins of Desert Cathay*' *Op. cit*, Vol. II, pp. 353 ff. For Stein's work in Lou-lan and Turfan areas, see his monumental work—*Innermost Asia*.

130. Eliot. *Hinduism and Buddhism*. Op. cit, p. 205. Pelliot suggests that Chotscho or Qoco is the Turkish equivalent of Kao-Chang in Tang pronunciation, the nasal being omitted (JA. 1912. 1 p. 579 quoted by Eliot, *ibid*, n.2).

131. Eliot. *ibid*, p. 206 quoting Chavannes. *Tou-Kiue Occidentavy*, p. 101.

when the army of Guchen attacked Turfan in the time of Wei-pei-ta. The trouble from the other side continued thereafter as well, because the two kingdoms were allied with two other warring powers. In A.D. 280, the king of Turfan sent his son to the Chinese court. From the beginning of the 4th century, the name of the southern part of the territory was changed to Kao-chang by the Chinese, and that constituted actual Turfan. In the fourth and fifth centuries A.D., Turfan had some relationship with two ephemeral states of Kansu—the Hou-liang and Pei-liang, the former founded by Lu-Kuang, the general who attacked Kucha. The other one was the creation of Men-haun of the Chu-chu tribe, related to the Hiung-nu. This tribe took a good deal of territory from the Hou-tiang in Turkestan as well as in Kansu. Its leader Men-haun devoted his later years to literature and Buddhism. Finally, the kingdom was conquered by the Wei dynasty in 439 and then its two members tried their fortune in Turfan where they ruled for twenty years. An-chou, the second one died in 480 and nine years after his death a temple to Maitreya was dedicated in his honour with a long inscription in Chinese.

Another line of Chinese rulers,[132] with the family name of Chiu, established itself at Kao-chang in A.D. 507, and one of them married a Chinese princess. Turfan continued to pay homage to the Tang dynasty but later on missions from this place stopped going to China causing suspicion and alarm. The Chinese forces, therefore, destoryed the kingdom in 640, as is recorded by Hsuan-tsang[133] who earlier on his outward transit visit had good reception from the king of Kao-chang. The political and cultural life of the kingdom, however, was not disturbed by the event. It was conquered later on by the Uighurs at an uncertain date. They had no doubt established themselves there in the

132. Bagchi mentions the names of the Kiu (Chiu) dynasty as known from different sources. These are Kiu-Kiu (497-520), Kiu-Kuang (521-30), Kiu-Kien (531-47), Kiu-Hiuen-li (548-54), Kiu-Meon (555-60), Kiu-Han-Ku (561-601); Kiu-Po-Ya (602-623), Kiu-Wen-tai (624-40) and Kiu-Che Mou (640-?). In 640 Turfan was brought under direct Chinese control.

133. In his biography there is a description of his reception by the king of Kao-Chang on his outward journey. But in the account of his travels written after his return he speaks of the city as no longer existent. (For the account of king's reception, see Beal : '*The Life of Hiuen-tsang*,' London, 1911, p. 37.)

eighth and ninth centuries. About 750, their Khan adopted Manichaeism as the state religion. The finds of manuscripts in Sogdian[134] and other Persian dialects at Turfan suggest its close connection with the west. Tibetan influence also affected Turfan in the eighth and ninth centuries since many Tibetan documents have been found here. About 843, this Uighur kingdom was destroyed by the Kirghiz.[135] Buddhist priests seem to have been massacred, as indicated by vaults filled with skeletons still wearing fragments of the monastic robe. Buddhism was not extinguished by this event, but lingered on here longer than in other areas of the Tarim basin. Even in 1420, the people of Turfan were Buddhists and according to the Ming Annals, there were more Buddhist temples than dwelling houses at Huo-chou (or Kara-Khoja).

Among the states of the Tarim basin whose history and personal relations have been sketched, Kucha seems to have played the most important role for nearly a thousand years. In their relations with China, while Turfan was nearest to bear the Chinese onslaught, Kucha seems to have offered stiff resistance. The Kucheans and their close allies Aksu and Uch-Turfan had many things in common, besides Buddhism, customs, literature and language. The Kuchean rulers are called 'Po' meaning white in Chinese, thereby pointing to their fair complexion. The names of the Kuchean rulers in the Tang period are also Sanskritised. The old Kuchean documents mention king Swarnate (Suvarṇadatta), transcribed into Chinese as Su-fa-lie and Ho-ti-pu-she-pi (Haripuṣpa). The Chinese pilgrim Hsuan-tsang also noticed Gold Flower (Skt. Suvarṇapuṣpa), a former ruler of Kucha. The names of individuals in ancient documents are also Sanskritised such as Wiryamitre (Vīryamitra), Wiryasene (Vīryasena), Jñānasena, Mokṣacandra etc.[136] This phenomenon must have been the result of Buddhist influence as also of Indian culture. There might have been Indian immigrants or their descendants in this part as well like those in Khotan.

134. Stein. *Ruins of Desert Cathay*. Op. cit. II. p. 359.

135. Eliot. *Op. cit*. III, p. 207.

136. Bagchi. *Op. cit*, p. 77.

The Regality & Buddhism in the Northern States

The exact date of the introduction of Buddhism in the Tarim basin kingdom is not known, but it could not have been later than the end of the 1st century A.D. A fuller picture of Buddhism in Kucha is available from about the third century onwards. According to the annals of the Tsin dynasty (265-316) there were a thousand Buddhist stūpas and temples in Kucha. Po-yen,[137] probably a member of the royal family, became a Buddhist monk and went to China in 256-60, and translated 6 Buddhist texts into Chinese in the famous Buddhist temple of Po-ma-sse at Lo-yang. Another Kuchean Po-Śrīmitra[138] went to China during 307-12 and then moved southwards He translated Buddhist texts between 335-342. Another Kuchean prince named Po-yen had gone to Leang-chou in 273. He was a Buddhist scholar of repute but no information is available regarding his literary contributions. A good bit of information is available about Buddhism in Kucha in the fourth century A.D. In one of the Chinese texts[139] of this period, reference is made to Kucha as a Buddhist city and the ruler's palace appearing like a monastery with standing images of Buddha carved in stone. The number of Buddhist monasteries and monks residing there are also recorded, as for instance Ta-mu had 170 monks. Po-shan hill also called Che-hu-li had 50 or 60 monks and the new monastery of the king of Wen-Su (Uch-Turfan) contained 7o monks. They were all under the direction of Fu-tu-she-mi (Buddhasvāmin), a scholar and follower of the Āgamas (Hīnayāna) school. His talented pupil Kiu-kiu-lo (Kumāra), however, became a Mahāyānist. Buddhist nuns too had their establishments at Kucha. Thus, the A-li (Āraṇyaka) monastery had 180 nuns, Liun-jo-kan had 50

137. Po-Yen, a Śramaṇa of the western region, translated some Sūtras in the White Horse monastery at Lo-yan in A.D. 257. (Nanjio—*Catalogue*. Op. cit, Appendix II No. 16, p. 387)

138. Poh-Sh-le-mi-to-lo-ye-Śrīmitra literally meaning a lucky friend was a śramaṇa of the western region who was an heir-apparent of a king of the country, but gave up his realm to his younger brother, and became a monk. He came to China in the Yun-Kia period A.D. 307-312 under the western Tsin dynasty. (Nanjio—*Op. cit*, ibid No. 36, p. 398)

139. Bagchi. *Op. cit*, p. 82.

and A-li-po had 30 nuns. These nunneries were under the direction of Buddhasvāmin, and the members were all drawn from royal families and households of nobles of the countries to the east of the Pamirs i.e. of the Tarim basin. The identity of Kumāra with the famous savant Kumārajīva[140] is certain, and his life history and contributions to Buddhism demand fuller and separate study in the text chapter covering 'Buddhism and Buddhist savants of Central Asia'. The monastery where Jīvā, mother of Kumārajīva, retired as a nun was called Tsio-li about 40 li to the north of Kucha. It was here that Jīvā learnt the language of India, might be Sanskrit. Kumārajīva was at that time seven years old; and the monastic environment had great impact on his personality as also acquisition of knowledge and breadth of learning. He was responsible for introducing Mahāyānism in the countries of the Tarim basin and also in China, rather in an authoritative manner. He was one of the greatest exponents of this school of Buddhism and also of the Mādhyamika philosophy. His compatriot Vimalākṣa[141] later on joined Kumārajīva in China in 404.

Another scholar from India, Dharmagupta,[142] visited Kucha towards the end of the sixth century and stayed there in the king's monastery for two years enjoying the patronage of the ruler who too was a great believer in Mahāyānism. He also taught various Śāstras in Kucha, including logic (*tarkaśāstra*) before leaving for China. Hsuan-tsang's description of Kucha and its Buddhist monasteries has already been recorded. The

140. Kumārajīva—called Thun-Sheu—meaning 'boy age' 'a longevity'—was an Indian Śramaṇa whose forefathers were successively ministers of the country. A fuller account of Kumārajīva's life and literary contributions is provided by Nanjio (Op. cit, II. 59, 406 ff) and also in *Encyclopedia of Religion and Ethics*.

141. Vimalākṣa, translated in Chinese Wu-Keu-Yen meaning 'without dirt-eye' was a Śramaṇa of Kublia (Kabul), who was a great teacher of Vinaya in Kwei-tsz i.e. Kharakar or Kuke where Kumārajīva was one of his disciples. He arrived in China in A.D. 406. (Nanjio—Op. cit No. ii, 44, p. 400)

142. Ta-mo-Kiu-to i.e. Dharmagupta whose name is translated Fa-mi literally 'law-secret' or 'law-repository' was a śramaṇa of the Lo-lo country or State of southern India (Nanjio—Op. cit. ii. 131. p. 434). Dharmagupta passed through Kucha about 584 and has referred to the king favouring Mahāyānism (Levi. J.A. 1913. II, p. 348 quoted by Eliot Op. cit, p. 204).

Chao-hu-li (same as Tsio-li of other accounts), about 40 li to the north of Kucha where Jīvā also studied, contained a beautiful image of Buddha. The Chinese pilgrim saw two standing images of Buddha about 90 feet high outside the western gate of the city. The quinquennial assemblies used to be held in front of these images. Hsuan-tsang mentions[143] another famous monastery called A-She-li-ni which was nearby, and was the meeting place of Buddhists from all countries. The chief priest of this monastery was Mo-cha-kiu-to (Mokṣagupta) who commanded respect from all for erudite learning and ability. He had travelled in India for twenty years and had also studied there. According to his version given to the pilgrim, the Buddhist libraries of Kucha were well equipped and contained valuable works such as *Saṁyukta-hridaya, Abhidharma-Kośa* and *Vibhāṣa.* Hsuna-tsang also describes the annual car festival when images of Buddha used to be carried in procession, with thousands of people participating in it, including the kings and nobles, who had great respect for Buddha and the Buddhist savants. Religious fasts were also observed by one and all and there were discourses on sacred teachings. Buddhism flourished in Kucha till the eighth century. When Wu-kong[144] visited Kucha in 751, he met a Buddhist teacher named Wu-ti-ti-su-yu (Utpal-tsirawne—Skt. Utpalavīrya). He knew a number of languages—those of India, the countries of the Tarim basin and also China. At the request of Wu-kong, he translated *Daśabala-sūtra* and two other works in collaboration with a Khotanese monk, Śīladharma. The pilgrim also furnishes information relating to Buddhism in the two states of Karasahr and Aksu. He mentions about 10 monasteries and 2,000 monks in Karasahr,

143. For Hsuen tsang's description see Beal. Op. cit, Vol. I, pp. 19 ff.

144. The last Chinese traveller to come to India in the Tang period, Wu-Kong left China on an official mission to escort the Indian ambassador, who had come to China from the kingdom of Kāpiśa. He passed through Kucha, Kashgar, Shignan in the Pamirs and Wakhan, and reached the Indus by the route of Yasin and Gilgit valley. He first came to Uḍḍiyāna and Gandhāra which were under the kingdom of Kāpiśa in this period. Here he was converted to Buddhism. A short account of his travels has been preserved (Bagchi. *India and China,* Op. cit., p. 78). This person Wu-Kong was also known as Dharmadhātu who remained some time in India, took the vows and ultimately returned to China with many books and relics (Eliot. *Op. cit.* III. 262).

all belonging to the Hīnayāna school of the Sarvāstivādins. The number of monasteries was the same in Ak-Su but the monks there were only a thousand. The monks of both the States as well as of Turfan were dependent on Kucha for religious leadership in the early period, but towards the end of the 5th century, with the establishment of the Chinese dynasty, the Chinese influence was more apparent. Buddhism continued to be the religion of the people till the middle of the seventh century in Turfan as recorded by Hsuan-tsang and enjoyed the hospitality of king Wen-tai in 630. There he came into contact with a Chinese Buddhist scholar who had studied at Chang-ngan. Hsuan-tsang stayed at Turfan and discoursed on the doctrine of the Prajñāpāramitā. The Chinese inscriptions of this period from Turfan provide good bit of information about the influence of Buddhism on the life of the people.

Buddhism flourished under the Uighurs as well. The Turks were equally familiar with Buddhism in Tokharestan and some of the rulers showed great interest in it. The Uighur Turks inherited that tradition and assimilated a good deal of Buddhist culture from the people of the northern area of the Tarim basin of Turfan, Karasahr, Kucha and Aksu, with whom they were in close contact in the 7th century. With the foundation of the new empire with Turfan as its metropolis in the 9th century, the old civilisation of Kucha-Karasahr had no doubt disappeared but the Uighurs had assimilated much of it. Buddhism continued to have its due place under the Uighurs despite the state patronage accorded to Manichaeism in this period. A large number of Tokharian Buddhist texts were translated into Uighur, forming the oldest literature of the Turks. Most of the Buddhist sites in Turfan belong to the Uighur period (750-550) of Central Asian history. Bezeklik contains the largest Buddhist sites of Turfan. There are cave temples and beautiful frescoes and numerous Buddhist shrines. The Buddhist sites of the Tarim basin (especially Bezaklik) are replete with stucco figures and frescoes, suggesting the Far Eastern expression of the Greco-Buddhist art of Gandhāra. The ancient sites in Kucha such as Kizil, Kumtura, Duldur, Akhur etc. contain vestiges of the ancient Buddhist art rather of a mixed character.

In a review of the political history of Central Asia in the

pre-Muslim period it may be suggested that the region lacked indigenous national unity though sometimes the Tarim basin was united under foreign rule. Cities or groups of towns, separated by deserts had their own way of life with political independence under native rulers. Chinese, Turks or Tibetans stationed troops in these places and appointed residents to supervise the collection of tribute. The main cities or oases were Kashgar in the west, Kucha, Karasahr, Turfan (Idiqutshahri, Chotsche) and Hami lying successfully to the north-east, and Khotan and Miran to the south-east. Inter-State confrontations were frequent though confined to neighbouring ones, and the interference of foreigners was not ruled out. Economic and political factors resulting in the clash of tribes and the displacement of the vanquished one necessitated migratory movements. These took the form of political upheavals and consequent formation of new kingdoms and empire. The roles of the Hiung-nu, and Yueh-chi are notable in this direction. The Chinese participation in the political affairs of Central Asia and its state was fairly active all through this period except when confronted with superior force or dissipated by internal troubles. The Chinese were equally interested in their trade with the west and wanted to have friendly relations with the States through which the route passed. Their concept of friendship was determined by the despatch of missions to the Imperial court with tribute and presents. Sometimes even royal princes were left there for Imperial service. The states were no doubt vulnerable to external pressures and there were cases of protéges of foreign powers ruling there. Thus, we find Kashgar becoming a Chinese protected state in the first century B.C. and on the relaxation of Chinese hold about the time of the Christian era, it was subdued by the neighbouring kingdom of Khotan. Chinese supremacy was restored with the conquest of Pan-chao, but the Yueh-chi interfered in the internal politics of Kashgar and placed a prince of their choice on the throne. Kaniṣka is also credited with the conquest of Kashgar and Khotan, and Hsuan-tsang refers to the princes of this state being kept as hostages. The Hephthalities, in turn, incorporated Kashgar in their dominions. The reference to the Indian rulers of Khotan with the prefix added to their names suggests Indian colonisation which is recorded in the Tibetan traditions. The history of the other kingdoms further east in the Tarim basin was in no way different except that those nearer to the Chinese border had greater control of the latter. Turfan in this sense was more receptive to Chinese influence—political as well as cultural. Kucha and the nearer states had much in common.

In this context the role of Buddhism and the part played by the royalty in its propagation are equally important. In fact, the religion of the Tathāgata was a cultural integrating force in Central Asia, despite the fact that according to Hsuan-tsang's religious conspectus of these regions, Kashgar, Osh and Kucha belonged to the small vehicle of the Sarvāstivādins, while Yarkand and Khotan mainly Mahāyānist. The small vehicle also flourished at Balkh and at Bamiyan. In Kāpiśa the Great Vehicle was predominant and there were many Hindu sects. The royalty played an active part in the propagation of Buddhism and also participated in Buddhist cultural activities. In Kucha, the royal palace appeared like a monastery with figures of Buddha everywhere in Hsuan-tsang's time. The Tibetans and Uighurs were no exception in their patronage of Buddhism. The contribution of Buddhist savants of Central Asia in that area as also in China where they translated many canonical texts into Chinese demands proper study in a separate chapter.

CHAPTER III

BUDDHISM AND BUDDHIST SAVANTS OF CENTRAL ASIA

A comprehensive study of Buddhism in Central Asia involving its introduction, expansion and branching off into several sects presupposes an investigation into the source material—literary, epigraphic, travel accounts as well as monumental remains of ancient Buddhist sites in this vast region. It is not a uniform phenomenon as different areas of Central Asia received the message of Tathāgata in different periods and, of course, through manifold channels—royal emissaries, individual scholars and even the trading and mercantile class who might have contributed materially towards its expansion. The zeal and curiosity of the indigenous element might as well have been a contributory factor in the expansion of Buddhism which, in a couple of centuries, became very popular not only in Central Asia but also in China, and thence eastwards in Korea and Japan. A long history of Buddhism and its expansion, however, demands regional study—namely that of the western region comprising Afghanistan, Bactria and Parthia, the central zone covering the present Russian Turkestan, and the eastern one assimilating both the northern and southern wings of Chinese Turkestan. Central Asia in general played an active role through its savants in the translation of Buddhist sacred texts into Chinese as also in other languages of the countries of its adoption. A long list of such scholars who worked in this direction is available from the catalogue of Chinese Buddhist Tripitakas in different periods. A study of the list would bring out the fruitful contribution of Buddhist savants from other parts of Asia including India in different centuries. Thus, according to the list of Nanjio,[1] among

1. See : *A Catalogue of the Chinese Buddhist Tripitaka*, Oxford (1882), Appendix II, pp. 379 ff. In his *Handbook of Chinese Buddhism*, Earnest J. Eitel refers to the contributions of different scholars in this context (Reprint—

72 translators who worked between 67 and 420 there were 15 Indians, 7 Yueh-chi, 5 Parthians, 7 Kubhans, 21 from the western countries and 17 Chinese; among them 22 worked in the south, of whom 5 were Chinese. Among 43 workers who worked between 420 and 550, 14 were Indians, 10 from Kubhā and other western countries, 4 Sinhalese and Indo-Chinese, and 4 of uncertain origin. Among them 27 worked in the south. A close study and scrutiny of the list would reveal the contribution of Parthians and these from Kubhā (Kabul) as eminent Buddhist scholars who went to China for Buddhism—its propagation through translation of sacred texts. The western countries include Central Asia and comprised of both the modern sectors of Russian and Chinese Turkestans. The two areas, however, demand separate treatment because of political considerations as also their separate archaeological investigations.

The history of Buddhism in Central Asia is also related to the political history of different regions and the hold of different political powers in later times, like that of the Chinese, Tibetans and Uighurs. The languages of these people have also left literary remains in Central Asia, which no doubt call for separate treatment. A brief notice of the languages represented in the manuscripts and inscriptions discovered will reveal many influences at work in Central Asia, and its importance as a receiving and distributing centre. Numerous Sanskrit writings have been found, all dealing with religious or quasi-religious subjects, as medicine and grammar. Relatively modern Mahāyānist literature[2]

Cosmos Publications, New Delhi, 1981; original edition 1888). This calculation is recorded by B.A. Litvinsky in his booklet entitled 'Outline History of Buddhism in Central Asia' prepared and circulated at the Diushandbe Session (1968) of the International Conference on the History, Archaeology and Culture of Central Asia in the Kushan Period, p. 13. Brough, J. suggests that certain Yueh-chih translators may have come not from the land of the Great Yueh-chih, but from the milieu of the Eastern Turkestan 'Little Yueh-chih' (quoted note 63, *Op. cit*, p. 83).

2. Central Asia, according to Eliot, has astonished the learned world with two new languages, both written in a special variety of the Brāhmī alphabet called Central Asian Gupta. One is called Nordarish, regarded by some as the language of the Śakas, and by others as the language of the Kuṣāṇas and of Kaniṣka's empire. The Mahāyānist literature translated into this language include the *Suvarṇaprabhāsa Vajracchedikā* and *Aparimātyus-sūtras*. It appears to have been spoken principally in the southern part of the Tarim

is abundant. Unknown forms of Prākrit are not unknown, while two new languages, written in Central Asian Gupta script, provide translations of Mahāyānist literature. Three other Iranian languages, all written in an alphabet of Aramani origin have left literary remains in Central Asia. Of the three, Iranian language, Sogdian with a more varied literary content also offers Buddhist texts, besides later Manichaen and Christian ones. It was originally the language of the region round Samarkand, but was used by merchants throughout the Tarim basin and spread even to China.[3]

As the Tibetans were the dominating power in the Tarim basin at least from the middle of the eighth until the middle of the ninth century, it is not surprising to record finds of Tibetan manuscripts in the regions of Khotan, Miran and Tun-huang. In Turfan, traces of Tibetan influence are fewer though not entirely absent. The documents include Buddhist translations[4] besides numerous official and business papers. At that time Buddhism seems to have shared with the Bon religion the allegiance of the Tibetans. Of course, there are no Manichaean or Christian translations in Tibetan. A large number of Chinese texts—both religious and secular—from the principal centres of Central Asia, including a series of dated documents ranging from 98 B.C. to 153 A.D. point to intercourse between China and Central Asia at this period. Some documents of the Tang dynasty are Manichaean with an admixture of Buddhist and Taoist ideas.[5]

Basin (Hoernle in JRAS, 1910, pp. 837 ff and 1383 ff; 1911 pp. 202 ff, 447ff.) The other language spoken principally on its northern edge is called Tokharian, associated with the Tokharas or Indo-Scyths. According to Eliot, it is safer of it as the language of Kucha or Kuchanese. It exists in two different dialects known as A and B whose geographical distribution is uncertain. Numerous official documents dated in the first half of the seventh century show that it was the ordinary speech of Kucha and Turfan. It was also a literary language and among the many translations discovered are versions in it of the *Dharmapada* and *Vinaya*. (Eliot. *Hinduism and Buddhism*—Op. cit III, pp. 190-91 with references to many articles including that of Sylvain Levi—'Tokharian B, Langue de Koutche' JA. 1913. II. p. 311)

3. Eliot : *Op. cit*, pp. 191-92.

4. Aurel Stein. *Ancient Khotan*—Op. cit, Appendix B—entitled Tibetan Manuscripts and Scraffiti discovered by M.A. Stein at Endere—edited by L.D. Barnett and A.H. France.

5. Eliot : Op. cit, p. 193. See also Chavannes—*Les documents Chinois decouverts par* Aurel Stein, 1913; also Appendix A entitled 'Chinese Docu-

Besides these languages and dialects used as mediums of Buddhist literature in Central Asia, another dialect Uighur[6] was used for Buddhist literature. It spread considerably when the Uighurs broke the power of Tibet in the Tarim basin about 860 and founded a kingdom themselves. It extended into China and lasted long.

Buddhism in Afghanistan, Bactria and Parthia

Monumental remains, as also reference to Buddhist savants in Chinese Buddhist literature point to the flourishing state of Buddhism in this part of Central Asia; and Alberuni[7], 'too, does not fail to record this fact. In his words, 'in former times, Khorasan, Persia, Iraq, Mosul, the country upto the frontier of Syria, was Buddhistic, but then Zarathustra went forth from Adharbayjan and preached Magism in Balkh (Baktre)'. His doctrine came into favour with king Gushtasp, and his son Isfendiyad spread the new faith both in East and West, both by force and by treaties. He founded five temples through his whole empire, from the frontiers of China to those of the Greek Empire. The succeeding kings made their religion (i.e. Zoroastrianism) the obligatory state religion of Persia and Iraq. In consequence, the Buddhists were banished from those countries, and had to emigrate to the countries east of Balkh. He also refers to the finds, of Buddhist idols, and their remnants from India, China and among the Toghuzghus. The people of Khorasan call them 'Shamanan' or (Sanskrit, Śramaṇa) while the shrine known as vihāra could be seen in the border district of Khorasan adjoining India. This is the impression about Buddhism and its monuments, as recorded by the talented Khoresmian Alberuni (973-1048), the author of *Tahkik-i-Hind* (Inquiry into India).

---

ments from the sites of Dandan Uiliq, Niya and Endere' translated and annotated by Eduvard Chavannes in *Ancient Khotan*—Op. cit, pp. 521 ff.

6. The name Uigur is perhaps more correctly applied to the alphabet than the language which appears to have been the literary form of the various Turkish idioms spoken north and south of Tienshan. The use of Uigur in China is evident from the printing of Sūtras in Uigur at Peking in 1330, and Uigur manuscripts were copied in the reign of Kang Hsi (1662-1773) (Eliot. Op. cit, p. 192).

7. 'Alberuni's India'—Translated by F.C. Sachau, Vol. I. London, 1888, p. 21.

The history of Buddhism in this part of Central Asia might be dated from the time of the Indo-Bactrians, although the teachings of the Lord might have found their way even earlier. In this context, the Kandahar bilingual edict[8] of Aśoka is rightly considered as an eloquent testimonial to the extension of Buddhism in the direction of Central Asia. The finds of other inscriptions in Afghanistan suggest that this part of Central Asia had come within the range of Mauryan cultural activities, it being a part of the empire of Aśoka. Buddhism as such must have had a substantial following in the Kandahar area of what is now southern Afghanistan by the middle of the 3rd century B.C. It is proposed by Bagchi[9] that Buddhism was introduced in Balkh in the time of Aśoka who, no doubt, speaks of his efforts to introduce his dhamma among the peoples of Gandhāra, Kamboja and Yona. The three peoples were neighbours, Kambojas were probably a branch of the Tukhāra people, while the Yonas were no doubt the Bactrian Greeks. In this context a legend recorded by Hsuan-tsang[10] refers to the first two lay disciples of Buddha, Trapuṣa and Bhallika as responsible for introducing Buddhism in that country. Originally these two were merchants of the kingdom of Bālhika, as the name Bhalluka or Bhallika probably suggests the association of one with that country. They had gone to India for trade and happened to be at Bodhgaya when the Buddha had just attained his enlightenment. Offering him cakes and honey out of their provision they were also ordained by the Tathāgata as his first two disciples. The progress of Buddhism to the north of Afghanistan is also borne out by a Kharoṣṭhī inscription on a clay object recovered from the Begram excavations

8. J. Harmata. 'Sino-Indica'—'Acta Antiqua', Vol. XII, No. 1-2, Budapest, 1964, p. 4.

9. *India and Central Asia*—Op. cit, p. 32. Foucher, however, holds that Buddhism did not appear in Bactria until the end of the 1st or the 2nd century A.D. (*La Vielle route de l'Inde de Bactres a Taxila,* Vol. II, Paris, 1947, pp. 280-84). Litvinsky, however, considers Foucher's view to be erroneous (*Outline History of Buddhism in Central Asia*, Dushanbe, 1968, p. 77 n.15).

10. T. Watters. '*On Yuan-Chwang's Travels in India*' (Photoprint edition, New Delhi, 1973, Vol. I, 112; II 131).

in the first layer, placed between the third and second centuries B.C. recording a Buddhist name.[11]

The foundation of the Greco-Bactrian state no doubt contributed to the expansion of Buddhism in this region in the first two centuries preceding the Christian era. Both Demetrius and Menander were interested in Buddhism.[12] The former is supposed to have attacked India to punish the Brahmin Śuṅga ruler for his anti-Buddhist activities and persecution of Buddhist monks, while the latter seems to have embraced the religion of the Tathāgata after his discourse with the Buddhist philosopher Nāgasena. The *Milindapañho* or 'Discourses with Menander' is the theme of the great work. This is both in Pāli and also in Chinese translation.[13] Its composition might have been of a later date, probably after Menander's death. It is now generally accepted that this Indo-Greek ruler was a devotee of the Tathāgata, and certain symbols like the stūpa on the coins of Agathocles, as also the legends on the coins of Menander are in agreement with the theory of infiltration of Buddhism in the realm of the Indo-Greek or Bactrian rulers.[14] It seems fairly evident that the Greco-Bactrian kingdom unified in one political state the north Indian regions, Afghanistan and several parts of western Turkestan. The political atmosphere was, thus, congenial for the Buddhist missionaries as also for the local followers in those

11. J. Harmata. Sino-Indica 'Ariana Antiqua', Vol. XII, No. 1-2, Budapest, 1964, pp. 4-5.

12. L. Levi. *Le Bouddhisme et les Grecs—Revue de l'Histoire de Religions*, XXIII, 1891 pp. 436-49; reprinted in *Memorial* Sylvain Levi, pp. 204 ff. *The Questions of King Milinda* SBE, XXXV; P. Denievitte. *Les versions Chinoises de Milindapañho* BEFCO, XXIV, pp. 168 ff.

13. The Chinese version of the *Milindapañha*, written several centuries later, describes Alasanda as 2,000 yojana from Sagala instead of 200 (Demieville—Op. cit; cf. Pelliot. J.A. 1914, Pt. II, pp. 413-19; Levi. IHQ. 1936, p. 126).

14. The Pāli texts represent the Greeks as taking part in missionary activities. We are told that after the conversion of Yavana (Greek) country to Buddhism, Moggoliputta Tissa went there and selected an elder Dharmarakṣita for missionery work. He was then sent to Aparāntaka where he made a large number of converts. The Greeks were also represented by this Elder Mahādharmarakṣita at the Great Stūpa ceremony in Ceylon, initiated by Duṭṭhagāmini in the middle of the second century B.C. (Levi. *Op. cit*).

areas to convey the message of the Lord outside the boundaries of this kingdom.

Further information regarding the association of Indo-Greek rulers as also the Yonas with Buddhism between the second and the first century B.C. is also available from other sources. Two Kharoṣṭhī inscriptions[15]—one from the ancient country of Uḍyāna (Swat valley) and the other from Bajaur (south-east of Jalalabad) record dedications by a Greek officer named Meridarkh Theodorus who enshrined the relics of the Lord Buddha, and the pious act of one Vīyaka-mitra—an *apracharājā* (Skt. *apratyagrāja*) respectively. The former was an officer of rank and the latter was a vassal—both probably under Menander or his successor. It is also proposed that the wheel on some coins of Menander is connected with Buddhism.[16] The association of these Indo-Greek rulers—Demetrius and Menander—was not a formality but an article of faith. According to a tradition cited by Tārānāth, Menander's association with Buddhism is independent of the *Milindapañho*. He refers to king Minara in the land of the Tukharas, who is identified with Menander by Lassen.[17] Further, the association of Greeks with Buddhism in the north-west area in the early first two centuries preceding the Christian era, is also evinced from the Ceylonese chronicles. It is said that when Duṭṭagāmini founded the Great stūpa (Mahāthūpa) in Ceylon, sometime in the middle of the second century B.C. he invited Buddhist teachers from various countries. The elder Mahādharmarakṣita represented the Greeks who came from the city of Alasandā.[18]

15. Sten Konow. Corpus Inscriptionum Indicarm (CII) II (i), These are discussed by K.A. Nilakantha Sastri: *A Comprehensive History of India*, p. 219.

16. J. Marshall : *Taxila*, 3 Vols, Cambridge, 1951, Vol. I, pp. 33-34; Narain : *Indo-Greeks*—Op. cit, p. 98. According to Tarn, the idea that Menander ever became a Buddhist in the sense of entering the order may be dismissed at once (Op. cit, p. 268).

17. This tradition as recorded by Tārānāth, refers to king Minnara in the land of the Tukhāras, and he is identified by Lassen with Menander (Narain, 98 n).

18. According to the *Mahāvaṁsa*, the Ceylonese king Duṭṭagāmini whose regnal years are assigned by scholars between 101-77 B.C. marked the laying of 'Great Stūpa' by a huge celebration attended by a large number of bhikṣus from many foreign lands (XXIX.29). These included wise Mahādeva from Pallavabhoga with 460,000 bhikṣus, and Yona mahādhammarakhita with

This place is mentioned in the *Milindapañho* as a *dvīpa* at a distance of 200 yojanas from Śākala (Sialkot) and it was in the village of Kalasi in this *dvīpa* that Menander was born. Both Alasandas seem identical and are supposed to be located at Charukar between Panjshiv and Kabul rivers.[19] Tarn, however, identifies the Alasandā of the *Milindapañho* with Alexandria of the Caucasus, and not with Alexandria in Egypt, as presumed by some French scholars. Buddhism, thus, appears to have flourished in Bactria and the neighbouring regions, and its savants could attract the attention of those interested in Tathāgata and his religion even in far off places like Ceylon. Coedes also records a local tradition connecting Menander with the origin of the famous statue of Buddha in Indo-China, the statue of Buddha of the Emerald produced by supernatural magical power by Menander's teacher Nāgasena.

Besides Bactria and its rulers, who it seems experienced the earliest infiltration of Buddhism in their areas, the Yueh-chi equated with the Tuṣāras and their later homeland Tokharistan also had the impact of this religious discipline more or less at the same time. The first inflow of Buddhist culture to China was from Tokharestan. It was in the year 2 B.C. that the Chinese ambassador Tsing-Kiang received Buddhist texts as presents to the Chinese court.[20] The passage recording this incident in the 'Wei-Lio', a third century source, has received different interpretations by the sinalogists. While the date is accepted as 2 B.C., it is suggested that the Yueh-chi crown prince acquainted the visitors with Buddhism. Some scholars, even question the historical authenticity of this account, but the role of the Yueh-chi in popularising Buddhism in China is not disputed. This

---

30,000 bhikṣus from Alasanda, the city of the Yonas (ibid, XXIX, 38-39). While the number of guests seems to be exaggerated, the participation of these foreigners might be accepted.

19. 'Quarterly Journal of the Mythic Society' (QJMS. LXXI, p. 180; Tarn : Op. cit, p. 141). The *Mahāvaṁsa* calls it a city of the Yonas (Yonanagaralasanda—XXIX, 37.). According to the *Milindapañha*, the town is mentioned as situated on an island in the Indus (III.7.4).

20. Chavannes. *Les documents Chinois decouverté par Aurel Stein*, 1973, Introduction. The earliest documents are of 98 B.C. See Eliot : *Hinduism and Buddhism*—Op. cit. III, p. 245.

must have been at the time of the composition of the 'Wei-lo' in the third century A.D. or again the early fifth century, when the commentaries on it appeared. The role of the people and savants of Tokharistan in the dissemination and elaboration of the Buddhist religion in the early centuries of the Christian era is also evident from other sources.

The famous scholar Ghoṣaka, born in Tokharistan, played a prominent part at the fourth Buddhist Council in Purushpura. He was the author of the commentary on the *Abhidharma-Vibhāṣa* which was compiled there. This theologian also composed an original treatise on *Abhidharma*—the *Abhidharmāmrita*—which is preserved in the Chinese translation of the third century, being one of the most clear expositions of the Abhidharma doctrines. Ghoṣaka had returned to Turkestan and was associated with the Vaibhāṣika school, later on divided into branch schools. One of such branch was connected with the country of Bālhika or Balkh and was called the western Vaibhāṣika school. The tradition of this school could be traced to Ghoṣaka. The importance of this school in Tokharistan is revealed from the first translation of its treatises into the Tokharian language by a local monk named Dharmamitra of Tarmita or Termez. The Vaibhāṣika school, a branch of the Sarvāstivāda sect of Buddhism was widespread in western Turkistan, although some important elements in the Vaibhāṣika doctrine are supposed to have brought it closer to the Mahāyāna school, paving the way for its introduction and flourishing nature in Khotan. Bālhika or Balkh was a great centre of Buddhist studies even in later times. The Nava-saṅghārāma of this place, according to the Chinese pilgrim Hsuan-tsang, was the only Buddhist establishment north of the Hindukush in which there were a constant succession of Masters who were commentators of the canon. The importance of the Vaibhāṣika school of the Tukhāra country is also evident from the finds of Tokharian literature to which fuller reference would be made later on. Āryacandra, who first translated the *Maitreya-samiti* into the Tokharian language, was a Vaibhāṣika.

The role of the Tokharian Buddhist monks in the propagation of Buddhism in China was consistent. The Chinese literature distinguishes these monks by prefixing the word Che (from Yueh-che) to their names. It is said that the first two missionaries to China in A.D. 68, Kāśyapa Mātaṅga and Dharmarakṣa, were met by the Chinese ambassadors in the country of the Yueh-chis.[21] The Chinese refer to a monk called Chu-Fan-lau who came from Central Asia and found some difficulty in obtaining permission to leave his country. He therefore followed shortly afterwards. Both were installed at Loyang, the capital of the dynasty, in the White Horse Monastery, so called because the foreign monks rode on white horses or used them for carrying books. The story does not state that there was no Buddhism in China before A.D. 62. On the contrary it only implies that it was not sufficiently conspicuous to the Emperor. It is very likely that Buddhism entered China half a century earlier. While political relation and the despatch of a Chinese mission to the Central Asian power of the Yueh-chi (129-119 B.C.) under Chang-Chian could be traced to the second century B.C., and the documents discovered by Aurel Stein in Central Asia confirm China's communition with this part of Asia, there is no reference to Buddhism in any of these source materials. The notice in the Wei-lue is the earlier reference to Buddhism in B.C. as pointed out earlier. The Later Han Annals also intimate that in A.D. 65, the Prince of Chu was a Buddhist and that there were *Śramaṇas* and *upāsakas* in his territory.

Tokharistan seems to have played a consistent and steady role in propagating Buddhism in China in the centuries following. A monk of rare learning named Lokaṣema of Tukhāra origin went to Loyang in A.D. 147 and translated there some of the most

21. The traditional date for the introduction of Buddhism is A.D. 62, when the chronicles tell how the Emperor Ming-Ti of the Later Han Dynasty dreamt of seeing a golden man fly into his palace, and how his courtiers suggested that the figure was Fo-to or Buddha, an Indian God. This was followed by the despatch of an embassy in 65 to the kingdom of Ta-Yueh-chih or India with instructions to bring back Buddhist scriptures and priests. On the return journey it was accompanied by a monk called Kāśyapa Mātaṅga, a native of Central India, followed later on by another person Chu-Fa-lan from Central Asia. The story does not state that there was no Buddhism in China before 62 A.D. According to Wei-lueh, which gives a brief account of the Buddha's birth in the year 2 B.C., an ambassador sent by the Emperor Ai to the court of the Yueh-chih was instructed in Buddhism by order of their kings. Also in 65 A.D. The Prince of Chu was a Buddhist and there were śramaṇas and upāsakas in his territory. (For the account of the Chinese mission, see—BEFCO, 1910; also Eliot : Op. cit III, 244-45.)

important texts of the Buddhist canon into Chinese. He worked at translations till A.D. 186. There are twelve translations ascribed to him.[22] Towards the end of the same century (190-220 A.D.), one of his young disciples, Che-kien, also of Tukhāra origin, was working in North China, but had to leave on account of political trouble and settled down at Nanking where he worked till the middle of the 3rd century A.D. He translated over a hundred Buddhist texts—yet another Buddhist monk named Dharmarakṣa (Chinese name Fa-hu) was born of a Tukhāra family. He had settled down in Tun-huang towards the middle of the 3rd century A.D. and after travelling far and wide in Central Asia, had picked up 36 different languages. He went to China in A.D. 284 and worked there till 313. He translated nearly two hundred Buddhist texts into Chinese, out of which 90 are still existing. Another Tukhāra monk named She-lun came to China in 373 and translated four works into Chinese. The last Tukhāra monk to go to China, as recorded in the Chinese works, was Dharmanandi[23] who went there in 384 and translated a number of works into Chinese.

While Tokharistan seems to have provided a number of Buddhist monks who went to China and translated canonical works into Chinese, Parthia and Kabul (Kubbā) also furnished a number of Buddhist scholars for the cause of Buddhism in China. That is possible only if the home country itself was iṇ a flourishing state. While reference has been made to the region of Kabul forming part of the territory of Indo-Greeks, Parthia and Drangiana demand consideration as centres of Buddhist activities in the early centuries of the Christian era. Reference has no doubt been made to Yona Mahādhammarakhita with 30,000 bhikṣus participating in the great celebrations at the laying of the 'Great Stūpa' in the time of king Dutta-gāmini of Ceylon. The *Mahāvaṁsa*[24] also refers to the visit of the wise Mahādeva from Pallavabhogga with 46,000 bhikṣu monks. There might be exaggeration in the number of foreign participants, and the Buddhist chronicle of the sixth century A.D. must have based its

22. Nanjio. *Catalogue*—Op. cit, ii. 3. pp. 381-82.
23. Nanjio—Op. cit, ii, 57, pp. 403-04.
24. W. Geiger. *Mahāvaṁsa*—Op. cit, XXIX. 29.

information on older material—primarily local chronicles, no longer available. The authenticity of the information according to Geiger[25] need not be questioned. The Pallavas are associated with Pahlavas i.e. the Parthians. Geiger takes it as a Persian name. As regards the wise Mahādeva and his *bhoggam*, he might have been from a satrapy (*bhoga*) of the Parthians and not Parthia itself. As such, this Ceylonese account could refer to Parthian Buddhism in the first century B.C. According to Bagchi,[26] real interest in Buddhism is shown by the Parthians only after its establishment in Tocharestan under the Kuṣāṇas. The Tokharians must have transmitted Buddhism to them. While there is no trace of old Parthian translations of Buddhist texts, the Chinese accounts do refer to a number of Iranian Buddhist scholars who went to China in the 2nd and third centuries A.D. and collaborated in the translation of Buddhist texts into Chinese. In the absence of any centre for Buddhist studies in Iran, it is suggested[27] that the Parthian monks had studied Buddhism and Buddhist texts in original at the Buddhist centres of Tokharestan before proceeding to China. It may, however, be presumed on the basis of reference[28] to the Parthian monk An-Shib-kao, who visited China in the second century A.D. that Parthia had already a long tradition of Buddhism. It is suggested[29] by G.A. Koshelenko that the Parthians made their acquaintance with Buddhism not later than the beginning of our era, and he also refers to the appearance of Buddhism in Margiana in the first century A.D. This could have been possible through the south-eastern territories of the Parthian kingdom of the 1st century B.C. at the latest.

25. *ibid*, pp. ix-x.

26. *India and China*, p. 30.

27. *ibid*, p. 37.

28. Nanjio. Op. cit, II.4, pp. 381-82. An-shi-Kao was a prince royal of the country of An-Si (Eastern Persia or Parthia or Arsak) which character is affixed to the names of other translators of the same country living in China. as their surname eg. An-Huen. When An-shi-Kao's father died, he gave up his kingdom to his uncle and became a śramaṇa. He came to China in A.D. 148 and worked at translations till A.D. 170.

29. 'The Beginning of Buddhism in Margiana' 'Ariana Antiqua' (Hungary), XIV, fasc. 1-2, Budapest, 1966, p. 180.

The names of Parthian Buddhist monks in Chinese are distinguished by the prefix An (Ngan) from the old Chinese name of Parthia An-She (Arsak), a name given to the country in the period of the Arsacid dynasty. The Chinese historian mentions the Parthian prince Ngan-She-kao (same as An-Sheh-kao) or Lokottama who appeared in the western frontier country of China with a burden of Buddhist texts, after the fall of the Arsacidan dynasty in A.D. 148. He is said to have left his throne in favour of his uncle, and left the family to become a Buddhist monk at an early age. He worked at translations till A.D. 170. He personally translated into Chinese more than a hundred Buddhist texts of which 55 are recorded by Nanjio.[30] Many of these texts are extracts from the Buddhist Āgamas, generally illustrating the fundamental doctrines of Buddhism. Another Parthian scholar, named Ngan-Hiuan,[31] came to Loyang as a merchant. He received royal favour in the form of military service with the designation 'Chief of the Cavalry'. He soon gave up his official position and became a Buddhist monk—an upāsaka of An-hsi. He collaborated with Yen-Fo-thiao,[32] a Śramaṇa (or an upāsaka) of Lin-hwai in China and translated two works at Lo-yang in A.D. 181. Besides these Parthians, there were some Sogdian monks belonging to the school of the royal prince Ngan-She-kao who laid the foundation of a school for systematic interpretation of Buddhism to the Chinese. The first Chinese scholar Yen-Fo-tiao[33] (Buddhadeva) was an assistant of An-Huen (Ngan-Hiuan). He learnt Sanskrit, the original language of the Buddhist texts from Central Asia, and could recite the whole of the *Prātimokṣa.* He was given the Sanskrit name Buddhadeva, and accorded the title of 'Ācārya'. Later on several other Parthian monks of minor importance went to China during the third and the fourth centuries A.D. They equally contributed to the spread of Buddhism in China as also to the work of translating texts into Chinese language.

The Sogdians originally from their centre at Samarkand to the

30. Nanjio. II. 4, pp. 381-2.
31. *ibid,* II, 6, p. 383.
32. *ibid.* II, 9, p. 384.
33. Bagchi. *La Canon Bouddhique en Chine*—Op. cit, pp. 48-50.

north of Tokharestan were famous traders, who had their colonies in different parts of Central Asia and had come into association with Buddhism and Buddhist culture. The Sogdian monks also cuntributed towards the transmission of Buddhist culture and religious thought in China. Their names are distinguished by the prefix *Kang*, as the ancient name of Sogdiana in China was Kang-kiu. Some of these monks had collaborated with Ngan-She-Kao. An illustrious Sogdian monk who worked in South China in the 3rd century was Seng-Hui.[34] His ancestors had at first settled down in India. His father was a merchant and he had to stay in Tonkin (Kiao-Che) where Seng-hin was born. After his father's death, this young boy left the world and became a monk. He soon proceeded to Nanking where he built a monastery and founded a Buddhist school. He was the first to introduce Buddhism in Southern China. Nanjio, however, refers[35] to his administrative background, as the eldest son of the prime minister of the country of Khan-Ku i.e. Kambo or Ulterior Tibet or Kamboja, whose family continuously resided in India. He came to the capital of the kingdom of Wu in A.D. 241. In A.D. 247 he had the Kien-Ku-Sh or Kien-Ku monastery built by order of Sun-Khuen, the first sovereign of the Wu-dynasty who named the place Fo-tho-li or the Buddha village. In A.D. 251 he began his translation work, continuing it for nearly thirty years till his death in A.D. 280. He translated nearly a dozen Buddhist texts into Chinese.

While the evidence from the Chinese sources records the contribution of Buddhist monks and savants from different nationalities towards the dissemination of Buddhism and translation of canonical Buddhist texts, epigraphic, numismatic and art and archaeological evidences might as well be quoted in this context. The oldest record[36] found in Tadjikistan from the site of Darshai in the west Pamirs by A. N. Bernahtam mentions Nārāyaṇa 'be victorious' in Kharoṣṭhī script of the end of the second or the beginning of the first century B. C. While Nārāyaṇa is another

34. Bagchi. *India and Central Asia*—Op. cit, pp. 39; *Toung-Pao*, 1909, 199.

35. *Catalogue—Op. cit*, II, 21, p. 39.

36. J. Harmata. 'The oldest Kharoṣṭhī inscription in Inner Asia' 'Acta Orientalia', Vol. XIX, No. , Budapest, 1966, pp. 1 -12.

name of Viṣṇu, and this inscription like that of Heliodorus at Vidisa could point to the acceptance of Bhāgavatism[37] by foreigners, here it is in the context of reverence to Buddha Nārāyaṇa. Buddha is noticed in the Khotanese-Śaka documents from Eastern Turkestan, and 'Narayana' the deva occurs in the Buddhist Sogdian documents.[38]

The spread of Buddhism in Central Asia was no doubt stimulated by the formation of the Kuṣāṇa empire, which at its zenith seems to have overshadowed the Greco-Bactrian kingdom. The first ruler Kujula Kadphises styles himself on his coins as 'steadfast in true law' (*Sacadhrama-thitasa = Satyadharma sthitasya*) and the figure of Buddha is depicted on his coins. His successor appears to be Śaivite, while Kaniṣka, the great Kuṣāṇa ruler, was definitely a Buddhist though publicly he professed Eclecticism. Buddha figures prominently on his coins with the legend CAKAMANO-BOYDO—BUDDHA SAKYAMUNI. Kaniṣka's name is also associated with a vihāra or monastery set up for the Sarvāstivādins in an inscription dated in the year 1 from Shah ji Ki Dheri[39] near Peshawar. Reference has already been made to the Buddhist theologian Ghoṣaka, born in Tokharistan, who was one of the leading figures at the Buddhist Council held in Kaniṣka's time at Puruṣapura, who belonged to the Vaibhāṣika school, a branch of the Sarvāstivādins. The finds of potsherds from Kara-Tepe, with inscriptions in Brāhmī point to the spread of the Sarvāstivāda school of Buddhism in the present Russian or Western Turkestan in the time of Kaniṣka.[40] The same site also yielded inscribed potsherds in Kharoṣṭhī reflecting the teachings of the Mahāsāṅghika school. The reference to pioneer Buddhist savants instrumental in translating Buddhist canons into Chinese, hailing from the country of the Yueh-chi indirectly points to the kingdom of the Kuṣāṇas as their homeland. It is suggested that

37. According to Dey, S.K., Nārāyaṇa is connected with the cult of the Sun (Bhagavatism and Sun-worship—*Bulletin of the School of Oriental and African Studies*, BSOAS, 1931, Vol. VI, Pt. 3)

38. J. Harmata : Op. cit, p. 6.

39. Sten Konow : *Corpus Inscriptionum Indicarum* (CII) Vol. II (I) pp. 134 ff.

40. Litvinsky, B.A. *Outline History of Buddhism in Central Asia*, Diushanbe, 1968, p. 10.

Buddhism also consolidated its position in Margiana in the first century A.D. and it reached Eastern Turkestan through the western part of it, and from there it went to China. Zurcher enacts[41] this process between the middle of the 1st century B.C. and middle of the 1st century A.D. Among the early Buddhist missionaries to China (Lo-Yang) were two Parthians (An-shib Kao and An-Hsuan), three Yueh-chih (Chih-lou-chia-Chien—Lokasena, Chih-vao and Chih-liang), two Sogdians (Kang-Meng. hsiang and Kang-Seng-hui). Reference has already been made to the life and literary activities of these savants.

At the beginning of the third century, the Sogdian monks again figure as translators and this process continued throughout the third century largely due to the efforts of those whose ancestors had emigrated from western Turkestan. One such scholar was Chih-Chien,[42] also known as Chih-Yueh, grandson of a native of the land of the Yueh-chi who had settled at Loyang. Another was the Sogdian Kang-Seng-hui[43] whose merchant father had settled down in Loyang. The famous scholar Yueh-chi Dharmarakṣa[43] who worked between A.D. 266 and 309 belonged to Tun-huang where his ancestors had settled down earlier. Among his disciples was a Sogdian. Reference is also made to the Parthian An-Fa-chin engaged in translations of canonical works between A.D. 281 and 306. Another scholar who had lost touch with the country of his forefathers was Kang-Seng-yuan[44], a Sogdian born

41. E. Zurcher. *The Buddhist Conquest of China. The Spread and Adaptation of Buddhism in Early Medieval China,* Vol. I (text) Leiden, 1956, pp. 22-33. (quoted by Litvinsky : Op. cit, p. 10, also note 43 p. 81).

42. Chih-Chien or K'Khien, who had the liberal appellation Kun-min, and also another Cognomen Yueh, was an upāsaka of the country of Yueh-K' who came to China towards the end of the Eastern Han dynasty which came to an end in A.D. 220. Afterwards he took refuge in the kingdom of Wu, where he was appointed as a professor by Sun-Knien, the first sovereign of the Wu dynasty. He translated numerous works in A.D. 223-253. (49 Sūtras according to San-Kwhan fasc. 1, fol. 9 BC). Nanjio : Op. cit, II, 18, p. 388.

43. Nanjio considers Khan San-hwui, as an Indian Śramaṇa who was the eldest son of the prime minister of the country of Khan-Ku i.e. Kambu or ulterior Tibet, or Kamboja whose family was continuously resident in India. He came to the capital of the kingdom of Wu in A.D. 241. In A.D. 251 he began his work of translation and died in A.D. 280. (Nanjio : Op. cit, II, 21, p. 390).

44. Ku Than mo-lo-Kha (i.e. Dharmarakṣa whose name is translated

in a foreign land. At the end of the 4th century one Dharmanandin from Tukharistan (Tu-ho-lo) came to China. He stayed there between A.D. 384 and 391 and translated five works in this period, including very important Hīnayāna ones.[45] It has been calculated that among the translators engaged in rendering the Buddhist scriptures into Chinese, some time before the end of the Western Chin dynasty (A.D. 265-316), there were six or seven of Chinese and six of Indian origin as well as sixteen belonging to various Central Asian nationalities—six Yueh-chi, four Parthians, three Sogdians, two Kucheans and one Khotanese. These appear to be only approximate figures, pointing to the interest of Central Asian Buddhist scholars in the propagation of Buddhism in China, as also its flourishing state in Central Asia. There are also indications of Central Asian monks engaged in Buddhist activities in north-western India and in the Taxila region in the Kuṣāṇa Period. The earliest reference is to a certain Bactrian (Bahlikena), a resident of the town of Noacha or Noachea (unidentified) in the Taxila inscription[46] of the year 136 of the unknown era (probably of 57 B.C.). It is recorded on a silver scroll in a vessel containing a small golden casket in which there were fragments of bones. It invokes wishes for the bestowal of health on the great king, the king of kings, the son of God, the Kusane, who is generally identified with Kujula Kadphises. The contents of the inscription show that the Bactrians acted as zealots of Buddhist religion in India. In this context it might be necessary to record the inscriptions relating to Buddhism—its different schools and protoganists in the Kuṣāṇa period.

The existence of the two important schools of Buddhism,

Fa-hu, literally 'law protection', was a śramaṇa whose family resided in the Thu-Kwan district (the western extreme of the Great Wall in Kan-Shuh in Nan-Si-Keu (China). He was a descendant of a man of the country of Yueh-chi. He became a disciple of the foreign Śramaṇa Ku-Kao-tso. He went to the western regions with his teacher, and was well acquainted with thirty-six languages or dialects. In A.D. 266 he came to Lo-yan where he worked at translations till A.D. 313 or 317 and died afterwards in his seventy-eighth year. He is supposed to have translated 90 works (Nanjio : Op. cit, pp. 391-92).

45. Nanjio : *Op. cit*, II, 57, pp. 404-05.

46. *Corpus Inscriptionum Indicarum* (CII.II(i)) Op. cit, pp. 70 ff.

namely that of the Sarvāstivādins and of the Mahāsāṅghikas is noticed in the Brāhmī and Kharoṣṭhī records of the Kuṣāṇa period. An earlier record from Mathurā—the Lion capital inscription of the time of Śoḍāsa,[47] however, points to rivalry between the two schools, and it also specifies the location of the headquarters of the Sarvāstivādins at Nagarahāra in Jalalabad (Afghanistan). This record is important from the point of view of history of Buddhism, as also for the conflict between the two schools. It refers to the import of dialectician (Khalula), the Sarvāstivādin monk Budhila from Nagara to teach the foremost Mahāsāṅghikas the truth. The Sarvāstivādins are also noticed in the Kalwan Copper plate inscription[48] of the year 134, probably of the old era. It records the enshrinement of relics in the stūpa shrine by Chandrabhī, the female worshipper in acceptance of the Sarvāstivāda for the attainment of *nirvāṇa*. The inscriptions of the Kuṣāṇa period connected with this school are the famous Taxila casket of the year 1, Zeda of the year 11 and Kurram of the year 20 of Kaniṣka's era.[49] The donors are Hipea Dhia (Zeda) and Yola Mira Shāhi (undated Tordher-Thal valley, Loralai Baluchistan) who appear to be foreigners. These records from the Kharoṣṭhī region suggest Sarvāstivādin establishments in Afghanistan, West Punjab and Sindh. Mathurā, of course, was the important centre of the Sarvāstivādins who were facing the stiff opposition of the Mahāsaṅghikas there and had therefore to seek the help of their fellow brother dialectician at the other end of the Kuṣāṇa empire.

The Mahāsāṅghikas, too, had their establishment in Afghanistan, as is evident from the Wardhak inscription dated in the year 51 of the time of Huviṣka. It refers to the deposit of the relics of Lord Śākyamuni in the Vagramarega vihāra, in possession of the Mahāsāṅghika teachers. There is no other Kharoṣṭhi record of this school, although quite a few from Mathurā[50] are associated with it. It appears that Afghanistan had several centres of Buddhism and Buddhist activities in the Kuṣāna period, as

47. *ibid*, pp. 30 ff.

48. Journal of the Royal Asiatic Society (JRAS), 1932, pp. 949 ff.

49. Puri, B.N. *India Under the Kushāṇas* (IUK) pp. 141 ff for consoildated references and comments.

50. *ibid*, p. 142.

is evident from these records in Kharoṣṭhī from that country. This is supported by reference to several monks from the Kabul (Kubha) region who went to China and translated Buddhist canonical works into Chinese, of course later on in the beginning of the fourth century A.D. This could not have been possible except for a strong base of Buddhism in the Kabul area, established during the period of the Kuṣāṇas. These included Khuthan San-Kie-ti pho[51] i.e. Gautama Saṅghadeva (A.D. 383), Pi-mo-lo-kha i.e. Vimalākṣa[52] a great teacher of Vinaya, with Kumārajīva as one of his disciples, who arrived in China in A.D. 406; San-kie-poh-khan[53] i.e. Saṅghabhūti who translated 3 works in A.D. 381-385; and Fu-zo-tu-lo i.e. Puṇyatrāta[54] who arrived in China in the Hun-sh period A.D. 399-415 and was a collaborator with Kumārajīva; Than-mo-yesho i.e. Dharmayaśas[55] who translated 2 or 3 works in A.D. 407-415.

Buddhism and the Southern States

While Western Turkestan, Bactria and Parthia as also Afghanistan and Kashmir contributed a lot towards the spreading and development of Buddhism during the first few centuries of the Christian era, the area now forming part of Chinese Turkestan —Kashgar, Yarkand, Khothan and various sites of Kroraina— was equally humming with Buddhist activities. The States on the

51. Nanjio. Op. cit, II, 39, p. 399. He was a Śramaṇa of the country of Ke-pin i.e. Kubhā. In A.D. 383 he arrived at Khan-an, then the capital of the Former Tshin dynasty of the Fu family where he translated two works. Between A.D. 391-398 he translated five other works in two different places.

52. *ibid.* II. 44, p. 400. He was a Śramaṇa of Kubha (Kabul) and a great teacher of Vinaya in Kwei-tsz i.e. Kharakas or Kuke, where Kumārajīva was one of his disciples. Afterwards in A.D. 406 he arrived in China and was respected by his former disciple Kumārajīva who was flourishing there. After the latter's death, which happened between 409 and 415, Vimalākṣa went southward and translated 2 works. He died at the age of seventy-seven.

53. *ibid*, II, 54, p. 404. A Śramaṇa of Kubhā (Kabul) who translated 3 works in 27 or 37 fascicule between A.D. 381-85.

54. *ibid.* II. 60, p. 408. He was a Śramaṇa of Kubhā (Kabul) who arrived in China in the Hun-Sh period (A.D. 399-415) and in A.D. 404 he, together with Kumārajīva, translated one work in 58 fasciculi (*Sarvāstivādavinaya*).

55. *ibid*, II, 62, p. 408. He also belonged to the country of Kubha and translated 2 or 3 works in A.D. 407-415.

northern route comprising of Kucha and Turfan seem to have been under the spell of a separate wave of Buddhism, and, as such, demand independent study in this context. Kashgar also included Kie-pan-to (Sarikol)[56] and Wu-sa (Yangi-Hissa) as Hsuan-tsang speaks of linguistic affinity of these states in his time. Ho-pan-to, the name given by Song-yun-to, is the same as Kie-pan-to of the later Chinese pilgrim. The Tang Annals accord it several other names : Han-to, Ko-kuan-to etc. besides Ho-pan-to. Its capital on the river site (Hsi-to) identified with the Yarkand Darya is located at modern Tashkurghan which contains ruins of earlier times. In Hsuan-tsang's[57] time there were more than 10 monasteries in the capital with 500 monks belonging to the Sarvāstivāda school. The ruler at that time patronised Buddhism and was a cultured scholar. A famous scholar of Takṣaśilā, Kumāralāta[58] was brought here and he was the founder of the Sautrāntika school of Buddhism, and a contemporary of Aśvaghoṣa, Nāgārjuna and Āryadeva. He is said to have written many treatises, but only one book the *Kalpanāmaṇḍitīkā*[59] a recast of the *Sūtrālaṁkāra* of Aśvaghoṣa, has been partially discovered from Chinese Turkestan. The local ruler had built a monastery for this Buddhist scholar which existed in the seventh century A.D. In the next country of Wu-sha which lay

56. The early Chinese accounts of Sarikol are recorded by Aurel Stein in his *Ancient Khotan*, Vol. I, pp. 27 ff. The Chinese transcriptions variously render the name as Chieh-pan-to, Han-pan-to etc. The Tang Annals also mention several names Ho-pan-to, Han-to, Ko-Koan-tan or Ko-lo-to. The Annals also notice the identical appearance and language of the people of this region with those of Yo-tien or Khotan. For Hsuen-tsang's account, see Beal : Op. cit, ii, p. 298, also *Life* (translated by Beal : Op. cit, p. 196).

57. Beal : Op. cit, II, p. 298.

58. Khotan, p. 37. The venerable Kumāralāta (labdha) was a native of Takṣaśilā. From his childhood he showed a rare intelligence, and in early life gave up the world. (Beal : Op. cit, ii, p. 302). Hsuan-tsang then records the spiritual excellences which made Kumāralabdha renowned as a great teacher in the north, like Aśvaghoṣa in the east, Deva in the south, and Nāgārjuna in the west. The king of this country (Chieh-pan-to), therefore, having heard of the honourable one and his great qualities raised an army, made his troops attack Takṣaśilā and carried him off by force. He then built this convent and thus manifested the admiration with which he (Kumāralabdha) inspired him.

59. See. H. Luders *Bruchstucke der Kalpanāmaṇḍitikā des Kumāralāta* Leipzig, 1926; Levi. *Journal Asiatique* (JA), ccxi, 1927, pp. 95 ff.

on way to Kashgar on the eastern slopes of the Tsung-ling (Pamirs), Hsuan-tsang noticed[60] 10 monasteries with nearly 1000 monks, all belonging to the Sarvāstivāda school. This country is identified with Yangi-Hissar in the extreme north-west of the Yarkand oasis.

Kashgar, besides of its strategic position, had played a significant role in the transmission of culture to the northern and southern states of the Tarim basin. It is mentioned by several names[61] in the Dynastic Annals of the Chinese, while the pilgrim to India calls it Kia-she, Kie-sha (Hsuan-tsang) or Kie-cha (Fa-hien). The place is supposed to be known to India as Khasa or Khasya and its script Khasyalipi is mentioned in the *Lalitavistara* (2nd or 3rd century A.D.), while Ptolemy calls it Kashaozi. The history of this kingdom has been recorded earlier. The position of Buddhism in Kashgar[62] is

60. Beal : Op. cit, ii, p. 304; for the identification on Wu-Sha, see Stein : *Ancient Khotan*, pp. 42.

61. From the time of the Former Han Dynasty, when the States of Central Asia were first opened upto the political influence of China down to the Tang period, the region of the present Kashgar was generally known by the name Su-le or Shu-le. Cf. accounts of pilgrims Sung-Yun, Kumārajīva (c. 400 A.D.), Fa-Yung (420 A.D.), Dharmagupta (c. 593-95 A.D.) and Wu-King. Hsuan-tsang and the Tang Annals record the name 'Chia-sha (transcribed as Kia-cha). According to Levi, *Shu-le—Chia-lo-shu-tan-le* in reality a transcription of Kharoṣṭhī was an ancient name of Kashgar from which the Kharoṣṭhī script received its designation (*Bulletin de l'Ecole d'Extreme* Orient (BEFFO. ii, p. 246 sq.); Stein—*Ancient Khotan*, Op. cit, pp. 48-49).

62. Legge. *Fa-hien* (translation) p. 23. According to a statement of Klaproth, gathered apparently from Chinese sources, the interference of the Yueh-chih in the affairs of Kashgar, towards A.D. 120, resulted in the introduction of Buddhism into that territory. Buddhism no doubt flourished in the Yueh-chi dominions on both sides of the Hindukush. It is proposed by Stein that the prolonged sojourn of the Kashgar prince, subsequently elevated to the throne, might have facilitated the spread of Buddhist propoganda in that part of the Tarim basin. This assumtion agrees with the tradition recorded by Hsuan-tsang making the princely hostages from the states east of the Tsung-king, including Sha-le or Kashgar reside in a Buddhist Convent and connects their stay with the reign of Kaniṣka, the renowned patron of Buddhism (Ancient Khotan. Op. cit, p. 56). Further, to whatever period the first establishment of the Buddhist church in Kashgar may prove to belong, it is far more probable that it was brought from the side of Baktria than from that of Khotan.

recorded by Fa-hien who visited the country towards the closing years of the 4th century. He found the religion of the Tathāgata in a very prosperous condition, and he also witnessed the quinquennial assembly (*pañcavārṣika*). In his time, Kashgar had more than two thousand monks, followers of Hīnayāna probably of the Sarvāstivāda school, following canonical rules strictly. The impressions of Fa-hien about Buddhism in Kashgar and the pageantry are confirmed by other Chinese pilgrims visiting this country shortly afterwards: Che-mong (404), Fa-yong and Tao-yo (420).[63] The number of Buddhist monks had swelled to 10,000 in Hsuan-tsang's time[64] without any deviation from their sectarian allegiance. They were all followers of the Sarvāstivāda school, and many of them could recite the Buddhist texts including the entire *Tripiṭaka* and the *Vibhāṣa*—all in Sanskrit. The place was also visited by Wu-kong who travelled back to China about A.D. 186.

Among the scholars from India or other parts of Central Asia were Buddhayaśa of Kashmir and Kumārajīva, born in Kucha, who had his education in Kashmir and on way back he stayed there for nearly a year. Buddhayaśa was of great help to Kumārajīva in his academic pursuits at Kashgar; and he stayed on there even after the departure of Kumārajīva, exercising great influence on the local ruler, named Pu-tu. His son Ta-mo-fo-to (Dharmaputra) was greatly influenced by Buddhayaśa's friendly approach. He maintained close relations with the regal family as also with his contemporary Kumārajīva who later joined in China. He had persuaded the local ruler to send an army to Kucha against Chinese aggression in 382, more for the sake of security of his friend Kumārajīva, and personally accompanied the force which reached there rather late after the fall of Kucha. The bond of academic union between these two Buddhist savants of Central Asia was so close that they joined hands in trans-

63. Bagchi : *India and Central Asia*, Op. cit, p. 46.

64. Beal : Op. cit, ii, p. 307. According to the Chinese pilgrims the writing (writing character) is modelled on that of India, while language and pronunciation are different from that of other countries. They have a sincere faith in the religion of Buddha, and give themselves earnestly to the practice of it.

lating several canonical works in Chinese.[65] As teacher of Kumārajīva, he was given the epithet Ta-pi-po-cha (*mahāvibhāṣa*). He translated four works into Chinese.

Another Buddhist scholar at Kashgar was Dharmacandra,[66] originally from Magadha who had gone to China in A.D. 730 from Kucha at the invitation of the Chinese ambassador. On his return journey from China in 741, he passed through Kashgar where he had to stay back on account of political trouble ahead of the route at Shughnan. Finally, he settled down at Khotan where he died two years later in 743 and a stūpa was erected in his memory. Only one work *Prajñāpāramitā-hridaya* is attributed to him. A number of old Buddhist stūpas found at various sites around Kashgar are suggestive of the importance of this place as a centre of Buddhist activities and its scholars.

The country of Che-kiu-kia, accorded different name in the Chinese sources and identified with Cokkuka in the Cenral Asian documents,[67] presently Karghahalik-Yarkand, was an important Buddhist settlement. According to the Chinese pilgrim Hsuan-tsang,[67] the people here were earnest Buddhists with tens of monasteries and more than 100 monks, all followers of Mahāyāna school of Buddhism. The Mahāyāna tradition here could be traced to the fourth century A.D. as two princes of Cokkuka, Sūryabhadra and Sūryasena had gone to Kashgar to receive initiation from Kumārajīva and to study Mahāyāna texts with him. It is quite likely that these princes belonged to an Indian ruling dynasty which had earlier settled down there.

Khotan and its origin and history have been recorded earlier. As regards the introduction of Buddhism here, it was done in the time of Vijayasambhava who was grandson of Kustana with the monk Vairocana, an incarnation of Maitreya coming here. He was responsible for bringing the relics of Buddha from Kashmir. The Khotanese ruler Vijayasambhava built for Vairocana the great monastery of Tsar-ma,[68] the first one in

65. Bagchi : *Le Canon Bouddhique en Chine*—Op. cit, pp. 200 ff; Also A. Stein : *Ancient Khotan*, I, pp. 47-48. Bagchi records the collaboration of these two savants in the translation of several works. (pp. 202-3).

66. Bagchi—*ibid*, pp. 565 ff.

67. Bagchi—*India and Central Asia*—Op. cit, p. 48 ff.

68. A. Stein—*Ancient Khotan*—Op. cit, p. 232.

Khotan, identified by Aurel Stein with Chelma-Kazan near Yotkan. A number of other monasteries were set up during the reigns of subsequent rulers. Three Arhats from India—Buddhadata, Khagata and Khagadrod—went to Khotan, and a later king Vijayavīrya built two monasteries for them. This was followed later on by another two built by the Chinese, princess Punesvar,[69] queen of king Vijayajaya, in honour of Kalyāṇamitra who had gone there from India. The ruler's eldest son Dharmānanda who became a Buddhist monk was a follower of the Mahāsāṅghika school and built several monasteries which kept on swelling in subsequent generations. In the time of Hsuan-tsang there were 100 monasteries in the capital with 5000 monks who were all followers of Mahāyāna school of Buddhism. The pilgrim also refers[70] to some of the important monasteries like those of Ti-ko-po-fa-na, Sha-mo-no, Gośriṅga and Mo-she. Earlier, Fa-hien refers [71] to the Gomati monastery to which 3000 monks were attached, and they were all followers of Mahāyānism. The Gośriṅga monastery built later on was supposed to be a spot formerly associated with the visit of Buddha. This monastery is also mentioned in the *Sūryagarbha-sūtra*,[72] a Buddhist canonical text translated into Chinese between A.D. 589 and 619.

Khotan, it seems, became an active centre of Buddhist studies

69. According to the 'Annals of Li-yul' (Rockhill : *Life of the Buddha*, pp. 238 ff), Vijayasiṁha, the third successor of Vijayavīrya married Princess Pu-nye-shar, the daughter of the ruler of China. She was responsible for raiming silk worms much against the wishes of her husband, who later on repented for his deeds. He called from India the Bhikṣu Saṅghaghoṣa and made him his spiritual adviser, and to atone for his wickedness he built the Po-ta-rya and Ma-dza caityas and a great vihāra. (Stein : *Ancient Khotan*, p. 230.)

70. Beal. *Buddhist Records of the Western World*. Op. cit, ii, pp. 309 ff. For an account of those monasteries, see p. 313 ff.

71. Fa-hien's account of Khotan is recorded in his *Travels* (Legge. *Translation*, pp. 16-20). The monks in Khotan were mostly students of the Mahāyāna. The pilgrim specially refers to the hospitable arrangements made in the Saṅghārāma for the reception of travelling monks, and notices the custom of erecting small stūpas in front of each family's dwellings.

72. The Chinese translation of the *Sūryagarbha-sūtra* made by Narendrayaśas between the years 589 and 619 A.D. in a list of holy places (*pīṭha*) sanctified by the presence of a Bodhisattva (Stein : *Ancient Khotan*. Op. cit, p. 186).

and activities. In the year 259, a Chinese monk named Chu-she-hing came to Khotan for the study of Buddhism, first hand under good teachers. In a few years time he collected 9000 bundles of original Buddhist texts and could manage to send these home through his disciple Fu-jo-tan (Puṇyadhana ?). He died in Khotan at the age of 80. These were translated by a Khotanese Buddhist scholar Mokṣala[73] who went to China in 291. He was assisted by an Indian monk, probably Sukta-ratna. The translated texts were *Pañca-viṁśati-sāhasrikā-Prajñāpāramitā*, *Vimalakīrtinirdeśa* and *Suraṅganasūtra*—all Mahāyāna canonical works. It appears from this account, as also from the reference to translation that Khotan was famous as a centre of Mahāyāna Buddhistic studies in the third century A.D. Fa-hien's account quoted earlier not only confirms this contention but equally points to the prosperity of this school of Buddhism in his time with 3000 monks in Gomatī monastery alone living a regulated ordained life. Dharmakṣema[74] of Magadha working in Liang-chou had to come to Khotan for tracing the lost portion of his incomplete manuscript of *Mahāparinirvāṇa-sūtra* which he translated into Chinese. His pupil Tsiu-kiu-king Sheng, a noble man of Liang-chou also came to Khotan, settled down in the Gomatī mahāvihāra and studied Mahāyāna Buddhism under an Indian scholar Buddhasena[75] who was noted for his academic attainments in all the countries of the west and was called *She-tseu* (Siṁha)—the lion of learning. On his return to China King Sheng translated the texts on *Dhyāna* which he had studied in Khotan and had brought with him.

A little later eight Chinese monks of Liang-chou came to Khotan in 439 in search of Buddhist texts. Their visit coincided

73. For an account of Mokṣala—see Bagchi : *Le Canon Bouddhique en Chine*—op. cit, pp. 119-120; Nanjio : *Catalogue*, Op. cit, ii, 26, p. 394. He was a Śramaṇa of Yu-then i.e. Kusutana (Khotan) who together with Ku-Shu-lan, an upāsaka of Indian descent born in China, translated one Sūtra in A.D. 291 (*Pañcaviṁśati-sāhasrikā-prajñpāramitā*). According to Eital, he was also the author of a new alphabet for the transliteration of Sanskrit (*A Sanskrit-Chinese Dictionary*, Op. cit, p. 100 B).

74. Bagchi : *Le Canon Bouddhique en Chine*, pp. 212-221.

75. Buddhasena (Fo-to-Sien) was probably the master of Buddhajur who came to China from Kashmir in 423 A.D. and worked at Nanking under the Sung (Bagchi—*ibid*, p. 179 n).

with the Pañcavārṣika assembly, and they attended the discourses of a few teachers and recorded some texts from dictation which they took back to China. This was not the solitary instance. A number of important Buddhist texts were taken to China from Central Asia. A monk named Fa-ling took a manuscript of the famous *Avataṁśaka-sūtra* which was translated by Buddhabhadra[76] in 418. He was a contemporary of Kumārajīva as well as of Fa-hien and cooperated with them in translation work. He met Kumārajīva in China and whenever the latter had any doubts, the former was always consulted for an explanation. He made some translations with Fa-hien. Between A.D. 398-21 he translated 13 or 15 works. He died in A.D. 429 at the age of 71. Namjio quotes 7 works of this savant—all Mahāyānist. This process of transmission of Buddhist thought and literature from Khotan—a great centre of Mahāyāna Buddhism—to China continued later on. A monk named Fa-hien brought from Khotan the manuscript of *Saddharmapuṇḍarīka* which was also translated by Dharmamati,[77] a śramaṇa of western origin, in 490. Among the Buddhist scholars of Khotan Śikṣānanda was the foremost who reached China in 695 and worked there till his death in 710. He translated in all 19 texts, the most voluminous one being the *Mahāvaipulya* or the *Avataṁśaka-sūtra*[78] in 80 chapters.

Literary evidence from the Chinese source material, the finds of Buddhist monuments—stūpas and sculptural figures, stucco statues of Buddha or Bodhisattvas as also painted panels from nearby sites do provide indication of the efflorescence of Buddhism in this part of Central Asia which was strong enough to transmit its offshoots in the form of its scholars and literature to China. It is proposed by Aurel Stein,[79] that Indian elements—the use of Sanskrit and Brāhmī script preceded Buddhism in Khotan. Even before the introduction of Buddhism Khotan's

76. Bagchi—*Le Canon Bouddhique en Chine*—Op. cit, pp. 341-46; Nanjio *Catalogue*, Op. cit, ii, 42, p. 399-400. His life history and achievements are recorded by Bagchi, Op. cit.

77. Bagchi. ibid, p. 409. He was a Śramaṇa who was invited by Cha-men Fa-hien to the monastery of *Wa Kouan-sse* in the capital for translating sacred texts. Nanjio : *Catalogue*, Op. cit, ii, 96, p. 42.

78. Bagchi : *India and Central Asia*, p. 61.

79. *Ancient Khotan*. Op. cit, pp. 163-64.

population had fusion of a strong Indian element and the cultural influences accompanying it. The finds of documents from Niya in Kharoṣṭhī—a script of the north-western India and written in Prakrit—tends to signify a later under-current of Buddhist influence.

Besides Khotan and the neighbouring areas, a number of old Buddhist sites excavated in the desert at Dandan-Uiliq have revealed stucco images and reliefs. Frescoes with Brāhmī inscriptions, manuscripts and other records mostly in Brāhmī and Chinese are fairly interesting pieces of evidence in the context of Buddhism in that region. The Brāhmī manuscripts include canonical works of Mahāyānism—The *Prajñāpāramitā* and *Vajracchedikā*[80] in Sanskrit. The Rawak stūpa[81] at a distance of only 7 miles to the north of Dandan-Uiliq has exposed Buddhist images mostly of the Gandhāra school. Ruins of Buddhist stūpas have also been found at other sites. Niya was an important Buddhist centre in the time of Hsuan-tsang. A large number of Kharoṣṭhī documents[82] from this site shed light on the material culture as also on administrative setup. The documents are in Kharoṣṭhī script of the 3rd century and their language is Prakrit allied to the one in the north-western Frontier of India in the Kuṣāṇa period. Later on, Kharoṣṭhī was ousted by Brāhmī, probably with the introduction of Sarvāstivāda Buddhism from Kashmir. Both the schools of Buddhism were introduced probably in the 4th century. Kumārajīva studied the Tripiṭaka of the Mahāyāna school and its Vibhāṣa in Kashgar—the gateway to Khotan. Reference has already been made to the country of Tu-ho-lo about 400 li to the east of Niya, represented, accord-

80. Ref. find of Prajñā-Pāramitā MS. at Dandan-Uiliq in Stein: *Ancient Khotan*, pp. 257-58. Hoernle's analysis proves that the fragments belong to the eighteenth and nineteenth chapters of a Mahāyāna text, written in Gupta characters of the seventh or eighth century. As regards the *Vajracchedikā* a famous treatise of the Mahāyāna school, first edited by Max Müller in the *Anecdota Oxoniensia*, fifteen out of twenty-four folia have been found intact (ibid p. 258).

81. Stein, A. *Ancient Khotan*. Op. cit, pp. 483 ff.

82. Stein, A. *Serindia*, Op. cit, I, pp. 433 ff. These documents have been edited by Boyer, Rapson and Senart and published under the title '*Kharoṣṭhī Documents discovered by Sir Aurel Stein in Chinese Turkestan*; Text and Translation (Oxford, 1928).

ing to Aurel Stein,[83] with the modern site of Endere. It seems to have been connected with the Little Yueh-chi, probably of some earlier time. The Chinese pilgrim calls it the ancient Tu-ho-lo (Tukhāra) country. Ruins of a Buddhist stūpa as also the finds of Kharoṣṭhī tablets and manuscripts similar to ones found at Niya, suggest that Buddhism flourished here. This place had close relations and contacts with Tsiu-mo or Tso-mo[84] of Hsuan-tsang, identified with Calmadana, now represented with Char-chen.

Further to its north-east was Na-fo-po,[85] in ancient times called Lou-lan in the region of Lobnor, situated on the oldest route connecting China with Central Asia. In the Han Annals, the name of the country is Shan-Shan. Loulan was the Chinese transcription of the original name Krorania or Kroranjina of the Kharoṣṭhī documents.[86] It was a stronghold of Buddhism and Indian culture. According to Fa-hien,[87] there were 4000 monks here, all followers of Hīnayāna in his time. The Kharoṣṭhī documents discovered at various sites of Kroraina are written in Prākrit, as was also current in Niya, and was the official language of the country. The names recorded in these documents appear to be of Indian derivation as well as of local origin.[88] Among the important sites is Miran—famous for its school of painting as also for its sculptures—mainly in Gandhāra style. The subject matter of painting is Buddhist and the style is linked with that of Gandhāra.

83. *Serindia,* I, p. 286. For Hsuan-tsang's reference, see Julien : *Memoirs,* II, p. 247; Walters : *Yuan Chwang,* ii, p. 304; also Stein : *Ancient Khotan,* I, p. 435. Stein also refers to Henry Yule's *Notes on Hsuen-tsang's Account* of *the Principalities of Tokharistan.* JRAS. N. S. VI, p. 95.

84. Julien, *Memoirs,* i p. 247; Walters : *Yuan Chwang,* i, p. 304; Stein : *Ancient Khotan,* i. p. 435 note 9; *Serindia,* I, p. 298.

85. Stein : *Serindia,* I, p. 321; See Julien : *Memoirs,* ii, p. 247; Beal, ii, p. 325.

86. See Inscriptions No. 754, 922 and 907, noticed by Aurel Stein in *Serindia,* I, p. 413.

87. Legge. *Travels of Fa-hien,* pp. 11 ff.

88. The Indian names are Ānandasena, Bhaṭisama, Budhamitra, Kumudvatī, Vāsudeva etc. Others of local origin are Cauleya, Kapgeya, Kalpisa, Kitsaitsa, Pulkaya, Varpeya etc. (*Serindia,* I, p. 414).

Buddhism and Buddhist scholars in the Northern States

The political history of the States on the northern route—Akshu, Kucha, Agnideśa or Karasahr, Kao-chang or Turfan, has already been recorded in the previous chapter. Attention could now be confined only to Buddhism and its propagators in these areas rather than to political figures and contacts. It has been proposed earlier that the people of the four states of Akshu, Kucha, Karasahr and Turfan were of one racial stock in ancient times, with a common language with slight dialectical differences of a local nature and a common culture. The language is termed as Kuchean. The specimens of this language were discovered from various sites in Kucha and Karasahr, with a large number of mural inscriptions in this language. Specimens of ancient Tokharian have also been discovered in the neighbourhood of Karasahr and in Turfan, probably as a result of the immigration of Buddhist priests in this area after the Arab conquest of Tokharestan. The Tokharestan texts were translated in Uighur, the language of the Turks who had set up a new empire with Turfan as the centre in the 9th century after the Arab conquest of their homeland. As such both Kuchean and Uighur texts are available in this area.

The exact date of introduction of Buddhism in Kucha is not known but it could not have been later than the end of the 1st century A.D. allowing it to take deep roots before blossoming in full form about the third century A.D. According to the Annals of the Tsin dynasty (265-316), there were nearly one thousand Buddhist stūpas and temples in Kucha at that time.[89] The Buddhist monks from Kucha started moving to China from this period, and the pioneer monk from the royal family Po-Yen[90]

89. As regards the early history of Kucha, it is mentioned in the Han Annals and when brought into contact with China, in the reign of Wu-ti (140-87 B.C.), its importance was realised because of its geographical location. It is, however, described as a seat of Buddhism only in the time of the western Tsin dynasty. According to the Tsin annals, it was enclosed by a triple wall and contained a thousand stūpas and Buddhist temples as well as a magnificent palace for the king. This does not, however, suggest any date for the introduction of Buddhism in that area. (Chavannes in Stein's *Ancient Khotan*, p. 544.)

90. For an account of the contributions of this Śramaṇa of the western region who translated some Sūtras in the White House Monastery at Lo-yan

came to Chinese capital in 256-260. He translated six Buddhist texts into Chinese in 258 at the famous Buddhist temple of Po-ma-sse at Loyang. The larger version of *Sukhāvatī-vyūha* was made by him. Another scholar from Kucha Po-Śrimitra[91] went to China during the period 307-312. The political troubles there compelled him to move to South China where he translated three Buddhist texts. Another Kuchean prince Po-Yen went to Liang-chou. Though a scholar of repute and conversant with a number of foreign languages he did not leave any translated canonical work.

The next century—fourth—is noted for great Buddhist activity in Kucha which was more or less a Buddhist city with the palace of the ruler looking like a Buddhist monastery with standing images of Buddha carved in stone. The city had a large number of monasteries, some special ones being founded by the kings. The monastery called Ta-mu had 170 monks, while that on the Po-Shan hill in the north, called Che-hu-li had 50 or 60 monks. The new one of the king of Wen-Su (Uch-Turfan) had 70 monks. All these monasteries were controlled by Fu-to-she-mi (Buddhasvāmin). Some information is available about the working of these monasteries as also on the activities of the monks from a Chinese text.[92] The head 'Buddhasvāmin' was a great scholar, a follower of the Āgamas—the Hīnayāna, while his brilliant disciple Kiu-kiu-lo (Kumāra) probably Kumārajīva of great fame in his time was a Mahāyānist. There were separate establishments

in A.D. 257, see Bagchi,: *Le Canon Bouddhique en Chine*, pp. 79 ff, as also Nanjio : *Catalogue*, ii, 16, p. 387. According to Sylvain Levi, the royal dynasty of Kucha from the first century A.D. was known as Po (J.A., 1913 p. 322), and the rulers have this prefix added to their names, such as Po-ying (124 A.D.), Po-Chang (285 A.D.) etc.

91. Po-Shi-li-mi-to-lo i.e. Śrīmitra—literally meaning 'lucky friend' was a Śramaṇa of western origin who was the heir apparent of a king of that country. He, however, gave up his kingdom to his younger brother and became a Śramaṇa. He came to China in the Yun-Kia period A.D. 307-12, under the western Tsin dynasty and translated 3 works at Kin-khan (Nanking) under the reign of Yuen-ti, A.D. 317-322 and died at the age of eighty in the Hhien-Khan period, A.D. 335-342. The works are *Mahābhishekārāddhidhāraṇī-sūtra, Mahāmayūrī-Vidyārāgnī* and in two Fascimulae (Nanjio: *Catalogue*, ii, 36, pp. 397-98).

92. Bagchi : *India and Central Asia*, p. 80. See also his *Le Canon de Bouddhique*, p. 155.

for the nuns at the monasteries of A-li (Avanyaka), Liun-jo-kan and A-li-po with 50 and 30 nuns respectively. These nunneries were also under the control of the head of Buddhist establishments, Buddhasvāmin. The nuns, mostly from the regal and noble families, led a strict disciplined life, observing as many as five hundred rules of conduct. The life and activities of Kumāra—Kumārajīva who played an important role in the dissemination and expansion of Buddhist ideals and canons both in Central Asia as well as in China, no doubt call for special reference and recording.

Kumārajīva—his life and contributions[93]

The name Kumārajīva is sometimes transcribed as Kiu-mo-lo-che and at others as Kiu-mo-to-tche-po with the Chinese translation Tang-cheu. He hailed from a noble family of ministers of state in India. His grandfather Ta-to had a great reputation while his father Kiu-mo-yen was equally intelligent. Kumārāyaṇa, as he was called, renounced his claim to hereditary succession in favour of his relations and joined the Buddhist order and left his home in search of learning and enlightenment. Crossing the difficult routes of the Pamirs he came to Kucha where he was appointed purohita (*Kouo-che*)—the royal priest. The sister of the king—a beautiful princess of 20, discarding other proposals, fell in love with this young Indian and they were married. Kumārajīva, taking the name after his father and also mother (Jīvā), was the issue of this union. Soon after Jīvā took holy orders and joined a nunnery. She retired to the Tsio-li monastery about 40 li to the north of Kucha and there learnt the language of India. Kumārajīva at that time was seven years old, but so sharp was his intellect that he committed to memory the sacred texts, and could recite a number of Sūtras as also a

93. For an account of Kumārajīva's life history and his contributions to Buddhist literature and canons, see, Nanjio : Catalogue, ii, 59, pp. 406-408; Bagchi : *Le Canon Bouddhique en Chine*, pp. 178-200; and also *Encyclopaedia of Religion and Ethics*, Vol. VII, p. 701 a; Sylvain Levi : JA. 1913, p. 335-338; Pelliot : *Toung Pao*, 1912, p. 392, in which he placed this savant between 344 and 413 A.D.; P. Wieger : *Histoire des Croyances religieuses en Chine* etc. (1922) p. 416 in which is given a resume of the notices of *Tsin Chou* on Kumārajīva.

thousand Gâthās. This was followed by learning Abhidharma. On attaining the age of nine, his mother took him to Kashmir for better education under Bandhudatta, Pan-teou-ta-to, the renowned scholar and a relation of the king. The young scholar studied with him Dīrghāgama and Madhyāgama and could discuss with the heretics. After three years of stay, Jīvā along with her son Kumārajīva decided to return to Kucha. Crossing the mountains and passing the kingdom of the Yueh-chi (Tokharestan) they reached Sha-le (Kashgar). An arhat in the way noticing the young boy predicted great future for him who, like Upagupta, would initiate a large number of people into the canons of Buddhism. Arriving at Kashgar, he stayed there for a year and studied the whole of *Abhidharmapiṭaka* with the Kashmirian scholar Buddhayaśa who was then in Kashgar. He also studied the four Vedas, five sciences, Brahmanical sacred texts as also astronomy, the *Śataśāstra* and the *Mādhyamaka-śāstra* etc. during his year's stay here. It was also the period of his ordaining two distinguished persons—the two sons of king Tsan-kiun, the son of the king of So-kiu (Chokkuka). These two princes were Sūryasama (Siuli-yeso-mo) and Sūryabhadra (Siuli-ye-poto).

Leaving Kashgar, the mother Jīvā and her son Kumārajīva then twelve years old and an erudite scholar, reached Wen-Su (Uch-Turfan) which was then the northern limit of Kucha. Here he defeated a Taoist teacher in discussions and this spread his fame. The king of Kucha, Po-Shui personally approached him at Uch-Turfan for taking him to his place. Kumārajīva was by that time well-versed in canonical literature, and he explained *Mahāsannipāta* and the *Mahāvaipulya* sūtras to the daughter of the king A-Kie-ye-mo-ti who had become a nun. He himself had not taken holy orders till the age of 20 when he was fully ordained at the king's palace. At that time there were more than 10,000 monks in Kucha. He was provided accommodation in the new monastery built by king Po-Shun. This young scholar was equally interested in exploring ancient manuscripts and he was fortunate enough to trace the *Pañcaviṁśati-sāhasrikā Prajñāpāramitā* in the old palace. His academic exercises were not at a standstill. Discourses and discussions with other scholars were part of his routine. He explained the Mahāyāna Sūtras in the great monastery of Tsio-li, and encouraged contacts with outside scholars. One such was Vimalākṣa from Kashmir who was received by this Kuchean savant and in turn the Indian scholar helped his host in the study of the Sarvāstivāda Vinayapiṭaka. Kumārajīva seems to have alienated his filial relations, and one gathers that Jīvā left for Kashmir to spend the rest of her life there.

The political expedition of the Chinese force under Lu-Kuang guided by the king of Kiu-che and that of Yar-khoto ransacked Kucha and carried numerous prisoners including Kumārajīva. This savant's merits and talents were recognised by this general who had at first ill-treated him. He stayed at Liang-chou till 401 and then at the request of Emperor Yao-Chang and his successor Yao-Hing, Kumārajīva after great hesitation finally left for Chang-ngan. He was warmly received by the new ruler who appointed him his purohita—priest-counsellor (Kouo-che). As his adviser and functionary, he exercised great power and influence on the ruler. He became a great admirer of *triratna* (San-pao) and asked him to arrange conferences in the royal palace as also to translate sacred texts. He was offered cooperation and collaboration from several distinguished monks in the task of editing, collecting and translating Buddhist Sanskrit texts. These included Seng-che, Seng-kien, Fa-kiu, Tao-liou, Tao-heng, Tao-piao, Seng-jovei, Seng-tchao etc. A little over eight hundred monks attended the assembly at Chang-ngan addressed by Kumārajīva.

Kumārajīva was well-versed with Chinese and the studies covered by him were vast. He had studied ancient works, some obscure and erroneous too. He had to make comparative studies of such works along with the monks from India (Tien-tchou) and those from Indo-Scythia (Yue-tche). He was able to remove doubts and dispel erroneous interpretations of monks from all quarters, including those of Che-Tao-chong of Long-kouang, Houei-yuan of Lou-chang. A monk of great intelligence and clear thinking Seng-jovei was always with him serving as his secretary and posed doubts and differences in texts before him. Explaining the differences between the literatures of India and China, Kumārajīva referred to literary composition, mixture of rhythmical phases with music, the universal songs of dedication (*vandanā*), and music always accompanying the visits of the images of Buddha.

While translating the Sanskrit texts into Chinese he refers to the loss of literary charm in translated texts.

Kumārajīva's stay at Chang-ngan was till his death in 413. There he translated 98 works, characterising his stay there as the glorious epoch in the history of Chinese Buddhism. Kumārajīva's Sarvāstivādin guru Vimalākṣa who was staying in Kucha all this time, joined him in A.D. 404. He was followed a year later by another Indian scholar named Dharmamitra who had come to Kucha for a few years' stay and then he came to the Chinese capital in 424 when Kumārajīva was no more. Other scholars who had earlier come in contact with him and later on joined him were the Kashmirian scholar Buddhayaśa under whom Kumārajīva had studied in Kashgar, and Buddhabhadra another scholar from Kashmir.

Several interesting details about Kumārajīva's life and activities are recorded about him. It is suggested that two years after his mother, who had already become a nun, brought her son to Kubha (Kabul), the young monk became the disciple of the famous priest, named Vandhudatta, a cousin of the king of that place. In his twelfth year when Kumārajīva was brought back to Karasahr by his mother, another Arhat told the mother that 'she should carefully guard this Śramaṇa against disorder till his thirty-fifth year when he would propagate the law of Buddha; but if he could not keep moral precepts (Śīla) he would not be more than a clever and skilful priest. Kumārajīva's study of the Sarvāstivāda Vinaya under Vimalākṣa, and later on that of Mahāyānism with Sūryasena, led him to exclaim that 'his former study of the Hīnayāna was like that of comparing a copper ore with the excellent golden one of which he was formerly unaware.' From that time he devoted himself completely to the propagation of the Mahāyāna, and he could convert his former teacher Vandhudatta as well. The Chinese general Lu-Kuang taking Kumārajīva with him compelled this young monk, then not yet thirty-five, to sleep with a daughter of the former Kucha king.

Kumārajīva stayed with Lu-Kuang in Liang-chu, China till A.D. 401 and on the twentieth day of the twelfth month of the same year he arrived at Chan-ang and was greatly welcomed by Yao-Hsin, the second ruler of the Later Tshin dynasty. Between

A.D. 402-412 he translated numerous works, and also wrote a treatise and some verses in Chinese. He is said to have had Chinese priests as his disciples, more than three thousand in number, among whom there were about ten great ones who wrote several works. Kumārajīva died in the Hun-sh period between A.D. 399-415, but the exact date is uncertain. Different traditions provide varying data between A.D. 405 and A.D. 411. There are, however, some of his translations of a much a later date.

Kumārajīva was responsible for introducing Mahāyāna in the countries of the Tarim basin and also in China in a more responsible and authoritative manner. He was one of the greatest exponents of this school of Buddhism and also of the Mādhyamika philosophy. He introduced texts relating to these systems into Chinese through translations, as also through interpretations sought by many Mahāyāna teachers of this period. His contemporaries included many savants of Kucha like Vimalākṣa who was staying there all this time and joined Kumārajīva in China in 401. Another scholar who was of Indian origin, Dharmamitra, came to Kucha and stayed there for a few years before leaving for Tun-huang in China, finally reaching the capital in 424. Buddhayaśa, the famous scholar of Kashmir under whom Kumārajīva had studied in Kashmir, was not only a contemporary but also a personal friend of Kumārajīva. He also joined him in China. Buddhabhadra was another Kashmiri scholar who joined Kumārajīva first in Kucha, and later on in the Chinese capital for a number of years. There might have been many more contemporaries of eminence. Kucha and its Buddhist savants deserve special attention for their contribution to Buddhism and its canonical texts with numerous recensions. As an example, the Chinese translation of the *Candraprabha-sūtra*, a part of the Mahāsannipāta we are told of 99 manifestations of Buddha while Akṣu had 24. According to this text, Kucha had her divine protectors, such as the constellation Sravana.

Kumārajīva is said to have introduced a new alphabet and translated some 50 works including *Pañcaviṁśati-sāhasrikā Prajñāpāramitā*, *Prajñāpāramitāhridaya-sūtra*, *Saddharmapuṇḍarīka*, *Sukhāvativyūha*, *Sarvāstivāda-prātimokṣa*, *Mahāprajñāpāramitā Sūtra-śāstra*, 'Life of the Bodhisattva Aśvaghoṣa'. 'Life of the Bodhisattva Nāgārjuna', and 'Life of the Bodhisattva Deva'. The translations ascribed to him are ranked as classical Chinese, and his translation of the 'Lotus of the True Law' (*Saddharmapuṇḍarīka*) remains the most valued and revered of the Chinese Buddhist scriptures. Kumārajiva was a monk but he is said to have led rather an irregular life. Yet his talents were so appreciated and his fame so high that his patron and the people honoured him despite his neglect of Buddhist discipline and in spite of attacks heaped upon him.

Kumārajīva and his contemporaries

Kumārajīva was not only a scholar; he was an institution in the true sense who drew votaries to his shrine of his learning both in Kucha as also in the Chinese capital where he lived till the end of his life. Reference might be made to the lives and activities of those mentioned earlier, namely, Vimalākṣa, Dharmamitra, Buddhayaśa and Buddhabhadra. The first one Vimalākṣa,[94] name translated as Wu-keu-yen meaning 'without-dirt-eye' was a Śramaṇa of Kubhā (Kabul). He was a great teacher of Vinaya in Karasahr where Kumārajīva was one of his disciples. When Kucha was invaded by Lu-Kuang in A.D. 383 he escaped to the western country. Later on, he went to China in the year 406 and was cordially received by his pupil Kumārajīva, but after the latter's death in 413 he left for the south and arrived at Cha-tchouen (Ting-yen) and settled down in the monastery of Tche-cheu-kien. With his sound knowledge he completed the Vinaya of the Sarvāstivādins which Kumārajīva had at first undertaken but could not complete. Amongst his collaborators was Huei-kouang, a monk of profound learning. Vimalākṣa died at the age of 77 years in the Kien-sse monastery. His two works are *Sarvāstivāda-Vinayanidāna* which exists, constituting a part of *Daśādhyāya-Vinaya*, and another one which is lost.

Dharmamitra,[95] originally from Kashmir came to Kucha where he was accorded due respect and he stayed in the capital for a couple of years. Then he wanted to leave for the East but the

94. For an account of Vimalākṣa's life and his contributions, see Bagchi : *Le Canon Bouddhique*, pp. 338-339; Nanjio's *Catalogue*, ii, 44, p. 400.

95. See Bagchi : *Op. cit*, pp. 388-391; Nanjio : *Catalogue*, ii, 75, pp. 414.

king was opposed to it. He had, therefore, to move in secret for Liang-chou from where he left for the South. He worked in China from A.D. 424 till 441 and died in his eighty-seventh year in A.D. 442. Ten works are ascribed to him, five of which are said to have been lost. Those works preserved in the Oxford collection and quoted by Nanjio include *Akaṣagarbha-bodhisattva-dhāraṇī-sūtra*, as also *Dhyāna-sūtra*, *Sarvadharma-rāga sūtra*, *Strī-vivarta-vyākaraṇa-sūtra* and *Samantabhadra-bodhisattva-dhyāna caryādharma-sūtra.*

Buddhayaśa,[96] translated in Chinese as Kio-ming, was from a Brahmin family of Kashmir or Kubhā, according to Nanjio. His father, not believing in the religion of the Tathāgata, had insulted a monk and he had to pay for this sin in the form of physical ailments. The son, however, was attached to a monk at the age of 13 and he made a serious study living in a monastery. At the age of 19, he could recite millions of words of Hīnayāna and Mahāyāna texts. A proud young man, as he was of his learning, he was not very popular and did not join holy orders till the age of 27. Being not satisfied with his knowledge he left Kashmir for the kingdom of Cha-le (Kashgar) where the Crown prince Dharmaputra appreciated his talents and invited him to stay in the palace. At this time Kumārajīva had also come there and he studied with him before returning to Kucha with his mother. The invasion of Lu-Kuang, the Chinese general, the fall of Kucha and the taking of Kumārajīva as a prisoner to China made Yaśa desperate and uncomfortable. Later on he went to Kucha and from there left for China to join Kumārajīva, ignoring the advice of the ruler and quitting secretly. At Chang-ngan, where he settled down with his former pupil, he collaborated with him, and translated four works into Chinese including the *Dīrghāgama* and *Dharma-guptaka-vinaya* between 410 and 413 A.D. He subsequently returned to Kashmir.

Buddhabhadra[97] was a contemporary of Kumārajīva. He was born at Nagarahāra and claimed direct descent from Amritodāna, the uncle of Buddha. He became an orphan at an early age, having lost his parents, and was admitted to the Buddhist order.

96. Bagchi : Op. cit, pp. 200-204; Nanjio : Op. cit, ii, 61, p. 408.

97. Bagchi : *Le Canon*, pp. 341-346; Nanjio : *Catalogue*, ii, 42, pp. 399-400.

He completed his studies at the age of seventeen and went to Kashmir along with his companion Saṅghadatta but did not stay there for long. He was interested in carrying the message of Buddha to different countries and also to study their customs. At that time Che-yen who was travelling in India with Fa-hien came to Kashmir and desired a scholar of repute to accompany them to China. Buddhabhadra availed of this opportunity and left with Che-yen on foot, not by the Central Asian route but probably through Burma to Tonkin from where they sailed by boat to China. When Kumārajīva learnt about his arrival in China and working at Chang-ngan, he personally went there to meet him. Buddhabhadra was a scholar of repute and was equally proud of his learning. He was invited by the Chinese Emperor to go to the capital and translate Buddhist texts there. He went to Nanking in 421 where he remained till his death in 429. This Indian scholar, whose name literally means 'intelligence-wise', translated between A.D. 398-421 13 or 15 works at two different places, namely at Lu mountain and Kien-khan, the capital. Kumārajīva acknowledged his superiority and whenever he had doubts, he always sought Buddhabhadra's explanation. He also collaborated with Fa-hien in the translation of *Mahāsāṅghika Vinaya* which he had brought from Pāṭaliputra. The general plan of the work is similar to that of other Vinayapiṭakas but it is much richer in cultural contents.

While some reference has been made earlier to Saṅghabhūti, Gautama Saṅghadeva and Puṇyatrāta who went to China by the end of the fourth century A.D., their contribution to Buddhism and its literature, as also collaboration with Kumārajīva no doubt call for detailed reference to their lives and activities. Saṅghabhūti[98] from Kashmir had reached the northern capital in A.D. 381. He was welcomed by some of the leading Buddhist savants of China; and at their request he translated a number of texts into Chinese, including a major one—an exhaustive commentary on the *Vinaya-Piṭaka* of the Sarvāstivāda school. He was there till A.D. 384. Another scholar from Kashmir—Gautama Saṅghadeva,[99] came to Chang-ngan in 384.

98. Bagchi : *Le Canon*, pp. 160-161; Nanjio ii. 54, pp. 404.

99. Bagchi : *Op cit*, 161-162; Nanjio : *Op. cit*, ii, 39, p. 399.

A profound scholar and a born teacher, he specialized in the metaphysical literature of Buddhism (*Abhidharma*). He remained in the north for a few years and availed of the opportunity in picking up Chinese language. In 391 Saṅghadeva went to China where a strong Buddhist school had been founded by the Sogdian monk Seṅghui. He was also invited at this time by a Chinese Buddhist scholar Hui-yuan to his institution at Lu-Shan. Here too Saṅghadeva left his impress translating a few Sanskrit texts. From Lu-shan he went to Nanking in 397 where he impressed the official circle, and one of the functionaries had a monastery built for him. With the assistance of his Chinese friends and followers from Kashmir he translated a number of important Buddhist texts into Chinese, probably staying there till his death.

Puṇyatrāta[100] and his pupil Dharmayaśa,[101] both from Kashmir, also went to China and were associated with the translation of a number of important Buddhist texts of the Sarvāstivāda school. Puṇyatrāta collaborated with Kumārajīva in China. His pupil Dharmayaśa, who had joined his master at the age of 14, soon attained great name and fame for his erudition. He left Kashmir at the age of thirty and having travelled in various parts of Central Asia reached China sometime in the last quarter of the fourth century A.D. He stayed there till 453, spending a number of years in the south as well, translating a number of works with his associates. Later on he returned to Central Asia, and finally was back home in Kashmir. It is said about Puṇyatrāta that he came to China towards the end of the fourth century and collaborated with Kumārajīva in A.D. 404. Probably both had met earlier in Kucha and Puṇyatrāta's visit to China might have been in response of Kumārajīva's invitation to his friend and past colleague for future collaboration.

Among the Buddhist savants of the first quarter of the fifth century A.D., more or less contemporaries of Kumārajīva, were Buddhajīva[102]—also from Kashmir—who had come to South China reaching Nanking in A.D. 423. His association and collaboration with Fa-hien need not be repeated here. It is fairly certain that

100. Bagchi : *Op cit*, pp. 176-177.
101. Bagchi : *ibid*, pp. 174-176; Nanjio, ii, 62, p. 408.
102. Bagchi : *Op. cit*, p. 363-364; Nanjio : *Op. cit*, ii, 73, p. 414.

he translated a couple of Fa-hien's manuscripts brought from India. He probably stayed in China till his death. He is called Ko-to-she translated as Kiao-she in Chinese literature. A great teacher of Vinaya in Kashmir, and a follower of the Mahīśāsaka School, he translated three works of the same school between A.D. 423-424. These include *Mahīśāsaka-vinaya* and *Prātimokṣa* of the Mahīśāsakas.

Guṇavarman[103], was another great scholar—a prince of the royal family of Kashmir—who reached China (Nanking) a few years later by the sea route. Both his father Saṅghānanda and grandfather Haribhadra were banished from their kingdom—the latter for his oppressive rule and the former for his father's lapses. This young prince left the house at the age of twenty and lived as a Buddhist monk. Mastering the Buddhist canon in all its sections, and the āgamas this young scholar, rejecting the offer of his paternal kingdom, left his country for Ceylon from where he subsequently went to Java. He was able to convert the Royal family to Buddhism. His name and fame attracted the attention of the Chinese Emperor, who personally invited him, and Guṇavarman reached Nanking in A.D. 431. During his short one year's stay at the Jetavana monastery he was able to translate eleven works into Chinese.

An inmate in the same Jetavana monastery was another scholar from Kashmir, named Dharmamitra,[104], who collaborated with him. His contributions are no doubt recorded earlier.

Later Buddhist Savants

The contribution of Buddhist savants from Central Asia to the history of Buddhism—its thought and literature—can be assessed in terms of their translation of texts in China. In the absence of detailed information about the life and activities of these scholars, one could only trace their origin, the period of stay in China as also their literary contributions in the form of translation of earlier texts. Dharmakṣema[105] (Chinese Tan-mo-chian

103. Bagchi: ibid, 370-375; Hastings: *Encyclopedia of Religion & Ethics*, VIII, 701-6; Eliot : *Hinduism and Buddhism*, III, pp. 176-177.

104. Bagchi : Op. cit, pp. 388-391; Nanjio, ii, 75, pp. 414.

105. Bagch: Op. cit, pp. 212-221.

or Tan-wu-Chian) translated as Fa-Feng—'land prosperity'—originally from Central India, was a follower of Mahāyāna Buddhism and at first went to Kashmir—then a great seat of Buddhist learning. From there he went to China through Central Asia reaching Liang-Chou in the beginning of the 5th century. He had to stay at Ku-tsang—then the capital of an independent kingdom—and translated 25 texts into Chinese. He wanted to returned to Khotan in A.D. 433 much against the wishes of the ruler. While attempting to do so he was killed in the way. He is also attributed the translation of the famous Kāvya of Aśvaghoṣa—*Buddhacarita* (Fo-Pen-hing-king) in five chapters. The incomplete manuscript of the *Mahāparinirvāṇasūtra*—which he had brought from India—was translated by him into Chinese. The rest of the manuscript which he wanted to get in his second visit to Khotan, actually cost him his life.

About the same time a pupil of Dharmakṣema Tsiu-kiu-Kingsheng[106]—a noble man of Liang-chou—went to Khotan—then a great centre of Mahāyāna studies—and studied the texts of this Buddhist school with an Indian scholar named Buddhasena who was a great Mahāyāna teacher, called She-tseu (Siṁha) in all the countries of the west. Kingsheng on his return to China translated the texts which he had studied in Khotan and had brought with him. Khotan's reputation as a Buddhist academic centre with its famous savants attracted many Chinese monks. Among them were eight monks from Liang-chou who came there in 439 in search of Buddhist texts. At that time the quinquennial assembly was being held there. These monks took dictation of texts which they carried with them to China. A Chinese monk named Fa-ling[107] brought from Khotan a manuscript of the famous *Avataṁśaka-sūtra* which was translated by Buddhabhadra

106. Bagchi : Op. cit, pp. 221-223; 394-398.

107. Fa-ling was a disciple of Hui-Yuan who was a great Sanskrit scholar, who did not translate any text into Chinese, but devoted a greater portion of his time to the work of organization. It was at his suggestion that the whole of the *Sarvāstivāda-vinaya* was translated into Chinese. He sent a number of scholars to Kumārajīva to be trained by him, and a batch of disciples, Fa-tsing, Fa-ling and others to the desert and snowy mountains (Central Asia) in search of Sanskrit manuscripts. After several years they came back with Sanskrit texts which were later translated into Chinese. (Bagchi : *India & China*, p. 100)

in 418. Another monk named Fa-hien[108] brought from Khotan in 475 the manuscript of the *Saddharma-puṇḍarīka* which was translated by Dharmamati into Chinese in 490.

Khotan continued to play an important role in the transmission of Buddhism to China in the Tang period (A.D. 618-907). One of the greatest scholars of this period was Śikṣānanda[109] who went to China from Khotan and worked there till his death in 710. He translated in all 19 texts, the *magnum opus* being the *Mahāvaipulya* or the *Avataṁśaka-sūtras*, in 80 chapters. The original text named *Buddhāvataṁśaka-mahā-vaipulyasūtra*, which was earlier translated into Chinese in the beginning of the fifth century by the Kashmirian scholar Buddhabhadra – Śikṣānanda translated it a second time in the seventh century A.D. Another scholar from Khotan was Devaprajña[110] or Devendrajñāna. He went to the Chinese capital in A.D. 689 and in all translated six works. According to Nanjio,[111] eight works are ascribed to him, including a part on the practice of compassion in the *Buddhāvataṁśaka-vaipulyasūtra*, a part on the *Acintya-viṣaya* and *Sarvabuddhaṅgavati-dhāraṇī*. Shih-Kiyen[112], a son of the king of Kustana (Khotan) was another dignitary, who became a Śramaṇa in A.D. 707. He went to China as a hostage. In 721 he translated four works into Chinese, including Sūtra on the good law determining the obstacle of Karman, *Anantamukha-sādhaka-dhāraṇi-sūtra* on the lion king Sudarśana's cutting his flesh to feed others, and a collection of important accounts taken from several sūtras on the practice of a Bodhisattva who practices the Mahāyāna.

There are references to several other Buddhist scholars from other parts of Central Asia who went to China and translated Buddhist texts. These include Mitraśānta[113]—translated Tsiu-

108. Bagchi : *Le Canon*, p. 409.

109. *ibid*, p. 517. This name is faithfully transcribed in Chinese as Cheu-nan-to. He was originally from the country of Yu-tien (Khotan) situated to the north of Tsong-ling (Pamirs).

110. *Bagchi* : *Le Canon*, pp. 514-16. He was a Śramaṇa of Khotan.

111. *Catalogue*, ii. 143, p. 439.

112. Nanjio : *Catalogue*, Appendix II, 152, p. 443. Shib-K-yen's original surname and cognomen according to Nanjio were Yu-Kh'lo.

113. ibid, II, 147, p. 440.

yiu, literally 'calm friend'. He was a śramaṇa of the country of Tu-kwa-lo i.e. Tukhāra who translated one work in A.D. 705, named *Vimalaśuddha-prabhāsa mahādhāraṇī*'. Ratnacinta[114] (Chinese O-ni-panna) translated as 'Jewel thinking' was a Śramaṇa of Kia-shi-mi-lo i.e. Kaśmīra. He translated seven works and died in A.D. 721 attaining the age of more than a hundred years. His works include *Pratibimbābhishiktaguṇa-sūtra*, *Amoghapāśa-hridaya-mantrarāga-sūtra*, Sūtra on the *Dhāraṇī-riddhimantra* of great freedom to be obtained by one who wishes for it. Another śramaṇa of Kia-Si-mi-lo or Kaśmīra was Thien-si-tsai—literally 'heaven or god' (= deva) 'stopping misfortune', who arrived in China in A.D. 980 and worked at translations for twenty years. In A.D. 982, he received the title Min-kiāo-tā-sh and died in A.D. 1000. Eighteen works are assigned to him which include *Ghanavyūha-sūtra*, *Sukarma-duḥkarmaphala-viśeṣaṇa-sūtra* etc. A śramaṇa from Kubhā (Kabul) named Pan-jo[115] or Prajña, translated as Che-hui, was educated in the Buddhist lore in Kashmir. He went to China in A.D. 781 and settled down at Chang-ngan in 810. He translated eight works into Chinese which include *Buddhāvataṁśaka-Vaipulya-sūtra*. A more prolific scholar was Dānapāla[116]—'the gift protector'—She-hu in Chinese. He was a Buddhist scholar of Uddiyana in north-western India and arrived in China in A.D. 980. He worked there at translations for some years. Two years later he received from the Chinese emperor the title of *Hien-kiaoa-ta-sh*. In the Nanjio's catalogue, 111 works are ascribed to him, including *Mahāsāhaṣra-pramardāna-sūtra*, *Mahāyāna-ratnacandra-kumāra-pariprikkhā-sūtra*, *Mahāyāna-cintyārddhiviṣaya-sūtra* etc.

Tibet too was not quiet in this direction, and there is a reference to a monk Pa-ho-sz-pa[117] or Pā-sz-pa—Bashpa—a śramaṇa of the country of Tu-po (Tibet)who was the Ti-sh, literally 'emperor's teacher'. He translated one work in A.D. 1271. He died in A.D. 1280 in his forty-second year. It is said that he had become a confidential adviser of Kublai Khan during the latter's career of conquest in China. In A.D. 1260 he was named Kwo-sh—

114. *ibid*, II, 148, p. 440.
115. Nanjio : *Op. cit*, II, 156, p. 448.
116. *ibid*, II, 161, pp. 453-454.
117. *ibid*, II, 169, pp. 457-458.

'Preceptor or Hierarch of the State', and recognised as the head of the Buddhist Church. In A.D. 1269 he constructed an alphabetic system for the Mongol language which was utilised for writing. In reward for his services he received the exalted title of 'Ta-pao-fa-wan' or 'Prince of the Great and Precious Law (of Buddha)'. His solitary contribution is *Mūlasarvāstivāda-nikāya-pravragyopasampadā-karmavāka.*

Buddhism and other Religions in Central Asia

The study of Buddhism in Central Asia is recorded on the basis of the accounts of Chinese pilgrims who passed through this vast region and have noticed the number of monasteries as also that of monks. The Chinese source material is equally rich in providing information on the lives and activities of these Buddhist savants of Central Asia who went to China to translate sacred texts. The archaeological finds of stūpas and sculptures as also paintings equally testify to the flourishing state of Buddhism—both Hīnayāna and Mahāyāna. It is equally proposed that there were two streams of Buddhism and there were running contacts between India and the Oxus region. The use of Prākrit and of various Iranian idioms point to actual colonization from these two quarters. According to the Chinese pilgrim, Shan-Shan (near Lob-nor), Turfan, Kucha and Kashgar were Hīnayānist, whereas Yarkand and Khotan were Mahāyānist centres. The *terminus a quo* of Buddhist art, religion and philosophy could be any time in the first century A.D., though traditional accounts, especially in relation to Khotan could place this event a couple of centuries earlier. The earliest Chinese notice of the Buddhism in Kashgar and Kucha date from 400 (Fa-hien) and the third century (Annals of the Tsin 265-317) respectively. In Turfan the first definite Buddhist record is the dedication of a temple to Maitreya in 469 and probably the history of Buddhism in this region was similar to that in Kucha. Khotan was probably the starting point of Buddhist activity in Central Asia, and it was carried from there to China. This Mahāyānist Buddhism of Khotan was a separate stream and, according to Hsuan-tsang, it came from Kashmir. While the

Mahāyāna school was predominant in Khotan, it was not to the exclusion of the other school. The Chinese pilgrim Fa-hien (c. 400) found the Hīnayāna prevalent in Shan-Shan, Kucha, Kashgar, Osh, Udyana and Gandhāra. Hsuan-tsang also notices its presence in Balkh, Bamiyan and Persia. Both the schools co-existed everywhere though disputations amongst their votaries were not unknown. An interesting passage in the 'Life of Hsuan-tsang'[118] relates his dispute with a Mahāyānist scholar in Kucha which was a centre of the Hīnayānists. This monk held that the books called Tsa-hsin Chu-She and Pi-Sha were enough for salutation(apparently referring to *Saṃyuktābhidharma-hridaya* (Nanjio 1287), *Abhidharmakośa* (ibid 1267), *Abhidharma-vibhāṣa* (ibid 1264) and *Yogikarabhūmi*(Nanjio 1170). He denounced the Yogaśāstra as heretical to the great indignation of the pilgrim, who no doubt accepted this work, its importance being revealed by Maitreya to Asaṅga.

Brahmanism

Besides Buddhism with its two most important schools that of the Hīnayāna and Mahāyāna, there are traces of other religions and cultures mingling in the Tarim basin and the lands of the Oxus. It is quite likely that besides Hinduism, Zoroastrianism and Christianity as also Manichaeism not only flourished but also interacted with their impact on Buddhism. The available evidence sheds light on the co-existence of these religions as also the mutual impact of Buddhism and Hinduism and of the former with the other two. Hinduism—in its two facets—Vaiṣṇavism and Śaivism with its gods and goddesses also came to be known in Central Asia quite early. The famous record from Vidisa[119] inscribed on the column refers to Heliodorus, son of Dion, as a worshipper of Bhāgavata. He had come there from the court of Antialkidas of Taxila, during the fourteenth year of the reign of the Indian king Kāśiputra Bhāgabhadra. This ruler of Taxila could be placed sometime in the last quarter of the second or the first quarter of the first century B.C. The Kriṣṇa legend seems to have travelled outside India during the second century B.C. according to Zenob's story of

118. S. Beal : *Life of Hiuen-Tsiang* (London. 1911), p. 39.
119. Luders : List of Inscriptions (EI.X. Appendix)

the Indians in Armenia. This story refers to two Indian chiefs called Gisane (Kisane) and Demeter (Temeter) having sought shelter with Valarashak or Valarsaces of Armenia (c. B.C. 149-127 B.C.). Later on, they were put to death, but their sons lived there and erected two temples of their gods (Gisane and Demeter). These were later razed to the ground by Saint Gregory despite stiff resistance.[120] It is suggested that both were Brahmanical deities—either Krişṇa and Balarāma or some solar ones.

The Nārāyaṇa cult, probably associated with Vaiṣṇavism, however, had not so uncomfortable an end—in another region of Central Asia. A fragment of an inscription discovered by A.N. Bernshtam in Tadjikistan in 1956 refers to the cult of Nārāyaṇa —'Nārāyaṇa be victorious'—*jayato*—as the inscription suggests. On palaeographic grounds the inscription can be attributed to the second-first century B.C. Harmata considers[121] the identity of this Nārāyaṇa at great length in his long paper. In case this Nārāyaṇa is equated with Viṣṇu, then the record points to Brahmanism preceding Buddhism in Central Asia. On the other hand, Nārāyaṇa, the Buddha, is mentioned in the Khotanese, Saka documents in Eastern Turkestan, and Nārāyaṇa, the deva, occurs in the Buddhist Sogdian documents.[122] In a Tun-huang painting Nārāyaṇa on Garuḍa is shown as attendant of Avalokiteśvara.[123] This vāhana Garuḍa is closely associated with Viṣṇu and it is likely that the artist had the Brahmanical deity in mind while painting his subject.

Reference to Viṣṇu worship along with that of Śiva and Sūrya is evident from the famous Nicolo seal which was first noticed by Cunningham.[124] According to him, the device consists of the four-armed Viṣṇu with a devotee standing by his side with folded hands showing obeisance. There is also an inscription, correctly

120. JRAS. 1904, p. 330.

121. *Acta Orientalia*, Hungary, Tome XIX, 1966, pp. 1-32.

122. For the Saka and Sogdian data, Harmata refers to Bailey, BSOAS. X. 1942, pp. 909 and 914; & E. Benveniste : *Vessantara Jātaka* (Paris 1916), pp. 58-59 and Texts Sogdiens (Paris 1940), p. 107.

123. Arthur Waley : *A Catalogue of Paintings recovered from Tun-huang* (1931), p. 54. See also P. Banerji's Paper entitled 'Hindu deities in Central Asia' in *India's Contribution to World Thought and Culture* (Vivekanand Memorial Volume, Madras, 1970, pp. 281-287.)

124. *Numismatic Chronicle* (N.C.) 1893, pp. 126-127, Pl. X, Fig. 2.

deciphered by Ghirshman.[125] This record in Tocharian language mentions the name of Mihira, Viṣṇu and Śiva. The devotee, according to the late French scholar, is not the Kuṣāṇa king Huviṣka, but some known Hephthalite chief, and the use of the Tocharian language and script suggests that a composite cult of Śiva, Viṣṇu and Sūrya was popular with certain peoples of Central Asia about 500 A.D.

Definite Vaiṣṇavite influence is also traced in a Buddha image from Balawaste[126] in the Domko region on the southern silk route. This image, now in the National Museum as part of the Stein collection of wall paintings, is assigned about the eighth century A.D. The body and arm of the figure are covered with symbols or devices including the Śrīvatsa, diamonds, mandara as churning rod, horse Uccaiḥsravā (suggestive of the story of the churning of the oceans), the sun, the moon, vajras, books, triangle and circles—all mystic elements depicting the *Viśvarūpa* aspect of the Buddha on the model of the Kriṣṇa Viśvarūpa of the Gītā. This painting is suggestive of the cosmic aspect of the Buddha, and not the Śākyamuni.

Śaivism, however, seems to be more popular in Central Asia with its amalgam with Buddhism effected by Asaṅga, the well-known philosopher of about A.D. 400. The Śaiva pantheon was accepted by the Buddhists, and it held the imagination of the Central Asian peoples for a long time and over a wider area. It is well-known that the figure of Śiva appears on certain coins of Gondopheres, Maves and others. An elaborate Śiva pantheon is represented on the coins of the Kuṣāṇa rulers with Wima calling himself Māheśvara—a devotee of Maheśa. Nanā is identified with Ambā or Umā as consort of Śiva.[127] Several Śaiva

125. Les Chionites : *Hepthalites*, pp. 55-58, Fig. 65 and Pl. VII.

126. Bussagli : *Central Asian Paintings*, Pl.; Banerji : *Op. cit*, p. 282.

127. For a study of deities on Kusana coins, see Puri: *Kuṣānas*, Appendix A, p. 213 ff. The epithet 'deva' applied to Gondophernes on coins is significant, likely to mean Śiva and no other god. Huang-tsang in his Si-yuki also refers to a Śiva temple outside the gate of the city of Puṣkalāvati, simply, as a Deva temple in the seventh century. An important Śaiva image is the so-called Trimūrtī with Śiva as the central Figure (c. third century A.D.) from Akhun Dheri near Charsadda, now in the Peshawar Museum. (Banerji : *Op. cit*, p. 283).

sculptures and Brahmanical figures are found in Afghanistan[128] like the head of Durgā overcoming Mahiṣāsura. They are all of the seventh or eighth century A.D. probably later of the time of the Hindu Sāhi rulers of Afghanistan. The inscribed Mahāvināyaka or Gaṇeśa with Ūrdhvameḍhra—phallus erectus—clad in a tiger skin—now in the Kabul Museum, is another Brahmanical divinity.

The popularity of Śaivism extended to Sogdiana and Eastern Turkestan, as is evident from a fragment of a wall painting from Penjikent[129] on the river Zervashan. In this Śiva is portrayed with a sacred halo and a decorated sacred thread (*Yajñopavīta*) and stands in *āliḍha* pose. He is clad in a tiger skin while his attendants are clad in Sogdian dress, ornamented long coat with open collar.

Certain finds in Dandan-Uiliq and neighbouring sites of the Taklamakan desert suggest extension of Śaivism to Eastern or Chinese Turkestan. A very interesting representation of Śiva on a painted wooden panel (D. VII.6) shows him three-faced and four-armed seated cross-legged on a cushioned seat supported by two couchant bulls. The rich diadem on the central head with the side ornament resembling a half moon, the third eye on the forehead, the tiger skin forming the loincloth (*dhotī*), and finally the bull as his *vāhana*, are all symbolical of the Brahmanic God Śiva.[130] Another panel from Dandan-Uiliq depicts a four-armed Trimūrti form of Śiva and his Śakti[131] kneeling on her right thigh. The god sits cross-legged, clothed in tight fitting long-sleeved white vest. Traces of the third eye are visible. Śiva is four-armed with a massive armlet on the left arm, the other resting on thigh and holding *vajra*. The lower right hand is thrown round the neck of Śakti. The deity has a long neck-cord tied into bows at intervals. His hair is long and wavy and the crown is of Iranian type. The face to the left is fearful and the third eye is clearly visible. The Śakti dressed in a long stola with

128. See Benjamin Rowland : *Ancient Art from Afghanistan*, pp. 107-108.

129. Banerji : Artibus Asiae. XXXI. 1969, also *Vivekanand Volume*, *Op. cit*, p. 284.

130. Stein : *Ancient Khotan*, I, p. 279.

131. Dandan Uliq panel No. D.8—ibid. p. 261, pl. LXII. It is now in the British Museum. (Banerji : *Op. cit*, pl. 52).

tight sleeves to wrist holds a cup in her right hand, which she is handing to the deity. She has well-drawn eyebrows—highly arched and long eyes, and is white-complexioned.

Another Trimūrti figure from Eastern or Chinese Turkestan, now in the National Museum, also points to the popularity of Śaivism in that area. The deity sits full face with head slightly turned to left. The other two heads project either side from behind ears. The central face has a third eye in the forehead and a long thin moustache. The eyes are heavy-lidded and dreamy. A skull is shown on the head against the back top knot. The deity has four arms, the two upraised ones are holding the sun to the left and the moon to right, a pomegranate in the lower right hand, and the left one resting on the thigh, probably grasping a vajra (?). The conspicuous Śaiva features are the third eye on the central head, the skull on the headdress and the three heads with four arms.[132]

Besides Śiva and Gaṇeśa, Kumāra, Kārtikeya, Brahmā, Indra, the sun, the moon and the lokapālas—all connected with Brahmanism, figure in Central Asian art. Brahmā is noticed, according to Coomarswamy,[133] on the caves of Kucha area. A fragment of wall painting from Balawaste, now in the National Museum,[134] is supposed to be that of Indra. The figure is either kneeling or sitting cross-legged, his body leaning forward and head tilting back. The eyes are downcast and hands folded and uplifted to neck-level. The head is covered with a close fitting cap with a head band in dark pink studded with pearls. The face is Indian and the figure puts on various types of ornaments and a *mukta-yajñopavīta*. The presence of the eye on the hand identifies the figure Indra.

The Tun-huang cave paintings depict Gaṇeśa, Kumāra, the sun and the moon. Gaṇeśa was no doubt very popular in Khotan as seems evident from a number of bronze tablets and painted wooden panels discovered by Stein at Endere, now in the British

132. Andrews : *Catalogue of wall Paintings from Ancient Shrines in Central Asia*. Bal. 0200, p. 87.

133. *History of Indian and Indonesian Art*, London, 1927, p. 150 n.

134. Andrews : *Catalogue*, p. 13. See also *Indo-Asian Culture*, XVII. No. 4, pp. 14 ff.

Museum.[135] This four-armed god with an elephant head is shown seated, wearing tiger-skin, dhoti and tight trouser. He has a rosary of dots, and holds a bowl or fruits or sweetballs, a spear-head, a turnip and an axe. Dandan-Uiliq has also certain wooden panels depicting Gaṇeśa,[136] and so also in Khadlik where he is shown seated on an open lotus. A fine figure of Gaṇeśa in cave 285 of Tun-huang[137] is equally interesting. Kārtikeya is represented in a wall painting from Bezaklik,[138] seated on a bird, with one leg hanging down and the other tucked up in front. Mahākāla and Garuḍa are shown carrying away the nectar after the famous sea churning. Mahākāla's image with a demon's head seated on a yak-tail (Nandī), and Lokapālas[139] fully absorbed in Buddhism also figure in paintings in Central Asia. The four well-known Lokapālas—Dhritarāṣṭra, Virudhaka, Virūpākṣa and Vaiśravaṇa were assimilated in Buddhist art and each was provided with a direction as its guardian. These protectors of the four quarters are shown in Central Asian art as warrior kings gorgeously dressed with armours, sometimes accompanied by Yakṣas or demons.

Besides Brahmanical divinities depicted in Central Asian art, and mythological legends faithfully brought out in artistic presentations, the Rāma legend as also the other epic stories were also known to the Central Asian people in ancient times. The story of Rāmāyaṇa in Khotan legend is somewhat different, but the reference to Rāma, Lakṣmaṇa, Sītā and Daśaratha and also Paraśurāma is significant. Prof. Bailey has gone[140] into the question of Rāmāyaṇa in Central Asia thoroughly. Scholars who have delved into Central Asian studies also took notice of many names of epic heroes—Bhīma, Arjuna and several others as proper names in Kharoṣṭhī inscriptions. There are scores of Brah-

135. Stein : *Ancient Khotan*, pp. 431, 442.

136. *ibid*, pp. 292 ff.

137. Basil Gray : *Buddhist Cave Paintings at Tun-huang*, pp. 1-20.

138. Andrews : *Catalogue of Wall-Paintings* (Op. cit), pp. 35-36.

139. Bussagli : *Central Asian Paintings* (Op. cit); also Stein : *Ancient Khotan*, I, pp. 494 ff.

140. See his paper 'The Rama Story in Khotanese' (Journal of the American Oriental Society. JAOS—LIX, pp. 460-8; also Bulletin of the School of Oriental and African Studies—BSOAS, 1949-50, pp. 121-39; 920-938.)

manical names in such records which might as well point to Brahmanism flourishing in Central Asia where these records were found. It is equally significant that the Yueh-chi and their descendants or associates, the Kuṣāṇas, should have so soon accepted Śaivism—Wima Kadphises calls himself Māheśvara or a devotee of Maheśa or Śiva while Śiva and his Nandī figure on the Kuṣāṇa coins all through from this Kuṣāṇa ruler onwards. Skanda, Kumāra and Vaiśākha are also depicted on the coins of Huviṣka. Gaṇeśa, another Brahmanical deity—son of Śiva—became very popular in Central Asia[141] as also in Mongolia, China and Japan, as the remover of obstacles (*Vighna nāśaka*). One might as well refer to the famous Mathurā inscription[142] of the year 28 of Huviṣka recording dedication of 550 Purāṇas each into the two guilds of *samitākara* and *dhaṅgika*—wheat flour and corn dealers respectively, for the exclusive benefit of Brahmins. The donor hailed from Wakhan or Badakshan. This religious impulse appears to have been deep-rooted.

The available evidence—artistic and epigraphic—no doubt suggests that Brahmanism—both Vaiṣṇavism and Śaivism with their divinities, epic heroes and legends, found their way to Khotan and other parts of Central Asia where Buddhism, of course, was the dominating religious force. Brahmanism came closer to Buddhism and several Brahmanical divinities figure independently. Lokapālas or guardians of the quarters were easily incorporated and assimilated in Buddhism, especially Mahāyānism. With the passage of time it came closer to Śaivism and Vaiṣṇavism—presenting the best of the Indian religious systems and the composite nature of Indian culture.

Manichaeism, Nestorian Christianity and Buddhism

Manichaeism, the religion of Mani[143] or Manes, is one of those systems, usually classed together under the name of Gros-

141. See Getty : *Ganeśa*, Oxford 1936, p. 40; Stein : *Ancient Khotan*, p. 221; Shivarama Murti : *Gaṇeśa*; also M.K. Dhavalekar: '*Gaṇeśa beyond the Indian Frontiers*' (Vivekanand Volume : Op. cit, pp. 1-15).

142. EI. XXI. pp. 55 ff.

143. Mani is said to be of noble birth, and like Zoroaster, the Buddha and Jesus, claimed to have been sent by God to fulfil what had been previously revealed. He preached a new universal religion which like Christianity em-

ticism. This religion arose in Babylonia about the middle of the third century A.D. and during many generations exercised great influence both in the East and in the West. Of course, very little of the Manichaean literature has survived. The fragments of manuscripts concerning this religion were discovered in Central Asia[144] thus confirming its existence in that area. The information about it being meagre, it is difficult to provide a fuller picture. Reference might as well be made to the writings of non-Manichaean authors most of whom wrote their accounts in a hostile manner. By far the most celebrated of the western authorities on Manichaeism is Augustine who was for nine years (A.D. 373-382) a professor of Manichaean thought. He represents Faustus as one of the ablest and the most influential among the Manichaeans, but it is doubtful if he could read the sacred books of his religion in the original Aramaic. The Mohammadan literature relating to this religion does not begin before the 9th century A.D. According to Al-Birūni,[145] Mani himself says that 'wisdom and deeds have always from time to time been brought to mankind by the messengers of God. So in one age they have been brought by the messenger called Buddha to India, in another by Zaradusht (Zoroaster) to Persia, in another by Jesus to the West. Thereupon this revelation has come down, the prophecy in this last age, through one Mani, the messenger of the God of truth to Babylonia.' Such was

---

braced all races and conditions of men. His doctrines were derived from the cults of Babylonia and Iran and were influenced by Buddhism and Christianity. Ghirshman : *Iran* (Pelicans), p. 315.

144. *Encyclopedia of Religion and Ethics* (ERE) VIII, pp. 394. These fragments are written in various languages (Persian, Turkish and Chinese). They have been published by F.W.K. Muller, A. Von Le Coq, C. Salemann, Chavannes and Pelliot. (Consolidated references provided in ERE, Vol. VIII, 394, Col. i, n. 1). The discovery of the Turkish version of the Khuastuanift— a Manichaean Confession prayer amidst Chinese Buddhist texts and monastic records from the Polyglot Library in the Turfan area is very interesting. It shows how easy it was for Mani's Church in Central Asia to share the same sacred site with Buddhist cult (Stein : *Serindia*, Vol. II, p. 819 and 921). The Chinese Manichaean texts were found at Chien-fo-tung. A Manichaean work in Chinese has been translated and annotated by Chavannes and Pelliot (JA. November-December, 1911, pp. 499-617).

145. Stein : *Serindia*, p. 819.

the claim put forward by Mani. The extreme simplicity of their cult, and in particular their abhorrence of idolatry, seems to have saved them from molestation. It is difficult to fix the exact date of introduction of Manichaeism into Central Asia and China. The finds in a polyglot library[146] at Tun-huang included a remarkable manuscript exhibiting a third variety of the Syriac script transplanted to Central Asia, and the one which discovered at the ruined sites of Turfan first revealed as peculiar to Manichaean writings. It was an excellently preserved narrow roll of paper about 15′ long containing the beautifully written and almost complete text of a Manichaean confession Prayer[147]—a Turkish version of the *Khvastuaniff*. The discovery amidst Chinese Buddhist texts and monastic record of this Manichaean relic was interesting. The Turfan excavations and finds point to the existence of Mani's church in Central Asia, sharing the same sacred site with the Buddhist cult, and with Christian worship too, though remaining for centuries a formidable rival to both of them.

The presence of the Turkish-speaking Manichaeans at Tun-huang is attested by another important find from the walled-up chapel—the perfectly preserved small book in Turkish 'Runic' script. The discoveries at Turfan sites furnish abundant proof for the existence of Manichaean and Buddhist worship existing side by side among a population which had come relatively early under Turkish influence as well as domination. Manichaean propaganda seems to have secured a firm foothold in that part of Central Asia as well as in China in Tang times. This is also confirmed by the finds of Chinese Manichaean texts found at Chien-Fo-tung. Pelliot discovered a fragment of a Chinese treatise setting forth points of Manichaean doctrine.[148]

146. Quoted by E.R. Bevan in his article in the *Encyclopedia of Religion and Ethics*, p. 396, Col. i, n. 3. He refers to Alberuni's book on *Chronology* (E. Sachau : Leipzig, 1878 and translated by him into English—*The Chronology of Ancient Nations*, London, 1879).

147. For an edition and annotated translation of this text, see Von Lecoq's paper '*Dr Stein's Turkish Khuastuanift from Tunhuang*', JRAS, 1911, pp. 277-314.

148. See Chavannes and Pelliot '*Un traite Manicheen retrouvé en Chine*'—JA. 1911. 1913, which is a most valuable contribution to our knowledge of

The admixture of Buddhism in Manichaeism is equally remarkable. The discoveries made in Central Asia seem to support the Chinese edict of 739 accusing Manichaeism of falsely taking the name of Buddhism and deceiving the people. This is not surprising since Mani is said to have taught, as pointed out by Al-Birūni, that Zoroaster, Buddha and Christ had preceded him as apostles and in Buddhist countries his followers naturally adopted words and symbols familiar to the people. Thus, Manichaean deities are represented like Bodhisattvas sitting cross-legged on a lotus. Mani receives the epithet Ju-lai or Tathāgata as in Amida's Paradise. There are holy trees bearing flowers which enclose beings styled Buddha, and the construction and phraseology of Manichaean books resemble those of a Buddhist Sūtra. The patrons of Manichaeism in Central Asia were the Uighurs who were established there in the eighth and ninth centuries A.D. and around 750 A.D. their Khan adopted Manichaeism as the State religion.[149] The many manuscripts in Sogdian and other Persian dialects found at Turfan show that it had an old and close connection with the west. Mani's teachings seem to be influential in Central Asia, but not before A.D. 700.

Nestorian Christianity also existed in the Tarim basin and was quite prominent in the seventh century A.D. This is in agreement with the record of its introduction into China by A-lo-pen

---

Manichaeism in Central Asia and China. (Eliot : *Hinduism and Buddhism*, III, p. 216 n. 3)

149. The most influential cultural event in the history of the Uighur Khanate was the conversion of the rulers to the Manichaean religion under the third Kaghan in A.D. 762. This event is recorded in the trilingual inscription of Qara Balgasun (E. Chavannes and P. Pelliot : *Un traite Manicheen retrouve en Chine. Journal Asiatique*, 1913, 177). The texts are in Chinese, Sogdian and Turkish, of which only the first is satisfactorily preserved. Apparently it was as a result of the Uighur occupation of the Chinese silk-route terminus of Lo-Yang that the Kaghan was brought into contact with Manichaean missionaries who had been established in China since A.D. 694. The new creed—a syncretistic one, including elements of Zoroastrian, Christian and Buddhist origin, was founded in Mesopotamia by its prophet Mani soon after the rise of the Sassanian Empire in Iran which took place in A.D. 224. The new creed penetrated early into Khurasan and Sogdiana under the leadership of the apostle Mar Ammo. It was carried by its devotees of Sogdian nationality and by tradition traders along the routes to China. (Hambay : *Central Asia*, Op. cit, pp. 60-61)

in A.D. 635, almost simultaneous with Zoroastrianism. Fragments of the New Testament have been found at Turfan mostly belonging to the ninth century, but one is of the fifth century. The most interesting document relating to the history of this faith is the Nestorian stone,[150] bearing a long inscription partly in Chinese and partly in Syriac, composed by a foreign priest called Adam or in Chinese King-Tsing. It provides a long account of the doctrines and history of Nestorianism. This inscription also contains many Buddhist phrases, such as *Seng* and *Ssu* for Christian priests and monasteries. It also omits references to the crucification and simply speaks of the creation that God arranged the cardinal points in the shape of a cross. It reviews in some detail the life and activities of Christ. It is suggested that the motive for omission must be the feeling that redemption by his death was not an acceptable doctrine, and the Nestorians as also the Jesuits were unwilling to give publicity to the crucification. It is equally interesting to find that king Tsing consorted with Buddhist priests and even set about translating a sūtra from the Hu language. Takakusu[151] quotes a passage from one of the catalogues of the Japanese Tripiṭaka which states that he was a Persian and collaborated with a monk of Kāpiśa called Prajña.

On the basis of manuscript finds, there is clear evidence of the co-existence of Buddhism and Christianity, and friendly relations between Buddhist and Christian priests in China. It is possible that in Western China and Central Asia Buddhism, Taoism, Manichaeism, Nestorianism and Zoroastrianism all borrowed from one another, though definite proof for this is wanting. Buddhism, no doubt, was in strength and the most important of all other religions. Its religious texts were translated much earlier. The happy land sūtra (*Sukhāvatīvyūha*) and *Prajñā-pāramitā* (Nanjio 23, 5) were translated before A.D. 200, and portions of the 'Avataṁśaka' and 'Lotus' (Nanjio 100, 103, 138) before A.D. 300. The principal doctrines of Mahāyāna Buddhism must have been known in Khotan much before the

150. Havert : *La Stele Chrestienne de Singan Fu in varietes sinologues*, pp. 7, 12 and 20 quoted by Eliot in reference.

151. I-tsing, pp. 169, 223.

presence of Christianity there.[152] So also were Turfan and Kucha centres of Hīnayāna Buddhism.

The association and contribution of Zoroastrianism might have contributed to the development and transformation of Buddhism since the two were certainly in contact with each other rather closely. Kaniṣka, the great Kuṣāṇa ruler, as also a patron of Buddhism, no doubt, portrayed many Zoroastrian deities[153] on his coins, and these are more copious and frequent than the figure of the Buddha. This could be possible only if Zoroastrianism was flourishing in his realm. According to the information available from the Chinese sources, the two religions co-existed at Khotan and Kashgar. The Tang Annals describe not only Buddhism as flourishing in Khotan—one of the Four Garrisons—but also the 'cult of the Celestial god' by which the Zoroastrian religion is to be understood.[154] An official Chinese document dating from the year 768 A.D., which was excavated at Danḍan-Uiliq, refers to the capital Kia-che (Kashgar) and its people. It mentions worship of the 'god of heaven' which according to Chavannes, recognizes a reference to the Zoroastrian cult.[155] Some hostile references to Buddhism are equally traced in Persian scriptures with Buiti and Gaotema called the heretic.[156]

Some New Trends in Buddhism

As a result of mingling of different religious ideas, the co-existence of denominational institutions and their patriarchs in Central Asia, mutual influence in a spirit of toleration and assimilation is understandable. Buddhism, as such, is supposed to have amalgamated with Zoroastrianism or Christianity, Confucianism and Taoism. Thus, the dated inscription[157] of the temple erected in Turfan, A.D. 469, is an amalgam of Chinese ideas—both

152. Eliot : *Hinduism and Buddhism*, Op. cit, III, p. 218.
153. Stein : Zoroastrian deities on the Kusana coins, I.A.
154. Stein : *Ancient Khotan*, (Op. cit, p. 172.
155. ibid, p. 155.
156. *Sacred books of the East* : SBE, Vol. IV, pp. 145, 209; XXIII, p. 184; Eliot : *Op. cit*, p. 218.
157. Eliot : Op. cit, p. 216. An Chou, the prince to whose memory the temple was dedicated, seems to be regarded as a manifestation of Maitreya.

Confucian and Taoist—with Indian ones. This record is in honour of Maitreya, a Bodhisattva, known to the Hīnayāna but regarded in that area not merely as the future Buddha but as an active and benevolent deity manifesting himself in many forms. According to a tradition, the works of Asaṅga were revelations made by him. This record also mentions Ākāśagarbha and the Dharmakāya, and equally speaks of heaven (tien) as appointing princes, and of the universal law (tao). The Central Asian Buddhism while borrowing many personages from the Hindu pantheon, has also many others—Buddhas and Bodhisattvas such as Amitābha, Avalokita, Mañjuśrī and Kṣitigarbha—without clear antecedents in India. These might have been the outcomes of other external factors. The most important Buddhist divinity is Amitābha. He does not figure in the earlier art and literature of Indian Buddhism. In the earlier part of the *Saddharmapuṇḍarīka*—'The Lotus of the True Law'—he is just mentioned without any special importance attached to him. The *Mahāyāna-śraddhotpāda-śāstra*[158]—'The Awakening of Faith'—ascribed to Aśvaghoṣa—though not certain—mentions Amitābha towards the end. Reference is made by Aśvaghoṣa to a sūtra (probably the Amitāyus-sūtra or *Sukhāvatīvyūha*) on Buddha Amitāyus or Amitābha and his Buddhakṣetra Sukhāvatī. Further Amitābha's paradise is just mentioned in the *Mahāyānasūtrālaṁkāra*[159] of Asaṅga. Amidst these cursory and meagre notices in Indian literature, and the nameless Buddha figures in the Gandhāra region providing uncertain inference about their identity with Amitābha, it is quite possible that Amitābha[160] and

158. Nanjio : Catalogue No. 1249, p. 274. This work composed by the Bodhisattva Aśvaghoṣa was translated by Śikṣānanda, A.D. 695-700 of the Than dynasty.

159. XII, p. 23; Eliot : Op. cit, p. 219. See Nanjio No. 1190, p. 262. This work composed by the Bodhisattva Asaṅga was translated by Prabhākaramitra, A.D. 630-633 of the Than dynasty, A.D. 618-907.

160. Lokesh Chandra in his paper entitled 'Iranian Elements in the Formation of Tantrik Buddhism' presented to the Symposium on 'The Silk Route and the Diamond Path' held on 7, 8 November, 1982 at the University of California suggests that the cult of Amitābha represents transcedental tendencies in Buddhism. Śākyamuni, the Man, was replaced by Amitābha. His historic Enlightenment was transcended into Supreme Enlightenment whose illumination became the new dynamised centre reflected in the new

his concept were evolved in Central Asia where his worship flourished in the early centuries of the Christian era. Two translations of the principal Amidist scriptures were made into Chinese in the second century A.D. and four in the third, all by native scholars of Central Asia.

According to the Tibetan historian of Buddhism,[161] Tārānāth, Amitābha's worship could be traced back to Sarāha or Rāhulbhadra, a great magician, and reputed to be the teacher of Nāgārjuna, who saw Amitābha in the land of Dhingkoṭa and died with his face turned towards Sukhāvatī. The name Sarāha does not sound Indian, probably a Śūdra represented in Tibetan scrolls with a beard and top knot and holding an arrow[162] in his hand. Thus, the first person whom tradition connects with the worship of Amitābha was of low caste and bore a foreign name. He saw the deity in a foreign country, and was represented as totally unlike a Buddhist monk. While it cannot be proved that he came from the lands of the Oxus or Turkestan, there seems little difficulty, according to Eliot, in accepting Zoroastrian influence on this cult or worship.[163] The main principles of Amidist doctrine are that there is a paradise of light belonging to a benevolent deity and those good men invoking his name would be led to that region. The highest heaven (following after the paradises of good thoughts, good words and good deeds) is called 'Boundless Light' or 'Endless Light'.[164] In this connection reference might be made to this region and its master, Ahura Mazda, who are constantly spoken of in terms implying radiance and glory. It is also a land of song, like that of Amitābhā's paradise

---

Tathāgata Amitābha, with Śākyamuni changing into Amitābha, the attendant acolytes also changed names. Brahmā became Avalokiteśvara and Śakra became Mahāsthamaprāpta (circulated paper, p. 55). Further, according to Lokesh Chandra, the development of triads Amitābha, flanked by Avalokiteśvara and Mahāsthamaprāpta, was influenced by the traditions of Mithra flanked by his companions Rasnu (the god of Justice) and Sraosa (the god of obedience) (ibid, p. 58).

161. Translation Schiefner, pp. 93, 105 and 303.

162. Eliot : Op. cit, p. 219.

163. ibid, p. 220.

164. Zenda-Avesta-trans. Dermesteter, Names. *Sacred Books* of the *East* (SBE), Vols. IV, p. 239; XXIII, pp. 317, 344.

re-echoing with music and pleasant sounds.[165] This paradise could be reached and Ahura Mazda and the Archangels would show the way to the pious.[166] Further, it is also said in the Zoroastrian text that whoever recites the 'Ahuna-variya formula', his soul would be led by Ahura Mazda to 'the lights of heaven.'[167] The repetition of Ahura Mazda's name is repeatedly reported to be efficacious enough to lead the person to paradise. It is proposed by Eliot,[168] that the chief features of Amitābha's paradise are Persian, only his method of instituting it by making a vow is Buddhist. While numerous paradises are the outcome of Indian imagination, and the early Buddhist legend tells of the Tushita heaven, the Sukhāvatī is unlike these early Buddhist abodes of bliss. It appears suddenly in the history of Buddhism as something exotic, 'grafted cleverly on the parent trunk, but sometimes overgrowing it'. Eliot equally poses the question of tracing connection between Sukhāvatī and the land of Saukavastan governed by an immortal ruler and located by the Bundehist between Turkestan and Chinistan. While there is no etymological relationship, it is likely that Saukavasta, being well-known as a land of the blessed, might have influenced the choice of a significant Sanskrit word with a similar sound.[169]

This Zoroastrian influence is traced by this British diplomat scholar even in the concept of Avalokita[170] who is also connected

165. Eliot : Op. cit, p. 220. It may also be noticed that Ameretat, the Archangel of immortality, presides over vegetation and that Amida's pardise is full of flowers.

166. SBE, XXIII, pp. 355-7.

167. *Saddharmapuṇḍarīka*, SBE, XXI, p. 261.

168. Op. cit, III, p. 220.

169. ibid, p. 221 n.

170. Avalokita is considered not only 'a great god' but a 'good providence'. The compound Avalokiteśvara may mean either 'the lord of what we see', i.e., of the present world, or 'the lord of the view' or 'the lord whom we see', the 'lord revealed'. He is placed along with a certain number of companions—the sons of Buddha—Avalokita Samantabhadra (the wholly auspicious), Mañjughoṣa (lovely voice=Mañjuśrī), Kṣitigarbha (earth womb) and Vajrin (thunderball holder=Vajrapāṇi). He is a Buddhist Śiva in visible form, while Amitābha is the Śiva Brahman. He is an ascetic, a magician and also a saviour; from his fingers flow rivers which cool the hells and feed the pretas (ghosts), terrifying all the demons. He is the refuge, Buddha-Dharma and Saṅgha all in one (ERE. II, pp. 256-261 n).

with Amitābha's paradise. His figure assumes distinct and conspicuous proportions in India at a fairly early date, and there is no ground for tracing his origin or association with Central Asia. Later works, no doubt, describe him as the spiritual son or reflex of Amitābha. This aspect recalls the Iranian idea of the Fravashi defined as 'a spriritual being conceived as a part of a man's personality but existing before he is born and independent of him belonging to divine beings.[171] The relationship between a Dhyānī Buddha and his Bodhisattva is compared with the Zoroastrian doctrine of the Fravashi.

Traces of Central Asian origin or affiliation of other Bodhisattvas is also noticed by scholars. Thus, Sylvain Levi suggests[172] the Tokharian origin of Bodhisattva Mañjuśrī. According to Eliot,[173] his worship at Wu-tai-shan in Shan-Si is ancient and later Indian tradition connects him with China, while local traditions also associate him with Nepal, Tibet and Khotan and he is sometimes represented as the first teacher of civilization or religion. His Central Asian origin could be probable but not very certain. E. Huber[174] was the first to observe that the canon of one of the Buddhist schools of the Little Vehicle or Hīnayāna contained traditions foreign to India, as for example, the legend about Khotan, and he wondered, therefore, whether this canon had not been considerably augmented and modified in Tukharistan itself. According to Louis de La Vallée Poussin,[175] it is now certain that Serindia—from the Pamir Mountains to the Great Wall and later China itself collaborated in the development of Buddhism. The story of Mañjuśrī is interesting. According to the Chinese pilgrim (I-tsing),[176] he dwells in China. He is represented in the miniatures of the Nepalese manuscripts as god worshipped in China and seems to have come from there to Nepal. Like the majority of Buddhist gods he is represented under various aspects

171. Eliot : Op. cit, III, p. 221.

172. Journal Asiatique (JA) 1912·1·p. 622; also Levi : *Le Nepal* pp. 330 ff.

173. Op. cit, III, p. 221.

174. Etudes de litterature Bouddhique, VIII. (Bulletin Ecolé France de l'extreme orient, VI (1906) 385, quoted in ERE. VIII, p. 4069.)

175. ERE. VIII, p. 4069.

176. *A Record of the Buddhist Religion*, trans. J. Takakusu, Oxford, 1896, p. 169.

—a Bodhisattva in the Mahāyāna or Great Vehicle and the principal 'exponent' of the Supreme Being in the 'Tantric Vehicle'. The cult of Mañjuśrī originating in India took a peculiar development in China. As a Tantric God, half a dozen Tantras (Kanjur) bear his name; among them is the List of the true Names of Mañjuśrī-Jnāña-sattva. Magical rituals are devoted to Mañjuśrī.[177]

The Bodhisattva Kṣitigarbha also receives similar treatment. He appears to be known but not very prominently in India in the fourth century A.D., but by the seventh century, if not earlier, his cult was flourishing in China and subsequently he became a popular deity second only to Kuan-yin in the Far East. This popularity, according to Eliot, was connected with his gradual transformation into a god of the dead. But it is uncertain if he was prominent first in Central Asia or in China. He was known as Ti-tsang in Chinese and as Jizo in Japanese. The devotion of the Chinese to their dead is suggestive of his great position among them. As a guide to the next world he has a parallel in a similar position with the Zoroastrian angel Srosh. Kṣitigarbha is always clearly distinguished by the shaven head of the monk and the barred or mottled mantle, the mendicant's garment. He has generally a flask in his left hand and elsewhere holds a more familiar emblem of the flaming jewel.[178] Kṣitigarbha was accepted by the Manichaeans as one of the 'Envoys of Light,[179] thereby suggesting impact or action of Buddhism on Manichaenism. Kṣitigarbha's paintings are interesting and important in respect of their iconography and artistic value. He stands as a possible rival to Avalokiteśvara in popularity among the Bodhisattvas of the Buddhist pantheon of the Far East. He is one of the Eight Great Bodhisattvas. Through innumerable incarnations he has been working for the salvation of living beings, and is especially honoured as the breaker of the power of hell. With his pilgrim's staff he strikes upon the doors of hell and opens them, and with the lustrous pearl that he carries he illuminates its darkness.[180] The Central Asian paintings from Tun-huang exhibit several aspects of his character. An analysis

177. ERE, Vol. VIII, p. 406.
178. Stein : *Serindia*, Vol. II, p. 364, n 16.
179. Eliot : Op. cit, p. 221, JA. 1911, II, p. 549.
180. Stein : *Serindia*, Op. cit, p. 965.

of the character of Central Asian paintings with references to thematic and stylistic aspects and the role of the Bodhisattvas and their maṇḍalas is reserved for consideration in another context in the chapter on Central Asian Art.

Central Asia was the earliest and, on the whole, the principal source of Chinese Buddhism. Reference has already been made to the Buddhist savants and monks who went eastwards from Central Asia to preach and translate the sacred scriptures into the language of the country. This aroused in the intellectual class a curiosity to proceed to the land of Buddha's origin—India—in search of truth and also to collect sacred texts which could be carried home for translation, thereby creating an atmosphere of Buddhism and Buddhist learning in China. Tibet and Mongolia, however, form independent areas of study of Buddhism, for synthesising local esoteric elements in Buddhism providing new colour as also in its expansion in the new form in areas coming under political influence of the Tibetans.

Tibetan Buddhism

The introduction of Buddhism[181] into Tibet is generally associated with the famous ruler of this land of snow-king Srong-tsan-gam-po, who ascended the throne in A.D. 629, a contemporary of king Harṣa and the Tang Emperor Tai-Tsung. The two queens of the Tibetan ruler—a Chinese princess and a Nepalese one were instrumental in persuading their husband to introduce Buddhism in Tibet as a necessary part of civilization.

181. The early history of Buddhism in Tibet is shrouded in nebulous legends. The missionaries sent by king Aśoka might have touched the Tibetan borders, but it is more than a hundred years later that there is legending account of the establishment of a Buddhist temple on the Tibetan side of the mountain range. This legend and the story of the miraculous descent of four caskets containing Buddhist treasures, in the fourth century A.D. might be suggestive of Tibet's contact with Buddhist mission. Definitive evidence for the introduction of Buddhism in Tibet is the 7th century in the time of Srong-btsan-Gam-po, who was married to a Chinese princess Wen-Ch'eng in A.D. 641. She brought with her Buddhist statues and books and probably some priests and, thus, established a firm footing for Buddhism in Tibet. The Nepalese princess, the ruler's second wife, was instrumental in introducing the occult worship of the Buddhico-Hinau goddess Tārā. This event determined to a great extent the nature of Buddhism destined to prevail in Tibet. (*Encyclopedia of Religion and Ethics*, (ERE), VIII, p. 702 a.)

The borrowing of the Tibetan alphabet from Indian Brāhmī, the fruition of the Sambhoṭa mission, are well-known. According to Eliot,[182] recent investigations, however, have advanced the theory that the Tibetan letters are derived from the alphabet of Indian origin used in Khotan and that Sambhoṭa made its acquaintance in Kashmir. The reign of Srong-tsan-gam-po and his two queens, regarded as the first patrons of Lamaism and worshipped as incarnations of Avalokita and Tārā, no doubt laid the foundation of Buddhism and civilization associated with it in Tibet. After his death in 650 there is little information about Buddhism here for some decades.

About 705 king Khri-gtsug-Ide-btsan took some interest in Buddhism, building a few monasteries, causing translations to be made and also inviting monks from Khotan, as recorded in the edict of 783 preserved in Lhasa. His zeal thus, paved the ground for further progress in Buddhism with the invitation extended to Padmasambhava by Khri-Sron-Ide-btsan and the arrival of this savant in Tibet.[183] This invitation seemed to have been extended at the instance of Saṅgharakṣita said to be the teacher of the ruler, though there was opposition by Chinese bonzes, while politically Tibetan influence had penetrated much beyond its natural frontiers with its predominance in the Tarim basin and rule over parts of Ssu-chvan and Yunnan; on the religious plane the Chinese influence consequent to the ruler's relation with that country was prominent. At this time Amogha,[184]

182. See Noernle MS *Remains found in E. Turkestan*, 1916, pp. xvii ff and Francke : EI.XI. pp. 266 ff; Contra see Laufer : JAOS. 1918, pp. 34 ff. According to Eliot, there is considerable difference between the printed and cursive forms of the Tibetan alphabet. He poses the question : Is it possible that they have different origins and that the former came from Bengal, the latter from Khotan ? According to F.W. Thomas, the mission of Sambhoṭa is made to precede the King's code of laws and his Nepal and Chinese marriages. The incentive to the acquisition of a script is said to follow the matrimonial alliance with Nepal which cannot be dated long after A.D. 634, while the king longed for a Chinese princess later on which materialised in 640. It was from Nepal that the Tibetan script was borrowed, since after the alliance with Nepal there was no need to go further in quest of a script. (*Festscriff Zur Feier des zoo jahriegen Bestchens der Akademie der Wissen Schaffen in Gottingen*, 1951, pp. 146 ff.)

183. See Waddel. JRAS, 1909, p. 931.

184. Amogha was a native of Ceylon (or, according to others, of Northern

a Ceylonese monk, was flourishing in China and he had introduced the Mahāyāna system or Chen-Yen in that country. This form of corrupt Buddhism was brought to Tibet where with its pliant nature amalgamated easily with local observance and demonolatry.

Padmākara or Padmasambhava, the Indian savant, belonged to then popular ritualistic and mystic yoga school at Nālandā, and he was skilled in Buddhist spells (*dhāraṇī*). Originally he was a native of Udyana (later known as Swat and Kafiristan) and he arrived in Tibet in 747 with several other Indian monks who were induced to settle in the country. Padmākara established the first monastery at Sam-yas in A.D. 749 on the left bank of the Brahmaputra river, about 30 miles to the south-east of Lhasa, and installed Śāntarakṣita[185] as its abbot, with seven Tibetan novices as the nucleus of the order. Padmasambhava 'the lotus-born' or 'the teacher treasure', the founder of the order of Buddhist monks in Tibet, was a believer in Tāntric mysticism with its prayers to various Buddhist gods and goddesses. While no

India) who arrived in China with his teacher Vajrabodhi. After the latter's death he revisited India and Ceylon in search of books and came back in 746. He wished to return to his own country, but was refused permission and so stayed in China until his death in 774. He received the title of *K'tsan* literally meaning 'wisdom-repository' which name is translated into *Prajñākośa.* According to Nanjio, he was allowed to go back to his own country in A.D. 749, but when he arrived at the South-sea district, he was ordered to stay in China by the Imperial command. In A.D. 756, he was called back to the capital. According to his version as recorded in his memorandum presented to the Emperor he translated 77 works. He died in 774 in his seventieth year, and received posthumous title of 'great-eloquence' correctwide-wisdom. He was held in high veneration at the court of successive sovereigns of the Than dynasty. (Nanjio : Op. cit, II, 155, pp. 444-447; Eitel : Op. cit, p. 8a; Eliot: Op. cit, pp. 39, 264, 327).

185. Śāntarakṣita, a native of Gaur, who was the High Priest of the monastery of Nālandā, was invited by king Thi-Srong-deu-tsang. He was received by the Tibetans with all the honour due to his position as the spiritual teacher of the king of Magadha and he was named Ācārya Bodhisattva. He was appointed as the High Priest of Tibet and under his direction, Buddhist monachism was introduced in Tibet. This came to be known as Lamaism. While Śāntaraksita attended to the moral and disciplinary part of the church, his eminent co-adjutor Padmasambhava, took charge of the Tantric part of the Buddhist liturgy. (S.C. Das : *Indian Pandits in the Land of Snow*, Calcutta (Reprint 1965), p. 51).

canonical translations are ascribed to him, he is the reputed author of several manuals of worship (*sādhanas*) and propitiation of deities by means of the repetition of spells (*dhāraṇī*) like the Brahmanical *mantras*. Padmākara or Padmasambhava[186] also initiated an era of great literary activity and scholarship with the translation of the Buddhist canon from Sanskrit. Several Tibetan scholars were sent to India to learn Sanskrit and Buddhist philosophy. These Tibetan translations of the Buddhist canonical texts preserve with remarkable accuracy the Indian texts, of which most of the originals have been lost in India.

The institution of the local order on these Indian lives was opposed by Chinese Buddhists in Tibet under a Mahāyāna monk named Hwa-shang (corresponding to Sanskrit *upādhyāya* or master). These Chinese, who were itinerant priests, moving from one place to another, were defeated in argument by the Indian Kamalaśīla and expelled from the country, leaving the Indian system to be developed undisturbed. Many monasteries and Buddhist temples were established all over the country and Buddhism became the state religion of the land. During the reign of Khri-Sron-Ide-btsan and the visit of Padmasambhava (which began in A.D. 747 according to the traditional chronology) the number of translations began to increase. Two works ascribed to the king and one to the Saint are included in the canon, but the most prolific writer and translator of the period was Kamalaśīla,[187] the hero of the intellectual bout between the

186. ERE.VIII, p. 745 a; Eliot : Op. cit, pp. 249 ff. Padmasambhava was one of the most celebrated exponents of Tantric Buddhism and in Tibet is often called simply the teacher (Guru or Mahācārya). His portraits represent him as a man of strongly marked and rather angry features, totally unlike a conventional monk. The account of his life, as read in Tibet, appears to be rather fantastic. Padmasambhava is not celibate but is accompanied by female companions. In Tibet where the older religion consisted of defensive warfare against the attacks of evil spirits, he assumes the character of a victorious exorcist, subduing demons. He preached a non-celibate and magical form of Buddhism, ready to amalgamate with local superstitions and needing new revelations for its justification. (Eliot : Op. cit, pp. 349-50)

187. Kamalaśīla, the great Buddhist philosopher of Magadha was invited to Tibet by king Khril-Sron-Ide-tsan at Śāntarakṣita's initiative to participate in the debate between the Indian Pandits and the Chinese *ho-shang*. After Kamalaśīla came to Tibet, a grand philosophical debate was organised between the Chinese priests and the followers of Śāntarakṣita with the ruler

Indian Pandits and the Chinese bonzes. Seventeen of the original works of this Buddhist savant from India are preserved in the *Tanjur* and he translated part of the Ratnakūṭa. This great period of translation commencing from the arrival of Padmākara, Padmasambhava with the active participation of Kamalaśīla and others is rightly called the Augustan age of Tibet. A solid foundation was laid by composing two dictionaries containing a collection of Sanskrit terms.

Padmasambhava was one of the greatest exponents of Tantric Buddhism and was known as the Guru or Mahācārya in Tibet. He is represented as a man of strongly marked and rather angry look, totally unlike a conventional monk. A popular account of his life is no doubt available and might contain some grains of truth, but it is difficult to account for the later events in his life. It is said that when he had finished his work in Tibet he vanished from there rather miraculously. His Interest in Tantric ideas was probably the result of his association with Bengal which was no doubt a centre of Tantrism. This took a more active and virulent form in Tibet where he is not only associated with female companions, but also assumes the character of a victorious exorcist against the attacks of evil spirits. Padmasambhava, therefore, preached a non-celibate and magical form of Buddhism[188] amalgamating local superstitions and needing new revelations

as the judge. Bu-Stan provides details of this debate. In the presence of the assembled court, Kamalaśīla came out victorious over the Chinese sage and was placed at the head of the metaphysical branch of the Buddhist church. Ho-shang, the Chinese contender in the debate was ordered to leave the country. (See, Das : Op. cit, pp. 51-52; Alaka Chattopadhyaya : *Atiṣa and Tibet*. Calcutta. 1967. pp. 228 ff.)

188. According to Waddel, there is no certain evidence regarding the character of his teaching. There is no certain evidence that it was of the flagrantly magical and necromantic type ascribed to him in the indigenous works on the subject, which are mostly late compositions of the 14th century onwards—when works of a similar nature were being issued by the Mahāyāna Buddhists in India ascribing precisely similar ritualistic spells to Buddha himself. From the high literary attainments of his contemporary pupils it seems probable that his teaching was more or less orthodox Indian Buddhism of the Mahāyāna type, and of the Middle Path School (*Mādhyamika*) to which he reputedly belonged, and that it afterwards became degraded in the hands of the converts from the indigenous Shamanistic Bar religion. (*Encyclopedia of Religion and Ethics* (ERE), Vol. IX, p. 591 a.)

for its justification. Reference has already been made to the monastery built by him at Samye and its abbot Śāntarakṣita, who is said to have laid the foundation of the order of Lamas. Samye became a great literary centre where many translations were made. A monk from Kasmir named Vairocana was one of the best translators.

The opposition to the new Buddhist order in Tibet both from the priests of the old native religion and also from Chinese Buddhists[189] might as well have accounted for the absence of Buddhist personal names and direct reference to Buddhism in Tibet in numerous Tibetan documents discovered in the Tarim basin. Buddhist priests (bon-da) are occasionally mentioned, but the title 'Lama' is not found. The writers of these documents no doubt seem to be familiar with the usages of the Bon-po religion and there are notices of religious struggles as well. This picture of Buddhism in Tibet from the time of Padmasambhava onwards could no doubt be visualised from the indigenous sources alone. When Padmasambhava vanished from Tibet, he left behind twenty-five disciples to propagate his teachings. They were no doubt sorcerers and the new religion flourished till the time of Ralpachan, the grandson of Khri-Sron-Ide-btsan. Monasteries multiplied with state endowments attached to them. They had the right to collect tithes and each monk was assigned a small revenue derived from five tenants. There was reorganization of the hierarchy.[190] Many translators were engaged in this period and a considerable part of the Buddhist canon was then rendered into Tibetan. The ruler's patronage of Buddhism, however, alienated disgruntled elements resulting in his murder[191] at the instigation of his brother

189. Numerous Tibetan documents discovered in the Tarim basin date from this period. The absence of Buddhist personal names in them as also the rarity of direct reference to Buddhism indicate that though known in Tibet, it was not yet prominent. Buddhist priests (ban-de) are occasionally mentioned but the title Lama has not been found. According to Eliot, the usages of the Bon-po religion seem familiar to the writers and there are allusions to religious struggles. (Eliot : Op. cit, p. 351. See also JRAS, 1914, pp. 37-59).

190. Rockhill : *Life of the Buddha*, p. 225.

191. Various dates are given for his death, ranging from 833 to 902 (Rockhill : Op. cit, p. 225; Bushell : JRAS, 1880, pp. 440). According to Eliot, the treaty of 82 was made in his reign (Op. cit, p. 351 n).

and successor Lang-dar-ma. He attempted to extirpate Lamaism by destroying monasteries, burning books and driving Indian monks out of Tibet. This process of persecution lasted for three years, finally leading to the murder of the anti-Buddhist king by a Lama. Political confusion, however, soon followed with the disintegration of the united kingdom, divided among clans and chieftains, and the collapse of Tibetan power in the Tarim basin. It is suggested that during this period of political turmoil and instability Buddhism had almost disappeared in Tibet, and the silence of ecclesiastical history during the tenth century confirms the gravity of the catastrophe. On the other hand, the preservation of translations made in the ninth century is suggestive of the existence and functioning of monasteries, for instance at Samye.

According to the chronicles,[192] foreign monks arrived in Tibet at the beginning of the eleventh century. This period of revival of Buddhist learning in Tibet is considered a separate or later one, *phyi-dar* in contrast to the earlier diffusion called *sna-dar*. The chief savants in the new diffusion were La-chen-Lo-chen, the royal Lama Yes'es and Atīṣa or Dīpaṅkara Śrījñāna. Lo-chen was from Kashmir which provided many other Lamas who were engaged in Tibet. The debased Tantrism passing on as Buddhism was instrumental in the despatch of young Lamas to India for instructions as also invitation to learned monks at centres of Buddhist learning. The initiative in this direction was taken by Yesesttod,[193] a king or chieftain of mNa-ris in Western Tibet. Atīṣa,[194] who came to Tibet under this programme was from Bengal, ordained at Odantapuri and studied in Burma or Suvarṇadvīpa. Subsequently he was appointed head of the monastery of Vikramaśilā. He stayed in Tibet for fifteen years. He reformed Tibetan Buddhism. With a view to introducing pure Buddhist monachism in Tibet, he selected intelligent lads,

192. Eliot : Op. cit, p. 352.

193. Lha Lama Yes'ehod, king of Tibet, was a devout Buddhist. He ruled peacefully for many years. About the year 1025 he founded the monastery of Thoding in Purang. (S.C. Das : *Indian Pandits in the Land of Snow*; Rep. 1965, p. 54)

194. For the Life of Dīpaṅkara Śrījñāna Atiśa, See Das : Op. cit, pp. 53ff; also Alaka Chattopadhyaya : *Atīṣa and Tibet*—Op. cit also *Encyclopedia of Religion and Ethics*, Vol. II, p. 1976.

each ten years old, and carefully trained them up in Tibetan and finally admitted them into the sacerdotal order with the consent of their parents. Not satisfied with the Buddhist teachers of Tibet, whose cults had become greatly debased by the admixture of Tantric and Bon mysticism, he sent these young monks to Kashmir and Magadha and other places of India. There pure Buddhism still prevailed, and they could study the philosophy of Ānanda Garbha of Kashmir and Vinaya code of monastic discipline. These young monks were also instructed to invite to Tibet, if possible, the renowned Kashmirian Pandit Ratnavajra and the Buddhist hierarch of Magadha and other holy men and savants. Out of the 21 Tibetan monks sent to India, Rinchhen Zan-po, the great Lochava and Leqspahi-Serab, were the only survivors who returned to Tibet after successfully completing their stay and study in India. The Lochavas had heard of Dīpaṅkara Śrījñāna who then occupied the highest position among the Buddhist scholars of Magadha. He was the second Sarvajña of the school of the 500 Arhats which was commonly called the Mahāsaṅghikas. On their report the king of Tibet ordered Rgya-tsar-gru-Senge to proceed to Vikramaśilā, with an invitation from him along with a large piece of bar gold as a present from the sovereign. The Indian Buddhist savant, however, refused to proceed to Tibet for quite some time. Lochava was sent again and he was finally successful in persuading the Vikramaśilā Abbot to visit Tibet in 1038. He remained there until his death fifteen years later. He introduced a new calendar[195] and inaugurated the second period of Tibetan Buddhism which is marked by the rise of successive sects in the form of reforms.

While stressing the importance of philosophical wisdom, Atiśa Dīpaṅkara felt that the most urgent task at that time in Tibet was that of moral reform—a *sine-qua-non* for any religion. He, therefore, laid great emphasis on moral reform in the *Bodhi-patha-pradīpa*. *Prajñā* or the highest wisdom, according to him, is that knowledge which is the realisation of the intrinsic nature

195. The Tibetan system of computing time is based on cycles of sixty years beginning in 1027, and not in 1026. In many dates there is an error of a year. Pelliot : JA, 1913.1. p. 633; Laufer : Toung Pao, 1913, p. 569; Eliot : Op. cit, 353 n.

of the void (*Svabhāva-śūnyatā*) of everything. He, however, insisted on establishing it on the secure basis of right conduct or *upāya*. Wisdom (*prajñā*) and right conduct (*upāya*) are indispensable to each other, and none can be ignored. He stressed on the supreme importance of moral conduct for a true Buddhist. He did not denounce Tantricism outright, but prescribed as preconditions of the Tantric initiations a correct insight into the real teachings of the Tantras, an extreme purity of moral conduct and correct guidance from an ideal teacher. He, therefore, concentrated on the reform of Tantric practices in Tibet. He retained the form of the Tantra but infused it with the content of classical Buddhism. His own knowledge of the Tantras was too imposing to be questioned even by the staunchest supporter of Tantrism. He was no doubt eager to preach in Tibet the Mahāyāna ideal of universal emancipation and the Mādhyamika philosophy called *Śūnya-vāda*.

Atiśa Dīpaṅkara introduced a new calendar and inaugurated the second period of Buddhism, with reforms introduced in the religion of the Tathāgata based on purity of conduct and moral disciplines, without wiping out completely the local influence based on superstitions and tantric rites. He professed the Kālacakra 'the wheel of death'. This symbolised the extreme Tantric phase introducing around the 10th century A.D., a rampant demonolatry with exacting priestly rites into a religion which in its origin was largely a protest against worship and ritual of every kind.[196] According to Eliot,[197] the Kālacakra tantra was introduced in 965 A.D. from Sambhala, a mysterious country in Central Asia. This system is said to be Vaiṣṇavite rather than Śaivite. It especially patronizes the cult of the mystic Buddhas such as Kālacakra and Heruka, all of whom appear to be regarded as forms of Ādi-Buddha or the primordial Buddha essence. Waddel however, presumes[198] that

196. *Encyclopedia of Religion and Ethics* (ERE), Vol. IV, p. 5926.

197. Op. cit, p. 386. In Tibetan the Kālacakra is known as Dus-Kyi-hkhor-lo and in Mongol Tsagun-Kurdun. It is also equated with Vajrayāṇa. According to Eliot, the system has some connection with the Turkish cycle of twelve animals used for expressing dates. (See Laufer : *Toung Pao*, 1907, p. 402).

198. ERE. IV. p. 5926.

the majority of these demons were monstrous 'king devils' of the most hideous Śaivite type with their equally repulsive spouses. The chief were Vajra-bhairava, Saṁvara, Hayagrīva and Gūhyakata. Their function was to be tutelaries (*Yidam*) to guard their human votary against the attacks of minor demons, while they acted as beneficiaries of their votaries. Some of them were also selected as defenders of the faith (*dharmapāla*) and also as guardians of particular monasteries and sects. The Kālacakra is described as the latest and most corrupt form of Indian Buddhism, but it was doubtless superior in discipline and coherency to the native superstitions mixed with debased tantrism which it replaced.

The great fame acquired by Dīpaṅkara in Tibet was due to several external factors, besides his personal scholarship and erudition. These include the patronage extended to him by the highly enlightened ruling family of Western Tibet, followed by his extensive tour of Tibet inspiring the nobles of the country and fostering a revival of Buddhism, as also his confrontation with Rin-chen-pzan-po,[199] the great Tantric scholar, much too senior to him. He humbled the pride of his adversary and thereby established his scholastic supremacy. His composition of the *Bodhi-patha-pradīpa* proved crucial not only for his successful career in Tibet, but also for the subsequent history of Tibetan Buddhism. This work, though extremely brief, consisting of only thirty-six verses, its impact on Tibetan Buddhism was all the more great. It contains in brief the essence of the whole *sūtras* and *tantras* paving the way for the spread of Buddhism. This was followed by another big work called *Bodhi-mārga-pradīpa-pañjikā*—the author's commentary on his previous one. The original was intended to be a manifesto of Buddhist reform in Tibet.

Atīṣa Dīpaṅkara's stay in Tibet was equally responsible for the assemblage of monks at a grand convocation and learned

199. Rin-Chen-bzan-po is said to be the first Tibetan scholar of Buddhism in the real sense. At the age of thirteen he was ordained by the Upādhyāya Ye-Ses-bzan-po. As a youngman he went to Kashmir and there studied numerous treatises in the Mantrayāṇa. His great fame as a scholar rested primarily on his knowledge of the Tantras and none could match him in scholarship. When Atiśa arrived in Tibet, this scholar was in his eighty-fifth year. (Alaka Chattopadhyaya : Op. cit, pp. 339 ff.)

translations of Sanskrit works into Tibetan as also for setting up of substantial structures to house monastic communities. The translators included Ssan-Kaar-Lochava, Rva-Lochava, Nau-Lochou, Lodan Serab, etc. The sage Marpa, Mila-Gonpo, and the famous Pandit Śākya Śrī of Kashmir, besides many other Indian Pandits were exponents of Buddhism in the following century. The monasteries became the largest and safest buildings in the land, possessing the strength of walls and inviolability. The most important was the Śākya monastery which had abbots of royal blood but not celibate. This monastery received royal benefactions. In the reign of Tagpa-de, the ninth in descent from Tse-de, an image of Maitreya Buddha costing 12000 Bot-shad or a million and half of rupees was set up.[200] He also got an image of Mañjuśrī made with seven *bre*—a measure equal to a tenth fraction of the English bushel—made. His son Asode, a greater Buddhist than himself, annually sent offerings and presents to the Vajrāsana at Bodh-Gaya (Dorje-dan) which was continued even after his death. His grandson Ananmal prepared a complete set of the Kangyur, written on golden tablets. His son in turn put the golden dome over the great temple of Buddha at Lhasa and set up the image of the God at an immense cost. The latter's grandson was initiated into Buddhism by the Sakyapa Lamas and subsequently became king. This dynasty of ecclesiastical statesmen practically ruled Tibet at a critical period marked by the conquests of Chingiz Khan and the rise of the Mongol Empire.

Buddhism in Mongolia and Tibet

There is no evidence that Chingiz favoured Buddhism in a special way. He believed in one king and one God, and thought of religions not as incompatible systems but as different methods of worship with their prayers in different languages. While there is no proof of the early Mongols invading or conquering Central Tibet, it is known that Kublai subdued the eastern provinces and through the Lamaist hierarchy established special relations between his dynasty and Tibet. This relationship began in the time of his predecessor with the summoning of the head Lama of the Śākya monastery—commonly called Śākya Pandit

200. S.C. Das : JRASB. 1881. p. 238.

or Sa-Skya-pan-cen to the Mongol Court in 1246-8; and he cured the Emperor of an illness. The favourable impression created by this great Lama—a man of great learning and influence—no doubt facilitated the achievements of his nephew and successor known as Bashpa or Paqspa. The Mongol Court already favourably impressed by Tibetan Lamas, became interested in Buddhism. The Emperor had a feeling that the intellectual calibre of the Mongols and the Tibetan was identical and it was politically easy as also expedient to conciliate the uncanny spiritual potentates ruling in a land which was no doubt difficult to conquer. He, therefore, summoned the abbot of Sakya to China in 1261 and was initiated by him into the mysteries of Lamaism. The role of Paqspa in this context is recorded by the Mongol historian Sanang Setsen,[201] while there are certain traditional accounts as well which suggest a greater degree of Śaivism incorporated in the religion first taught to the Mongols.

It is said that before Paqspa's birth the god Gaṇeśa had an eye on the land of Tibet and he helped Paqspa at the Chinese court with Mahākāla helping him with mystery which he imported to Kublai. It is called Hevajravasita—a magical formula which compels the obedience of spirits or natural forces. It is associated with Hevajra—the same as Heruka—conceived as manifestations of Buddhas and Bodhisattvas, made for a special purpose and closely corresponding to the manifestations of Śiva. Paqspa received the title of 'Kuo-Shib' or 'instructor of the nation' and was made the head of all Buddhists, Lamaists and others. He was recognised as the head of the Church in Tibet, and a tributary ruler with a lay council to assist him in the government run through three heads of provinces.

Paqspa was also charged by the emperor to provide the Mongols with an alphabet[202] as well as a religion. He used a square

201. See Schmidt : *Mongol History of Senong Setsen*—quoted by Eliot : Op. cit, p. 355. Paqspa or Bashpa—a title equivalent to Ārya in Sanskrit, was the nephew and successor of Śākya-Pandit (or Sa-Skya-pan-cen). He made great achievements in Mongolia.

202. The Mongolian alphabet was received from the Uigurs, a Turki people, in the 13th century. The latter took it from the Sogdians, an Iranian people. The Sogdian alphabet was an adaptation of a Semetic alphabet

form of the Tibetan letters written not in horizontal but in vertical lines. This experiment of introducing Tibetan script fell into disuse and was replaced later on after Paqspa's death by an enlarged and modified form of the Uighur alphabet. This was already employed by Śākya-Paṇḍita for writing Mongol. Its definitive form for that purpose was elaborated by the Lama Chos-Kyi-hod-zer in the time of Kublai's successor.

This alphabet, supposed to be of Aramaic origin had already been utilized by Buddhists for writing religious works. Its application to Mongol is supposed to be merely an extension of its general currency in Asia. Paqspa also supervised the preparation of a new edition of the Tripiṭaka in Chinese, not in Mongol; and its learned editors were scholars well-up in Sanskrit, Chinese, Tibetan and Uighur. This comprehensive work also records references to Chinese texts in Tibetan, wherever available. The Tibetan influence also extended in the field of fine arts and appointed a Lama called Aniko, skilled in both sculpture and painting as the head of the bureau of fine arts.[203] The direct influence of Lamaism in Mongolia through parts of northern China, however, seemed superficial and temporary. It appears that the first growth of Mongolian Buddhism as part of a political system died down with the end of the Yuan dynasty.[204] The Strong Lamaist influence was partly, if not wholly, responsible for this political debacle. The subservience to the clergy and extravagant expenditure on religious buildings and ceremonies depleted the royal chest. The role of the later Lamas after the departure of Paqspa, holding a high position at the Peking Court and exercising considerable influence might as well have added to the political malaise. Chos-kyi-hod-zer and Gyun-ston-rdo-rje-

---

(Aramaic). The Mongolian alphabet was written vertically downward. (*Encyclopedia Britannica*, Chicago, 1972, Vol. XV, p. 734.)

203. Eliot : Op. cit, p. 356.

204. The fall of the Mongol empire in China in 1368 led to the weakening of the Tibetan Buddhist faith throughout Mongolia. The old popular religion of Shamanism gained ground again and Taoist beliefs spread to Mongolia. The reformed version of Tibetan Buddhism, the Geng-pa was introduced by Neyica toyin (1557-1653)—the first Buddhist missionary to eastern Mongols, and the first Jaya Pandit (1599-1662)—the two most prominent representatives of the new west Mongolian Buddhism.(*Encyclopedia Britannica*: Op. cit, XV, p. 730 a.)

dpal were two such figures. The latter was a great exponent of the Kālacakra system and also the teacher of the great historian Bu-ston who is said to have arranged the Tibetan canon.

Despite royal favours heaped upon priests and monasteries, Buddhism does not appear to have flourished in Tibet during the fourteenth century. From 1270 to 1340 the abbots of Śākya were rulers of both church and state. All the abbots were appointed or invested by the Emperor and their power declined with the Yuan dynasty. Mutual conflicts were not unknown. In 1320 the Śākya abbots burnt the rival monastery of Dikung; but in due course other monasteries increased in importance and a chief known as Phagmodu succeeded after many years of fighting in founding a lay dynasty which ruled over parts of Tibet until the 17th century.

The Ming dynasty supplanting the Yuan in 1368 was not pro-Buddhist. Its rulers had no preference for Lamaism but were equally anxious to maintain good relations with Tibet treating it a friendly but vassal state. They recognised the dynasty of Phagmodu and also the abbots of eight monasteries, of course with and implication of suzerainty. The primacy of the Śākya monastery, at one time a reality, was reduced to only one among several great monasteries. The advent of the Ming dynasty also coincided with the birth of the reform movement leader Tsong-Kha-pa in the district of Amdo on the western frontiers of the Chinese province of Kansu. He absorbed instructions from many teachers and as a youth went to Tibet where he studied at Śākya, Dikung and finally at Lhasa. Noticing the discrepancy between Lamaism in theory and in practice, he decided to undertake the work of reform, which became visible in the Geluga—the sect presided over by the Grand Lama. It acquired paramount importance in both ecclesiastical and secular matter and came to be known as the 'Established Church of Tibet,' also conveniently called the Yellow Church.

Tsong-Kha-pa's reforms were on two lines. Firstly, he stressed on strict monastic discipline, insisting on celibacy and frequent services of prayer; secondly he greatly reduced the Tantric and magical elements in Lamaism. An effective organization was set up to perpetuate these principles. The great monastery of Gandan near Lhasa was set up by him and he became its first abbot. Three others at Sera and Depung near Lhasa and Tashilhunpo were also set up in his life time. Tsong-kha-pa[205] seems to have ruled by virtue of his personal authority, and after his death in 1417 his nephew and successor Geden-dub claimed the said right. The Lamas had gained considerable prestige and the Ming Emperors utilized their position for gaining political influence in Tibet. The Kanjur was printed in China in 1410.

The ecclesiastical and political hierarchy was vested in the Grand Lama, the abbot of the Tashil-hun-po monastery, residing at Lhasa. The theory of successive incarnations which is the characteristic of Lamaism was developed and defined. Two ideas were combined in it—the first being the appearance of divine persons in human form, and secondly the real continuity of life in a school, sect or church. Accordingly, a great teacher is reborn in the successive occupants of his chair. The hereditary soul is identified with a Buddha or Bodhisattva, as in the great incarnations of Lhasa and Tashilhunpo. These incarnations are not confined to the great Lamas of Tibet. The heads of most large monasteries in Mongolia also claim to be living Buddha. A long record of the Lamas of Tibet need not be mentioned here, but reference might be made to their association with the Mongols in ecclesiastical and political matters.

The Mongols were no doubt converted to Buddhism when their capital was at Peking and mainly affected these Mongols residing in China. When the Yuan dynasty was dethroned with the Mongols driven back to wild regions, they relapsed into their original superstitions and beliefs. About 1570 Altan Khagan, the powerful chief of the Tumed became acquainted with Tibet through some Lamas captured in a border fray and taken to his court. He thought it politically expedient to invite the Grand Lama to his court.[206] The Lama set out on his travels with great pomp and

205. Tsau-Kha-pa, the founder of the Dge-lugs-pa sect, was in fact the same (i.e. the incarnation of) Jo-bo-rje (Atīśā). In the eyes of the common people he appeared to receive the *upadeśa* or *mārgākraṇa* of the bka-gdams from mahāupādhyāya Nam-kha-rgyal-mutshan and Chos-skyabs-bzan-po. He removed the dirt of doubt and distortions and made changes in Jo-bo's *upadeśa* in course of time. (Alaka Chattopadhyaya : *Op. cit*, p. 12).

206. The visits of the third Dalai Lama in 1557 to Tumed and Ordos and in 1587 to the Kharatsin tribe led to the mass conversion of these Mongol

appeared to the bewildered Mongols in the guise of Avalokita with four arms and the imprint of his horse's hoofs showed the six mystic syllable *om mani padme hum.* A great congregation was held near Lake Kokonor. The Lama bestowed on the Khagan high sounding titles and himself received the epithet 'Dalai' or 'Talai', the Mongol word for 'sea', signifying vast extent and profundity. This is the origin of the name Dalai Lama. The hierarchy was divided into four classes corresponding to four ranks of Mongol nobles. The use of meat was restricted and the custom of killing men and horses at funerals forbidden. The observance of Buddhist festivals was madecompulsory, and native gods were more or less assimilated in the new pantheon. The Grand Lama specially recommended to the Mongols the worship of the Blue Mahākāla, a six-armed representation of Śiva standing on a figure of Gaṇeśa. He left with the Mongols a priest who was considered an incarnation of Mañjuśrī, and a temple and monastery were built for him in Kuku-Khota. The Grand Lama returned to Tibet but made a second trip to Mongolia after the death of Altan Khagan in 1583, to ensure allegiance of the new chiefs. He also received an embassy from the Chinese Emperor Wan-li as also the honorific titles similar to those received earlier by Pagspa from Kublai. This move was politically motivated to neutralise the Tibetan-Mongolian alliance.

This Grand Lama died at the age of forty-seven and was born in the Mongol royal house, as a great-grandson of Altan Khagan. Till the age of 14 he lived in Mongolia and then moved to Lhasa. A Lama was appointed as his Vicar and Pruniate of all Mongolia with residence at Kuren or Ugra. About this time the Emperor of China issued a decree that these hierarchies must be reborn in Tibet and not reappear in a Mongol family for fear of too close unionism of religion and patriotism. The church of Lhasa became

---

tribes. The old popular religion of Shamanism was suppressed, its ideas being incorporated in the doctrine of popular Buddhism. The foundation of many Buddhist monasteries; the conversion of many members of the Mongol nobility to religion and their entry into the monastic life; the formation of an educated class able to read and write and to translate into Mongol from Tibetan and Sanskrit; and the translation of religious works into Mongol and the subsequent creation of a written secular literature in the Mongolian language are the peculiar features of this period. (*Encyclopedia Britannica*, 1972, Vol. XV, p. 731 a.)

a powerful religious and political force with the ascending influence of the Grand or Dalai Lama. Lozang, the fifth Grand Lama, established his temporal and ecclesiastical sovereignty over Tibet. He built the Potala and his dealings with the Mongols and the Emperor of China are of considerable importance for political relations with the neighbouring states. China was equally anxious to enter into friendly relations with Tibet with a view to contain Mongol pressure on its borders. Their negotiations finally culminated in the visit of Lo-Zang to Peking in 1652-3 and he was treated as an independent sovereign and received from a long title contained in the phrase 'Self-existent Buddha', 'Universal Ruler of the Buddhist faith'. The later history of Tibet—ecclesiastical and political—is modern and could be studied in the contemporary context. One need, however, take fuller notice of canons connected with Lamaism as also the different sects of Buddhist groups.

Lamaism is defined as a mixture of late Indian Buddhism which itself is a mixture of Buddhism and Hinduism—with various Tibeton practices and beliefs. These include, in the main, demonophobia and the worship of human beings as incarnate deities. Religion and magic are expected to protect against fierce and terrible spirits in the atmosphere. Even benevolent deities assume a terrible form in order to strike fear into evil spirits and keep them away. The worship of incarnate deities common in eastern Asia acquires a new dimension and extent in Tibet. An ancient inscription[207] applies to the kings of Tibet the word *hphrul* meaning the transformation of a deity in a human form. This term was applicable to the Grand Lamas and the Yellow Church officially recognized the Emperor of China as an incarnation of Mañjuśrī. India provided terrible deities, like Kālī and her attendant fiends, and also the concept of divine incarnation in human form. It is, therefore, proposed that Tibetan Buddhism is not so much as amalgam, as a phase of medieval Hindu religion disproportionately developed in some directions, with the Lamas acquiring the same status as the Brahmanas serving as intermediaries between gods and men. In Tibet Buddhism acquired more life and character than it had in Bengal. The native

207. Waddell : JRAS, 1909, p. 941; Eliot : Op. cit, p. 383.

character had something monstrous and fantastic with features similar to the oldest form of Tibetan religion called Bon or Pan. Books and images introduced from India did not assume any national character prior to 747. The arrival of Padmasambhava in that year marks the first phase of Lamaism. The Nying-ma-pa or old school claims to represent his teaching. He brought with him the late form of Indian Buddhism called Mantrayāna, closely allied to the Chen-Yen of China, and transported to Japan under the name of Shingon and also to Java. Padmasambhava's teachings included toleration and incorporation of local cults, free use of spells (*dhāraṇī*) and magical figures (*maṇḍalas*) for subduing demons and acquiring supernatural powers, the belief in assuming divine form through such methods. The worship of Amitābha, among other deities, and a belief in his paradise, presentation of offerings and the performance of sacrifices on behalf of the departed souls and finally the worship of departed and perhaps of living teachers. According to Grünwedel,[208] the later corruptions of Buddhism in northern India, Tibet and Central Asia are connected with the personage known as the eighty-four Mahāsiddhas or great magicians.

The next phase of Buddhist activity in Tibet with the visit of Atiśa in the eleventh century A.D. and some others, is associated with the Kālacakra system also known as the Vajrayāna. While a legend[209] credits the Śākyamuni promulgating this system in Orissa (*Dhānya-Kaṭaka*) and that Sucandra, king of Sambhala, writing the Kālacakratantra in a prophetic spirit, Tibetan authorities state its introduction in Nālandā by a Pandit called Tsilu or Chilo. It was accepted by Narotapa, then the head of the University and from there it spread to Tibet. Its promulgation is also ascribed to a personage called Siddha Pito. Since it means Islam and Mohammad it is perhaps connected, according to Eliot,[210] with anti-Mohammadan movement which looked to Kalki,[211] the future incarnation of Viṣṇu as their Messiah. The mythology of this school is Viṣṇuite, not Śaivite. It may as well

208. *Mythologic des Buddhismus*, p. 40; Eliot : Op. cit, p. 385.

209. JASB, 1882, p. 225, quoted by Eliot Op. cit, p. 386.

210. Eliot : Op. cit, p. 387.

211. See Kalkipurāṇa; Viṣṇupurāṇa IV. XXIV; Bhag. Purāṇa XII. ii. 18; Eliot · ibid.

be mentioned that the Pañcarātra system which had some connection with Kashmir, lays stress on the wheel or discus (*cakra* or *sudarśana*) of Viṣṇu, which is said to be the support of the universe and the manifestation of creative will. The Kālacakra is mentioned as a special form of this cosmic wheel having six spokes. The Buddhist Kālacakra stresses on an Ādi-Buddha or primordial Buddha God from whom all other Buddhas are derived. Under the influence of Kālacakra the Lamas did not worship one Supreme God but they identified with the Ādi-Buddha some particular deity, like Sāmantabhadra, who usually ranks as a Bodhisattva. It also adopted all the extravagances of the Tantras and provided the principal Buddhas and Bodhisattvas with spouses, including one for the Adi-Buddha himself.[212]

In the last phase of reformation Tsong-Kha-pa disciplined the priesthood and enabled the heads of the Church to rule Tibet. It no doubt imported new ideas but emphasised the worship of Avalokita as the patron of Tibet and systematized the existing beliefs about reincarnation. It created a powerful hierarchy and restricted Tantrism without abolishing it. The Tibetans also elongated the number of deities from the Nepalese Buddhist original pantheon. A single deity was represented in many forms and aspects for purposes of art and popular worship. The adoration of saints and their images is also more developed than in Nepal. The later doctrines of Indian Mahāyānism are naturally prominent. The three bodies of the Buddha are well-known and also the series of fine celestial Buddhas with corresponding Bodhisattvas and other manifestations. In fact, Lamaism[213] accepted the whole host of Indian Buddhas and Bodhisattvas with additions of its own. Among the Buddhas those most worshipped are Amitābha, Śākya and Bhaiṣajyaguru or the Buddha of Healing ; among the Bodhisattvas the popular ones are Avalokita, Maitreya and Mañjuśrī. The peculiarities of Tibetan Buddhism lie in the Tantric phase which is eschewed

212. Waddell : *Buddhism*, p. 131.

213. For a comprehensive study of Lamaism, see the Bibliography provided in L.A. Waddell's article on the subject in the *Encyclopedia of Religion and Ethics*, Vol. VII, pp. 784 ff. See also Eliot : *Hinduism and Buddhism*, Vol. III, Chapter LII relating to the Doctrines of Lamaism, pp. 382, ff.

elsewhere. All the deities turning familiar spirits are coerced by spells. Great prominence is given to goddesses either as the counterparts of male deities or as independent. These deities appear in various forms—as mild, angry or fiendish and even the benevolent ones are not immune from furious frenzy. The tutelary deities of individuals are called Yi-dam like the Iṣṭa-devatās of the Hindus. The most efficacious tutelaries are tantric forms of the Dhyānī Buddhas, especially Vajrasattva, Vajra-dhara and Amitāyus.

Another class of tutelaries consists of the so-called Buddhas, accompanied by Śaktis and are terrific in form. Some of them such as Mahākāla and Saṁvara seem to reveal their identity from their name while there are others like Hevajra, Buddha-kapāla and Yāmantaka who have grotesque features. Several of these are well-known figures in Hindu mythology. Hayagrīva, the horse-necked god, appears to be connected with Víṣṇu rather than Śiva. The Mongols regard him as the protector of horses. Other gods include Yama, the Indian god of the dead, Mahā-kāla, the form of Śiva who inspired Paqspa to convert Kublai Khan, Lha-mo the goddess Devī the spouse of Śiva and Cam-Sran, a war god, a Tibetan form of Kārttikeya. Other deities frequently included in this group are Yāmantaka, Kubera or Vaiśravaṇa, and a deity called white Brahmā (Thsangs-pa-akarpo). The Lamaist books mention numerous other Indian divinities such as Brahmā, the thirtythree Devas, the kings of the four quarters etc. as also Nāgas, Yakṣas and Rākṣasas, rather a part of the old folklore of Tibet. The great goddess Tārā is described in Lamaist theology as the spouse of Avalokita. Originally benevolent and depicted with the attributes of Lakṣmī she is transformed into various terrible shapes.[214] Twentyone Tārās are often enumerated. Amongst them the Green Tārā is

214. Tārā is a goddess of India, Nepal and the Lamaist Church and almost unknown in China and Japan. Tārā means 'a star' as also 'she who causes to cross', that is who saves life and its troubles. It is not known if the name was first used by Buddhists or Brāhmaṇas but after the seventh century, there was a tendency to give Tārā the epithets bestowed on the Śaktis of Śiva and assimilate her to these goddesses. Thus, in the list of her 108 names she is described among other more amiable attributes as terrible, furious, the slayer of evil beings, the destroyer and Kālī. (Eliot : Op. cit, Vol. II, 18-19)

the commonest form in Tibet while the White Tārā is the favourite of the Mongols. The goddess Mārīcī is often depicted with Tārā.

Reference might as well be made to the use of praying wheels and the famous formula *Om mani padme hum.*[215] The origin of both seems obscure. They were unknown in India. The total absence of praying wheel in India as well as in the ruined cities of Central Asia negates their origin or association with both these places. The praying formula appears to be a Dhāraṇī and seems to have come to Tibet with the first introduction of Buddhism. The first and last words are mystic syllable *Mani Padme* which are generally interpreted to mean the jewel in the lotus. The formula was originally an invocation of the Śakti under the title of Manipadma, although it is considered by the Tibetans as an address to Avalokita. It is even suggested that its prominence might be due to Manichaean influence, but in the absence of the formula being in use in the Tarim basin, this suggestion is negatived.

There is no reference to sects[216] in Tibetan Buddhism prior to Lang-darma's[217] persecution in the 9th century nor till more than a century and a half later. The sectarian movement seems to coincide with the visit of the great Indian Buddhist monk Atīśa in 1038. Atīśa while clinging to Yoga and theistic Tantri-

215. Many scholars think that the formula *Om maṇipadme huṁ*, which is supposed to be addressed to Avalokita, is readily an invocation to a form of Śakti called Maṇipadma. (Eliot : op. cit, Vol. II, p. 17 n, cf. ERE, Vol. II, p. 260 and JA. IX. 192). Waddell quotes a similar spell known in both Tibet and Japan, but addressed to Vairocana *Om Amogha-Vairocanamahāmudrā maṇipadma-jvalapravarthtayā huṁ*—Buddhism, Op. cit, p. 149; Eliot : Op. cit, p. 395 n.

216. For a study of sects in Tibetan Buddhism, see *Encyclopedia of Religion and Ethics*, Vol. VII, pp. 787-788; also Eliot Op. cit, Vol. III, chapter LIII on 'Sects' in Tibetan Buddhism pp. 397 ff.

217. The last and perhaps the worst of Tibetan monarchs, Landarma, commenced his reign by persecuting the Buddhist whom he considered his mortal enemies. He was joined in his wicked plans of persecution by his prime minister Batagna (Sbas-Stag-Sans). He reviled the first Chinese princess, wife of king Sron-tsan-Gampo as an evil goblin (a Yakṣinī) who had brought the image of Śākya Muni into Tibet. It was for that inauspicious image that the Tibetan kings were short-lived. The country was infested with maladies and often visited by famines and wars. (Das : JASB, 1881, p. 229).

cism, at once started a reformation movement on the lines of the higher Indian Mahāyānism enforcing celibacy and high standard of morality and denouncing the Bon rites which had crept into some of the priestly practices of the Buddhist monks. Atīśa identified himself with the Ka-dan or 'those bounded by the orders'. This sect three and a half centuries later in Tsong-Kha-pa's hands became less ascetic and more ritualistic under the title of Ge-lug or 'Virtuous Order', the Yellow Hals.[218] While Atīśa or the 'Lord' (Jo-bo-rje) was the great reformer of Tibetan Buddhism, other parallel reformations were initiated by his pupils. These were Kar-gyu and Sas-kya sects which were directly based upon Atīśa's teaching to a great extent. These two sects may be considered as less austere in their stress on morality and discipline.

The remaining members of the Buddhist Church, bereft of the best and most intellectual members, were called the 'Old' or Nying-ma, still adhering to the old corrupt practices. These Nying-ma Lamas began to discover hidden revelations (ter-ma), or fictitious gospels, ascribed to Guru Padmākara, authorising these practices. The revelations treat mainly of Bon rites and they prescribe forms of worship mostly of the Buddhist model.These gospels formed the starting point for further sub-division of the semi-reformed and the old unreformed sects. The distinctions between the various sects are partly theistic and partly ritualistic. None of them relate to the personality or doctrine of the historical Buddha as is totally accepted by all. The differences are confined to the personality and title of the primordial deity or Ādibuddha, special source of divine inspiration and the transmitters, meditative system of mystical insight, special *tantra*-revelation, personal tutelary (yi-dam) or Śaivite Indian protective demon and the guardian demon Dharmapāla, sometimes of the Tibetan type.

The Ge-lug or dominant yellow Hats have as their primordial deity Vajradhara (holder of the thunderbolt) and they derive their divine inspiration from Maitreya, the next coming Buddha, as revealed through the succession of Indian saints from Aśaṅga down to Atīśa, and then through the Tibetan saints Bronton,

218. Waddell : ERE, Vol. VII, p. 787.

Atīśa's pupil downwards to Tsong-nha-pa. Their tutelary Indian demon (Yi-dam) is the fearful thunderbolt (Vajrabhairava)—Tib Dorje-jig-je, supported by Saṁvara and Gūhyakāla; and their guardian demon (Dharmapāla) is the six-armed lord (Gon-po) or the horse-necked (*Hayagrīva*— Tib-Tam-ch'en) both of them Indian. The yellow-robe Lamas carried a begging bowl which was soon dropped out of use. The 'yellow Hat' distinguished them from the other sects who wore red hats in sharp contrast to the black caps of the Bon priests.

The next sect Kar-gyu[219] was founded in the later half of the 11th century by the Tibetan monk Mar-pa who had visited India. Its distinct features are its hermitage, practice of meditation in caves and other solitary places, and certain other peculiarities. Its primordial Buddha is also Vajradhara and its tutelary Saṁvara. Its mystical insight is Mahāmudrā (pyag-rgya-chen) of the Middle Path, its Tantra Sun-Kar-bsdus, its guardian 'the lord of the black cloak (Bar-bag)', its hat has a frontal badge, to symbolise that meditation with crossed knees is its special feature. With these is associated a stricter observance of the Indian monastic rules. The strict hermit features rendered it rather unattractive and several sub-sects arose out of it which dispensed with the necessity of hermitages.

The third great reformed sect is the Sas-Kiya[220] or Sa-Kya, named after the monastery of that place, founded in A.D. 1071. It became under imperial Chinese patronage the first great hierarchy in Tibet and in 1251 attained for a time the temporal sovereignty, until eclipsed by its later rival, the Ge-lug sect. Its special source of inspiration is the Bodhisattva Mañjuśrī, through the Indian saints from Nāgārjuna to Vasuputra (Vasubandhu). Its mystic insight is the deep path (*gambhīra-darśana*), its tutelary Vajra-phurpa, and its guardians are 'the tent-lord' and 'the presence-lord' (Gon-po-Zhab). The Śākya sect connected with the great monastery of the same name had acquired great political importance from 1270 to 1340 with its abbots as the rulers of Tibet. The historian Tārānātha belonged to one of its sub-sects and about 1600 settled in Mongolia with a monastery

219. ibid, p. 788.
220. ibid.

founded at Ugra. The main distinction is between the Gelugpa or yellow Church and all other sects. The use of the yellow cap and the veneration paid to Tsong-Kha-pa's image are its external manifestations.

As Buddhism was carried from Tibet to Mongolia, there seems no difference between Tibetan and Mongolian Lamaism in deities, doctrines or observances.[221] Mongolian Lamas imitate the usages of Tibet, study there when they can and recite their services in Tibetan, although they have translations of their scriptures in their own language. It is proposed by some scholars that Lamaism was equally responsible for the political and military decadence of the Mongols with the substitution of priestly for warlike ideals. There may be many other factors for this decadence. An analogy could be cited of other tribes like the Turks and Tartars equally dissipating and collapsing. The role of religion in this direction could be only marginal. The Mongols were not only interested in Buddhism, as they continue to be, they are equally anxious to frequently use Sanskrit words, such as Mañjuśrī or slightly modified forms such as a Dara, Maidari (Tārā, Maitreya) as pointed out by Eliot.

In a long review of the history of the expansion of Buddhism in Central Asia, one is likely to come across certain interesting features. Different areas of this vast region received the message of the Tathāgata in different periods, and, of course, through manifold channels—emissaries, scholars and the trading class. The zeal and curiosity of the native elements was also a contributory factor to the expansion of Buddhism in those areas of Central Asia. A regional study of Buddhist activity in these parts with particular reference to the monastic establishment, schools, scholars and their contributions in the translation of Buddhist sacred texts has, no doubt, been attempted. With the western region comprising Afghanistan, Bactria and Parthia, the Central one including the present Russsian Turkestan, and the Eastern one assimilating both the northern and southern wings of Chinese Turkestan, and Tibet at the one end and Mongolia at the other, the stage of Buddhist activities was set for a proper

221. Eliot : Op. cit, p. 401.

display of this religion as also for a fuller projection of the personalities of the actors. The centres of Buddhist learning in Kashmir as also in Afghanistan acted as feeders of Buddhist monks and missionaries, and similar ones at Nālandā with Vikramaśilā and their eminent savants equally contributed towards the expansion of Buddhism in Tibet and through it in Mongolia.

The history of Buddhism in the western region of Central Asia might be dated from the time of the Indo-Bactrians, though the teachings of the Lord might have found their way there even earlier. In this context the Kandahar bilingual edict of Aśoka is considered as an eloquent testimony to the extension of Buddhism in the direction of Central Asia. The progress of Buddhism to the north of Afghanistan is also evident from a Kharoṣṭhī inscription on a clay object recording a Buddhist name. It is from the first layer of the Begram excavations dated between the third and second centuries B.C. Further, the association of Demetrius and Menander with Buddhism is well-known, as also the contribution of the Kuṣāṇa ruler Kaniṣka. In his time the famous scholar Ghoṣaka, born in Tokharistan, played a prominent role in the deliberation of the Fourth Buddhist Council. The Vaibhāṣika school, traced to Ghoṣaka, had its treatises first translated into the Tokharian language by a monk named Dharmamitra. In this context the role of the Tokharian Buddhist monks in the propagation of Buddhism was consistent with the pioneer work undertaken by Lokasena, a monk of rare learning who went to Loyang in China in A.D. 147 and translated many works. Parthian and Kubhan scholars also distinguished themselves, the former being signified with the prefix *An*. A Parthian Mahādharmarakṣita is said to have participated in the great celebrations in the time of Duṭṭagāmini in Ceylon.

The Sogdians, originally from Samarkand, had their colonies in different parts of Central Asia and their monks were equally interested in the profession and propagation of Buddhism. Senghui, a Sogdian, was the first to introduce Buddhism in Southern China. The southern States of Central Asia experienced active Buddhist activities in the first few centuries of the Christian era. Of course, those lying on the southern silk trade route, Kashgar, Yarkand, Khotan and other sites of Kroraina, were predominently Mahāyānist, while those on the northern one comprising Kucha and Turfan were centres of Sarvāstivādins. This regional predominance of different schools could be suggestive of two separate waves of Buddhist activities in Central Asia. The Chinese pilgrims have recorded the number of monasteries of different schools and the places visited by them.

The band of Central Asian Buddhist scholars, from Kumārajīva onwards who contributed towards the dissemination of Buddhist religion and thought in Central Asia and also in China through expositions and translations of sacred texts, comprised scores of such galaxy of savants. Their list, fortunately, is available in the catalogue of Chinese Buddhist texts. Each century produced its own set of scholars who tried to emulate the examples of their predecessors. Buddhabhadra, Saṅghabhūti, Gautama Saṅghadeva and Puṇyatrāta might be quoted as some of the best specimens of Central Asian Buddhist scholars, whose life and academic activities are properly recorded and assessed.

The study of Central Asian Buddhism and its savants would no doubt be incomplete without reference to Tibet and Mongolia which continue to be strongly Buddhists. Their native and indigenous beliefs and practices were assimilated in Buddhism in such a fine manner that the original ethos is not completely obliterated. Buddhism became the religion of the people, thanks to Indian savants like Padmasambhava, Kamalaśila, Atīśa Dīpāṅkar and the contribution of hosts of Indian Buddhist Pandits in the land of snow. Mongolia accepted Tibetan Lamaism in its totality. Their religion—hierarchic in character and equally symbolising control over political affairs—is defined as a mixture of late Indian Buddhism and Hinduism with various Tibetan practices and beliefs incorporated in it. The position of the Dalai Lama with his ecclesiastical prestige and political importance as a temporal sovereign of Tibet and the fiction of continued existence, was a stabilising factor in both countries. The Tibetan Buddhists were no doubt divided into three sects, but the Yellow Hat ones predominate.

A study of Buddhism in Central Asia in proper historical perspective from the early centuries of the Christian era and the period slightly preceding it, to about the seventeenth century

A.D., has no doubt been made with particular reference to men and matters connected with it. The finds of Buddhist manuscripts as also objects of art and artistic importance no doubt call for separate studies. These could as well be made in the context of different areas and schools of religion as also of art. The material culture, associated with Buddhism and its believers—the lay members—who played an active role in their socio-economic activities, as also contributed to the development of their personality in an organized and effective manner, demands independent and separate study.

CHAPTER IV

LANGUAGE AND LITERATURE

The manuscript finds in Central Asia by different missions engaged in activities of exploration and excavation in the course of a fairly diversified and long period[1] reveal certain interesting features worth noticing. Firstly, these are primarily concerned with Buddhism—both of the Sarvāstivādin as well as of the Mahā-saṅghika (Mahāyāna) schools, as also of the later ones in their more evolved esoteric forms. These manuscripts include fragments not only of Sanskrit texts, but also of translations of Indian

1. The history of exploration of Central Asia, particularly Chinese Turkestan is traced in full by J.K. Dabbs in his book *History of the Discovery and Exploration of Chinese Turkestan*, London, 1971. Earlier, Kali Das Nag in his work '*Greater India*', Bombay, 1969, described in brief explorations in Central Asia, beginning from A. Regal, a German Botanist in the service of Russia, in the oasis of Turfan in 1879. The acquisition in 1891 of the famous birch-bark codex by Col. Bower caused a great sensation amongst the Indologists. It is now preserved in the Bodlein Library at Oxford. It contains seven texts of which three have medicinal contents. It is said to belong to the second half of the 4th century A.D. (JASB, 1891, pp. 79 ff). Several manuscripts of a still earlier period were found in later explorations, like the dramatic fragments of Aśvaghoṣa, collected by the German mission and the manuscript of the *Udānavarga*, a Sanskrit version of the Dhammapada, brought by the French mission. Both are written in quasi-Kusana character of the 2nd century. There was a regular campaign among scholars of different nationalities for the collection of manuscripts at government representative's levels as well as at private ones. These were done through agents. The British collection was catalogued by Rudolf Hoernle, who could publish only the first volume entitled '*Manuscript Remains of Buddhist Literature found in Eastern Turkestan*, London, 1916. In this context the names of Dutrevil de Rhines of the French mission in 1892, the founder of the birch-bark manuscript of the Prakrit Dhammapada at a place not far from Khotan, Aurel Stein, the Great Hungarian explorer, leader of several Indian missions, and A. Von Le Cog of the German expedition may be recorded for their pioneering work in the fields of exploration and excavation of ancient sites in Central Asia, as also for the discovery and acquisition of manuscripts including those from the famous Tun-huang library.

works in Central Asian languages, like Kuchean and Khotanese, named after the regions where these were spoken. A brief catalogue of the languages represented in the manuscripts and inscriptions suggests that many influences were at work in Central Asia which was notable as a receiving and distributing centre. As such, the number of tongues simultaneously in use for popular or learned purposes was fairly large. This might be evident from the huge collection of manuscripts in different languages from Tun-huang as also from a small one at Toyog, representing Indian, Manichaean, Syriac, Sogdian, Uighur and Chinese books. The writing material includes imported palm leaves, birch bark, plates of wood or bamboo, leather and paper, in use from the first century A.D. onwards.

It appears that with the establishment of the centralised authority of the Kuṣāṇas over this vast area of Central Asia touching Meru, Tashkent and Kashgar with base in the Northern Indian Sub-continent, cultural, commercial and religious contacts were closely established between one region and the other. In this period Buddhism became very popular in Central Asia, now represented by the Soviet and Chinese Turkestan, and with it were introduced Indian thoughts, languages and literatures, as also the writing media—first Kharoṣṭhī, widely prevalent in the North-Western part of the Indian Sub-continent and later on Brāhmī as well. The Indian impact on the literary horizon of Central Asia was heightened by the contributions of Indian Buddhist scholars to that region and further to China, as also by the visits of savants from these countries to India in search of manuscripts as also for satisfying their religious urge. This age of Buddhist intellectual curiosity lasted for several hundreds of years with the contributions of men of different nationalities—all wedded to the religion of the Tathāgata—trying to translate the life activities and teachings of the Lord. The code of discipline and conduct introduced by him as well as the philosophical and mysterious element in Buddhism, passed into practice as also in their languages.

In this context it may be mentioned that the translators were probably not unfamiliar with the original Pāli texts although they indented on the Buddhist Sanskrit ones. The Sarvāstivāda school of the Hīnayānists had its adherents especially in Kashmir and Gandhāra, from where this school spread to Central Asia, Tibet and China. It had a Sanskrit canon of its own.[2] In wordings and in the arrangement of the texts, this Sanskrit canon evinces great similarity to the Pāli canon, of course, with many points of difference as well. This might be due to both having a common source, probably the lost Māgadhī one, as proposed by Winternitz, from which first the Pāli canon branched off in one part of India, and then, later on, the Sanskrit canon in another one. Here reference might be made to fragments of the Prātimokṣa-sūtra[3] of the Sarvāstivādins, as well as other texts of the Vinaya-piṭaka of the Sanskrit Buddhist texts, which were found in Central Asia (Eastern Turkestan), and a few in Nepal as well. The Chinese and Tibetan translations are no doubt helpful in reconstructing the *Prātimokṣa-sūtra*. The Sanskrit texts of the Sarvāstivādins and the Vinayas of the Mahiśāsakas, Dharmaguptas and Mahāsāṅghikas, evidently show manifold difference and divergences in separate details from the Pāli Canon and from one another, though the original stock of rules is one and the same.

Numerous Sanskrit writings have been found, all dealing with religious or quasi-religious subjects, such as medicine and gram-

2. According to Winternitz, though no complete copy of this canon has come down to us, we know it firstly from many fragments, large and small, which have been discovered among the manuscripts and block-prints brought from Eastern Turkestan by Stein, Grunwedel, Von Le Cog, Pelliot and others; secondly from quotations in other Buddhist Sanskrit works, such as *Mahāvastu*, *Divyāvadāna* and *Lalita-vistara*, and lastly from Chinese and Tibetan translations. The principal texts of the *Mūla-Sarvāstivādin* canon were translated from Sanskrit into Chinese by the Chinese pilgrim I-tsing in the years 700-712. There are, however, translations of single texts dating from the middle of the 2nd century onwards, and these were adherents of the Sarvāstivāda in India, as early as the 2nd century B.C. Winternitz: *History of Indian Literature* (HIL), Vol. II, p.232 with references to papers of other scholars on the subject.

3. The Sanskrit text of this work is edited by Finot on the basis of the fragments of manuscripts found by Pelliot in Central Asia and it is translated into French, with the Chinese version of Kumārajīva, by Huber (JA.Ser.II, t. 11, 1913, pp. 465-558). A fragment from Stein's collection is translated by Louis de La Valée Poussin in JRAS, 1913, p. 843; a fragment in the Kuchean language by S. Levi in J.A., S. 10 t. XIX, 1919, pp. 101 ff; JRAS, 1913, pp. 109 ff; Hoernle, *Manuscript Remains* (*op. cit*) pp. 357 ff. Waldeschmidt in his *Bruchsticke des Bhiksuṇi-Prātimokṣa der Sarvāstivādins*, Leipzig, 1926, has edited the fragments of manuscripts of the Prātimokṣa of the nuns, which were found at Turfan, comparing these with the corresponding texts of all the other schools. (Winternitz : Op. cit, p. 233 and n).

mar. While the Central Asian manuscript finds are mostly Mahāyānist, greater interest attaches to portions of an otherwise lost canon which agree in substance though not verbally with the corresponding passages in the Pāli canon, and is apparently the original text from which much of the Chinese Tripiṭaka was translated. The published manuscripts[4] from Central Asia include Sūtras from the Saṁyukta and Ekottara Āgamas, a considerable part of the Dharmapada, and the Prātimokṣa of the Sarvāstivāda school. Interest in Sanskrit—its use and popularity—among the monks of Central Asia is also recorded by Fa-Hsien,[5] who states that the monks of Central Asia were all students of the language of India.[5] The other Chinese pilgrim Hsuan-chuang passing through Kucha in the seventh century confirms the statement of his predecessor.[6] Portions of a Sanskrit grammar were found near Turfan, and it is

4. The published material includes fragments of the Sanskrit canon discovered among the Manuscripts found in Eastern Turkestan, and edited by Pischel (SBA 1904, pp. 808 f, 1138 ff; Levi in Toung Pao, S.2, Vol. V, 1904, p. 1297 ff; JA. S 10 t XVI, 1910, pp. 433 ff, 450 ff; JRAS, 1911, p. 764 ff; L de La Vallee Poussin in JRAS, 1911, p. 772; 1912, p. 1063 ff; 1913, p. 569 ff; Hoernle : *Manuscript Remains*, pp. 16-52). A fragment of the Srong-Sūtras of the Saṁyukta-Āgama (cf. *Saṁyuttanikāya* 22, 49 f = Vol. III; p.48 ff') has been edited by La Vallee Poussin from Mss of Cecil Bendall's collection in JRAS 375 ff. Quotations from the Saṁyutta and Ekottara Āgamas have been traced by S. Levi in the commentary on Asaṅga's Mahāyāna-Sūtrālaṁkāra. (Winternitz : Op. cit, p. 234, n. 3). According to Winternitz, who records points of agreements and divergences, it may be suggested that the Sanskrit Āgamas and the Pāli Nikāyas were compiled from the same material, but were arranged in different ways in the different schools (ibid, p. 235).

5. Beal : *Buddhist Records of the Western World*, Vol. I, p. xxiv. Describing the country of Shen-Shen (Lou-lan), the king of this place is said to honour the law (of Buddha). There are some 4000 priests, all of the Little Vehicle belief (learning). The laity and the śramaṇas of this country wholly practise the religion of India. From this proceeding westward, the countries passed through are all alike in this respect, only the people differ in their language (*Hu words*). The professed disciples of Buddha, however, all use Indian books and the Indian language.

6. *ibid*, p. 17. Noticing the country of Kiu-chi (Kuche), this Chinese pilgrim refers to a hundred convents (*saṅghārāmas*) here with five thousand and more disciples, all these belonging to the Little Vehicle of the school of the Sarvāstivādins (Shwo-Yih-tsai-Yu-pu). Their doctrine (teaching of the Sūtras) and their rules of discipline (principles of the Vinaya) are like those of India, and those who read them use the same (originals).

suggested[7] that in the earlier period Sanskrit was probably understood in polite and learned society. This is also evident from the finds at Ming-oi of some palm leaves containing fragments of two Buddhist religious dramas, one of which is the *Sāriputra-prakaraṇa* of Aśvaghoṣa.[8] The handwriting seems coeval with the period of Kaniṣka, thus pointing to the oldest specimen of Indian dramatic art as also of the antiquity of Sanskrit manuscripts in Central Asia. The dramas are no doubt written like the Indian classical ones in Sanskrit and also various forms of Prākrit. Another Prākrit text found in Central Asia is the version of the Dharmapada written in Kharoṣṭhī letters. It was discovered by the Dutrevil de Rhins mission near Khotan.[9] The same region also provided numerous official documents in Prākrit written in Kharoṣṭhī.

7. Eliot : *Hinduism and Buddhism* (Eliot : Op. cit), Vol. III, p. 190. The Kuchean and Tokharian fragments—all translations of Sanskrit Buddhist texts—contain some bilingual pieces with original Sanskrit by the side of translations. These bilingual texts must have been used as handbooks for teaching Sanskrit to local Buddhists. A Buddhist scholar of Kucha named Li-yen compiled in the 7th century a Sanskrit lexicon which is preserved in the Chinese Tripiṭaka. The lexicon modelled after Sanskrit *kośas*, also contains some words of Central Asian origin (Bagchi. *India and Central Asia*, pp. 106, 111); also Bagchi. *Deux Lexiques Sanskrit Chionis*, Vols. I and II (Paris, 1929-37; B.N. Mookerji in the *Cultural Heritage of India*, Vol V, pp. 710-11).

8. Among the works of Aśvaghoṣa, a fragment of the *Buddha-caritra* brought from the Turfan region shows that the text was studied by the Buddhist monks of Central Asia. A drama entitled *Sāriputra-prakaraṇa* discovered in the same region, and not known from other sources, is also ascribed to Aśvaghoṣa. Only portions of the original work have been found, but they clearly point to its remarkable character. It is the oldest Indian drama known to us. It is in Sanskrit but there are dialogues in Prākrit. See Luders : *Bruckstucke buddhistisclar Draman* (1911); Keith : The *Sanskrit Drama* (London, Rep. 1959) pp. 80 ff.

9. This important manuscript in three small oblong birch-bark leaves was acquired in the spring of 1892 by the French traveller Dutrevil de Rhins in Komari Mazar in the valley of the Karakash Daray, 21 Kilometres (about 13 miles) from Khotan and was sent to France along with other finds. The text was published by M. Senart with palaeographic and philological notes in the 'Journal Asiatique' for the year 1898 (IX e Serie, tome XVI, pp. 193 ff). Several scholars made important contributions on its date and place of origin. According to Buhler, it belonged to the first century A.D. and it was brought from India to Chinese Turkestan by a Buddhist monk. (*On the origin of the*

Languages

It is equally evident from the Central Asian literary finds that in the early centuries of the Christian era two distinct languages prevailed—one spoken in the north and the other in the south. These are differently named by scholars, as for instance, the northern one is named 'Tokhari' by Muller, and the Southern one 'Nordarisch' by Leumann, and 'Saka' by Lüders. These have not found favour with scholars, and it would be preferable to accept the suggestions of Sylvain Levi and Sten Konow to name these according to the centres or capitals of the territories with which the northern and southern ones were associated, namely Kucha or Kuchar and Khotan respectively.[10] Kuchean is supposed to be an Indo-European language of extremely early affinities with the two great western and eastern groups. Spoken principally on the northern edge of the Tarim basin, it is also called Tokharian which name implies its association with the Tokharas or Indo-Scythians.[11] There is, however, no proof of this and it

Indian Brāhmī Script, Strassburg, 1898, p. 122.) Jules Bloch on philological grounds places its origin in the N.W. part of India (JA. Xe Serie, tome XIX, pp. 331 ff). Sten Konow suggests its composition in a dialect of North-Western India, but was written down in Khotan where it was discovered (*Festschrifb Windisch*. Leipzig, 1914, pp. 85 ff). The manuscript has also been edited by B.M. Barua and S.N. Mitra, with adjustments and notes (Calcutta, 1921). The Kharoṣṭhī Manuscript of the Prākrit Dhammapada figures as a section in Kalidas Nag's work (*Greater India*, op. cit, with fuller references, pp. 245-247).

10. A.F.R. Hoernle in the General Introduction to his work on *Manuscript Remains of Buddhist Literature found in Eastern Turkestan* discusses this question in detail, taking into account the views of other scholars on the subject with proper references. Eliot in his work (op. cit, p. 191) as well records the views of Luders (*Die Sakas und die Nordarische sprache'* Sitzungsber de Kon Preuss Akad. 1913); Sten Konow. Goffing Gel Anz. 1912, pp. 551 ff; and Hoernle in JRAS, 1910, pp. 837 ff; and 1283 ff; 1911 pp. 202 ff; 447 ff.

11. P.C. Bagchi notices in detail Kuchean or western Arsi—a forgotten language of the Indo-European family in his *India and Central Asia* (op. cit, pp. 152 ff) with Sylvain Levi's work entitled *Fragments des Texts Koutcheans* including a section in Hoernle's work (op. cit) pp. 357 ff and some fragments belonging to the collection of the Pelliot's Mission, some to the Stein, and a few others to the Russian Mission. Of the two dialects marked A and B, the first has been deciphered and interpreted from the manuscripts of the German collection of Grunwedel and Von Le Cog by Sieg and Siegling. The second dialect has been deciphered and interpreted by S. Levi from the French

is safer to speak of it as the language of Kucha or Kuchanese. It exists in two different dialects called A and B, of course, with uncertain distribution. Numerous official documents dated in the first half of the seventh century suggest that it was the ordinary speech of Kucha and Turfan. As a literary language it was in use for many translations, including versions of the *Dharmapada* and *Vinaya*. As pointed out earlier, it belongs to the Aryan family and is related more clearly to the western than the eastern branch, showing affinities to Latin, Greek, Celtic, Slavonic and Armenian.[12]

The other language associated with the southern region of the Tarim basin, sometimes called Nordarisch and regarded by some scholars as the language of the Sakas, is designated the Khotanese language. The manuscript remains in this language suggests two stages in its evolution—the earlier and the later. In the earlier one it is associated with the Buddhist Canonical literature[13] while the later stage is confined to the official documents of the eighth century. This divergence could be explained with reference to the introduction of Buddhism into this part of Central Asia from north-western India as early as the beginning of the Christian era. This was soon followed by the translations of the principal Buddhist Canonical texts from the original Sanskrit, or, as supposed by Hoernle, from the Indian vernacular of those days into the language of the native people of Khotan. The process continued from time to time with the growth of Sanskrit Buddhist literature.

---

collection along with those collected by other Missions. The documents written in A dialect came from the region of Karasahr and its neighbourhood whereas those in the B dialect were from the region of Kucha and its adjoining places. According to Bagchi, it is risky to connect the two dialects with the Indo-Scythians (op. cit, p. 125).

12. Eliot, (op. cit) p.191. While the numerous papers on this language are naturally quickly superseded, the two important ones : Sieg and Siegling '*Tokharisch*', 'Die Sprache der Indoskythen' (*Sitzungsber—der Berl.*. Ak. *wiss*, 1908 p. 815) and that by Sylvain Levi 'Tokharian B, Langue de Koutcha' J.A. 1913, II, p. 311 may be mentioned, according to Eliot.

13. Hoernle, Op. cit, p. xii. According to this scholar, Khotanese must be classed with the Iranian languages. Its study has been facilitated through the recovery of several complete texts by Aurel Stein in the immured library of Tun-huang. This language continued to flourish as a spoken one in the territory of Khotan as late as the eighth century A.D.

According to Eliot,[14] the basis of the Khotanese language is Iranian but strongly influenced by Indian idioms. Many translations of Mahāyānist literature, as for instance, *Suvarṇaprabhāsa*, *Vajracchedikā* and *Aparāmitāyus*-sūtras were made into it. This language appears to have been in use as a spoken one principally in the southern part of the Tarim basin.

Besides these two languages in use in Central Asia and connected with the Buddhist literature, three other Iranian languages have left literary remains in Central Asia. These are all written in an alphabet of Aramaic origin, unlike the Brāhmī and Kharoṣṭhī scripts associated with the earlier two. Two of these Iranian languages are supposed to represent the speech of south-western Persia under the Sassanids and of north-western Persia under the Arsacides, as suggested by Eliot.[15] Both these languages have preserved only Manichaean texts, but the third one, called Sogdian, offers a more variegated literary content with Buddhist, Manichaean and Christian texts. It was originally the language of the region around Samarkand but soon acquired an international character.[16] It was used by merchants throughout the Tarim basin and from there it spread even to China.

14. Eliot. Op. cit, p. 191 n. 1. See Luders 'Die Sakas und die Nordarische Sprache' *Sitzungsber der Kon Preuss Akad*, 1913; Konow. *Gotting Gel. Anz*, 1912, pp. 551 ff.

15. Eliot. Op. cit, p. 191. According to Aurel Stein, the languages represented in these Brāhmi texts from the walled-up board are mainly Sanskrit and that 'unknown' tongue of Iranian type for which the term' Khotanese' now recommended by Sten Know and Hoernle, appears the most convenient provisional designation (*Serindia*. Op. cit, Vol. II, p. 814, 914; III, p. 1289). This Iranian-Unknown so-called North-Aryan language is tracedin MSS from Khadlik (*ibid*, Vol. I, pp. 155, 158, 164); on wooden tablets from Mazar-toghrak, 205 Sq.

16. Aurel Stein discusses the language and script of the early Sogdian documents from Tun-huang. He suggests that from the outward appearance of these strange documents, it appears that the writing was in the same unknown script, resembling early Aramaic, like the one noticed on a small piece of paper from the Loulan site (LA. VI.ii.0104). This Semitic script found on the border of China might probably have been used for an Iranian language (*Serindia*, op. cit. II. p. 675). The original homeland of this Sogdian language seems to be *Scythia intra Imaon* of Ptolemy of the first century of Christ, and it was probably carried by traders to the Tun-huang region. Further, Stein quotes Robert Gauthiot's views that the language of the documents was an early form of that Sogdian, first revealed in Buddhist manuscripts recovered

A Turkish dialect written in Uighur alphabet, derived from the Syriac, was (like Sogdian) widely used for Buddhist, Manichaean and Christian literature.[17] Uigur, named after the alphabet, appears to have been the literary form of the various Turkish idioms spoken north and south of the Tien-Shan. The use of this dialect for Buddhist literature gained momentum when the Uighurs supplanted the Tibetan power in the Tarim basin about 860 and founded a kingdom of their own there. This language was in use in China as well, with the Sūtras printed in it in Peking in 1330 and several manuscripts were also copied in this language much later on.

The Tibetans with their hold over the Tarim basin from at least the middle of the eighth until a century later, were not slow in providing Buddhist canonical literature in their language. Tibetan manuscripts[18] have been found in the regions of Khotan, Miran and Tun-huang. Traces of Tibetan influence in Turfan are fewer though not completely absent. The Tibetan documents

---

from Turfan. Their writing was shown to represent a cursive Aramaic, intermediate between the Aramaic proper and the Sogdian script from which the Uigur script had been evolved (*Serindia*.II.p. 675).

17. The name Uighur (Uighur) is perhaps more correctly applied to the alphabet than the language which appears to have been the literary form of various Turkish idioms. A variety of this alphabet written in vertical columns is still used, according to Eliot (op. cit. III. 192) in some parts of Kansu where a Turkish dialect is spoken, and this appears to have been introduced into Khotan only after the Moslem conquest. Several Buddhist manuscripts in Uigur were recovered from many sites in Central Asia, including Turfan sites (Stein : *Innermost Asia*—op. cit, 1147), and Khara-Khoto (ibid) 1049. A translation of a portion of the *Saddharma-puṇḍarīka* was found at Turfan (Eliot. Op. cit. III.p. 192 n; Winternitz. Op. cit 304 n) and also of *Diśa-svāstika-sūtra* from the same area, Turfan (ibid, 384 n). Fragments of Uighuric texts were edited by W.K. Muller in his *Uigurica* (*Abhandlungen der Berliner Akademie der Wissen Schaften* ABA.1908, pp. 10 ff; and Luders : *Sitzunqsberichte der Preussischen Akademieder Wissenchaften*—S.B.A. 1914, p. 99—quoted by Winternitz. Op. cit, p. 304 n.).

18. The abundance of Tibetan texts in the walled-up Hoard at Tun-huang suggest that Buddhism there must have been subject to an even more powerful influence from the South during a certain period (Stein, *Serindia*.II.p.816). Pothi's Manuscripts in Tibetan were recovered from M ran (ibid.I.p.462), Chen-Fo-tung (ibid.II. pp. 816, 823, 919 Ser.). See Notes on the Tibetan Manuscripts by F.W. Thomas—Appendix R. *Innermost Asia* (op.cit, pp. 1084-86), *Serindia*, pp. 1410-7. See also Stein. *Khotan*—op. cit—Appendix B and Franke. JRAS. 1914, p. 37).

discovered are anterior to the ninth century and comprise numerous official and business papers as well as Buddhist translations. These are important for the history of the Tibetan language as also for the association of Tibetans with Buddhism and their allegiance to the Tathāgata, without completely alienating themselves from the traditional religious ethos—the Bon religion of the homeland.

A large number of Chinese texts—both religious and secular—have also been recovered from the principal religious centres.[19] These are interesting for providing political information. particularly relating to old military outposts near Tun-huang, and intercourse between Central Asia and China between 98 B.C. and A.D. 153. Sọme documents of the Tang dynasty are Manichaean in character with an admixture of Buddhist and Taoist ideas.[20]

The use of Gāndhārī Prākrit[21] written in Kharoṣṭhī seems to

19. For the finds of Chinese manuscripts from Central Asian sites, see Stein : *Innermost Asia*, p. 358 (Chen-Fo-ting); p. 449 (Khara-Khoto); p. 636 (Murtuk) pp. 647, 652, 665, 689 (Astana). See also E. Chavannes 'Chinese inscriptions and Records—translated and annoted'—Appendix A. *Serindia*.III. pp. 1329-1339; Pelliot. BEFEO. 1908. pp. 508 ff; Chavannes : *Documents Chinois decuverts par Aurel Stein*. 1913 (quoted by Eliot. Op. cit. III. 197).

20. See Chavannes and Pelliot 'Trait Manichaen' in J.A. 1911 and 1913, Eliot. Op. cit, p. 193 n. The discoveries at Turfan sites have furnished ample reason for belief that Manichaen and Buddhist worship had existed there probably side by side among a population which had come relatively earlier than Turkish domination as well as racial influence. Pelliot discovered a fragment of a Chinese treatise manifestly setting forth points of Manichaean doctrine (*Serindia*—Op. cit.III.p 922; See Pelliot. BEFFO. VIII. p. 518; also Chavannes—Pelliot—'Untraite Manichaen retrouve' en Chine'. JA novembre-decembre. 1911. pp. 499-617).

21. This form of Prākrit, now called by scholars as Gāndhārī Prākrit, agrees closely with the language of the post-Aśokan Kharoṣṭhī inscriptions of the north-western part of the Indian sub-continent (including Gandhāra). It differ from other varieties of Prākrit according to the degree of modifications in its inflectional system. It was subjected to two foreign influences viz. Iranian and that of the native language of Krorania. Loan words from several non-Indian languages like Iranian (including Sogdian), Greek, Tibetan etc. may be traced in Gandhārī Prākrit. Several innovations were made in the Kharoṣṭhī script in writing Gāndhārī Prākrit, and so also was the pronunciation of Prākrit words affected by the Phonetic structure of the Koraini: (See J. Brough : *The Gāndhārī Dhammapada*, London 1961; H.W. Bailey : Gandhārī, BSOAS. Vol. XI, part 4, pp. 764ff; Mookerji. B.N. : *The Cultural Heritage of India*, Vol. V, Section on Central Asia Literature, pp. 703 ff).

mark the beginning of the introduction of Buddhism and Buddhist literature in Central Asia. This is evident from the finds of manuscripts as also of numerous inscriptions—all in Kharoṣṭhī—which seems to have been introduced in Central Asia earlier than Brāhmī. According to H.W. Bailey,[22] the name Gāndhārī has a sufficiently wide scope and includes the Buddhist literary text. The Dharmapada found in Khotan, written likewise in Kharoṣṭhī, the Kharoṣṭhī documents on wood, leather and silk from Niya (Cadota) on the border of the ancient kingdom of Khotan representing the official language of the capital Krorayina of the Shan-Shan kingdom; and one document, no. 661, dated in the eign of the Khotana *mahāraya rayātiraya hinajha deva vijida siṁha.* With this more copious material must be grouped the scattered traces of the some Middle Indian dialects in Khotanese, Tibetan, Agnean, Kuchean, the earlier Buddhist translations, as in particular in the Dirghama of the Dharmaguptaka sect and the remains in Sogdian, Uighur, Turkish and in Mongol (in living use), and also in Manchu texts. It appears that this Gāndhārian Prākrit text played an active role in the dissemination of Buddhism and its literature in Central Asia and China. The same medium language and script seems to have been employed in the northwestern parts of India for recording donations and dedications for the faith of the Tathāgata.

Besides the Prakrit recension of the Dharmapada[23] in Gāndhārī, of which fragments were found in Khotan in 1892 and 1897, there are traces of a fairly good literature in this language and script in Central Asia. Some literary pieces are noticed in a few

22. BSOAS.XI.iv. p. 764.

23. J. Brough : *The Gandhārī Dhammapada* (Op. cit). The Dhammapada texts in their various recensions were very popular in Central Asia and China. Besides the Prākrit one, and the text of *Udānavarga* written in Sanskrit, a collection akin to the Dhammapda, in some places more extensive, there are four separate Chinese translations. These are based on four different recensions of the text, three of which had been carried to China from Central Asia. They are *Fa-Kiu-King-Dharmapada-sūtra* translated in 224 A.D.; *Fa-Kiu-pi-yu-king-Dharmapada-avadāha*-sūtra translated between 290 and 306 A.D.; (iii) *Chu-yao-king* translated in 398-99 A.D. The first two translations were probably based on a text similar to that of the Prākrit Dhammapada (Bagchi : *India and Central Asia*—Op. cit, p. 99).

Kharoṣṭhī records,[24] and one such record mentions the subjects of study like grammar, music, astronomy and science of poetics. This language seems to be known to early translators of Buddhist texts into Chinese. The earliest Chinese versions of the *Sukhāvatīvyūha* (c 3rd century A.D.) shows influence of Gāndhārī. It is also suggested that the Buddhist texts like the *Dīrghāgama*, rendered into Chinese in A.D 413, were translated from Gāndhārī Prākrit. This rendering might be due to the association of the earlier translators with the Gandhāra region.[25] It is calculated from the catalogue of Chinese translations of Buddhist canonical works that until A.D. 316 among the translators were six Yueh-chis, four An-hsin (Parthians), three Sogdians and six Indians, who should have been familiar with the Gandhārian Prākrit. The practice of writing Gāndhārī Prākrit in Kharoṣṭhī seems to have continued till the sixth century A.D.[26] when Brāhmī became popular in Khotan—the centre of Mahāyānism and seems to have replaced Kharoṣṭhī.

Scripts

The introduction of the Brāhmī script in Central Asia and its association with Buddhism might be dated earlier than Kharoṣṭhī[27] Brāhmī inscriptions—donative and didactive—have been found

24. Rapson, Senart and Boyer—*Kharoṣṭhī Inscriptions Discovered by Sir Aurel Stein in Chinese Turkestan* (Oxford 1920) Nos. 501, 516 and 204, 514.

25. Mookerji—Op. cit; cf. BSOAS. XII. p. 764; XVIII. p. 609; XXIV. p. 527 and Asia Major (old Series) Vol. II, pp. 270-7.

26. While the *terminus ad quem* for the use of writing Gāndhārī Prākrit in Kharoṣṭhī may be placed in the sixth century A.D. the earliest use of Prākrit in Soviet Central Asia is suggested by a Kharoṣṭhī record from Tajikistan, dated c. first century B.C. Reference might as well be made to Kharoṣṭhī inscriptions from Wardhak and Qunduz in Afghanistan and at Fayaz-Tepe and Kara-Tepe near Termez in Tajikistan for the use of Kharoṣṭṇī script and the Prārit language for the dissemination of Buddhism in those areas. (*Corpus Inscriptionum Indicarum*, CII. Vol. II (1) p. 170; B.A. Litvinsky. Op. cit, p. 8; BEFEO. Vol. LXI (1974) pp. 22 and 58; Mookerji. Op. cit, pp. 76-77 n).

27. This statement might be true in the context of Kucha and Karasahr regions. In the southern one, Brāhmī supplanted Kharoṣṭhī. The finds of Aśvaghoṣa's dramas in Brāhmī script from Turfan area suggest its *terminus a quo*. The manuscript is written in Kushan character and may be placed on palaeographic groups about the middle of the second century A.D. There

at Kara Tepe Soviet Central Asia.[28] The script was used for recording Sanskrit texts and three varieties of its alphabets are traced. The first is a purely Indian variety of the time of the Kuṣāṇas and the Guptas. The second and third ones are development of the later Gupta scripts. The purely Indian Brāhmī script is found in various Sanskrit manuscripts—the earliest being the fragments of the dramas of Aśvaghoṣa. On paleographic grounds it may be placed about the middle of the second century A.D. The manuscript containing fragments of the *Kalpanāmaṇḍitikā* of Kumāralāta, written in Gupta characters, seems to be of the first half of the fourth century A.D. The famous Bower manuscript also belongs to the fourth or the fifth century A.D.[29]

The other two distinct scripts used in the manuscripts from Central Asia are technically known as the 'slanting' Gupta script and the upright Gupta script, associated with the Kuchean or Tokharian and Khotan region respectively. According to Hoernle,[30] the northern or Kuchean Brāhmī script, noted for its upright ductus, was imported from India through immigrants. In the hands probably of the natives of the country, the upright type of Indian Gupta developed a more or less starting *ductus*. This northern or Kuchean slanting type of Gupta script must have originated at a very early period since some of the fragments exhibiting it were found along with those having the true upright Gupta of the fourth or fifth century A.D.[31] The deve-

---

are fragments of a birch-bark manuscript in the French collection, written in a quasi-Kushan character, and may be dated about the end of the second century A.D. (Ghoshal : *Greater-India*—Op. cit, p. 255).

28. B. Y. Stavisky. *Novuie Nahodici na Kara-Tepe V Staram Termez* (Moscow. 1975) p. 70; Mookerji, B.N. Op. cit, p. 707. Of the two Indian languages, Prākrit and Sanskrit, known in Central Asia in the first millennium A.D. Sanskrit was written in Brāhmī. An isolated inscription containing the whole text of the *Pratītya-samutpāda-sūtra* discovered from Tun-huang area is also in this early Brāhmī (Bagchi : *Op. cit*, p. 93).

29. The manuscript containing fragments of the *Kalpanāmaṇḍitikā* of Kumāralāta—edited and published by Luders has been placed in the first half of the fourth century A.D. The Bower manuscript is also supposed to belong to the fourth or fifth century A.D. (Ghoshal : Op. cit, p. 258).

30. *Manuscript Remains* (Op. cit) p. xiii. This is evident, according to Hoernle, from the Vinaya fragment, No. 149, found in the vicinity of Bai, west of Kuchar in the northern area of Eastern Turkestan.

31. Hoernle : *Op. cit*, p. xiii n. 14.

lopment of the southern, or Khotanese type of Gupta script did not commence quite as early.[32] In that part of Eastern Turkestan, the slanting type was never in use. The Indian upright Gupta script prevailed. Later on, gradually some of its letters, notably those for the initial vowels or vocalic radicals were modified in a calligraphic and a cursive form. The former type was in use for writing the sacred books of the Buddhist canon, and the latter one for literary works of non-canonical nature and more commonly for the writing of public and private letters and documents. The area covered by the Brāhmī script for canonical purposes was extensive. Meru seems to have been the western-most point since it yielded a Sanskrit manuscript.[33] In the north-eastern region, Brāhmī was regularly used for writing not only Sanskrit, but also Kuchean, Agnean (language of ancient Agnideśa or the Karashar area) and Saka-Khotanese in the southern part of Central Asia. Brāhmī was sometimes used along with other scripts on the same leaves of manuscripts, as for instance, some paper leaves from Khara-Khota, Turfan and Mazar Taqh bear Chinese or Uighur with internear Brāhmī writing. The relationship of the Brāhmī script with the Chinese language is traced in a manuscript containing a Buddhist Chinese text written in Brāhmī characters similar to those used in Saka-Khotanese documents.[34]

32. The use of Brāhmī in the Khotan area seems to be later than in the northern zone. Of course, sporadic use of Brāhmi in Southern Chinese Central Asia in the early centuries of the Christian era could be traced in three lives in Brāhmī characters of the Kuṣāṇa period recorded on a wooden tablet with a Kharoṣṭhī inscription on the other side. (Stein : *Ancient Khotan*, Vol. I (Oxford 1907 p. 369.) The testimonies of Sung-yun as well as of Hsuan-tsang suggest that Brāhmī seems to be popular in Khotan in the sixth/seventh century A.D. Saka (including Khotanese) manuscripts, written in Brāhmī, are datable between the seventh and the tenth centuries A.D. There are no doubt a few traces of earlier use of Brāhmī. A mutilated folio and a fragment of a Palm-leaf *pothī* in Sanskrit from Miran (No. M.11.0011) are written in the upright Brāhmī script of the early Gupta age. The *pothi* seems to be a part of a glammatical text. Hoernle dates these to c. A.D. 400 (*Serindia*. Op. cit, p. 489). It is, however, evident that Kharoṣṭhī was in use in Khotan and Shan-Shan etc. before Brāhmī became popular (Bagchi : Op. cit, 93).

33. B.A. Litvinsky : *Op. cit*, p. 65; *Journal of the Asiatic Society* (JAS), Vol. XI (1969).

34. Stein : *Innermost Asia* (op. cit) Vol. III, pl. cxxv; *Serindia* (Op. cit) pl. cii.

Sanskrit in Central Asia

The role of Sanskrit in the propagation and preservation of Buddhism and its canonical works can well be ascertained from the finds of Central Asian Buddhist manuscripts and documents in this language in different parts of that region. It is not connected with any particular Buddhist school, like the association of Pāli with the Theravādins and their canonical works, but it is patronised by the Sarvāstivādins, Mahāsāṅghikas as well as the Dharmaguptikas. It was no doubt introduced into Central Asia by the Sarvāstivādin school of the Hīnayāna sect which had its adherents more especially in Kashmir and Gandhāra. This school had a Sanskrit canon of its own. While no complete copy of this canon has come down to us, its existence is confirmed by many fragments, large and small, discovered among the manuscripts and block prints brought from Eastern Turkestan by Stein, Grunwedel, Von Le Coq, Pelliot and others.[35] Quotations from this religious text can as well be traced in other Buddhist Sanskrit works, such as *Mahāvastu*, *Divyāvadāna*, and *Lalitavistara*, and also from Chinese and Tibetan translations.[36] The principal texts of the Mūlasarvāstivāda canon were translated from Sanskrit into Chinese by the Chinese pilgrim I-tsing between A.D. 700-712.[37] The sacred literature of this school of Buddhism in Sanskrit was studied by scholars of several Buddhist kingdoms

35. cf. W. Geiger 'Die archaeologischen und literarischen Funde in Chinesisch Turkestan und ihre Bedeitung Fur die Orientalistische Wissenschaft' (Rede bein Antritt des Prorektorats) 1912; H. Oldenburg in Nachrichten Vonder Kgl. Gesellschaft der missenchaften Gottingen—NGGW 1912, 171ff; H. Luders 'Uber die literarischen Funde Von Osturkestan in Sitzunqs-berichte der Preussischen Akademie der Wissenschaften in Berlin—SBA; A.F.R. Hoernle : *Manuscript Remains of the Buddhist Literature found in Eastern Turkestan*—Op. cit., I, Oxford, 1916; Winternitz : Op. cit, II, p. 232 n. 1. See also Stein : *Serindia* and *Inner Asia* (Op. cit)—relevant references to literary works in the Index, as also the Appendices.

36. cf. Oldenburg in ZDMG 52, 1898, 654 ff; 662 ff; M. Anesaki in Transactions of International Congress of Orientalists (O.C.) Hamburg, 1902, p. 61; JRAS. 1901, pp. 895 ff; Winternitz : *Op. cit*, p. 232 n. 2.

37. J. Takakusu. *A Record of the Buddhist Religion by I-tsing*, translated, p. xxxvii, cf. Ed. Huber in BEFEO VI, 1906, pp. 1 ff.; S. Levi in 'Toung Pao' Ser. 2, t. V. 1904, pp. 297 ff.

such as Kucha and Agnideśa in Central Asia, as recorded by Hsuan-tsang.[38] It is called the language of India. The Mahāyāna school of Buddhism introduced into Khotan, Kashgar and Kucha in the fourth century has also its literature in Sanskrit. A Kharoṣṭhī inscription[39] discovered by Stein in southern Sinkiang and datable to third/fourth century A.D. actually refers to Mahāyāna. Thus, Sanskrit occupied a pre-eminent position in respect of both the schools of Buddhism in Central Asia. It is mentioned as *ārṣa=ārya* in a Tokharian manuscript.[40] It was methodically taught in Central Asia in the monastic schools of Kucha as also in other places. Some bilingual documents containing Sanskrit texts and their Kuchean or Agnean or (Saka) Khotanese versions have also been found. Finds of manuscripts of dictionaries, such as a Sanskrit-Tokharian vocabulary (c. A.D. 700) in the Kucha area and a Sanskrit-Chinese lexicon undertaken by a Kuchean scholar in the seventh century A.D. fully testify to the extensive and elaborate study of Sanskrit in Central Asia.[41] Its study by local scholars enabled them to translate Sanskrit Buddhist texts into regional languages. In this context reference might as well be made to the discovery of several manuscripts of the *Kātantra-vyākaraṇa* or Sanskrit grammar according to the school of Kātantra.

Canonical Literature

The Central Asian manuscript finds have clearly established the use of Sanskrit language by the Buddhists, thus providing authentic canonical literature. Pāli is not the sole repository of Buddhist thought, nor are the Theravādins its custodian. Even the conservative school of the Hīnayānists in Central Asia has its sacred works in Sanskrit. A complete Tripiṭaka or the three baskets is no doubt lost, but Central Asian fragments of the

38. Thomas Watbers : *Op. cit*, I, pp. 53, 60; Bagchi : Op. cit, p. 94.

39. Boyer, Rapson and Senarb : *Kharoṣṭhī Inscriptions discovered by Aurel Stein*—Op. cit (No. 390.

40. Mookerji 'Central Asia' in *Cultural Heritage of India*, Vol. V, Op. cit, p. 711; quoting BSOAS. VII. p. 895.

41. Bagchi : *India and Central Asia*—Op cit, pp. 106, 111. The Sino-Sanskrit lexicons were apparently meant for the Chinese scholars or those conversant with Chinese who were interested in learning Sanskrit.

canonical text belong to this lost Sanskrit Tripiṭaka—consisting of the *Sūtrapiṭaka*, *Vinayapiṭaka* and *Abhidharmapiṭaka*. The first one has this difference with the corresponding Pāli Nikāyas that it contains only four Āgamas in contrast to five in Pāli. A study of these Āgamas (A-han in Chinese) literature is possible with the help of translations done by the Buddhist scholars of Central Asian origin[42] in Chinese or by the local scholars in China. The four Āgamas, mentioned earlier, were translated into Chinese at different dates between the fourth and sixth centuries. Thus, the *Dīrghāgama* was translated by Buddhayaśas in A.D. 412-13, the *Madhyamāgama* by Saṅghadeva earlier in A.D. 397-98, *Saṁyuktāgama* by Guṇabhadra in A.D. 420-7, and *Ekottarāgama* by Dharmanandi in A.D. 384-85. Incidentally all the translators hailed from Kashmir which was a strong centre of Buddhist learning[43] and its scholars. The collections of the Āgamas seem to have completed in Kashmir before the fourth century and these were deeply studied there before being carried to Central Asia and China along with the Sarvāstivāda school of Buddhism towards the end of the fourth century A.D. The Central Asian manuscripts belong to the same period. The *Sūtrapiṭaka*—the Sanskrit Tripiṭaka canon of the Sarvāstivāda school—being a collection of Āgamas,[44]—has left fragments of Sūtras of at least three Āgamas as following.

42. For the relation of the Chinese translations to the Pāli Tripiṭaka and to a Sanskrit canon now preserved only in a fragmentary state, see *inter alia* Nanjio Catalogue—Op cit, pp. 127 ff. In class I—covering O-lian-pu or Agamclar—No. 542—noticing *Madhyamāgama-sūtra* and its translators—Dharmanandi (A.D. 384-391) and Gautama Saṅghadeva (A.D. 397-98) No. 543. *Ekottarāgama-sūtra* by Dharmanandi (A.D. 384-85); No. 544—*Saṁyuktāgama-sūtra* by Gaṇabhadra (A.D. 420-479); No. 545—*Dīrghāgama-sūtra* by Buddhayaśa together with Ku-Fo-nien A.D. 412-413.

43. The importance of Kashmir as a great centre of Buddhist learning is an accepted fact. The Mūlasarvāstivādin Vinaya contained many legends having reference to the conversion of Kashmir and North-Western India to Buddhism. cf. Przyluski and S. Levi in JA.S.II t. IV. p. 493 ff; Winternitz : Op. cit, p. 233 and n. 2; also Bagchi : Op. cit, p. 95. See also Bagchi. *Le Canon —Op. cit*, p. 200.

44. The fragments of the Āgamas are probably the oldest of the canonical texts discovered in Central Asia. These were carried there by monks and traders from Kashmir and Gandhāra. The Āgamas were Buddha 'vacanas' or 'sayings' of the Buddha. Their selection and division, as also modification

Dīrghāgama[45] (Tā-o-han in Chinese): The Sūtras forming part of this Āgama and recovered from Central Asia include *Saṁgiti sūtra*, which enumerates different dharmas into ten classes according to the number of items constituting such dharmas. It is in agreement more with the *Saṁgiti-sūtra* of the *Dīrghāgama* in Chinese translation than with the *Saṁgitisuttanta* in the Pāli Dīgha-nikāya. So also another Sūtra of this Āgama—the *Āṭanāṭīya-sūtra*—is very much different from the Pāli *Āṭanāṭiyasuttanta*, while a similar text under the title *Mahāsamaya-sūtra* is noticed in Chinese Dīrghāgama. The *Āṭanāṭīya-sūtra* might be an elaboration of this text.

Madhyamāgama in the Central Asian manuscript finds[46] include *Upāli-sūtra*—different from the corresponding Pāli text, but in agreement with the Chinese translation and *Śukra-sūtra*—dealing with the doctrine of Karma retribution.[47] This fragment

---

and enlargement of the Sūtras followed later on. The compilation of the Āgamas might have been done in the time of Kaniṣka, a great patron of Buddhism. These differ from the Pāli Nikāyas of which they are not the exact copies. While missing in India or in Nepal, a complete set of the Āgamas is available only in Chinese, being translations from the Central Asian Sanskrit texts by the Buddhist scholars in China who had immigrated there from Kashmir through Central Asia. A detailed account of the Āgama translations is given by Nanjio in his *Catalogue* (op. cit) pp. 127 ff; see also Bagchi : *La Canon Bouddhique en Chine* (Op. cit) under individual translators. Kshanika Saha notices Āgama literature in China, Tibetan translation of the Āgama literature and early and later Buddhist texts in her work *Buddhism in Central Asia* (Op. cit, pp. 351 f).

45. The Dīrghāgama Sūtra of the Hīnayāna school included in Hoernle's *Manuscr pt Remains* (pp. 16 ff) are *Saṅgiti-sūtra* and *Atanatīya-sūtra*—which does not figure in the Chinese *Dīrghāgama* (Bagchi : Op. cit p. 95; K. Saha—Op. cit, p. 47).

46. For a detailed reference to the contents of Madhyāgama-Sūtra in its Chinese translation see Nanjio— Op. cit, No. 542, pp. 127 ff; No. 556, p. 140—by Than-Kwo (Dharmapāla) together with Khan-Man-Sian, A.D. 207. This is said to be an extract from a full text of the Dīrghāgama (No. 545).

47. See Nanjio : Op. cit No. 544, p. 135. It was translated by Guṇabhadra of the earlier Sun dynasty. Two other translations are noticed in the same Catalogue (Nos. 546 and 547). Both are extracts from a full text as that of No. 544. The names of the translators are lost, though one was done under the three Tshin dynasties, A.D. 350-431 (No. 546), and the other ones earlier under the Wei and Wu dynasties (A.D. 220-280). See also Bagchi : Op. cit, pp.95-96; Saha:Op. cit, pp. 36-37. In the Saṁyuktāgama the division into

agrees with the corresponding text in Chinese Madhyamāgama, but differs from the Pāli one—more elaborate and with a different title—*Chulla-Kammavibhaṅga*. The Sanskrit text was popular in Central Asia with its translation in Kuchean language and so was the case in China with its four separate translations.

The *Saṁyuktāgama* has a quite good many sūtras left in Central Asian manuscript finds. These include *Pravāraṇa-sūtra* agreeing with the Chinese translation of Guṇavarman. Two other translations of the text were made in Chinese by Dharmakṣema (266-317 A.D.) and Fa-hien (Dharmabhadra) in the 10th century. The text is in general agreement with the Pāli *Vangīsa-therasamyutta* of the *Samyutta-nikāya*. The next sūtra—*Candropama* too, is in general agreement with Pāli Saṁyutta (third sūtta of the Kassapa Section) but agrees more closely with the Chinese translation. *Śakti-sūtra* and *Nidāna-sūtra* are also in agreement with their Pāli counterparts—Pāli *Satti-sūtta* of the *Opamma* section of *Saṁyuttanikāya*, and *Nidāna-saṁyutta* of the *Saṁyutta*-nikāya (XIII.15) respectively. Both are also translated into Chinese, while there is also an independent translation of the Nidāna-sūtra which deals with the chain of causation and with the means of its destruction. The other sūtras of this *Saṁyuktāgama* include *Kokanada-sūtra*, *Anāthāpiṇḍaka-sūtra*, *Dīrghakaṇṭha-sūtra*, *Sarabha-sūtra*, *Parivrayāka-sthavira-sūtra* and *Brāhmaṇa-Satyamsūtra*. These correspond to their Pāli counterparts and are as well translated into Chinese.

Ekottarāgama and its fragments are no doubt missing in the Central Asian literary finds, but the Chinese *Ekottarāgama*[48] was first translated by Dharmanandin of the Tukhāra region. He went to Chan-an in A.D. 384 and completed the translation of

---

'vargas' and 'samyuktas' is totally different and there are Saṁyuktas in the 'Pāli which are missing in the Chinese version and vice-versa (Winternitz: Op. cit, p. 235 and n). The Sanskrit fragments of the Saṁyuktāgama found near Turfan contain parts of six sūtras arranged in the same order as in the Chinese translation and are apparently the original from which it was made. (Eliot : Op.c it, p. 297).

48. Nanjio : Op. cit, No. 543 ff. It was translated by Dharmanandi A.D. 384; but it was lost already in A.D. 730, while a later translation in existence is said to have been made by Gautama Prajñāruci A.D. 397. See Bagchi : Op. cit, pp. 93, 94, 95; Saha : Op. cit, pp. 35, 38, 41, 42.

this Āgama with the assistance of two Chinese monks. The translation was revised by Saṅghadeva who hailed from Kubhā. In the Sanskrit of canon an Ekottarāgama corresponds to the Aṅguttara-nikāya. Literally meaning 'yet one more', it is synonymous with *Aṅguttara.* The absence of finds of fragments of this Āgama in Central Asia need not preclude us from presuming its literary existence in that region when there are positive evidences of its translation in Chinese, where it is divided into 51 sections containing 454 sūtras as against the *Aṅguttaranikāya* in Pāli with eleven *nipātas* i.e. sections containing 169 Sūtras.

The canonical rules embodied in the *Vinaya-piṭaka* of the Sarvāstivāda school seem to have been scrupulously followed. Fragments of texts of this work have been recovered from the northern parts of Eastern Turkestan. Written in Sanskrit, a complete text of the *Prātimokṣa-sūtra*[49] belonging to Sarvāstivāda Vinaya was discovered by the French Mission in the ruins of Duldur-Aqur at Kucha. Other texts of the Vinayapiṭaka of the Sarvāstivādins have also been found in Central Asia, and a few in Nepal too. It is possible to reconstruct the *Prātimokṣa-Sūtra,* from Chinese and Tibetan translations.[50] Both the Sanskrit canons of the Sarvāstivādins and the Vinayas of the Mahiśāsakas, Dharmaguptas and Mahāsaṅghikas, reveal manifold differences in separate details from the Pāli canon and from one another, though the original stock of rules is one and the same.

49. Bagchi : Op. cit, p. 96; See Nanjio : Op. cit Nos. 1110 (p. 245) and 1160 (p. 255); Eliot p. 214; 323. The ten primary commandments are called Prātimokṣa and he who breaks them is Parajika, who automatically leaves the road leading to Buddhahood and is condemned to a long series of inferior births. For Central Asian finds of Prātimokṣa fragments and their translation in European languages—see reference No. 3 (Op. cit) of this chapter with fuller information as recorded by Winternitz. S. Levi has edited the Kuchean fragments of *Prātimokṣa Prāyaścittika* and *Prātideśanīya*—with a French translation in Hoernle's *Manuscript Remains*, pp. 357 ff.

50. The *Prātimokṣa-vinaya* (or Sūtra ?) was translated by Gautama Prajñāruli A.D. 543 of the Eastern Wei dynasty, A.D. 534-550. (Nanjio 1108, p. 245). The Mūla-Sarvāstivādin (nikāya) Vinaya (or Prātimokṣa). Sūtra was translated by I-tsing A.D. 710. It agrees with the Tibetan 'K-Yuen-lu' (Nanjio. No. 1110, p. 245). There was also an earlier translation by Kumārajīva c. A.D. 404. (Nanjio 1160 p.255). In Tibetan there is a literal translation of the whole of the Vinayapiṭaka of the Mūla Sarvāstivādins (See Banerji : *Sarvāstivāda Literature*—quoted by K. Saha : Op. cit p. 65).

The Mūla-Sarvāstivādin Vinaya contained many legends referring to the conversion of Kashmir and North-western India to Buddhism. The Vinayapiṭaka also includes the *śikṣās* and *saṅgha-karmas* corresponding to the Pāli *sukkhas* and *kammavacas*, and fragments of these have been found in Central Asia. Reverting back to the text of the *Prātimokṣa-sūtra*, one could trace agreements with its Pāli counterpart. The text contains all the sections such as Nidāna, Parajika, Saṅghādiśeṣa etc. and agrees literally with its Chinese translation by Kumārajīva in A.D. 404. In this context reference might as well be made to the other canonical work of the Sarvāstivādins—the *Bhikṣuṇīprātimokṣa*[51] of which fragments were discovered in the Kucha region by both the French and the German missions.

Another important text entitled *Mahāparinirvāṇasūtra*, belonging to the Mūla-Sarvāstivāda Vinaya and written in Sanskrit, has been restored from a number of fragments discovered from the ruins of Sorcuq near Turfan, and of Tumshuq near Maralbashi by the German Mission. Parallel texts were also discovered from the ruins of Kizil near Kucha. The *Mahāparinirvāṇa-sūtra* is an important piece of Pāli *Suttapiṭaka*, but here it figures in the Vinayapiṭaka and agrees with the Mahāvagga of the Pāli literature. The Chinese Tripiṭaka contains ten different translations of the *Mahaparinirvāṇa-sūtra*. Three of these belong to the Hīnayāna[52] and seven to the Mahāyāna with the external form

51. Bagchi : Op. cit, p. 96; Saha : Op. cit 65. The *Bhikṣuṇī-prātimokṣa-sūtra* forms one of the six parts of the Tibetan 'Dulva'. This fourth part of *Bhikṣuṇī-Prātimokṣa-sūtra* agrees substantially with Pāli Bhikhuni Pāṭimokkha Sūtta with which there is close agreement of the Central Asian *Bhikṣuṇi-prātimokṣa-sūtra*, edited by Louis de la Valleé Poussin and Waldschinidt. (Saha : p. 66 quoting Banerji). For the Chinese translation of this work see Nanjio : Op. cit No. 1149 (p. 53); and No. 1160 (p. 255).

52. Bagchi : Op. cit, pp. 96-97. The *Mahāparinirvāṇa-sūtra* corresponds to *Mahaparinibbāna-sutta* or 'Great lecture on the Complete Nirvāna', a continuous account of the last days of Buddha. It supplies the earliest beginnings of a biography of the Tathāgata. The Chinese translations contain speeches which the Buddha is supposed to have uttered prior to his death (*parinirvāṇa*)—Winternitz : Op. cit 236 and n. For the Chinese translations of the '*Mahāparinirvāṇa* of the Hīnayāna', see Nanjio No. 118fp. 40 translated by Fa-hian of the Eastern Tsin dynasty A.D. 317-420; and No. 119 (ibid) also translated by the same author in the same period. The third one of this

as the only common factor and contains the speeches which the Buddha is supposed to have uttered prior to his death. On a comparison of the Pāli, Tibetan and Chinese versions with the Central Asian one, it is suggested that it was the choice of the Buddhist sects to place it either in the Sūtrapiṭaka or in the Vinayapiṭaka. Mūla-Sarvāstivādins and the Chinese Buddhist scholars included the whole text in the Vinayapiṭaka including the account of the two councils originally forming the concluding part of this Sūtra.

The Central Asian finds also include *Abhidharmapiṭaka*[53] fragments. This *piṭaka* consists of seven texts which are preserved in Chinese translations. A fragment of the original Sankrit text of the *Saṅgītiparyāya* was found in the Turfan oases area, and some were also discovered in the caves of Bamiyan in Afghanistan. This text corresponding to *Saṅgīti-sutta* appears among the Sarvāstivādins as a book of the Abhidharmapiṭaka. The script of this fragment is slanting Gupta which was in use in the northern part of Eastern Turkestan.

Fragments of a few sūtras belonging to the *Sūtrapiṭaka* of Hīnayāna, but not strictly included in any of the Āgamas are also identified.[54] These include *Daśabalasūtra, Mahāvadānasūtra* and *Saptabuddhaka* etc. The *Daśabalasūtra* agrees partially with the Pāli *Dasakanipāta* of the Aṅguttara-nikāya, and the *Daśaka* section of Chinese translation of Ekottarāgama. It was a very popular text of the Sarvāstivādins. A separate translation of this text was made at Kucha towards the end of the eighth century A.D. by the Chinese envoy Wu-kong in collaboration with a Kuchean monk named W-ti-ti-si-yu.

---

school No. 552 (Nanjio: Op. cit, p.139) was translated by Po-Fa-tsu, A.D. 290-306, of the Western-Tsin dynasty A.D. 265-316. This is an earlier translation and it agrees with the Tibetan, K'yuen-lu.

53. Bagchi : Op. cit, p. 97. A text corresponding to the *Sangītisutta* entitled *Saṅgitiparyāya* appears among the Sarvāstivādins as a book of the Abhidharmapiṭaka of J. Takakusu. Pali Text Society (PTS) 1905— p. 99ff; Winternitz : Op. cit, p. 44, n. 2. See also Nanjio : Op. cit No. 1276 p. 281. The work entitled '*Abhidharma-sangīti-paryāyapāda*' (*Śāstra*) was composed by the venerable Sāriputra. According to Yaśomitra's *Abhidharma-kośa-vyākhyā*, its author is Mahākausthila. This is the first of the six Pada works of the Sarvāstivādins.

54. Bagchi. *Op. cit*, p. 97.

Another important canonical text is the *Udānavarga*[55]—a complete text in Sanskrit found by Pelliot and Grunwedel from Eastern Turkestan. Stein could get only its fragments. The text is a collection similar to the Prākrit Dhammapada found in the Khotan area.[56] The title literally means a collection of Udānas or the utterances of the Buddha. It was earlier known through its translation into Tibetan and Chinese. It is a work of the Sarvāstivāda school of Buddhism. It is divided into 33 chapters of varying lengths, each bearing a separate title as we find in the Dhammapada—beginning with 'Anityavarga' or the chapter on Impermanency, and ending with 'Brāhmaṇa-varga'. The work contains about 1000 verses. Its author is Dharmatrāta, said to be the maternal uncle of Vasumitra. The popularity of this work is evident from its translation in the past into several languages. It was first known through its Tibetan translation done by an Indian named Vidyākaraprabha or Vidyaprabhākara in collaboration with a Tibetan scholar named Lotsava Rin-chen-mchog. Apart from the Chinese and Tibetan translations, the work was also translated into other Central Asian languages. The fragments of this work found by Stein are in the Central Asian form of Brāhmī as was prevalent in Kucha about the seventh century A.D.

55. Fragments of a Sanskrit anthology have been found in Central Asia which were at first regarded as passages from recensions of the Dhammapada, but which in reality belong to the Udānavarga, known to us from a Tibetan translation. It was compiled by Dharmatrāta, who, according to Tārānātha, is supposed to have lived in Kaniṣka's days (Winternitz. *Op. cit* p. 237). These fragments of the Udānavarga from finds in Central Asia were published by R. Pischel, 'Die Turfan-Rezensinen des Dhammapada' SBA. 1908 p. 968 ff.; Sylvain Levi and Louis de la Vallée Poussin in JAS. t. 10, t. XVI. 1910 p. 444 ff; t. XVII, 1911, 431 ff; t. XIX, 1912, p. 311 ff; JRAS. 1911, p. 758 ff; 1912, p. 355 ff. The Tibetan version of the Udānavarga was translated by W.W. Rockhill, London, 1883 and the Tibetan text was published by H. Beckh, Berlin 1911.

56. *Ancient Khotan*, Oxford, 1907, I, p. 88; S. Konow (Fest-schrift Windisch, p. 85 ff) suggests that though this anthology was composed in a dialect originating in the north-west of India, it was written in the neighbourhood of Khotan. Fragments of this anthology have come down to us in a few leaves of a manuscript written in the Kharoṣṭhī script which M. Petroffsky and J.L. Dutreuil de Rhins had found at Khotan (for reference see Winternitz. Op. cit, p. 238 n). See also Ghoshal. Op. cit, pp. 260 ff in which N.P. Chakravarti traces the history of the compilation of the Sanskrit Udānavarga.

The finds of Mahāyāna Sūtras and fragments as also *pothīs* represent a new stratum in the history of Sanskrit Buddhist literature in Central Asia. The Mahāyāna school is not supposed to possess a canon of its own, since it does not represent one unified sect. It is doubtful if the Buddhist council held in the time of Kaniṣka could establish any canon, and even if so, in which language and by which sect.[57] A Chinese text translated by Hsuan-tsang mentions a Bodhisattvapiṭaka consisting of a long list of Mahāyāna texts, a Vinayapiṭaka and an Abhidharmapiṭaka, and the same text also enumerates a lengthy list of Mahayānasūtras.[58] The so-called nine Dharmas or texts in Nepal are not the canon of any sect, but a series of books which were compiled at different times and belonged to different sects. The title of these nine books are *Aṣṭasāhasrikā-Prajñā-Pāramitā, Saddharma-Puṇḍarīka, Suvarṇa-Prabhāṣa, Gaṇḍa-vyūha, Tathāgatagūhyaka* or *Tathāgataguṇajñāna, Samādhirāja* and *Daśabhūmīsvara.* All these works are also called 'Vaipulya-Sūtras'. *Saddharmapuṇḍarīka*[59] or the 'Lotus of the true Law' is the most important as well as the most popular Mahāyānist work, highly respected in China and Japan. According to Nanjio, there were eight or nine translations of this text into Chinese, of which only three are available. The earliest (A.D. 286) is that of Dharmarakṣa, a Yueh-chi scholar from Kan-su.

57. Winternitz. Op. cit, pp. 294 ff. According to Takakusu (JRAS. 1905 p. 414 f), the Council dealt with Hīnayāna and not the Mahāyāna. It is proposed that the object of the alleged Council of Kaniṣka was not to establish a canon, but to collect explanations (Commentaries). (Winternitz. 294 n. 2).

58. See Levi and Chavannes in JA. 1916.S.11 t. VIII. p. 5 ff. The Buddhist dictionary Mahā-vyūtapatti (Bibl. Buddh. XIII) p. 65 mentions 105 separate Mahāyāna texts, No. 12 of which is a 'Bodhisattva-Piṭaka'. It is also quoted in the *Śikṣā-samuccaya* pp. 190 and 311.

59. The Sanskrit text has been edited by Kern and Nanjio in *Bibliotheca Buddhica*, X, translated by Burnouf (*Le Lotus de la bonne Loi*) 1852, and by Kern (*Saddharmapuṇḍarīka*) in the Sacred Book of the East, Vol. XXI, Oxford. There are several translations in Chinese. Nanjio. Op. cit. No. 134 p. 44; Translated by Kumārajīva A.D. 384-417; No. 135 p. 44 (translator's name lost); No. 138 p. 45 translated by Ku-Fa-hu (Dharmarakṣa) of the western Tsin dynasty, A.D. 265-316; No. 139 p. 45 translated by Jñāngupta and Dharmagupta A.D. 601 of the Sui dynasty A.D. 589-618, with an introductory preface.

The next (400-2) is that of Kumārajīva, the famous Buddhist scholar monk of Kucha, who was taken as a prisoner to China, where he translated several Buddhist works into Chinese. The third translation (A.D. 601) is of Jñānagupta and Dharmagupta—the two Indian Buddhist scholars who followed the Nepalese manuscripts. It was also translated into Tibetan. A number of fragments of this work were found at different sites in Central Asia.[60] In Hoernle's '*Manuscript Remains of Buddhist Literature*' there are fragments of the manuscripts of this text found at Khadlik and edited by F. W. Thomas (one) and Luders (two). It purports to be a discourse delivered by Śākyamuni at the Vulture Peak (*Griddhakūṭa*) to an assemblage of Bodhisattvas. The 'Lotus' clearly affirms the multiplicity of vehicles, or various ways of teaching the law, and also the eternity of the Buddha. The fragments of the *Saddharmapuṇḍarīka* found in Eastern Turkestan and presenting a text diverging from that of the Nepalese manuscripts, suggest that there were two recensions of the work.

The next Mahāyānist work in importance and in popularity is the *Prajñāpāramitā*[61] or 'transcendental knowledge'. This generic name is given to a whole literature consisting of treatises on the doctrine of Śūnyatā, which vary greatly in length. They are

60. See Stein. Inside Asia p. 1018; No. 0153 from Domoko near Khotan; Fragments from Khadlik (*Serindia* I.p. 163) from Shrine F.12 in the Khotan region (*Serindia* p. 1254) and from the ruined shrines at Khadlik (*Serindia* pp. 1433 ff). Several manuscripts and fragments of this works are noticed in Appendix F. by A.F. Rudolf Hoernle, containing the Inventory List of Manuscripts in Sanskrit, Khotanese and Kuchean.

61. For the finds of Manuscript fragments of this Buddhist Mahāyānist text, see Stein : *Serindia*, 814, 914, 1432-50; Khotanese 1454; Tibetan 1470 Sq. & Chinese 163 Sq, 687, 914, 925; *Prajñā-pāramitā* means both the perfection of 'wisdom' and the writings treating it. 'Prajñā' not only means knowledge of the absolute truth, that is to say of Śūnyatā or the Void, but is regarded as an ontological principle synonymous with Bodhi and Dharmakāya. The Buddhas not only possess this knowledge in the ordinary sense but they are the knowledge manifest in human form, and 'Prajñā' is often personified as a goddess (Eliot. Op. cit. III. p. 52). According to Aneski, the innermost qualities of Buddhahood can be sought nowhere else than in the profound abyss of the prajñā. (ERE. IV. p. 837). The six *pāramitās* include behaviour (*śīla*), contemplation (*samādhi*), wisdom (*prajñā*), deliverance (*vimukti*) and the realization of the knowledge leading to it (*Vimukti-jñāna-darśana*).

classed as Sūtras, being described as discourses delivered by the Buddha on the vulture peak (Griddhakūṭa) at Rājagriha. The Prajñāpāramitās belong to the earliest Mahāyāna-sūtras regarded with greatest reverance and equally of the greatest importance from the point of view of the history of religion. Being in the nature of philosophical treatises, they talk of six perfections (Pāramitās) of a Bodhisattva, finally aiming at the highest one called 'wisdom'. This wisdom consists of the knowledge of 'Śūnyatā', 'emptiness' i.e. the unsubstantiality of phenomena—all objects being endowed with a conditional or relative existence. Since a Prajñāpāramitā was already translated into Chinese[62] as early as A.D. 179. This class of Mahāyānist literature seems to be the earliest one. Presented in a dialogue form, similar to those of the Pāli Suttas, the Buddha called Bhagavān, 'the Lord', generally appears in conversation with one of his disciples, especially Subhūti. In other Mahāyāna-sūtras Buddha usually talks to a Bodhisattva.

A considerable number of Prajñā-Pāramitā of all texts were already in existence in India and their number increased even more in China and Tibet. Hsuan-Tsang translated 12 different *Prajñā-Pāramitā-sūtras* in his *magnum opus*, *Mahā-prajñā-pāramitā-sūtra*,[63] the longest is that of 10,000 ślokas or verses and the shortest that of 150. The following have come down to us in Sanskrit : *Śatasāhasrikā-prajñā-pāramitās* of 1,00,000 ślokas,

62. Amongst the Sūtras of the Mahāyāna, the Pāramitā class called Pan-zo-pu, is the foremost. The earliest translation of the '*Daśasāhasrikā-prajñā-pāramitā*' was done by Leu-Ki-Khan (Lokarakṣa ?) of the Eastern Han dynasty, (Nanjio No. 5 p. 4) followed by several others including Kumārjīva (ibid) No. 6 p.5) in A.D. 408, Dharmapriya together with Ku-Fo-Knien and others, A.D. 382 (ibid No. 7 p. 5) and then repeatedly till the 10th century (Nanjio Nos. 927, 935, 988, 1033, 1034).

63. See Nanjio. ii. No. 133 pp. 435-37 noticing the Chinese translations of Buddhist Canonical works by Hsuan-Tsang who received his ordination at Chan-tu in A.D. 622 and died in A.D. 664 in his sixty-fifth year. According to Nanjio, there are 75 works of this Chinese śramaṇa of which he gives the list that of *Mahāprajñapāramitāsūtra* (No. 1). According to Eliot, there are ten collections of Prajñāpāramitā, besides excerpts sometimes described as substantive works. See Wallesser. *Prajñāpāramitā in Quellen der Religion geschite*, pp. 15 ff. SBE. XLIX. Nanjio *Catalogue* Nos. 1-20 and Rajendra Lal Mitra's *Nepalese Buddhist Literature*, pp. 177 ff. See also Winternitz. Op. cit, p. 314 and 315 and n. 1.

Pañcaviṁśatisāhasrikā—of 25,000, *Aṣṭasāhasrikā* of 8,000; *Sārdhadvisāhasrikā* of 2,500, *Saptaśatikā* of 700, *Vajracchedikā Pāramitā*, 'the diamond cutter Prajñā-pāramitā cutting as sharp as a diamond; the *Alpasāra-prajñā-pāramitā* and *Prajñā-pāramitāhṛdaya Sūtras* are only used as protecting magic formulae (*Dhāraṇīs*).

In Central Asia a few fragments of the Prajñāpāramitās have been found. Those of the *Aṣṭādaśasāhassrikā prajñā-pāramitā*[64] comprise of nine folios found at Khadlik. The leaves belong to four different manuscripts of the seventh-eighth centuries A.D. Another fragment of a Prajñāpāramitā manuscript consisting of 48 leaves from Central Asia is in upright Gupta characters and is supposed to be earlier than the sixth century A.D. Its language is Sanskrit. Despite the numerous epistemological and metaphysical discussions on Śūnyatā, its religious character is also emphasised in several chapters. Great merit is supposed to be acquired by the hearing and understanding of it, and the learning and teaching of the Prajñā-pāramitā is praised repeatedly and extraordinarily.

The manuscript of *Vajracchedikā-prajñā-pāramitā*[65] discovered by Stein is written on nineteen folios. In this work, too, we come across the same paradoxes as in the *Aṣṭasāhasrikāprajñā-pāramitā* and the longer *Prajñā-pāramitās*. The work seems to be an

64. See Central Asian fragments of 'Aṣṭādaśa-sāhasrikā' and of an unidentified text edited by Sten Konow in Memoirs of the Archaeological Survey of India No. 69. Calcutta. 1942. cf. the Sanskrit edition of the work edited by Rajendra Lal Mitra—Bibliotheca Indica, Calcutta 1888. According to Winternitz, the '*Aṣṭa-sāhasrikā-prajñā-pāramitā* is the earliest of these writings which was, on the one hand, expanded into the larger works, and the contents of which were, on the other hand, condensed in the shorter texts. (Op. cit 316 and n 6 for the references).

65. *Ancient Khotan*—Op. cit, Vol. I p. 258; Hoernle. Op. cit p. 176 for the Chinese translation see Nanjio Op. cit No. 10 p. 5 translated by Kumārajīva; Bodhiruci (A.D. 508-535 in China) No. 11 p. 6; Hsuan-Chuang No. 13 p. 6; I-tsing No. 14 p. 6; and Dharmagupta No. 15 p. 5; cf. also *Vajracchedikā-sūtra Śāstra*, a commentary on Nos. 10-15 compiled by the Bodhisattva Asaṅga and translated by Dharmagupta A.D. 590-616 of the Sui dynasty (No. 1167 p.257), and a commentary on No. 1167 under the same title compiled by the Bodhisattva Vasubandhu, translated by Bodhiruci, A.D. 509 (ibid No. 1168 p. 257). The Khotanese texts from Central Asia include *Vajracchedikā* (Hoernle. Op. cit p. 214).

abridgement of the exposition of the doctrine of Śūnyatā propounded in the 'Hundred-thousand prajña-pāramitā'. It has a commentary translated into Chinese by Dharmagupta (A.D. 590-616) and Vasubandhu, brother of Asaṅga, a convert from Hīnayāna to Mahāyānism is said to have written a commentary on this canonical work, as well as on *Saddharmapuṇḍarīka* and *Mahāparinirvāṇa-sūtra* as a penance for his previous calumniation of the Mahāyāna school of Buddhism. According to chapter 13 of the *Vajracchedikā,* Buddha is made to say words to the effect that one who selects merely one four-footed verse here from this sermon and explains 'it to others' acquires greater religious merit than a person who might sacrifice his life day by day for aeons.[66]

Suvarṇaprabhāsa-sūtra—Literally meaning the 'Splendour of Gold', this later Mahāyāna Sūtra contains partly philosophical and ethical matter and many legends. While there are many beautiful passages such as the confession of sins and the praise of love (*maitrī*) towards all beings, the doctrine of Śūnyatā is developed in a full chapter (VII). Its major portion consists of a glorification of the *Suvarṇaprabhāsa* itself. The work enjoys great reputation and popularity in all countries professing Mahāyāna Buddhism. In Central Asia, too, fragments of this work were discovered.[67] Its Chinese translators were Dharmakṣema (413-33), Paramārtha and his pupils (552-557) and I-tsing (703). There are also fragments of Uiguric texts[68]—

66. See Walleser. *Prajñā-pāramitā* p. 146 f, 149 ff. In a fragment of the *Adhyardhaśatikā-prajñāpāramitā* from Khotan (Leumann 'Zur nordarischen Sprache und Litteratur' p. 89) it is even said that he who 'even while still in the womb' hears this section of the Prajñā-pāramitā, is freed from all attacks and dangers, and never goes to hell or is reborn in any other evil form of existence (Winternitz, p. 320 n).

67. Hoernle. Op. cit p. 108 edited by Sarat Chandra Das and Sarat Chandra Sastri, Calcutta, 1898 (Buddhist Text Society of India). See also Rajendra Lal Mitra—*Nepal Buddhist Literature* pp. 241 ff; cf. Burnouf. *Introduction* pp. 471 ff, 490; Bendall. *Catalogue* p. 12 f; M. Anesaki in ERE p. 839; Winternitz. Op. cit p. 339 n; for the Chinese translations of this Buddhist text, see Nanjio Op. cit No. 126 p. 41 by I-tsing which agrees with the Tibetan; No. 127 p. 42 by Dharmarakṣa which is an earlier and incomplete translation of No. 126, though the most popular one in China.

68. An Uiguric translation appeared in Bibliotheca Buddhica in 1914. For fragments of Uiguric texts see F.W.K. Muller. 'Uigurica' in ABA. 1908,

Ratnadhvaja-sūtra,[69], *Ratnarāśi-sūtra*,[70] *Bhadrapāla-sūtra*[71]. The fragments of these Sūtras are all in upright Gupta characters. The text of the first one is identified by Watanabe with *Ratnadhvaja* of the Mahāsannipāta Sūtra. It was translated into Chinese by Dharmarakṣa, a native of Central India between A.D. 414-21 under the Northern-Lian dynasty. The next one—*Ratnarāśi-sūtra* is also in upright Gupta characters. Its Tibetan version is to be found in the Bkah-hgyur. The Sūtra was translated into Chinese in A.D. 397-439. Passages from the Sūtra, outside this fragment are cited in the *Śikṣāsamuccaya* of Śāntideva. The *Bhadrapāla-sūtra* also in upright Gupta characters has been identified by Watanabe. Jñāngupta translated it into Chinese. Besides these there is a fragment of *Candragarbhā*[72] of the Mahāsannipāta class.

Fragments of Dhāraṇīs : Dhāraṇīs or 'protective spells' constitute a large and important part of Mahāyānist literature. According to the *Saddharmapuṇḍarīka*,[73] the *dhāraṇīs* are taught for the protection, safety and shelter of the preachers. The

p. 10 ff; Luders. SBA. 1914 p. 99; Winternitz p. 341 n. This work was translated from the Indian language into Chinese, and from the Chinese into Turkish (Winternitz. Op. cit p. 341 n).

69. Hoernle. *Manuscript Remains*—Op. cit p. 100; Stein. *Serindia*, III, p. 1432. The text has been identified by Watanabe as from the second chapter of the second part of *Ratnadhvaja* of the *Mahāsannipāta-sūtra* (Nanjio No. 84; ZDMG. LXII p. 100). It was translated into Chinese by Dharmarakṣa (Nanjio App. II. No. 67).

70. Hoernle. Op. cit p. 116; *Serindia*. III. p. 1439. The Sūtra was translated into Chinese in A.D. 397-439—Nanjio No. 23 (44) p. 19.

71. Hoernle. Op. cit p. 88. See Nanjio. Op. cit No. 75 p. 31. It was translated by Jñāngupta, Dharmagupta and others of the Sui dynasty, A.D. 589-618.

72. Hoernle. Op. cit p. 103. According to Bagchi, the *Sūryagarbha* and the *Candragarbha* are two important Sūtras of the 'Mahāsannipāta' collection. They are preserved in Chinese translation of about the middle of the sixth century by Narendra Yaśas (op. cit p. 109).

73. Kern. Op. cit p. 99. See Burnouf. *Introduction* pp. 466, 482 ff; Wassiljew. *Der Buddhismus* pp. 153 ff; 193 ff, La Valee Poussin. *Buddhisme* Belgium 1898 p. 119 ff; J. Haver. *Die Dhāranī im nordlichen Buddhismus* Tubingen 1927; Tuchi. IHQ. IV. 1928 pp. 553 ff; Winternitz pp. 380 ff and notes for references. See also Waddel 'The Dhāraṇī Cult' in 'Ostasiat Zisft' 1912 pp. 155 ff. Formulae or spells called 'Dhāraṇī' are said to possess a mysterious efficiency and potency.

protective and salutary magical power of *dhāraṇī* is primarily due to some piece of wisdom contained in it, and not to any occult mystical significances of the words and syllables, though these Dhāraṇīs include magic words (*mantrapadāni*) of this kind. The Prajñā-Pāramitā-Sūtras in their shortest form were used as Dhāraṇīs. In this context special mention might be made of the *Prajñā-Pāramitā-hṛdaya Sūtras*.[74] These sūtras teach the heart (*hṛdaya*) of the Prajñā-Pāramitā i.e. 'the Mantra which alleviates all pain', contain the perfection of wisdom. Many Prajñā-Pāramitā texts appear in the Tibetan *Kanjur*. There are Mahāyāna Sūtras which are only recommendations of Dhāraṇīs. Thus, in the *Aparamitāyuḥ-sūtra*[75] in Sanskrit and old Khotanese, as also in Chinese and Tibetan translations there is nothing more than the glorification of a Dhāraṇī. The growth of the Dhāraṇī literature might be placed between the fourth and eighth century A.D. In the early Mahāyāna text *Saddharmapuṇḍarīka* there are a few Dhāraṇīs for recitation ensuring protection against evils. In the twenty-first chapter of this work, Bhaiṣyarāja Bodhisattva approaches the teacher for a protective spell needed for the Dharmabhāṣakas engaged in handing down the texts of this canonical work. In the *Suvarṇaprabhāsa sūtra* (chapters XI, XII) there is a section exhorting the gods and demons to protect those reading and writing the sūtra from any harm.

Among the Dhāraṇī fragments found in Central Asia, mention maybe made of the *Anantamukhadhāraṇī*[76] and *Nīlakaṇṭhadhāraṇī*[77]

74. Edited by F. Max Muller and B. Nanjio in 'Anecdota Oxoniensia' Aryan Series, Vol. I, Part III, 1884, and translated by Max Muller in SBE Vol. 49. Part II, p. 145 ff; translated from the Tibetan by L. Feer in 'Annals du Musie Guimet' (Paris) V, 176 ff; Winternitz. Op. cit 316 n. 5.

75. *Serindia* p. 914; Hoernle. Op. cit pp. 289 ff. It is a Dhāraṇī' which has long been known to exist in Sanskrit manuscripts and in Tibetan. A complete manuscript of this version was found by Stein in the cave temples at the Halls of the Thousand Buddhas which also yielded the manuscript of the '*Vajracchedikā*. Sten Konow provides the Sanskrit text and Tibetan version as also the Khotanese one.

76. Hoernle. Op. cit p. 86. See Nanjio. Op. cit Nos. 353-360 pp. 89-90. The earliest one (No. 353) is by C'Chien of the Wu-dynasty, A.D. 222-80.

77. The fragment of Nīlakaṇṭhadhāraṇī' brought from Central Asia by Aurel Stein, with the Sanskrit text in Brāhmī script and in Sogdian transcription has been edited by La Vallee Poussin and R. Gauthiot in JRAS 1912 pp. 629 ff. (Saha. Op. cit p. 96). See Nanjio. Op. cit Nos. 318, 319. pp. 81-82.

and *Sitātapatrā Mahāpratyaṅgiradhāraṇī*[78]. The first text has been identified be Watanabe as part of the *Anantamukha-dhāraṇī*, of which the Chinese Tripiṭaka includes eight translations, the earliest being by C'chien, whose date is A.D. 222-80. The fragment of Nīlakaṇṭhadhāraṇī, brought from Central Asia by Stein, is in Sanskrit written in Brāhmī script and in Sogdian transcription. This Dhāraṇī was popular in China between A.D. 650-750. The fragment of *Mahāpratyaṅgiradhāraṇī* contains only a small portion of it and also a series of epithets of the goddess Tārā. It is written in upright Gupta characters similar to those of the *Saddharma-puṇḍarīka* manuscripts. The whole of the Sanskrit text of this Dhāraṇī was transcribed in Chinese characters by the famous mystic teacher Amoghavajra (A.D. 704-774). Another manuscript of this Dhāraṇī in the peculiar corrupt Sanskrit current in certain parts of Eastern Turkestan, was recovered from the Temple Library near Tun-huang. There are also Nepalese manuscripts of this Dhāraṇī. Fragments of another Dhāraṇī—*Surāṁgama-samādhi*—are also noticed in Hoernle's manuscripts.[79] In fact, the text of this manuscript is the conclusion of a *Surāṁgama-samādhi-sūtra* followed by a Dhāraṇī.

Non-Canonical Texts : Besides religious texts in Sanskrit Central Asian finds include non-canonical ones as well. These include poetical works of the two great Buddhist poets—Aśvaghoṣa and Mātriceṭa. The German mission brought fragments of the works of this contemporary of Kaniṣka. Aśvaghoṣa was a poet, philosopher and dramatist of excellence. His two long Kâvyas—*Buddhacarita*[80] and *Saundara-*

78. Aurel Stein. *Serindia* p. 918; Hoernle. Op. cit pp. 52 ff. These are the Nepalese manuscripts Nos. 61 and 77 of the Asiatic Society, Bengal Collection, as also the Cambridge Collection (Cat. pp. 63, 68). There is also the Roll. Ch. 0041 from the Temple Library near Tun-huang in the Stein Collection which is noticed in the Journal of the Royal Asiatic Society 1911 pp. 460 ff., containing this *Dhāranī* in the peculiar corrupt Sanskrit. There are further two Chinese translations, one of which is noticed in Nanjio (No. 1016 p. 223). There is reference to an earlier translation by Amoghavajra A.D. 746-771.

79. Hoernle. Op. cit p. 125. It was translated into Chinese in A.D. 384-417. Nanjio No. 399 p. 98. Hoernle also quotes the Tibetan version.

80. A fragment of the 'Buddhacarita' brought from Turfan region shows that the text was studied by the Buddhist monks of Central Asia (Bagchi.

nanda[81] are well-known in original. A third one *Śāriputraprakaraṇa*[82], the earliest specimen of Sanskrit drama was discovered in the Turfan region. Only portions of the original work have been found. As the oldest Indian drama known to us it presupposes a great development of Indian dramatic art. This work is in Sanskrit, but the dialogues are in Prākrit—older than the ones used in classical Sanskrit dramas. Aśvaghoṣa is credited with the authorship of another work, the *Sūtrālaṅkāra*[83] preserved in Chinese translation of Kumārajīva, as also a philosophical work entitled *Śraddhotapāda-śāstra* which, too, has been preserved in Chinese translation.[84] The German mission discovered another poetical work in Sanskrit, the *Sūtrālaṅkāra* of

---

Op. cit p. 100). See *Serindia* I p. 163; III, 1437. See Winternitz. Op. cit pp. 258-265. This is the Fo-Sho-hing-tsan-king, translated from Sanskrit into Chinese between A.D. 414 and 421 by Dharmarakṣa and translated into English by Cowell in SBE Vol. 49. There is also a translation by E.H. Johnston. Oxford. 1936; see also M. Aneski in ERE. II. 1909 p. 159 ff.

81. No fragment of this work is found in Central Asia nor is it translated into Chinese. It was discovered and edited by Haraprasad Shastri Bibl. Ind. Calcutta 1910; critically edited and translated into English by E.H. Johnston, Oxford 1928, 1932; which gives full bibliography.

82. Ref. No.8. The discovery of fragments of manuscripts on palm-leaf, of great antiquity at Turfan, has revealed the existence of at least three dramas. One, of course, is *Sāriputraprakaraṇa* of Aśvaghoṣa, son of Suvarṇākṣī. It gives also the fuller title *Saradvātiputra-prakaraṇa,* and the number of acts is nine. The same manuscript which contains portions of this drama of Aśvaghoṣa has also fragments of two other dramas. There is no evidence of their authorship, but they appear in the same manuscript as the work of Aśvaghoṣa, and they display the same general appearance as the work of that writer. It is more probable that they are contributions of Aśvaghoṣa rather than of some unknown contemporary (Keith. *Sanskrit Drama* O.U.P. 1959 Reprint pp. 80 ff).

83. Fragments of this work were discovered in Central Asia. Its authorship is controversial. The Chinese translation of the work made by Kumārajīva about A.D. 405 assigns it to Aśvaghoṣa (Nanjio No. 1182 p. 261), but the finds of the fragments of the same work in Sanskrit in Central Asia and identified by Luders accords it to Kumāralāta, probably a junior contemporary of Aśvaghoṣa. Some scholars hold that Aśvaghoṣa was the real author, and Kumāralāta only refashioned it. According to S.N. Dasgupta, Aśvaghoṣa had nothing to do with its composition (*History of Sanskrit Literature,* Calcutta, Reprint 1977, p. 72 and n. 4.

84. Nanjio No. 1249 p. 274 translated by Sikhanand A.D. 695-700, and earlier by Paramārtha (No. 1250 ibid).

Aśvaghoṣa as known from the Chinese translation of the work by Kumārajīva. The colophon of the Turfan manuscript, however, ascribes the work to Kumāralāta, a well-known Buddhist scholar. According to Luders who translated this work, its name is *Kalpanāmaṇḍitikā*[85] and its author is Kumāralāta. According to him, the Chinese tradition ascribed the work to Aśvaghoṣa by mistake. Kumāralāta's name is transcribed in Chinese as Ku-mo-lo-to meaning 'tong-show' 'boy received'. The Tibetan tradition associates him with the school of the Sautrāntikas. Luders, however, advanced the hypothesis that Aśvaghoṣa did actually write a work entitled Sūtralaṅkāra, which was not translated into Chinese but soon got lost, and was subsequently confused with the *Kalpanāmaṇḍitikā*.

The *Kalpanāmaṇḍitikā* is a collection of pious legends on the pattern of the Jātakas and Avadānas, and they are told in prose and verse in the style of ornate poetry. It contains old legends and parables, while others breathe the spirit of the Mahāyāna or at least reveal Buddha worship. In this work itself, the teachers of the Sarvāstivādins are honoured and many of the stories in the Kalpanāmaṇḍitikā are taken from the canon of the Sarvāstivādins.[86] King Kaniṣka, as a ruler of the past, appears in two narratives. It mentions the two epics—Mahābhārata and Rāmāyaṇa, and confutes the philosophical doctrines of Sāṁkhya and Vaiśeṣika, and the religious views of the Brāhmaṇas and Jains, and also contains all kinds of reference to script, art and painting. Kumāralāta is further described in Chinese tradition as a 'Master of Comparisons' (*driṣṭānta*) and as a 'founder of comparison' (*Dārṣṭāntika*). As such the principal work of

85. Luders. *Bruchsticke der Kalpanāmaṇḍitikā des Kumāralāta* (Kon. Preuss Turfan-Expeditions Kleinere Sanskrit Texte II). Leipzig 1926. Both 'Kalpanāmaṇḍitikā' and 'Kalpanālaṅkṛtā' appear as titles in the Colophons (Winternitz. Op. cit 267 & n). For the French translation of this work in Chinese see *Sūtrālaṅkāra* tranduit en francens sur la version Chinoise de Kumārajīva par Ed. Huber, Paris 1908. cf. La Vallee Poussin in Le Museon N.S.X. 1909, 86 ff.

86. Winternitz p. 269 and n. 1; cf. S. Levi in JA. 1968. S.10. t. XII. 91ff; 184; Huber (in BFEO) 4, 1904, pp. 709 ff has traced three stories in the Divyāvadāna. The Sautrāntikas originated with the Sarvāstivādins and that explains why there is no contradiction for Kumāralāta, as a Sautrāntika to honour the Sarvāstivāda teachers (Luders. Op. cit, p. 22).

Kumāralāta is mentioned in the Chinese texts as *Yo-man-lun—Driṣṭānta-mālā* (paṅkti) Śāstra. Levi, therefore, expresses the opinion that the name of the Turfan text was really *Driṣṭānta-paṅkti* (as found in the Colophon) and that *Kalpanāmaṇḍitikā* is its adjective. This text is considered by Levi to be a new edition of the *Sūtrālaṅkāra* of Aśvaghoṣa expanded by the addition of moral lessons and apologues in the form of examples (*driṣṭānta*) according to the practice of the Dārṣṭāntika school. The Turfan text, therefore, represents partially the Sūtrālaṅkāra of Aśvaghoṣa.[87]

Mātriceṭa[88] is another Buddhist scholar of eminence whose hymns—the fragments of the poems—were brought to light in Central Asia both in Sanskrit original as well as in Tokharian translation. Like Kumāralāta's work—the *Kalpanāmaṇḍitikā*—some poems by Mātriceṭa—have likewise been ascribed to Aśvaghoṣa in Tibet. It is proposed by Winternitz that Mātriceṭa who wrote the 'Mahārāja Kanika-lekha', which has come down to us in Tibetan language was an old contemporary of Aśvaghoṣa. His most famous hymns are the *Catuḥ-śataka-stotra*—'the hymn of the Four Hundred Verses' and the *Śatapañcāśatika*[89] 'the hymn of the

87. Bagchi. Op. cit p. 101; cf. Levi in JA. 1896, S. 9, t. VIII, pp. 444 ff.

88. For the life and works of contributions, see, F.W. Thomas' article on 'Matricheta' in the *Encyclopedia of Religion and Ethics* Vol. VIII, pp. 495-97. Mātricheta, the Buddhist author, is identified by Tārānātha with Aśvaghoṣa, while a much older writer, the Chinese traveller I-tsing (2nd half of 7th cent. A.D.) plainly distinguishes the two. The sole reason for the identification is the fact that both writers stood in relation to Kaniṣka. Aśvaghoṣa was no doubt a figure at the court of Kaṇiṣka, where the epistle from Mātricheta declining upon grounds of old age and sickness, to visit the king, make the possibility of their identification untenable. See Winternitz. Op. cit p. 270 & n. 2.

89. Hoernle. Manuscript Remains, p. 58 ff and 75 ff. The *Śatapañcāśatika-Stotra* folios were found in three different localities (Jigdalik-Bai, Tun-huang and Khora), as well as in different sizes. Besides introductory remarks of Hoernle regarding this work and this author, see the comprehensive Introduction to the *Śatapañcaśatika*—Sanskrit Text, Tibetan translation and commentary and Chinese translation by D.R. Shaekleton Bailey, Cambridge, 1951. The *Catuḥśataka* or Hymn of 400 verses is also noticed by Hoernle *Op. cit* pp. 75 ff. Three fragmentary folios of this work came from two different localities—Khora near Karashahr and Jigdalik near Bai. The two from Jigdalik have the same author and the same number of lines in a page. The three

one hundred and fifty verses'. Fragments of both these were found amongst Central Asian manuscripts. According to I-tsing,[90] the Chinese pilgrim scholar of the seventh century, 'it is delightful to hear both the Hymns recited in the assembly of monks'. These charming compositions are equal in beauty to the heavenly flowers, and the high principles which they contain rival in dignity the lofty peaks of a mountain. He is admired by later poets who imitate his style considering him as the father of literature. His poems were part of the Syllabi for both the Mahāyānist and Hīnayānist monks when they were initiated. Besides Asaṅga and Vasubandhu, who admired him, Dignāga—the 'Bodhisattva Jina' compiled a hymn of 300 verses, known as 'mixed Hymn of Praise' in praise of the first work—'Hymn of 150 verses', whichwas also translated by I-tsing into Chinese. Manuscripts of the Sanskrit original of the *Śatapañcāśatika-stotra* were recovered from various sites in Central Asia such as Jigdalik-Bai, Tun-huang and Khora, while Tokharian translations of the texts have also been brought by the German expedition from Turfan. Fragments of the other works of Mātriceṭa, the *Catuḥśataka-stotra* have also been recovered from Central Asia. There is no Chinese translation of the text but the Tibetan translation gives the name of the work as *Varṇanārha-varṇana-stotra*. Fragments of Sanskrit manuscript were discovered from Khora (near Karasahr) and Jigdalik (near Bai). The colophon of the chapters give the full title of the work as *Varṇanārha-varṇanā-Buddha-stotra-catuḥśatakam*.[91]

Among other works of a literary nature and non-canonical in character may be mentioned Āryaśūras *Jātakamālā*.[92] Its manus-

---

fragments are written in the slanting type of the Gupta script. I-tsing to whom both this and the hymn of 150 (*Śatapañcāśatika*) appear to have been well-known, translated only the latter into Chinese (No. 1456 p. 321) and not the former.

90. For I-tsing's praise of the work see Takakusu—Op. cit pp 156 f, 166.

91. Bagchi. Op. cit, p. 103.

92. Edited by H. Kern in Harvard Oriental Series I, 1891; translated by J. S. Speyer in Sacred Books of the Buddhists Vol. I 1895, Oldenburg; JRAS. 1893 p. 308 ff. A. Gawronski, *Studies about the Sanskrit Buddhist Literature*, Krakou, 1919, pp. 40 ff. Winternitz. Op. cit p. 273 n for other references. I-tsing praises the Jātakamālā (or Jātakamālās) among the works which were particularly popular.

cripts have been found at Murtuq and Toyoq. It resembles in style the Kalpanāmaṇḍitikā. This garland of Jātakas as the generic name Jātakamālā suggests, does not include or invent new stories, but retells the old legends in ornate, elegant language in the Kāvya style—lofty and refined and more artistic than artificial. The work contains 34 Jātakas like the 35 Jātakas of the Cariyā-piṭaka, intended to illustrate the 'Pāramitās' or 'perfections of a Bodhisattva'. The boundlessness of the Bodhisattva is also glorified in many narratives.

Along with the Kāvyas, two works on Sanskrit metrics and grammar *Chandoviciti* and *Kātantra* are supposed[93] to have been in use in the northern area of Chinese Turkestan. It is proposed on the basis of Sanskrit literary compositions in official donatory records from Kucha and Agnideśa of about the seventh/eighth century A.D. that Sanskrit works were composed in Central Asia. The Jātakastava preserved in a Khotanese metrical translation by Vidyāśīla seems to have been written in Sanskrit as indicated by the Syntax. Its Khotanese translation was done in the second half of the tenth century in the Sainanya monastery in Khotan.[94] In this context a Kharoṣṭhi inscription refers to the study of grammar, poetics and astronomy. Another inscription[95] notices the names of twelve nakṣatras named after twelve animals, also recorded in a portion of the *Mahāsannipāta-sūtra*, translated in the second century A.D. The text is supposed to have originated, at least partly, in Central Asia and appears to be a fragment of an astrological treatise written in a more or less barbarous Sanskrit.[96] It is an unidentified fragment and the text written in a curiously debased dialect, is astrological. Its name is Rishi Kharuṣṭa, said to be the reputed inventor of the Kharoṣṭhī script.

The literary remains brought from the ancient sites include a large number of fragments of Sanskrit medical texts, testifying to the conveyance of Indian medical literature in Central Asia. The

93. Mookerji. Op. cit p. 714.

94. ibid.

95. *Kharoṣṭhī Inscriptions* (Ed. Boyer-et-others) (Op. cit) No. 514.

96. Hoernle. *Op. cit* pp. 121 ff.

earliest discovery was by Col. Bower[97] of three different medical texts from an old stūpa near Kucha. One of these texts, named after him, deals with the origin, use and efficacy of garlic which is said to cure many diseases as also extending the longevity upto 100 years. The text also deals with digestion, an elixir for longevity, correct mixing of ingredients, other medicines, lotion and ointment for eyes etc. The second text contains 14 medical formulae for external and internal use, while the third one —the largest one—called Navanītaka (cream) contains an abstract of the earlier medical literature, including those of Agnideśa, Bheda, Jātikarṇa, Kṣarapāṇi, Parāśara and Suśruta. The text deals with the preparation of powder, decoctions, oils and also with injections, elixirs, aphrodisiacs, nursing of children etc. The instructions at the beginning of the text enjoin that it should not be given to anyone who has no son, nor to anyone who has no brother, nor should it be taught to anyone who has no disciple. The last part suggests provision for medical instructions. There is also a treatise on a charm against snake-bite. The Indian medical texts were also translated into Kuchean and Khotanese languages, thereby pointing to the prevalence of Indian system of medicine and its popularity.

Local Translations

The northern and southern regions—with their separate languages—Kuchean and Khotanese—have also provided local translations of Buddhist canonical and non-canonical texts in these languages. The language of Kucha—known to the Uighur Turks as *Kusana*, was spoken in the region from Aksu (ancient Bharuka) to Turfan (ancient Agnideśa). The French Mission discovered literary remains in different parts of this area. A few fragments in this language were also recovered by Aurel Stein, and some others by the German and Russian explorers. The Kuchean texts of the German collections have not been published, but fragments of the Stein and Russian Collections were published along with the French one by Sylvain Levi and later on by Jean

97. For an account of the discovery of this manuscript and its contents in a summarised form see Ghoshal. Op. cit p. 266; Bagchi. Op. cit, p. 104.

Filliozat.[98] Fragments of texts in the other dialect, called Tokharian, were discovered by the German mission in Karashar and Turfan region. The spoken language, however, was Kuchean. It is suggested[99] that the Tokharian literature was probably developed in some other area most likely in Tokharestan and the texts were brought to this region during the Uighur period. The major part of the German collections is from Shorchuq in Karasahr and the rest from the sites of Bazaklik, Murtuq, Sangim and Idikutshari at Turfan.

The Kuchean and Tokharian fragments are all translations of Sanskrit Buddhist texts with some bilingual extracts in original Sanskrit as well. These pieces were helpful in interpreting the Kuchean language extracts and in the identification of the fragments. These fragments include Kuchean translation of Sarvāstivāda-Vinaya like *Prātimokṣa*,[100] *Prāyaścittika* and *Prātidesanīya*.[101] These canonical rules in the language of use were meant for those monks who could not follow the Sanskrit texts. The bilingual texts might as well have been used for teaching Sanskrit to the members of the Buddhist order in that region. The Kuchean translations of *Udānavarga*,[102] *Udānastotra* and *Udānālaṅkāra* were very popular with the Buddhists. Fragments of Kuchean translation of a very extensive work called *Karmavibhaṅga*—a text

98. Textes Koutcheens : *Fragments de Textes Kouctcheens de Medicine et de Magie*—Paris 1948.

99. Bagchi. Op. cit p. 106.

100. Hoernle. Op. cit p. 357; Stein. Ancient Khotan I p. 483 edited with translation in French by S. Levi. The very earliest Buddhist literature must have included a Prātimokṣa. It is known in a Sanskrit version and in one Tibetan and four Chinese versions. The Prātimokṣa is to be recited twice a month in an assembly of atleast four monks, who confess their sins to each other before the ceremony. This disciplinary code is at the same time a formulary of confession (Kern : *Manual of Buddhism*—Reprint—Delhi 1968 p. 74); cf. the Chinese translation of the Prātimokṣa of the Sarvāstivādins by Kumārajīva about A.D. 404. (Nanjio No. 1160).

101. Hoernle. Op.cit p. 365 with a French translation of both the fragments by S. Levi.

102. Fragments of the *Udānavarga* from finds in Central Asia have been published by R. Pischel 'Die Turfan-Resensionen des Dhammapada'. SBA. 1908 p. 968 ff; S. Levi and La Vallee Poussin JA.S.10 t. XV. 1910 p. 444 ff; t. XVII, 1911, 431 ff; t. XIX. 1912 p. 31 ff; JRAS. 1911. p. 758 ff; 1912 p. 335 ff; Ref No. 55.

on the retribution of acts (Karma) were in use by the Buddhist priests, as a handy text expounding the doctrine of transmigration.

The non-canonical translations in the Kuchean language include those of medical and Tantric Sanskrit texts. One such is *Yogaśataka*, a medical work in about one hundred verses. It is an excellent abridgement of standard medical texts and a convenient medical handbook which could be used with profit and by practitioners. While Caraka and Suśruta Saṁhitās are not available in Kuchean translation (even in fragments), there are no doubt fragments of local translations of medical texts from Pelliot, Weber and Stein collections. Sanskrit names of drugs are transliterated with phonetic changes which could be easily adopted in local language.[103] Besides Kuchean, fragments of translations of Buddhist texts in the other dialect called Tokharian have also been traced though not closely studied. They contain bilingual texts and include such popular texts as the Udānavarga.

Buddhist texts were also translated into the Khotanese language, called by some as the Saka language. It continued to be in use even as late as the seventh-eighth centuries when there was no trace of the Sakas in Central Asia. Khotanese—as this language is designated—is associated with the translation of Mahāyāna Sanskrit Buddhist[104] texts. These translations include those of the *Suvarṇaprabhāsa-sūtra*, *Vajracchedikā*, *Aparimitāyus-sūtra*,[105] *Bhadracaryādesanā*, *Jātakastava* and *Maitreya-Samiti-nāṭaka*. The non-canonical texts include translation of two Indian medical texts : the *Siddhasāra* and *Jīvakapustaka*.[106] The former is attributed to one

103. Bagchi. Op. cit p. 106.

104. H.W. Bailey : *Khotanese Texts*, pp. 94 ff; Bagchi. Op. cit p. 107.

105. Stein. *Serindia*—Op. cit—II p. 914.

106. Bagchi. Op. cit 107. The name Jīvaka appears in the Sanskrit portion of a manuscript of medical treatise, written in a form of crude Sanskrit, and also in Śaka Khotanese. Fragments of this manuscript were found in the cave of Thousand Buddhists near Tun-huang. On the folios available each phrase of words in Sanskrit is followed by a full translation in Śaka-Khotanese. There are some medical formulaeas well, which are not traced elsewhere. Neither the name of the text nor that of the author is known (Mookerji. Op. cit p. 715 quoting R.G. Bhandarkar Commemoration Volume, Poona 1917 pp. 415 ff).

Ravigupta. The rendering is based on the Tibetan translation and contains portions concerning *tantra, dravya, arśa, bhagandara, pāṇḍuroga, mūtrakricchra, netra-roga* etc. The original of the other text, the *Jīvakapustaka*, however, is not traced, but it must have been in Sanskrit as the interlinear Sanskrit verses show.

There are also Buddhist texts in Sogdian[107] language which was spoken not only in ancient Sogdiana (north of Tokharestan with its centre at Samarkand), but also in other parts of Eastern Turkestan, which had colonies of Sogdian merchants. It was fairly popular in that part of Central Asia, and was used by the Buddhist priests and later on in the 9th and 10th centuries by the Manichaean priests as well. The Sogdian translations of Buddhist texts include those of *Dīrghanakha-sūtra, Vassantara-Jātaka, Vimalakīrtinirdeśa, Dhyāna-sūtra, Dhutasūtra, Nīlakanṭhadhāraṇī*[108] and *Padmacintāmaṇi-dhāraṇī-sūtra.* The translation of Buddhist Sanskrit texts into the major languages of Central Asia is evident from Uighur manuscripts[109] as well besides those mentioned earlier. Tokharian translations of *Maitreya-samiti-nāṭaka, Suvarṇaprabhāsa-sūtra,* Jātakas, *Sūtra of Kalyāṇaṁkara* and *Pāpaṁkara* etc. were rendered into Uighur-Turkish. The Turfan area provides fragments of three other manuscripts whose colophons refer to a work called *Daśakramapudarutanamal* (= *Daśakarma-pathāvadānamālā*), belonging to the Avadāna class. It is supposed[110] to have been first imported into Kucha or might have been composed there. It was translated from WKW Kwys'n (= Sanskrit) into Toyari or Toxari (Tokharian = Kuchean) and from that into the Uighur-Turkish language.

The Indian Buddhist texts are also supposed to be amplified in Central Asia[111] at the hands of local scholars who might have

107. *Serindia.* II. p. 920 ff.

108. Among the rolls with Sanskrit texts, *Nīlakaṇṭhadhāraṇī* with an interlinear Sogdian version deserves special mention since its publication by Louis de la Valleé Poussin and Gauthiot. Sylvain Levi has suggested strong reasons for placing the date of this bilingual manuscript between A.D. 650-700 (JRAS. 1912 pp. 629 Sq. 1063 Sq.).

109. For the Vigur manuscript, see *Serindia* p. 925; Bagchi. Op. cit, p. 108.

110. Mookerji—*Op. cit,* p. 716.

111. Central Asia is supposed to have provided new aspects to Buddhist

been Indian immigrants or had their education at centres of learning in India. The Chinese evidence does provide some information on these points. The story about the search by Dharmarakṣa in Khotan for a complete text of *Mahāparinirvāṇa-sūtra*, even though he had already found the text consisting of ten chapters, suggests its amplication in Central Asia. Besides this canonical work, according to the Chinese evidence, manuscripts of the *Mahāsannipāta-sūtra*, *Avataṁśaka-sūtra*, *Vaipulya-sūtra*, *Ratnakūṭa-sūtra*, *Laṅkāvatāra-sūtra*, *Sāriputra-dhāraṇī*, *Mahāprajñāpāramitā*, *Aṣṭasāhasrikā-prajñāpāramitā* etc. were preserved in the Chokkuka area. The contents of the Chinese versions of *Candragarbha-sūtra* and *Sūryagarbha-sūtra* in the absence of the Indian originals could be suggestive of their being recast in Serindia. This contention could as well be true in the case of the other Chinese translations of Buddhist canonical works noticed above.

The Buddhist literature in the course of its migration from India to China assumed some new aspects in Central Asia. In this direction the famous monasteries, their abbots and dons, seem to have played an effective role for preservation and propagation of Buddhist canonical literature as also its reconstitution. They seem to have made active and conscious efforts to naturalise the canon by introducing in it such elements as could bear the stamp of Sea-Indian literary contribution. Thus the *Sūryagarbha-sūtra*[112] in one of its sections mentions Buddhist Holy places which include besides those in India, Cīnasthāna (China), Khasa (Kashgar ?), and Gomalaśālāgandha Caitya on the Gośriṅga mountain of Khotan—one of the holiest places visited by the Buddhist devotees. The fragmentary manuscript of Prākrit *Dharmapada* in Kharoṣṭhī writing was procured from the Gośriṅga monastery site built on the slopes of the mountain of this name. The *Candragarbha-sūtra*[113] also mentions the kingdoms

---

literature in course of its migration from India to China. These are discussed in details by Bagchi (pp. 108 ff). Unfortunately references are not provided by him.

112. See Nanjio—*Op. cit.* No. 62 p. 28. It was translated into Chinese by Narendrayaśas of the Sui dynasty A.D. 589-618.

113. See Nanjio—*Op. cit* No. 63 p. 29. Translated by the same person Narendrayaśas but under the Northern Tsi dynasty A.D. 550-577.

of Central Asia supposed to be visited by the Buddha. These include Aśoka, Darada, Khasa, Cokkuka, Shalei (Kashgar), Khotan, Kucha, Bharuka, Hecyuka, Yi-ni (Agnideśa), Shan-Shan (Kroraina) and Chinasthan in the first list. The second one enumerates the number of incarnations of Buddha in various countries, including those outside India. Judging by the number of these incarnations, Khotan, Kucha and China are given places of the greatest honour in the Buddhist world.

A Buddhist scholar of Kucha named Lu-yen[114] compiled in the seventh century a Sanskrit-Chinese lexicon which has been preserved in the Chinese Piṭaka. This lexicon modelled on the Sanskrit Kośas also contains words of Central Asian origin such as *kalam* (pen), *kakari* (paper), *makara* (monkey), *kavasi* (sandal), and names of places in Central Asia and China such as Truṣaka (Turk), Korttana (Khotan), Kuchnia (Kucha), Wu & Shu (provinces of China), Kunudana (Khumdan i.e. Ch'angngan, Capital of China). There is also a Sanskrit-Khotanese text, useful for literary and colloquial purposes.[115] While its text in Sanskrit is corrupt, it is much influenced by Khotanese pronunciation.

The development of Buddhist literature in Central Asia and the contribution of its savants could not have been possible without the patronage of its rulers, some of whom bore Indian names like Vijayakīrti, Vijayasambhava etc. of Khotan, Haripuṣpa, Suvarṇapuṣpa, Suvarṇadeva etc. of Kucha, Indrājuna, Candrājuna etc. of Agnideśa. The Indian element in the local population and in the royalty appears to be fairly conspicuous and that accounts for the patronage accorded to Buddhism and its literature in Central Asia. This could as well be ferreted out from a study of the material culture of the Central Asians—an area of detailed study in the next chapter.

Bactria in Northern Afghanistan, with its language written in Greek script, was also the centre of Buddhism and this script was used in the records of certain Buddhist monasteries. Sanskrit seems to be understood in this part of Central Asia, as is evident

114. Bagchi—*Le Canon Bouddhique en Chinese*—Op. cit pp. 565-66; cf. *India and Central Asia*, pp. 110-111.

115. Bagchi—*ibid* p. 112.

from the discovery of a fragment of the Sanskrit text of the *Saṅgītaparyāya*[116] in a cave at Bamiyan. It is written in the North Turkestanese script of Chinese Central Asia. While it might have been imported there for use by the local monks, it nevertheless points to the understanding of Sanskrit canonical literature by the Buddhist monks of Bactria, who might not be having any literature in their language. Prākrit was used there in the early centuries of the Christian era in Buddhist donative records. In this context a record from the Tochi valley—now in Pakistan—uses both Bactrian and Sanskrit.[117] A Bactrian inscription on a vessel found in the ruins of a monument near Termez suggests philosophical or religious impact in that region. It is translated as : 'He who makes no distinction between his own 'I' and that of others is on the proper road'. Like the Bactrians, the Parthians, although followers of Mani, are also supposed to have been influenced by Buddhist literature in their amulatic text, with a list of Yakṣas closely resembling those in the Buddhist *dhāraṇī* texts. It is claimed that there is evidence revealing a strong influence of the literature of Northern Buddhism on Manichaean-Parthian literature.[118] A Manichaean-Parthian text refers to Mani as the Buddha.

Tibetan Buddhist Literature

It would not be out of context to take notice of Buddhist literature in Tibetan from Central Asia as well as from Tibet, based on Sanskrit Buddhist literature, as also the contribution of important Indian scholars to Tibetan Buddhist literature. The two main divisions of Tibetan literature are Kañjur and Tañjur.[119] The first one includes works esteemed as canonical, including Tantras. The second is composed of expositions of scriptures and also of many treatises on such subjects as medicine, astronomy and grammar. The canonical part is smaller but the commentaries and miscellaneous writings are more elaborate.

116. Mookerji. Op. cit p. 718.
117. ibid. p. 718.
118. BSOAS. XII. pp. 47-48.
119. The Tibetan orthography is bKah-hgyur (the translated command) and bsTan-hgyur (the translated explanation). Various spellings are used by

The great literary epoch of Tibet was in the ninth century. The Tibetan scriptures reflect the late Buddhism of Magadha when the great books of the Hīnayānist canon were neglected and a new Tantric literature was flourishing with exuberance. That accounts for the absence of the Abhidhamma works of the Hīnayāna and none of the great Nikāyakas. The whole collection of the Kañjur is commonly divided into seven parts : The Dulva,[120] equivalent to the Vinaya, is stated to be the Mūla-

European writers such as Kah-gyur, Kandijour, Bkahgyur etc. Weddel writes Kah-gyur and Tan-gyur (Eliot. Op. cit III p. 372 ff and n .1). See also Waddell: *Buddhism and Lamaism of Tibet*—Reprint, New Delhi 1974, pp. 157 ff. While the two terms are suggestive of two forms of Tibetan canonical Buddhist literature—the first one including Tantras also, the second one is composed of exegetical literature and also of many treatises on such subjects as medicine, astronomy and grammar. This distinction seems to hold good on the whole, yet it is not strictly observed. Thus, the work called Udāna and corresponding to the Dhammapada is found in both the 'Kañjur' and 'Tañjur' (Eliot. Op. cit, III, p. 372 n 2). The Lamaist Scriptures are faithful translations from the Sanskrit texts and a few also from the Chinese made mostly in the eighth and ninth, and the eleventh to the thirteenth centuries A.D.

120. Eliot. Op. cit, p. 373 and note for references. The Dul-va (Skt. Vinaya), or 'Discipline' is said to be compiled by Upali in thirteen volumes. It deals with the religious discipline and education of those adopting the religious life, and also contains Jātakas, Vyākaraṇas, Sūtras and Nidānas. It is sub-divided into seven parts :—

(1) The basis of discipline or Education (dul-va-gzi-Skt. *Vinaya-vastu*) in four volumes translated from the Sanskrit in the ninth century by Sarvajñadeva and Dharmakāra of Kashmir and Vidyākara-prabha of India, assisted by Tibetan scholars.

(2) Sūtra or Emancipation ('So-Vor-tar-pai-mdo' Skt. *Prātimokṣa-sūtra*) in 30 leaves.

(3) Explanation of Education ('Dul-va-nam-par-byod'pa Skt. *Vinaya-Vibhāga*) in four volumes. It also provides directions for dress and etiquette.

(4) Emancipation for Nuns ('dGe-Shon mahiso-Sar thar paimod' Skt. *Bhikṣuṇī-prātimokṣa-sūtra.*) 36 leaves in the ninth volume.

(5) Explanation of the Discipline of the Nuns (Skt. *Bhik. Vinaya-Vibhāga*) in preceding volume.

(6) 'Miscellaneous Minutiae concerning Religious Discipline' (Dul-va pran-tseqs-Kyi-gzi, Skt. *Vinaya-kṣudraka vāstu*) in two volumes.

(7) The highest text book on Education (Dul-va gzunv-bla-ma—*Vinaya-uttara Grantha*) in two volumes. (Waddel. Op. cit, p. 160).

For the analysis of the Dulva etc. four parts in *Asiatic Researches*, Vol. XX, 1836, by A. Cosund Korosi; Translated into French by Feer '*Annals dumusee*'

Sarvāstivāda Vinaya and agrees with the Chinese translation of Kumārajīva and to a great extent with the Sanskrit Prātimokṣa found at Kucha.[121] The second division Ser-chin corresponds to the *Prajñāpāramitā*[122] containing its longer and shorter versions. In this group the *Vajracchedikā* is very popular. Phal-Chan, equivalent to Avataṁśaka and *dkon-brtseqs* or *Ratna-kūṭa* are the two other divisions. The former in its sub-divisions appears as separate treatises in the Chinese Tripiṭaka called Hua-yen.[123] The next one agrees closely with the similar section of the Chinese Tripiṭaka despite its shorter form.[124] The other three sections are *mdo* equivalent to Sūtra,[125] comprising important works as the 'Lalitavistara', 'Laṅkāvatāra' and 'Saddharma-puṇḍarīka'; '*Myang-hdas*' or Nirvāṇa[126]—describing the death of the Buddha and *rGyud* or Tantra,[127] with many of its texts

---

Guimet loin zme, 1881; also Waddele '*Tibetan Manuscripts and Books*' in *Asiatic Quarterly*. July 1912 pp. 80-113. Eliot. Op. cit III p.373n for other references to several editions and translations of short treatises.

121. See Nanjio. Nos. 1115-1119, 1112, 1132. Rockhill. *Prātimokṣa-sūtra selon la version Tibetanie*, 1884. Finot and Huber.

122. Transcendental wisdom (Skt. *Prajñā-pāramitā*) in twenty-one volumes contain speculative doctrines which the Mahāyāna school attributes to Buddha's revelations in his mythical discourses. There is no historical matter, all is speculation and metaphysical (Waddell. Op. cit p. 161). Estimated by the Tibetans to be the Abhidharma, it is said to have been first collected by Kāśyapa, representing the teachings delivered by the Buddha in his fifty-first year (Eliot. Op. cit p. 374).

123. Waddel in *Asiatic Quarterly* 1912, XXXIV p. 98 renders the title as 'Vata-sangha' which according to Eliot probably represents *Avataṁśaka*. S.C. Das identifies Phal-Chen, Sde pa with Mahāśaṅghika. Feer notices its forty-five sub-divisions (Eliot p. 374).

124. cf. Nanjio—Op. cit No. 1234 p. 271. It enumerates several qualities and perfections of Buddha and his doctrine (Waddel Op. cit. p. 162).

125. Of the 270 works contained in this section about 90 are *prima facie* identical with works in the Ching division of the Chinese Tripiṭaka and probably the identity of many others is obscured by slight changes of title (Eliot. Op. cit, p. 374). The subject of the works is various. The greatest part of them consists of moral and metaphysical doctrine of the Buddhist system, the legendary accounts of several individuals etc. etc. (Waddel. Op. cit p. 162).

126. It consists of only one work, corresponding to Nanjio 113 (*Mahā-parinirvāṇa-sūtra*) p. 39.

127. It consists of twentytwo volumes containing about 300 treatises, out of which between thirty and forty are *prima facie* identical with those in

agreeing with treatises comprised in the Chinese Tripiṭaka. Among the Tantras[128] may be mentioned the *Mahāgaṇapati-tantra*, the *Mahākāla-tantra*, the *Ārya-Mañjuśrī-mūla-tantra* and *Śrī-Guhyasamāja*', the more important being *Paramādi-buddha-uddhrita-Śrī-kālacakra* on which the Kālacakra[129] system is founded.

The Tañjur[130] is a considerably larger collection than the Kañjur consisting of 225 volumes as against a 100 or 108 of the

---

the Chinese Tripiṭaka. Many of these are Brahmanic in spirit rather than Buddhist, like the *Mahāgaṇapālitantra* and *Mahākālatantra*) (Eliot. Op. cit, p. 375).

128. The idolatrous cult of female energies grafted upon the theistic Mahāyāna and the pantheistic mysticism of Yoga equally resulted in the evolution of Tantric Buddhist literature in Tibet. The difference between the 'Dhāraṇīs and the Mantras' belonging to the Tantras became more and more obliterated and finally the Dhāraṇīs were completely supplanted by the Mantras. In the Tibetan *Kañjur* the *Dhāraṇīs* are to be found both among the Sūtras (Mdo) and the Tantras (Rgyut). There are four classes of Buddhist Tantras : *Kriyā-Tantras, Caryā-Tantras*—teaching of the practical cult, *Yoga-Tantras*—dealing with the practice of Yoga and *Anuttarayoga-Tantras* which deal with higher Buddhism (Winternitz. Op. cit p. 389 and n. 1 for reference).

129. For the reference to Tibetan literary texts see Eliot Op. cit III p. 375. The extreme development of the Tāntric phase was reached with the Kālacakra which, according to Waddell, is a coarse Tantric development of the Ādi-Buddha theory combined with the puerile mysticism of the Mantrayāna. It attempts to explain creation and the secret powers of nature by the union of the terrible Kali, not only with the Dhyānī Buddhas, but even with the Ādi-Buddha himself. The demoniacal 'Buddhas' created through this union under the names of Kālacakra, Heruka, Achala, Vajra-Vairabha etc. are credited with powers not inferior to those of the celestial Buddhas themselves. They and their female spouses—ferocious and blood-thirsty—are to be conciliated with offerings and sacrifices, magical circles, special mantra-charms etc. (Op. cit p. 131).

130. The Tibetan commentary or Tañjur is a great cyclopedic compilation of all sorts of literary works, written mostly by ancient Indian scholars and some learned Tibetans in the first few centuries after the Introduction of Buddhism into Tibet commencing with the seventh century A.D. Divided into the *rGyud* and *mDo* (Tantra and Sūtra) classes, the former covers tāntrika rituals and ceremonies in eighty-seven volumes, while the latter concentrates on science and literature in one hundred and thirty-six volumes. One separate volume contains hymns or praises on several deities and saints, and another is the index for the whole. The first sixteen volumes of the mDo (Sūtra) class are all commerntaries on the *Prajñā-pāramitā*, followed by several volumes explanatory of the Mādhyamika philosophy (of Nāgārjuna) founded on the

latter. It is known to contain a great deal of relatively late Indian Buddhist works such as those of Aśvaghoṣa, Nāgārjuna, Asaṅga, Vasubandhu and other Mahāyānist scholars, and also secular literature such as the Meghadūta of Kālidāsa together with a number of works on logic, rhetoric, grammar and medicine. While some treatises, such as the Udāna (Dhammapada) occur in both the collections, the Tañjur group is considered as a thesaurus of exegetical and scientific literature. While grammar and lexicography are helpful in understanding the scriptures, the study of secular law demands an amplification of the Church rules and code of conduct. Medicine is useful in establishing the influence of the Lamas. History compiled by theologians suggests that true faith is progressive and always triumphs. Art and ritual are very close to each other. It is, therefore, incumbent on a learned person to be familiar with these disciplines. That accounts for all-pervasive character of the Tañjur literature.[131] Both the compilations have Tantric compilations of later times closer to the Mahāyāna Sūtras than the teachings of the Buddha. Further, the great majority of works in both the collections have the Sanskrit name first prefixed in transcription followed by its translation. The Indian proper names are generally translated. There are some translations from Pāli and a few from Chinese. One work is translated from the Bro-za language (perhaps from Gilgit) and another from the language of Khotan. Some works in the Kañjur literature have no Sanskrit titles and are perhaps original works in Tibetan. The Tañjur literature contains many such works.

Prajñāpāramitā. One volume contains the Tibeto-Sanskrit dictionary of Buddhist terminology, the bye-brag-tu-rtogs—the *Mahāvyutpatti.* Later commentaries, such as the Bodhi-pāṭha (in Mongolian Bodhi Mur) are also included under this heading. Its contents include rhetoric, grammar, prosody, mediaeval mechanics and alchemy (Waddell. Op. cit p. 165).

131. Huth's analysis of Vols. 117-124 of the Tañjur shows that they contain *inter-alia* eight works on Sanskrit literature and philosophy besides the Meghadūta, nine on medicine and alchemy with commentaries, fourteen on astrology and divination, three on chemistry (the composition of incense), eight on gnomic poetry and ethics, one encyclopaedia, six lives of the saints, six works on the Tibetan language and five on painting and fine art (*Sitzungsber Kon Preuss Akad Wiss. Berlin.* 1855—quoted by Eliot p. 376 n. 3).

Both the Kañjur and Tañjur as a whole represent late Buddhism of Bengal and also resemble in arrangement with the Chinese Tripiṭaka replacing the old Piṭakas and Āgamas. Being later than the Chinese, the Tibetan Canon lacks the Abhidharma but adds a large section of Tantras. Both the Tibetan and the Chinese canons recognise the divisions known as 'Prajñāpāramitā', 'Ratna-kūṭa', 'Avataṁśaka' and 'Mahāparinirvāṇa' as separate sections.[132] The Tibetan translation of all this literature falls into three periods: from the seventh century until the reign of Ralpachan in the ninth; the reign of Ralpachan, described as the Augustus age of Tibet, and some decades following the arrival of Atīśa in 1038. The first period includes contributions of Thonni Sanbhoṭa who was sent to India in 616 and made renderings of *Kāraṇḍa-vyūha* and other works. A Tibetan manuscript of the *Śālistambha-sūtra* (not later than A.D. 740) was discovered by Stein at Endere.[133] Padmasambhava and Kamalaśīla also contributed during this period. The former translated three works while seven of the latter's original works are preserved in the Tañjur. He also translated a part of the 'Ratnakūṭa'. It was also the beginning of the great period of translation to follow and two dictionaries containing a collection of Sanskrit Buddhist terms were also composed, namely the *Mahāvyutpatti* and an abridgement.[134]

Ralpachan[135] who ruled in the ninth century summoned from Kashmir and other parts of India many Buddhist savants for revising the then existing translations with the assistance of

132. Eliot. Op. cit p. 378.

133. *Ancient Khotan* pp. 426-9 and App. B; cf. Pelliot. BEFEO. 1908, pp. 507 ff.

134. The Mahāvyutapatti edited by Minayeff in *Bibliothica Buddhica* and an abridgement. (Eliot 379 n. 2).

135. Ralpa-Chan who ruled in the ninth century is described as the Augustus of Tibet. It is probable that at least half of the works now contained in the Kañjur and Tañjur were translated or revised at this time and that the additions made later were chiefly Tantras (rGyud). It is also probable that many tantric translations ascribed to this epoch are really later. According to Feer (*Analyse* p. 325), the Tibetan historians state that at this epoch kings prohibited the translation of more than a few tantric works (Eliot. Op. cit III p. 379 and n).

native monks and also adding many more of their own. The most prolific translator was Jinamitra, a Vaibhāṣika scholar from Kashmir, who translated a large part of the Vinaya and many sūtras assisted by Ye'ses-sde and Dpal-brTsegs commonly described as Lo-tsa-va. The death of Ralpachan was a great blow to Buddhist activities for a century. The revival that followed was distinctly Tantric with the arrival and contribution of Atīśa[136] from Vikramaśilā. During the eleventh century a great number of Tantric works were translated. Atīśa is credited with the revision of many works in the Tantra section of the Kañjur as also twenty others composed by him. Atīśa's disciple Bu-ston is credited with the compilations of the Kañjur and Tañjur with definitive arrangement. The Kañjur was later on translated into Mongol by order of Khutuktu Khagan[137] (1604-1634).

In a broad survey of the Buddhist literature in Central Asia and Tibet, based on the literary finds in Chinese Turkestan as well as in the western region comprising of Soviet Central Asia and Bactria, reference has been made to the contribution of Indian scholars and savants who first carried the message of the Tathāgata. A brief notice of the languages represented in manuscripts, fragments and inscriptions would no doubt provide reference to many influences at work in Central Asia which served both as a receiving as well as a distributing centre. The number of tongues simultaneously in use for popular as also for religious purposes was fairly large. The writing materials employed included palm leaves, birchbark, plates of wood or bamboo, leather and paper. Numerous Sanskrit writings all dealing with religious or quasi-religious subjects such as medicine and grammar—have been found amidst the literary relics. While the Mahāyānist literature is abundant, that relating to the Hīnayā-

136. Atīśa while clinging to Yoga and Tantrism, at once began a reformation on the lines of the pioneer Mahāyāna system by enforcing celibacy and high morality, and by deprecating the general practice of diabolic arts. Perhaps the time was now ripe for the reform, as the Lamas had become a large and influential body, and possessed a fairly full and scholarly translation of the bulky Mahāyāna Canon and its Commentaries, which taught a doctrine very different from that practised in Tibet (Waddell. Op. cit, p. 54).

137. Eliot. Op. cit p. 401.

nist school is not missing. Sūtras from the Āgamas, a considerable portion of the *Dharmapada* and the *Prātimokṣa* of the Sarvāstivādin school, fragments of two Buddhist religious dramas—one such being *Sāriputra-prakaraṇa* of Aśvaghoṣa, many translations of Mahāyānist literature such as the *Suvarṇaprabhāsa*, *Vajracchedikā* and *Aparimitāyus-sūtra* found in the southern part of the Tarim basin, are all suggestive of Sanskrit being understood in polite and learned society in Central Asia. Kuchean and Khotanese—the former in two dialects—were as well employed for local translations written in Brāhmī and Kharoṣṭhī scripts. While the use of Kharoṣṭhī could be traced rather to earlier times in the southern Tarim area, Brāhmī dominates the literary scene for a longer period and on a wider horizon.

The Buddhist literature in Central Asia, like its architecture, represents several periods distinguished by their contents, scripts and fine spots. Fragments of the Sanskrit Āgamas found at Turfan, Tun-huang and in the Khotan area represent the first period, followed by fragments of the dramas and poems of Aśvaghoṣa from Turfan, the Prātimokṣa of the Sarvāstivādins from Kucha and numerous versions of the anthology called Dharmapada or Udāna. Its Prākrit version found in the neighbourhood of Khotan and fragments in Tokharian and Sanskrit are all supposed to represent the canon, as it existed in the epoch of Kaniṣka representing its old stratum.

The new stratum includes Mahāyānistic Sūtras either written or re-edited in Central Asia. The popularity of the *Prajñāpāramitā*, the *Saddharma-puṇḍarīka* and the *Suvarṇaprabhāsa* is evident from finds of their fragments or part manuscripts from different areas. As Buddhism seems to have co-existed with other systems, its literary impact on those religions might not be denied. The construction and phraseology of Manichaen books resemble those of a Buddhist Sūtra. Some similarities could be traced between Buddhism and Nestorian Christianity, Taoism and even Zoroastrianism. A fuller study of this point is of course beyond the purview of literary enquiry in this context.

Reference to Buddhism and its canonical literature in Tibet is also traced here with a fuller review of the literary contribution of Indian scholars to Buddhist literature in the 'land of the snow.' It is not possible to provide a more comprehensive and elaborate study of Central Asian literature, especially with reference to Buddhism, till the huge stock of manuscripts and fragments still lying unexposed are studied and published. One need only wait patiently and be content with the available material on the subject.

CHAPTER V

MATERIAL CULTURE

Central Asia presents a picture of rich and assimilative cultural pattern. Its complete isolation from oceanic influence resulting in extreme aridity, physical configuration of a vast area covered by the deserts, and mountainous and hilly tracts making communication terrain difficult, have no doubt contributed to the development of local cultures along the oases fringing the Tarim Basin. Its two zones—sharply divided into nomadic and sedentary ones—were occupied by peoples of different ethnic origin and engaged in separate avocations. The former included nomadic hordes of Aryan stock—the Scythians at the one and the Turco-Mongol at the other end in the region now known as Outer and Inner Mongolia and Manchuria. In the South, the region between the Jaxartes and the Oxus was occupied by the people of Iranian origin. The area known as Eastern Turkestan from the Pamirs upto the frontiers of China was under the occupation of Aryan speaking people of different affiliations. Movements of the nomads of the steppes either in the west or in the east affected the sedentary life of the people in the south through the ages. This historical process, therefore, accounts for the evolution and development of local cultures along the routes of communication, with the impact and influence of the stronger one on the weaker, and equally resulting in the assimilation of the former in the local ethos. Cultural adaptability was not an unknown phenomenon. It ensured man's security and survival in his new environment. With this diversity provided by geographical factors in the cultural history of Central Asia, two things, however, contributed towards cultural integration, namely Buddhism and the Silk trade. Trade contacts between China and the West through Central Asia seem to have been established earlier than the introduction of Buddhism into Central Asia and through it into China. Central Asia played its role in the transmission of cultural traits from one part of the old world to another. The horse culture of Central Asia was, however, its own and the use of long boots, stirrups as also fur was carried from Central Asia to other parts of the world. New inventions, new ideas, new manners and customs continued to spread from one direction to another through this area. Alexander's campaign also provided cultural stimuli to this move, with the impact and influence of classical art, while Graeco-Roman glass influenced Chinese craftsmanship. The Chinese contribution was in terms of peach and apricot, carried through Central Asia and Persia to the European world. The most important product was the silk from China which was exported through two routes in Central Asia—the northern one passing through Turfan, Karashahr (old Agnideśa) and Kucha, and the southern one through Miran, Niya, Khotan and Yarkand. The terminal points of the two routes at the eastern end were Tunhuang and at the western one Kashghar. Trade provided stimulus and incentive to merchants of different personalities for participation in it and settling down at vantage points on the trade routes. This afforded opportunities not only for the people of northern and southern regions in Central Asia but also of other nationalities in fostering a bond of amity and understanding.

Along with trade and commerce, missionary activity and cultural transmission followed Buddhism which spread through its missionaries, and was successful in carrying the message of peace and understanding along with the sermons and scriptures of the Lord. Buddhism, and with it Indian culture, finally succeeded in establishing its firm hold throughout Central Asia, as is evident from archaeological finds and traces of hundreds of Buddhist shrines, stūpas and monasteries all along the two routes. Reference has already been made to the finds of Buddhist texts as well as to secular writings. Besides these, hundreds of documents from Loulan, Endere and Niya on the southern routes in Kharoṣṭhī shed light on different aspects of material culture of this part of Central Asia. Excavations, explorations and finds of literary texts and documents from sites on the northern routes are equally helpful in presenting a faithful picture of the cultural life of the people and impact of Indian culture on the local population. The accounts of the Chinese travellers who passed through Central Asia on their way to India in search of manuscripts equally furnish interesting details.

Cultural Integration

Both Buddhism and trade relations contributed towards the integration of social forces in Central Asia to a considerable extent. The plurality of local cultures consequent to geographical factors did stay, but the plantation of Indian colonies and that of others on the trade routes necessarily set the process of fusion into operation. Buddhism and its introduction, however, accelerated the process. There are traces of Indian names in records and manuscripts both in the northern and in the southern areas of exploration. In this context the role of the Buddhist missionaries[1] was effective in converting the local population

1. The role of the Buddhist missionaries in Central Asia and China is traced in M. Anesaki's article in the *Encyclopedia of Religion and Ethics*, Vol. X, pp.700-704. It is proposed that the spread of Buddhist missions in Central Asia was close on the heels of Aśoka's missionary enterprises. Historical records, however, agree in assigning to A.D. 67 the first official introduction of Buddhism into China with the coming of Kasyata Matanya and Dharmaraksa along with Buddhist statues and scriptures to China. Conversions *en masse* are said to have taken place in 71, many nobles and Taoist priests being among the converts. The new religion was received with open arms and heart; the way must have been long prepared for it. There is a gap of about eighty years between the mention of the first missionary and the advent of two other monks, one of whom was Shib-Kao of Parthia who came to China in 148. He is said to have been of royal blood and to have left his country because of the fall or decline of his family. This is one of the evidences that Buddhism had a strong foothold in Parthia and Central Asia. The Sogdians—a branch of the ancient Iranian people living in Samarkand and Bokhara—were equally propagators of Buddhism in Central Asia and China, and Seng-hui (Saṅghabhadra) was a great Sogdian Buddhist scholar. Reference has already been made to the role of the Indian Buddhist scholars from Kashmir. Kumārajīva son of Kumārāyaṇa and the Kuchean princess nun—Jīvā symbolises the spirit of cultural collaboration and synthesis between India and Central Asia. Saṅghabhūti, Gautama Saṅghadeva, Puṇyatrāta and his pupil Dharmayaśas are some of the other scholars who contributed to Buddhism and its cultural ethos in Central Asia and from there to China. The glorious days of Buddhism seem to have ended about the beginning of the eleventh century when the religion of the Tathāgata was in a tottering state in the land of its birth. Personal mysticism had weakened the community and the brethren were no

to a considerable extent. The Chinese pilgrims who passed through these routes between the fourth and the seventh centuries A.D. have noticed this fact and have recorded domination of Buddhist thought and way of life, sometimes in totality at some of the places. There are also references to rulers bearing Indian names in both the sectors. The Tibetan Annals,[2] however, record introduction of Buddhism in Khotan much earlier than is generally supposed. These record foundation of this kingdom to a son of Aśoka—born there—Ku-stana. Buddhism was first introduced in Khotan during the reign of Vijayasambhava, the grandson of the founder. All the successive rulers in the Annals have the names beginning with Vijaya, such as Vijayavīra, -jaya, -dharma, -siṁha, -kīrti, -samgrāma, -bala, -vikrama and so on. The Annals also speak of the Buddhist foundations attributed to various rulers.

---

longer bound by any unbreakable tie. The internationalism of Buddhism had lost its *raison-d'etre* with the decline of Buddhism in India and Buddhist missionary forces ceased to operate. (See also Bagchi—*India and China*—Chapter II on Buddhist Missionaries of India to China, pp. 28 ff.)

2. The history of Khotan is traced in Rockhills—*Life of the Buddha*—London 1884 pp. 230ff; by Abee Remusat in his *Histoire de la ville de Khotan;* and also by A. Stein—in his *Ancient Khotan* (Oxford. 1907). The Tibetan Annals include *Li-yul-gyi-lo-rgyus-pas*, *Li-yul-lung bstan-pa*, *Dgra-bchom-pa-dge-hdun-hphelgyi-lung-bstan-pa*—quoted by Stein (and noticed by Bagchi —*Op. cit* pp. 51 ff). According to Thomas, the first introduction of Buddhism is attributed to a śramaṇa by name Vairocana, who by a miracle was over the king Vijaya-Sambhava and under whose influence the first monastery in the country, that of Tsar-ma, was built. He agrees with Spect and Levi (JA. 1896-97.I. pp. 14 Sq.; II. pp. 166 Sq.) in rendering c. 60 B.C. for the first appearance of the Buddhist religion in Tibet. He further poses the question : Can one point to any specific matters of Indian culture which may have come to Khotan during its pre-Buddhist Period ? He suggests that certain Greek terms occurring in Shan-Shan inscriptions, viz. *Sadera* and *trakhma* = Stater and *drachme*, barracks—*parambula*—may have been brought from the Indian side. Further the division of the country into parishes (*sīmā*) and further into hundreds (*śata*), as also the ornate, formal, epistolary style noticed in inscriptions is certainly Indian, and might have developed into Mauryan Chancelleries. Further, the terms *lekha*—letter, *lekha-hāraka*—letter carrier, *pothī*—book noticed in records are Indian and so also *nagarka*—the town—mayor. (*Indianism and its Expansion*—Calcutta University Readership Lectures—Calcutta. 1942. pp. 60-61).

In analogy to the Indian rulers at Khotan, those at Kucha[3] on the northern route include Haripuṣpa, Suvarṇapuṣpa, Haradeva, Suvarṇadeva and others. The famous Buddhist savant of Central Asia Kumārajīva also belonged to this place. His father Kumārāyaṇa, a great scholar, came to this place from Kashmir and had married Jīvā, a royal princess. Another Indian colony on the northern route was at Karasahr—Karashar (Agnideśa) with its rulers bearing Indian names like Indrārjuna and Chandrājuna. Other important personalities noticed in manuscripts or in fragments include Yaśomitra, associated with a Kuchan monastery and one of the writers of the medical texts contained in the famous Bower manuscript.[4] The Indian missionaries included Gautama Saṅghadeva who arrived from Kabul in 383; Buddhayaśa, a Kashmiri Brahmin who collaborated with Kumārajīva; Buddhabhadra, a Śākya from Kapilavastu; Dharmarakṣa, a Mahāyānistic monk from Kashmir, who arrived in Kucha and then went to the court of a local king of Kan-su; Jīvagupta (528-605), born of a Kṣatriya family in Gāndhāra; and Dharmagupta from South India who spent a couple of years in Kashgar, Karashar and Turfan and finally went to Lo-Yang in China. The process of Indian missionaries coming to Central Asia and then moving on to China continued for a long time.

The Sung Annals[5] mention by name several Buddhist monks

3. The Chinese accounts name the ruling dynasty of Kucha as 'Po' meaning 'white'—probably to distinguish the rulers and their family from others. The old Kuchean documents mention the Sanskritised names of the rulers in the Tang period, like king Swarnate (Suvarṇadatta), transformed into Chinese as Su-fa-tie who ruled in the first quarter of the 7th century. His brother's name was Ho-li-pu-she-pi (Haripuṣpa), while that of his father was Su-fa-pu-kiue (Svarṇa or Suvarṇa-). The names of private persons had also been Sanskritised in the Karasahr area in this period, such as Wiryamitre (Vīryamitra), Wiryasene (Vīryasena), Jñānasena, Mokṣacandra etc. (Bagchi—*India & Central Asia*—Op. cit, p. 79).

4. The Bower Manuscript is supposed to be a very interesting document of the Indian cultural heritage in Central Asia. It contains seven medical texts written by four different persons, all obviously residents of a Kuchan monastery. It was in the memorial stūpa of its last owner, Yaśomati by name. According to Sten Konow, Sanskrit played the same role in Khotanese medicine as Latin in European. (Aalto : 'On the spread of Central Asia in the spread of Indian cultural Influence'—*Vivekanand Volume*, pp. 251-52).

5. Aalto : *ibid*, p. 254. A detailed account of the life and activities of the Buddhist missionaries who went to China from India through Central Asia

who around 1000 A.D. arrived in Kaifeng either from India or from Khotan, Turfan or Kucha, bringing with them holy relics and sculptures. The Indian Buddhist scholars were not inactive in the south-western sector of Western Asia. An Indian mission group headed by Prabhākaramitra is said to have converted the Yabu of the western Turks around A.D. 622. Earlier, according to the Chinese sources, a Chinese monk had persuaded the Quran of the Eastern Turks To-Po (572-591) that the greatness of China was based on Buddhism. The Quran founded a saṅgh-ārāma and received from the emperor Buddhist Sūtras translated into Turkic by Liu-Che-tsing.[6] Jīvagupta, the famous Buddhist scholar, lived for ten years in the Turki court until A.D. 575. Later Bilga Quran around 720 planned to build a Buddhist temple but he was dissuaded by his prime minister Tonyukuk who pointed out that Buddhism did not promote warlike spirits in the people.

These references to Indian regnal names and those of Buddhist scholar missionaries in different sectors in Central Asia suggest that Buddhism played quite an effective role in bringing about cultural integration among the peoples of Central Asia. The royal patronage extended to this religion and its propagation did bring about cultural evolution in the life style of the people. It was not a one-way traffic as would be evident from a study of the data provided by the Kharoṣṭhī records from Lou-lan, Endere and Niya, mentioning Indian names, mixed names and indigenous ones[7]—all forming part of the native cultural ethos.

---

is recorded in the earlier chapter dealing with Buddhism and Buddhist Literature.

6. BEFEO-1905. p. 253; JA. 1895. p. 355, quoted by Aalto—*ibid.* p. 251.

7. Aurel Stein in his note on the Kharoṣṭhī documents from the Lou-lan site, notices similarity of names with those in the Niya Series. Just as in the Niya ones, numerous names of unmistakably Buddhist or Indian derivation, such as Ānandasena, Bhatisama, Bhimaya, Buddhamitra, Dhammapāla, Kumudvatī, Pumnadeva, Caraka, Rutra, Sujada, Vāsudeva, are noticed side by side with others which seem of local origin eg. Cauleya, Cuvalayina, Kapgeya, Kalpisa, Kipsa, Kitsaitsa, Lampurta, Maldraya, Porbhaya, Pulkaya, Signaya, Tasuca, Tameca, Varpeya. Besides names, the official titles of Cojhbo, Gusura, Korī, Vasu are common to both Lou-lan and Niya records. Peculiarities of style, phonetics and spelling have no doubt as to identical standards

There was stamp of Indian thought and way of life quite perceptible from these records in matters of family life, position of women, professional avocations, and other items of material culture. The academic side and attainments as also the relations between the individual and the State are some other areas where one could trace Indian impact. The Indian names appearing in records are Ānandamitra, Buddhamitra, Dharmapāla, Puṇyadeva, Vāsudeva. Epic names like Arjuna, Bhīmasena, figure in several records and suggest familiarity with the Mahābhārata story. The Rāmāyaṇa lengend[8] in Khotan and its popularity is equally well-known. The documents from Niya and Lou-lan suggest the co-existence of Indians as well as the natives in these areas. Thus, one finds names of unmistakably Buddhist or Indian derivation, such as Bhatisama, Bhūmaya, Budhamitra, Dhammapāla, Kumudvatī, Pumnadeva, Caraka, Rutra, Sujada, Vāsudeva, occurring side by side with others, seemingly of local origin, like Cauleya, Cuvalayina, Kapgeya, Kalpisa, Kipsa, Kitsailsa, Lamputra, Maldraya, Porbhaya, Pulkaya, Signaya, Tasuka, Tameca, Varpeya. The official titles of Cojhbo, Gusura, Kuri, Vasu are common to both Lou-lan and Niya records. These are local ones in contrast to the Indian titles like *mahārayasa rayātirāsa* Skt. *mahārājasa rājātirājasa*, and *avijidasimhasya* Skt. *avijitasiṁhasya* and *devaputra.*[9] These seem to be based on the appellations used by the Kuṣāṇa monarchs. The association of names—Indian and native—in records suggest their active participation in administrative functions. Thus, one inscription (318) mentions Cozbo Indra-

been followed by the chancelleries, from Khotan to Lop at the period to which these records belong (*Serindia.*I.p.414).

8. The Rāmāyaṇa legend in Khotan is discussed in detail by H.W. Bailey in the Journal of the American Oriental Society (JAOS. LIX.pp 460-8) as also in the Bulletin of the School of Oriental and African Studies (BSOAS) 1940-42 pp. 365-76; pp. 559-605.

9. See nos. 204, 209. 332. The term Cozbo occurs in the maximum number of records—about forty. The imperial title—*mahārājasa rājātirājasa mahānuava rājadevaputrasa* is accorded to Rāja Tajaka (no. 422); and Rāja Mihira (500), and Rāja Anguvaka carries only the titles of *mahānuava* and *devaputra* (572). These may be compared with the same set of titles used by Kaniṣka and his successors.

sena and Kīrtisama, with the *ogus*[10] Asuraga, Piteya, Rohana, Camkura, Pūrṇadeva, and Cozbo Mitrapāla who heard the case of theft. Apparently the names are suggestive of both indigenous people and Indians who must have settled down there for long, participating together in sharing administrative responsibilities. Another inscription (418) records a priest Sariputra receiving an adopted child from Dewga Amto—named Sirsateyae—and marrying her to the priest Buddhavarma in lawful marriage. The daughter from this lady was given in marriage to the priest Jivalo Athane. Reference to three generations of cross relations in this record reveals many interesting features of social life. These may now be viewed in the context of family life, marriage, position of women, social gradations, pastime and recreations, food, dress and ornaments, agriculture and industries, pastoral avocations, weights and measures, communications, labour and finally, a review of material culture.

Family Life

The family, as an institution, is found in all human societies. There could be differences over its constitution and functions, but its general concept is a widely accepted phenomenon. In the modern western concept, a married couple and their own children—socially recognised, form the family group. A joint family, according to oriental standard and norms, however, consists of two or more lineally related kinsfolk of the same sex, their spouses and offspring occupying a single homestead and jointly subject to the same authority or single head. It is a cohesive unit forming a solid group. The evidence provided by the records from Central Asia is suggestive of the traditional joint-family system prevailing in this area. The family included father, mother, brothers and younger sisters (Kudi) (Nos. 164, 195) with the headman exercising authority over them (450, 562). Terms used are primarily Indian like

10. Ogus, Gusura, Kala and Cankura are prefixed with the names, probably suggesting their position in administrative hierarchy. It is, however, not possible to determine their social or administrative status, or assess their position. The Cozbo Sañjaka in one record (272) is enjoined to finish his administrative work at full speed, and anybody interfering in his functioning was to be punished.

mātu, *mādu* for mother, *putra* and *suta* for son, *pitūmaha* for grand-father, *prapotra*, *prautra* for grandson; *nāpata* for daughter's son; *bhrāta*, *bhrātu* for brother; *brhrāta-putra* for brother's son; *jāmāta* for son-in-law, *svasu* for sister, *bhāryā* for wife; *putrī* and *dhitū* for daughter. *Kula* and *parivāra*, suggesting family as a unit, are also noticed. One inscription refers to *Visatitaga* Skt. *Viśa*—suggesting a family. There is evidence of familiarity and closeness among kinsmen and relations. Letters to near and dear ones[11] are addressed in familiar tones, informative in nature particularly concerning the family problems. It was natural to be communicative with brothers on domestic problems. A Buddhist monk addresses his brother in an affectionate manner (646) without alienating himself completely from his family. Two letters (499, 612) addressed to friends are in sincere and well-wishing tone (*kalyāṇakārī*), soliciting an early reply. A lady communicates with her sister (No. 316) pointing to literacy among upper strata of society and addresses her as a pleasing personality (*priyadarśinī*). Letters are addressed to daughter and son-in-law (690), wife's brother (syālā) (140, 475), conveying good and bad news.

The head of the family was enjoined to restrain the other members from raising any settled issue in future, failing which he had to renounce his control over them (No. 621). He had to look after their safety and see them settled down comfortably elsewhere in period of emergency or distress (No. 362). There could be addition to the family through adoption as also through purchase of slaves who were also a part of the family. Children—both boys and girls (nos. 331, 542 etc)—could be given in adoption after payment of proper consideration (*Kutīchara*) in cash or in kind (11, 31). Even elderly ladies could be accepted in adoption (528) and provision was made for their share in inheritance. The birth of a son was an occasion for rejoicing in the family (no. 702), that of a girl, of course, was not one of distress or depression, since she could as well be helpful to the family in future. Several terms used for girls

11. The list of such letters is very long (106, 109, 435, 476, 512 etc.) and primarily concerned with domestic affairs or personal matters involving the communicating parties (nos. 139, 152, 157, 499, 519 etc). They are addressed in a very affectionate manner, signifying close family ties.

and ladies suggest their position in society. A young girl is called *Kuḍī* and when grown up is known as *dhitū* (279), in Sanskrit *duhitrī* or *ghihare* (no. 46) *grihaṇī*. After marriage she is called *bhāryā* and *mātu*—Skt. *mātri* when she has children. A sister is known as *Svasu*—Skt. *Svaśru* and maternal aunt—*māhulā*—Skt. *mātulī*. Certain other terms associated with ladies denote their status and position in society like *vesiṣṭrī* (709), probably *veśyā*—a public woman and *khakhonistrī* or *khasorṇa* (Nos. 58, 63, 248) identified with *svasurānī*, *anitī* or *anitā* probably synonymous with *bhāryā* and finally *dāsī* (621) signifying female slaves. Some insteresting information about the position of ladies is available, as for instance, the father's responsibility to marry his daughter for which he could demand bride's price called *lote*, from the son-in-law.[12] He could legally claim it, but not if the girl had run away with her suitor (No. 621). As part of the family, she had no doubt her position, but being treated as the property of her husband she could be given in exchange, or be a salable commodity and her value was determined on the basis of her height and in cash or in kind (nos. 587, 437) etc. As part of the sale transaction or gift (no. 380), or in exchange (no. 551), as also for payment of debt (no. 114), she could be transferred to the other party without hindrance. Women could amass money over which they had full rights and on their death it was to be shared equally among their children (no. 474). Girls were generally married to persons of the same avocational group. A Buddhist monk married his daughter to another monk rather legally (no. 18, 474), but another such girl defying her father eloped with a potter's son (no. 621). Marital relations among close relatives were not unknown and sometimes these were on a mutual exchange basis (*vinimaya*).[13] This was fairly

12. The demand for the bride's price seems to have an accepted principle in society. In the Ārṣa form of marriage, mentioned in the Hindu Dharmaśāstras, the bridegroom had to provide a pair of oxen. On the other hand, in the *Brāhma* form the father-in-law catered to the needs of the daughter and the bridegroom. In China, the acceptance of any bride's price was banned by the Tang Emperor Kao-Sung, but if such money was accepted , it was to be spent on the bride's necessities alone. (For a detailed account of marriage in different countries see *Encyclopedia of Religion and Ethics*, Vol. 8 pp. 423 ff.)

13. In the first century A.D., A Hūṇa noble Jiji had married the daughter of Kanga-gu and in exchange had given his daughter to his father-in-law.

common among the Hūṇas probably more for political reasons. Communication difficulties encouraged near distance or rather marriages in the same locality with the mutual offering of girls in exchange (nos. 279, 481). The status of a woman in the family was rather limited. She could not participate in social and public activities. Her husband had full right over her person—from use of violence (no. 279) to pledging her or disposing her in satisfaction of debt clearance (no. 719). Her value was assessed in terms of rolls of silken cloth (no. 3), the price of a camel (nos. 209, 578), carpets of different sizes and even household goods (no. 706). She along with her children could be the subject of robbery and easily disposable (no. 415). Dissolution of marriage (no. 34, 621) was possible in cases not covered by monetary payment to the girl's father. A term *vivega*[14]—meaning probably 'separation' is recorded in an inscription (no. 34). Ladies of the upper strata in society seem to have been better off—educated and capable of free communication with friends and relations (no. 316). They could as well send presents. Administration no doubt accepted their credentials and they could be called for evidence in legal matters (nos. 3, 420).

Slaves—male and female—as well formed part of the family. Several terms are used for such slaves like *dāsa* (nos. 345, 491), *dāsī* (no. 621), *dajha* (no. 569), *dhaja* (no. 227), dhajhī (no. 39, 45) with the master known as *bhatare* (no. 147), *bhataraga*→Skt. *bhaṭṭāraka*. A servant is called *presi* (no. 204) who seems to be different from *dāsa* or slave. Another term for a domestic employee is vathayaga— *vadhaya* (no. 118) equated with Khotanese *vakṣaya*[15] and Tokharian *upasthayaka*. Some records (no. 19, 54, 401) mention his scale of emoluments in terms of salary and perquisites—*parikraya bhojana*(*pacevara*)—food, and clothes (*co-*

(McGovern : *Early Empires of Central Asia* p.190). An inscription (no. 279) notices a girl of Yave-avana being married to a native of Ajiyama—Avanā, on an exchange basis. A similar case is recorded in another inscription (no. 481). For discussion on the terms *lote* and *mukeśa*, see BSOAS. 6. pp. 523 ff.

14. Burrow. *Language of the Kharoṣṭhī documents from Chinese Turkestan*, Cambridge, 1937, p. 116.

15. Burrow derives *Vatayaga* or *Vathayaga* from *upāsyaka*, and it was accepted in Khotanese as *vathiaya* (*Languages*—Op. cit, p. 118). In Hindi it is accepted as *bhritya* or *anucara*. Bailey equates Khotanese *vaḍhaya* with *vakṣaya*, or *vaghayarha* (BSOAS. Vol. II, p. 791).

daga), and he was required to look after the grazing cattle. The slaves received only food and clothing. A record (no. 25) mentions 3 milim rice and another (no. 470) 10 *khi* rice as the remuneration for such a servant. Carriers on their back *prithabhārika* > Skt. *priṣṭhabhārika* (no.396) transported short distance goods. The slaves and servants looked after the farms of their masters as also their household. The slaves were bonded for a specified period like ten years (no. 550) or twelve years (no. 364). The breach of agreement was punishable (no. 764). Slaves could even otherwise be punished for theft (no. 518) or stealing of clothes, cattles etc. (345, 561). Sometimes the punishment inflicted was exemplary and caused their death (no. 144). Abduction of slaves was not an unknown phenomenon (no. 36, 324, 491). One who returned to his original master did not involve any payment by the abductor to the former lord, otherwise money payment (*lote*) was necessary. Slaves were marketable as well as presentable commodities (nos. 491, 324). A couple of inscriptions record sale of girls and men (*pruṣdhaya*) transferring ownership as also the right to sell, pledge, exchange and present the slaves (nos. 589, 590, 591). The master was liable for the lapses of his slave, and for theft he had to make good the loss involved (nos. 345, 561). The slaves could adopt someone only with the consent of their master. The longer stay at a farm away from the master's home occasionally generated a spirit of defiance and an urge for independence in a slave. He could, however, purchase his freedom by paying back *lote* and *mukeśi* to his master (no. 585). A benevolent master sometimes transferred his interest in the farm in favour of his favourite slave (no. 36). This concession enabled the slaves to build up some strength in terms of money and cattles as also clothes (nos. 24, 327). The master could not illegally appropriate his slave's earned property (no. 24), nor could this be executed in payment of debt (no. 49). The monks also kept slaves to look after their farms and property interests (no. 152) and there could be change of masters.

Food & Food Habits

The records provide interesting information regarding items of food and food habits. The village economy was fairly developed and the agriculturists fairly experienced. Wheat, rice and corn were produced as items for staple food. The term generally used for these products is *pacevara.* Flour (*aṭa-āṭā* and *śaktu*) (no. 359) and rice (*dhānya*) were commonly used. One record (no. 359) notices provisions consisting of 2 *milima,* 15 *khi* of meat and 5 *khi* of *maka* and one vest (*Kavasti*). Condiments and saucy stuffs made food delicious with the addition of pepper (*mārica*), ginger (*orakhing*), *arakhima* of pepper (*pipali-pipala*), *svaca* and cardamons (*susmela*) (no. 702), milk, sugar (*śarkara*) and ghee (*ghridra*) are also noticed in records (nos. 13, 15). The nonvegetarian food was far nutritious than the vegetarian one (no. 514). Jars of ghee and a hundred jars of oil are no match, according to the author of this record, to a sixteenth of one piece of meat. Food was meant to sustain one's body and maintain his existence (*nisaganam*) (nos. 478, 641). Provision was made for soldiers in the capital in the form of corn and sheep (no. 478). Spirituous liquor was in common use as is recorded in several inscriptions (nos. 175, 244, 317, 329, 343), and the state administration realized cess on its production and sale. A record (no. 175) refers to the supply of old wine to the ruler and the people taking only three *khi* of ordinary drink. This might have been the restricted limit. Another record mentions cultivation of grape vineyard, but there is no reference to the wine shops for ths supply of drinks or bars. The wine supplied to the ruler had to be sealed to ensure its genuineness (no. 247).

Dress and Ornaments

The dress of the Central Asians conformed to the climatic conditions, as also to the impact of Indian as well as Chinese cultures. Some information on this aspect of material culture is provided by the accounts of the Chinese pilgrims who passed through this region on their way to India. The data from the records under consideration as also the sculptures and paintings from different sites have much to reveal. These people, according to Hsuang-Chuang, used clothes of wood and fur, as also silk and cotton.[16] The ladies' dress consisted of a trouser and a petty-coat type of covering *pamzavanta* made of *prigha*—a kind of silk (no. 316). Another inscription (no. 318) mentions an

16. Stein—*Ancient Khotan* (*op. cit*) p. 139.

embroidered *viḍapa*—a jacket made of white silk, a *samimna*, a *lyokmana* of many colours, a yellow coloured *Kharavaraṇa, a patovarṇaga* garment, golden dave, a *varsara*, fine hasta of woollen cloth (Umna = Ūrṇa), bluedyed kigin. *Cotaga* or *codaga* was the coat or the upper covering, since the term is used with reference to males as well as females (no. 19, 506). Another inscription (505) mentions *caṭoga* which is another form of cotaga and is translated as 'cloth' which was universally used. Several other terms suggestive of items of clothing are *kavāsi, kuñchali, kacavadha, candri. Kavasi* appears to be inner clothing—same as *kavaji*, while *kañculī* could be equated with the Sanskrit *kañculikā* meant to cover the upper part of the ladies' body. This was made of silk (*kauśeya*) as well as of wool (*ūrṇa*) and was dyed as well (no. 318). A small jacket was known as *kañcabandha* (no. 149). This inscription also makes reference to roughly woven clothes, woollen clothes, two jackets, two sanstamni (?), two belts and three Chinese robes in some context. The head dress is suggested by a term *Cīnabeda* (no. 353)—a kind of Chinese head covering. Two inscriptions (nos. 272, 714) mention a term *candri-kammata*, which, according to Bailey,[17] is suggestive of some sort of trouser made from a sheet of cloth. Others take it to signify some tax or cess or jade. The *cīna-cīmara* (no. 149) →Skt. *Cīna-cīvara*-is suggestive of Chinese overcoat, although *cīvara* is a term used for the upper covering of Buddhist monk. Several other terms, probably connected with dress, are noticed in inscriptions (no. 714) like *kacikumuṭa* Khotanese *komadayi*—a form of trouser; *puchama* (534)—some sort of cotton night dress, *pasamvamta* (no. 534) made of cloth; *lastuga* (nos. 144, 298, 566) made of many-coloured silk—probably some kind of scarf. The Indian blanket (*kambala*) is noticed as *loyi*—Hindi *Loyī*, and also as *kojava* (no. 583, 593, 599). An inscription (660) refers to rolls of silk.

Some idea of the dress and its style can be had from the Central Asian paintings as well with the male and female donors and devotees dressed in their traditional costumes and head dress. Thus, in a painting of the *Parinirvāṇa*—'the dying Buddha scene' at Bezeklik[18]—a Chinese dignitary wears the head dress of a judge,

17. BSOAS. Vol. XI. p. 793; cf. Burrow. *Op. cit.* p. 143.
18. F.H. Andrews. *Wall Paintings from Ancient Shrines in Central Asia* (henceforth—Andrews. *Paintings.*) p. 75.

another Chinese has a broad-brimmed conical hat, while an elderly person puts on a loosely tied white turban (*pagrī*). The same scene depicts an unmistakable Persian figure with grotesquely long and bulbous nose, full beard and flowing moustache, wearing the typical wing-shape Persian hat. Similarly (the figures) in the pictorial remains from the caves of the thousand Buddhas, the head gear and robes of the donors and donatries suggest 'Chinese translation of the quasi-secular forces'.[19] In a scene from Kizil[20] (7th century) showing the preaching Buddha (17, 850), a lady sits on a low chair, her hands in the *añjali* mudrā. She wears a white blouse with blue spots and a green under-garment. The young monk behind her puts on his brown robe. The main group in the foreground consists of a man laden with jewellery, and wearing only short dhoti reaching to his thighs, and to his right a woman dressed in a green jacket with fancy embroidery and wide brown oversleeves under which green borders are noticeable. Her blue speckled skirt reaches down to her ankles and the upper part of the body is covered with a short piece of white cloth. Similarly Vajrapāṇi from Kizil[21] is shown elaborately draped in chains and strings of beads or metal disks. He wears a brown skirt with ruffled green borders, and the ends of long green scarves suspended from his head dress almost touch the ground.

Portrayals of princes and their families are an interesting feature of the art of Central Asia, and these also provide an insight into the aristocratic life style. The finest painting of a Uighurian prince[22] on cloth, now in the Berlin Museum, depicts him dressed in a fine robe, patterned with a large floral design. It is a long-sleeved, round-necked garment reaching to the feet with a belt fastened in front, with rectangular decorative pieces containing a slit from which to hang straps with objects of daily use. A slit in the side of the garment reveals a black knee-length boot. On his head the prince puts on a three-pronged cap, held by a strap under the chin, with a shoulder-length veil hanging

19. Stein—*Serindia*. Vol. II. p. 850.

20. Martin Lerner. *Along the Ancient Silk Routes—Central Asian Art* (New York. 1982) p. 96.

21. *ibid*. p. 68.

22. Bussaghli. *Paintings of Central Asia*, p. 106.

down behind. Along with an attractively curled moustache, he has a beard covering his chin and framing his cheeks.

The Miran paintings—in all probability Indian in conception and execution—depict Indian garments[23] and bare feet. They wear loin-cloths (*dhotī*) gathered about their legs, and stoles draped over the shoulders. The drapery is shaded or contoured with a suitable colour; red with black lines, green with dark grey; white with pale grey, and yellow with red. The dhotī is traced in the painting from Toyuk[24] near Turfan in the northern part of Central Asia. The costumes are of two kinds; one with a long dhotī covering the legs to the ankles; the other short, leaving the legs bare. A loin-cloth is usual and a kind of *upavīta* or narrow shawl crosses from the left shoulder and passes round the body below the left arm. A stole, passing over the shoulders and winding round the arms, with freely flowing ends, seems common to all. Most of the figures wear a simple headdress (*mukuṭa*). In the Turfan area costumes are either the loose draperies customary in India, or elaborately 'tailored' garments[25] conforming to fashions of the intruding communities. The use of sandals or shoes of more or less elaborate fashion is a notable feature. The highly decorative shoes, an imbricated pattern in red on a white ground, may be a form of plaiting or quilting, are noticed in Bezeklik paintings.[26]

Ornamentation of the body for both male and female is noticed in paintings and a few Kharoṣṭhī inscriptions from Lou-lan, Niya and Endere also mention some items. Thus, one record (no. 566) mentions seven-stringed pearl/ornament (*muṭilaṭā*) and one ear pendant (*sudī*). Reference to a silver ornament is recorded in another inscription (no. 149). While the costumes are simple and there is absence of jewellery in Miran paintings, in the later ones, are noticed different kinds of jewellery in general use. These include armlets, anklets, bracelets, ear-rings, garters, *mukuṭa*, carcanet, armlets and bangles, adorning the male figures along with pearl studded garlands or necklets. A prince in a

23. Andrews. Op. cit. p. XXII, also p. 8.
24. *ibid*, p. 42.
25. *ibid*, p. xxvi.
26. *ibid*, pp. 58, 60.

Bezeklik painting[27] has the long, slit lobes of his ears carrying gold rosettes from which hang bunches of five coloured beads. His necklet is of chased gold and red in alternate sections, with red and green beads. Beads in bunches are also attached to armlets, and to ear-rings. The *mukuṭa* or tiara also presents a prominent look with its varied compositions—crown like, jewelled and decked with flowers[28] or composed of a group of three gold bosses at the centre, one at each side and a red and green palmettes above.[29] Coiffure and head-dress are varied and significant at Bezeklik, floral and pearl studded.[30]

Pastime and Recreations

A sophisticated life style enjoins provision for recreation in a dignified manner. It could be outdoor games or hunting exersions, rather more masculine exercises or indoor gatherings with music, dancing and other items of recreations. A solitary inscription (no. 13) enjoins stoppage of wounding mares and horses in hunting. This negative approach in the form of issuing injunctions against slaughter of useful animals could imply people's interest in hunting. The painting scenes,[31] no doubt, depict some of the animals, as for instance, lions, wild goats—their horns as votive offerings, elephants, bulls (139), camels—noticed in inscriptions as well. In the famous cowherd Nanda scene from Kizil[32], two cattle, one dark in colour and the other white, lie on the ground, while in another painting of seated Vajrapani from the same cave one notices two sharp-beaked falcon-like birds. A hunting scene is depicted in a clay sealing from Farhad — Beg-Yailaki with a man on horseback galloping

27. *ibid*, Bez. iii. A.B. p. 71.

28. *ibid*, pp. 31, 55, 58.

29. *ibid*, p. 72.

30. ibid, pp. 52, 84, 88. Stein notices the headdress of a princess in the mural painting in Cella V at Miran. Her hair descends in black tresses below the neck, with love-locks in front of the ears and two fringes crossing the forehead. In another figure two strings of red beads crossing the hair obliquely are fastened with a large circular jewel ornament above the middle of the forehead. (*Serindia*, Vol. I p. 519)

31. Stein. *Serindia*, pp. 506, 891, 950, 943, 1024 Sq. etc. for reference to these animals in painting.

32. Lerner. *Along the Silk Route*—Op. cit, p. 67; Bussagli. *Op. cit* p. 72 (ill.)

with a sword in his uplifted right hand. A lioness is shown behind the horse and a goat or deer is shown running.[33] The swimmer's scene[34] from Kizil shows persons in some pool among water lilies, while the middle one seems barely able to keep his head above water; the man on the right swims with powerful strokes. His expression and gestures reveal great determination and skill in swimming.

Khotan and Kucha were noted for their music, as is evident from certain paintings from these regions, as also from the account of the Chinese pilgrim Hsuan-tsang. This Chinese pilgrim records that the green-eyed people of Khotan were very fond of music and dancing. In the famous 'attainment of Parinirvaṇa' painting[35] from Bezeklik, four musicians contribute to the sounds of lamentation, with professional enthusiasm and energy. The drummer holds the drum under his right arm and beats it with a ball-headed stick. To his left the cymbal player clashes his box-like instrument above his head. Another, whose head is missing, plays a flute with the left hand fingering the notes while the last one—the white-haired *biwa* player uses the classical plectrum. The animated poses of the legs suggest time beating. The divine musician from Kizil[36] suggests the continuation of the musical traditions at Kucha which was the centre of Indian influenced music in Central Asia from where it spread to China. It is reported that when Chinese rule was extended to this region in 382, the General Protector Lu-Kuang brought groups of performers—actors, musicians and dancers—back to China as booty. Among the instruments used were the five-stringed lute, the harp, the mouth-organ, drums, cymbals, gongs, and the four-stringed Kucha lute.[37] In China one of the teachers

33. Stein. *Serindia*, p. 1257.

34. Lerner. *Op. cit.* p. 75.

35. Andrews. Bez. xii. A.1.pl. XXVII. pp. 95 for a detailed account, including reference to the Chinese pilgrim Hsuang Tsang's account.

36. Lerner. *Along the Silk Route—Op. cit.* p. 93.

37. The musical traditions at Kucha are mentioned in early Chinese records. Chang-Chien, whom emperor Wu-Ti sent to the West in 138 B.C. is said to have brought back musical instruments and melodies from Kucha to the capital Ch'ang-an (Liu-Mau-tsai. *Kutscha and seine Beziehungen Zu China*—Wiesbaden 1969—quoted by Hertel—*Along the Silk Route*, p. 93).

of this lute was a brahmin, and another lute player Sujīva who went to China in 568 bore the family name of Po of the royal house of Kucha. It appears that along with Buddhism, Indian music was brought to Kucha, an inference that is supported by the many musical subjects depicted in the wall paintings. In this scene, the fragment shows the head of a dark skinned divinity playing the flute.

Agricultural Economy

The Central Asian socio-economic structure seems to be related to the land economy, cattle rearing and a few productive avocations. The State was no doubt the owner of the land with the upper class people (no. 120) enjoying it on payment of rent in terms of produce. They cultivated this land with the help of hired labourers and slaves. The existence of a slave-owning society is fairly evident from numerous inscriptions recording their status. Besides payment of salary, food and clothing were also provided to the labourers (no. 25). Payment of wages was necessary (no. 50) but there could be disputes as well. Slave women too were not denied these perquisites though they could be purchased. An inscription (no. 591) assesses a male slave's value (*prusdhaya*) in terms of a five year old camel, a horse of the same age and 25 *altga* (not known). He could be pledged, exchanged and utilised as desired by his master, but he had certain rights as well, as for instance acquisition of property through one's savings (no. 671) and its alienation as well (no. 419). This right extended to female slaves as well. The use of violence against working women (no. 20, 29, 53) and appropriation of their land produce was not unknown (no. 36). The master was not responsible for the debts of his slave (no. 24). There are references to several kinds of lands. The arable one was called *mishi*[38] (no. 572) while the barren one was known as *akri*. Land

38. *Misi*, according to Aurel Stein, is some crop. He also notices the full proprietory rights over this *mlsi*—the full enjoyment of all its benefits in whatever way the purchaser desires, whether for ploughing or sowing or for giving to another as a gift or as a *namanya* (*namaneya*, tenancy ?). Further, if at any subsequent time a *vasu ageta* (*vasu*, a common title; *ageta* also apparently the title of some official) shall give any order concerning it, such a verbal order shall be invalid at the king's court (*Serindia*, Vol. I. p. 232).

left unploughed could be barren. The ploughing (*krisitam—krisṇata*) and sowing (*bavitaga—vapānta*) operations are recorded (no. 320). While reaping and winnowing processes are not mentioned in any record, the reference to barn-house (*gothada*) in a record (no. 36) used for storage is interesting. This belonged to a slave who had complained to the authorities for theft. The term *kurora* (no. 514) is also noticed in connection with land and is defined as 'the earthern boundary line of the ploughed land'. The amount of seed required in a measured plot of land is also recorded in several inscriptions (nos. 422, 519, 580), and the price of the land was accordingly determined and paid for in kind or in barter (no. 715). There is no reference to cash payment. One inscription (no. 366) records collective farming, since the land in dispute was returned to villagers.

Irrigation was equally important after the sowing of the seed, and several records notice it. Tibetan documents from Chinese Turkestan mention irrigation of fields by the labourer called *chun-pa*. These documents also mention the ploughing of fields and threshing of the grain, and announce punishment for those who let the water dry up. An ordinary field labourer was called *zhing-pa*.[39] The wheat crop (*goma—godhuma*) needed at least two-three waters (no. 72). Canals carried water to distant areas urgently needing it and payment had to be made for it (no. 368). One inscription notices payment both for seeds as well as for water (no. 160) which was not to be misappropriated or allowed to go waste (no. 502). The land owner had to be careful by not allowing the water to flood the adjacent land and the farm house attached to it (nos. 47, 125). Seeds borrowed had to be returned with interest (no. 140) or in double the quantity (no. 142). Land disputes were fairly common (nos. 90, 124). There are also references to state farms (nos. 272, 278) and also to the collection of revenue—one-third of the produce (no. 291) through the state collecting agency (no. 198) every year (nos. 275, 295). There is a reference to interest on tax (no. 211). Geographical factors with paucity of rainfall could no doubt endanger agricultural economy resulting in famine, noticed in a record (no. 581). The drought impelled its owner to sell his

39. Stein. *ibid.* p. 1464.

vineyard to the scribe just for a carpet (*tavastaga*) six feet long, one *kavaji*, two sheep and one milima of corn. It appears to be a case of exploitation in adverse circumstances. The ownership of land was unfettered with the right to plough, to exchange, to sell, to mortage it (nos. 586, 587). Slaves and women were not denied this right to sell their land (nos. 574 & 677). There are also references to land disputes which necessitated affirmation on oath by witnesses on behalf of the contesting parties (nos. 90, 124). Sometimes land was put under the care of someone, probably some minor official either in the case of disputed ownership or that of failure to pay state dues (no. 278).

There are also references to crops other than the cereal ones—like growing of cotton, hemp, fruits and vegetables. Grape vineyards were equally productive and remunerative. The major portion of Central Asia being arid desert, it was only the hunted area which could be utilised for cultivation and the steppes could cater for grazing purposes. The Khotan area was productive of cotton and hemp. Animal husbandry, closely connected with pasture lands, equally engaged Central Asians in their economic activity. Among the animals some were useful for transport and others like sheep for the by-products. Camel or *ūṭa* is mentioned in several records (nos. 4, 6, 10, 16 etc.). It was extremely useful for transport of goods as also for conveyance of traffic on hire (nos. 6, 16, 21). Heavy loading could sometimes prove fatal for which the person engaging the animal on hire was responsible (no. 52). Veterinary help was available during transit (no. 40). Camels and horses were also used for military transport (nos. 125, 367) and the state also looked after their maintenance and upkeep. Camels also served as medium of exchange and could be accepted in payment of taxes (nos. 589, 592, 715). Horses were used for ploughing as well as for transport and could be loaned as well (nos. 24, 119). They formed items of presentation (no. 243) and were equally exchanged with other animals. Sheep provided wool, while rams could be used for carrying light goods (nos. 568, 633). Cows yielded milk as well as ghee, and there are several references to presentation of cows and also their sale (nos. 13, 122, 439, 514). The state cowpans were looked after by the keeper called *gopālaka* (no. 439). *ghrid—ghrita*—ghee was made on a grand scale, probably under state supervision. An inscription records the production of a hundred jars (no. 574) which could be possible only in a co-operative or state enterprise, and its theft was not an unusual feature (no. 15).

The grazing grounds called *kaboḍha* were outside the town area and were generally enclosed (no. 392) while the open one was called *lathanam.* One inscription (no. 55) records provision to be made for the royal camel in all cities. This included fodder and water. This might not have been on payment. The responsibility for the upkeep of animals was on their owners and cruelty to animals was punishable. A record (no. 13) bans hunting of the mares and horses. Cattle rearing seems to be encouraged because of the utility of animals in day to day life and economic necessities. These also provided avenues for ancilliary avocations like those of blanket and carpet makers and of other items. The sheep wool provided the raw material for rough texture. Milk and its products like ghee were in great demand; and this industry seems to have contributed quite a bit to the economic life of the people. Hsuan-Tsang has referred to the enormous cattle population in Khotan, especially camels.

Handicrafts and other Industries

There are references to several industrial arts and artists and economic professions. The makers of gold and silver ornaments were quite conspicuous (no. 578). Reference has no doubt been made to different types of ornaments and beads found in Khotan and at other places in Central Asia. The finds of wooden tablets—recorded and painted—are suggestive of workers in wood as also painters and sculptors. Leather and its goods, especially long boots, point to this professional class of workers. Weavers and tailors looked after the cloth industry and the making of garments. The silk industry was very prominent, and the famous scene of a Chinese princess secretly bringing silk cocoons to this region sheds light on the introduction[40] and subsequent prosperity of this industry. One inscription notices coloured silk

40. Stein, *Innermost Asia.* pp. 471, 598; 232 Sq; The Chinese princess is credited according to a legend reproduced by Hsuan-tsang, for the introduction of sericulture into the kingdom of Khotan (Stein—*Ancient Khotan.* 1.pp.229 Sq; Beal. Si-Vu-Ki. II. pp. 318 Sq).

(no. 566) of which a *lastuga*-gown was made. The finds of paintings on silk,[41] as also silken fabrics with weaves and designs and embroidered point to the skill of the silken weavers. This industry has a long history and even the trade route between China and Persia was known as the famous silk trade route.[42] The local industries included manufacture of other necessary items of use including utensils, shoes, comb and mirror which are noticed in inscriptions and were also found in excavation. Stein mentions several kinds of shoes made of leather, cotton, wool and hemp—the prominent type being the long boots with straps.[43] The use of comb and mirror is evident from a record (no. 566) as also from their finds of both.[44] The Kharoṣṭhī records mention a term *tavastaga* (no. 431) meaning 'carpet' while another term *thavastaye* (no. 714) is supposed to suggest a cloth carpet.[45] This part of Central Asia was noted for carpet making[46] and these were exported from there. Rolls of silk were imported as well as exported (no. 660), with the Chinese traders playing an important role (no. 35). *Paṭa* is the word used for silk which was used for making clothes, and its rolls also served in barter transactions. One record (no. 3) values a woman's price in terms of 41 rolls of silk. Another record (no. 489) prescribes the fine of a roll of silk as punishment for breach of monastic order rules, like non-participation in the *posatha* or joining it in the dress of a householder.

41. See Stein : *Innermost Asia*, pp. 471 ff; and also for references to silken fabrics (ibid 232 Sq.), weaves and designs (ibid 673 Sq), and embroidery (ibid 235, 489).

42. Ptolemy furnishes interesting information on the subject of silk trade from China during the first century A.D. (*Geographia*. I. XI. 7; XII.8 Sq). Stein records the importance of the route for trade during the centuries before and after the beginning of the Christian era, when Baktra was a chief emporium for the great silk trade passing from China to Persia and the Mediterranean. It led from Kashgar to the Alai valley and thence down the Kizil-su or Surkh-ab towards the Oxus. Nature favoured the use of this route, since it crossed the watershed between the Tarim basin and the Oxus where it was the lowest. (Stein. *Innermost Asia*. Vol. II. p. 848)

43. *Serindia*. II. pp. 704, 719, 813; *Ancient Khotan*, p. 297.

44. *Serindia*. pp. 943, 967, 721.

45. Bailey. BSOAS. II. p. 793.

46. McGovern. *Early Empires*—Op. cit, p. 53.

There were dealers in items of food and drinks. Several records (nos. 175, 244, 317 etc.) notice wine and its trade with other countries. The vineyards supplied grapes for processing and the industry had the support of the administration. It was also accepted by way of tax and collected by officials appointed for this purpose (no. 206) who sometimes misappropriated the accumulated tax (no. 272). There was a special department for this old and new wine tax collection (no. 567). Another record notices selling of wine (no. 247). As a medium of exchange and barter, it could be used for payment of debt and also as the price of some commodity (nos. 168, 244). Like the state distilleries there were dairy farms as well which were looked after by the administration. An inscription (no. 314) refers to state cows probably suggesting public sector enterprises in ghee and oil. An officer called 'Satavida' looked after this state enterprise and he was expected to provide full account of its export. Sometimes there was misappropriation of the state revenue. One record (no. 621) notices *kulāla* or *kutala*—a potter, who manufactured clay utensils and tablets. Jars were made of clay and these were used for storage purposes.

National Economy and Medium of Exchange and Barter

The Central Asian economy seems to be properly planned, with a fair amount of gold reserve. The yellow metal and its sale is mentioned in a record (no. 140) and reference has been made to the manufacture of gold ornaments. Another record (no. 177) mentions presentation of gold. The reference to 'Suvarṇa satera' might be suggestive of gold coin equivalent in value to Greek Strateros—Stater. While barter was fairly common, the medium of exchange or even the collection of state dues could be in the shape of animals and commodities. This might be a primitive way of economic activity in the absence of coinage, but it seems to have worked. One inscription (no. 586) records despatch of cows in exchange for some commodities purchased. Another record (no. 180) mentions 6 regal camels probably received in trade transaction or in tax. There are many references to land deals in terms of barter and exchange with productive animals like cows, sheep, camels and horses. Some types of coins were also in use as is evident from references in inscriptions (nos. 43, 324, 419, 431). These are *sadera—stater*, *trasya*, *muli*, *kampomasa*, *ghare*, *mamaka*.[47] A *sater* and two *trakhma—drachm* was the price paid for a slave (no. 324), while a single sater could bring a vineyard (no. 419)—rather an unusual or a very cheap deal, when another record (no. 702) notices sugar worth 4 *sadera* and pepper worth 2 *trachma—drachme*. These coins must have reached Khotan area through trade transactions from the western region. There is no reference to the ratio between gold and silver coins but one of the Tibetan documents provides the equation : $\frac{1}{2}$ zho of gold = 3 zho of silver.[48] A Kharoṣṭhī record (no. 43) mentions a term *kampo* along with the golden *sadera*, probably suggestive of some kind of silver denomination. Several records (nos. 500, 149) notice the term *masa* (*māsa*)—*māṣa* of the ancient Indian coinage which appears to be of a small denomination since it appears in big numbers as 8000, 2800, 2500 in inscriptions. Another term noticed in records is ghane (no. 702) which might have been a quarter of *drachm* or four times the value of a *kārṣāpaṇa* as supposed by some scholars. *Muli* of the inscriptions (431, 579) might have been the local form of *mūlya* or value although its denominational value is proposed as the twelfth part of a *sadera-stater*, since a carpet of certain length is valued in both the denominations in two records separately. Yet another term *mamaka* is supposed to denote some coinage since Tita—Titus the painter was paid 300 in this denomination for his work.[49] In the absence of finds of local coinage, the information available from the Kharoṣṭhī records alone is considered in this context.

There are several terms relating to weights and measures which are recorded in inscriptions (nos. 25, 98, 162). *khi* and *milima* are the two weights which are supposed to be primarily used for weighing purpose. Their ratio was 20 : 1. These were

47. These terms are considered by several scholars like Thomas, F.W., Sten Know, and H.W. Bailey in their papers in JRAS 1926 pp. 507 ff; ibid. 1924 pp. 671 ff; A.O. VI pp. 255 ff; BSOAS. 1948 pp. 128 ff; R.C. Agrawala has also contributed a few papers in this context. These are 'Numismatic Data in the Kharoṣṭhī documents from Chinese Turkestan' JNSI, 1953, pp. 103 ff; ibid 1954 pp. 229 ff; and a study of weights and measures in the Kharoṣṭhī Documents from Chinese Turkestan—JBRS. Vol. 38. pp. 365 ff.

48. Stein. *Serindia*. III. p. 1465 n. 6.

49. *ibid.* p. 530.

uniformly used for weighing purposes as also for transactions relating to wine (no. 168, 175). One record (no. 175) notices people taking 3 *khi* of wine, probably in illegal drinks. Another one (no. 168) prescribes 30 *khi* of seed in a plot of land for sowing purpose. Salary was also paid in this denomination (no. 210) and so also was tax paid accordingly. Even the load prescribed rather the maximum—to be carried by a camel—3 milima (no. 200). One record (no. 76) associates another word '*casaga*' with *khi*. It might be the local form of Sanskrit *caṣaka*. The drinking bowl also used for measuring liquid things including ghee. Yet another term *sparṇa* connotes measuring of *suki* wine (no. 169). It was smaller than *khi*. *Vacari* is another term mentioned in several records (nos. 159, 214, 295). It might have been a kind of measuring pot, as proposed by Burrow.[50] The *prasta* (no. 721) could be equated with the Sanskrit *prastha*. *Hasta*—the term of measurement is noticed in several records (nos. 581, 578, 83) and is generally used for carpet's measurement. The height was measured in *dithi* (no. 187)→Skt. *diṣṭi*, while another term *kuṭhala* is noticed (no. 327) along with *misi* in land transaction (nos. 419, 582). These weights and measurements seem to be based on the Indian pattern while some might have been derived from the current ones in other neighbouring regions.

Labour and Transport

Labour poses a very important problem in the economic activity of any country. The labourer has to be paid for his services, otherwise associated with profits in an enterprise. The payment of salary for work done seems to have been quite a normal feature (no. 25) along with food and clothing (no. 50). There could be wage dispute (no. 54). Labourers and slaves formed the corps of workers (nos. 20, 29, 53) and they could keep their earnings with them or invest these in land (no. 677), but exploitation of labour was not an unknown feature of economic life and so was recourse to violence against women. Labour was comparatively cheap and its mobility from one place to another at the command of the master or in exchange

50. Burrow. *Translation*—Op. cit p. 77.

is also recorded (nos. 491, 324). Bonded labour for a stipulated period of ten to twelve years (nos. 550, 364) is also noticed. Their purchase is recorded in inscriptions. A slaves price is mentioned as 25 *alta* along with a five year old camel and a horse of the same age (no. 591). There is no reference to skilled labourer. An inscription (no. 272) prohibits immigration as also over-crowding in the city, possibly in some period of emergency.

Information about trade routes and medium of transport is provided by the accounts of the Chinese travellers as well as from inscriptions. The geography of Central Asia no doubt forbids communication between China and the Western world because of the Lop and Gobi deserts in the east, the long chains of the Tien-shans and the Kun-luns to the north and south; and the Pamirs linked to the Kun-luns by the Karakoram ranges in the south-west. These to-gether form a pair of pincers around the heart of Chinese Central Asia. Further, the sands of the Taklamakan desert with its deadly perils were equally deterrents for traders and pilgrims. However, the foot-hills of the mountain slopes in the north and south provided the ground for traffic, facilitated by human habitations along the course of the Tarim river. The famous 'Silk Road' or 'Silk Route' traversed this region of Central Asia, and catered to the main traffic between China and the West with several stopovers. The route started from the capital Chang-an (modern Sian) in the province of Shansi and crossed the Gobi desert to the oasis of Tun-huang from where it bifurcated in two directions. The northern route passed through Hami, Turfan, Karashahr, Kucha, Aksu, Tumshuk and Kashgar to Samarkand. The southern one was via Miran, Cherchen, Keriya, Khotan and Yarkand to Herat and Kabul.[51] The means of transport along these routes were camels and mules. There are references to hiring of camels (nos. 52, 195). Any harm done to this precious animal—rather the ship of the desert—constituted an offence for which compensation had to be paid to the owner. On a complaint by the owner, the culprit was sent under escort (no 262). Another record (no. 195) awards com-

51. Lerner. *Along the Ancient Silk Routes*—Op. cit p. 18.

pensation for the lost animal. The rates for hiring a camel for transport seem to have been fixed. The hiring of the animal even by the State had to be done at regular rate (no. 272). Escorts were provided on certain routes (no. 14). Another record (no. 35) expresses regret that at that time the Chinese traders in silk had not come there and so some dispute regarding advance on silk could not be settled in Court. Yet another record (no. 223) notices the use of horses for transport. In this case the mule was taken on hire since local arrangements could not be made for transport. The states seem to have maintained camels for transport (no. 248), and the local officials were forbidden to use them for their families (no. 362).

Administration and Rural Economy

The Kharoṣṭhī records as well provide a good deal of information relating to the administrative setup in these areas and the officials associated with it. While it may not be necessary to record the powers of the Cozbo—the ruling local authority and his associates, in this context, it might be desirable to take into account measures affecting economic activity as part of administration. These include taxation and officers connected with assessment and realization of rent and the role of officials in regulating economic enterprises. The local official's functions included collection of land tax and other cesses in kind every year. Assessment is recorded in several inscriptions (nos. 42, 57, 206, 275, 714 etc.) and the tax was paid in kind—grain, wine, animal, ghee and other commodities (no. 714) which were deposited in the State storage depots (nos. 279, 59, 291 etc.). The despatch of tax was not to be delayed although pilfering of objects was not unknown (no. 567). Local cess (*dranga*) was laid on articles of consumption. There are several references of defaults (nos. 42,158, 165) for which interest was added to the arrears (no. 211). One inscription (no. 450) records the case of a land holder who had not paid tax for four years. It involved serious punishment with his land and house being auctioned and he was required to work on the state farms along with his wife and children. Two types of taxes—*rottana* and *churma*—are also mentioned in this context. One can gather from these records that tax collection agencies had to be firm and strict and the defaulters had to undergo privation in the form of services to be rendered at the state farms. There are also instances of royal scribe (*divira*) purchasing such defaulters or slaves farm or vineyard. Feudalistic tendencies and exploitation of labour were normal features. The officials seem to have been paid through land and its perquisites and it was quite natural to make use of the available labour.

In a review of the material culture of Central Asia one notices several features; Firstly the impact of the local population on the foreigners who had settled down there as immigrants—Indians, Iranians, Uighurians and Chinese, as also foreign influence on the local ethos. The Indian element was forceful, as is evident from numerous Indians, probably descendents of Buddhist monks, traders and scholars as also some princes who trekked into various parts of Central Asia, and set up some kingdoms there. This is evident from the use of Indian regal titles as also from the Indian administrative norms traced in inscriptions. The association of some Indian names with the local ones suggests understanding and spirit of co-existence between the natives and the immigrants. There are references to Brahmins and also to upper class people—probably the ruling class or those belonging to the administrative hierarchy. The impact of Buddhism seems to have eliminated caste consciousness of which there is hardly any trace. Of course, class consciousness did exist. Native chiefs, feudal lords, affluent householders and administrative officials constituted the upper and the middle class, while slaves in general and other workers and artisans belonged to the last group. The well born and the noble class included natives as well as Indians, as is evident from the names—Vasu Mogiya, Vasu Kekeya and Jeyaka (no. 588). The exploitation of the slave class is evident from a record (no. 591) which notices the owner's right to sell a purchased slave just for a camel, a horse and 25 atga, as also to pledge him, to exchange him, to give him to others as a present, and do whatever he likes with him. The feudalistic society based on vocational status and economic division seems to have cast its shadow on the Buddhist order, since one finds the Buddhist monks owning lands as well as keeping slaves and also entering into matrimony. Rural economy seem to have been shaped accordingly, with the upper crust of society and the bureaucracy owning land and farms, which they managed with the help of labour and slaves, paid and provided for. Some slaves could manage to set up their own farms and vineyards but these could be purchased or appropriated in lieu of arrears of taxes by the scribe or other tax-collecting officials. There were also artisans and workers who contributed to the national economy in their own way. The international trade popularly called the silk trade between China and the West had no doubt contributed to the material culture of the people of Central Asia since it passed through both the Northern and the Southern areas. The material finds at the places excavated and explored reveal a fairly good standard of socio-economic life of the people dipped in native traditions and cultured with the impact of Buddhist scholars from India firmly pressed on the local ethos. The Chinese influence is equally traceable in those parts which lie in close proximity to China and is deeper in periods of its political hegemony in Central Asia. It is no doubt difficult to sift or apportion the contributions—Indian, Iranian and Chinese as also that of the later period—in the composite culture of the peoples of Central Asia till about the tenth century, when Islam had spread its influence and gradually changed the tenor and temper of the people in these areas.

CHAPTER VI

THE ART OF CENTRAL ASIA[1]

Central Asia provides the best example of a complex fusion of peoples and ideas of different nationalities in the realms of material culture and art. This vast area insular in nature, noted for its virtually, unrelieved deserts and steppe, witnessed the development of two types of human society—the nomadic one

1. The art of Central Asia is located at several centres on the northern and southern silk trade routes. The peoples in these regions took over the art forms of the great sedentary civilizations around them: those of the semi-classical cultures of the East, of Iran, of Indo-Greek and Indo-Scythians, of China, and of Gupta India. The borrowings, no doubt, vary in extent and intensity from minute reminiscences of detail to essential concepts of style and iconography. The Iranian element predominates in the western region, while the Chinese influence in the figurative arts is prominent in the eastern area of Central Asia nearer to or forming part of the Tang empire. The Indian influence associated with Buddhism and Gupta art made itself felt in Khotan and other places, varying, of course, in degree and dimension. Stylistic currents emanating from Central Asia itself are supposed to be instrumental not only in shaping Indo-Iranian trends of North-west India and Afghanistan, considered the southernmost offshoot of Central Asian art. They also reacted on the artistic evolution of Kashmir, on much of the ancient art of Tibet (particularly painting) and even on Chinese Buddhist painting (Bussagli : *Op. cit*, p. 16-17). Several scholars have made a general study of Central Asian Art—sculptures and paintings, as also of specific areas. These include : Bussali, Mario : *Painting of Central Asia*—translated from the Italian by Lothian Small, Geneva, 1963; Talbot Rice, Tamara : *Ancient Arts of Central Asia*, London, 1965; Montebello, Phillippe de : *Along the Ancient Silk Routes—Central Asian Art from the West Berlin State Museums*, New York, 1982; Rowland, B : *The Wall Paintings of India, Central Asia and Ceylon*, Boston, Mass. 1938; F.H. Andrews : *Wall-Paintings from Ancient Shrines in Central Asia recovered by Sir Aurel Stein*, London, 1948; Nobuo Kumagai : *Central Asian Painting*, Tokyo; Gray, B : *Buddhist Cave Paintings at Tun-huang*, London, 1959; Hackin, J. : *Buddhist Art in Central Asia, London*, 1936. For a comprehensive bibliography on Central Asian art, see Hambi's Article on the subject in the *Encyclopedia of World Art*, Vol. I, pp. 837-38.

in the north and the sedantary one in the south where there was water and equal facilities for irrigation. In this settlement complex the development of civilization was influenced by the more vigorous cultures that flourished on the southern borders. The cultures of the permanent settlements of the southern region, vitalized by exchanges and contacts with the western world—as also Persia, India and China, seem to exhibit a degree of consistency in their artistic development, which those in the northern areas, however, were influenced less by the major Eurasian civilisations. Buddhism and its expansion from India to Central Asia and the Far East, no doubt, provided the base for the artistic activities in both the regions. It acted as a centripetal force for devotees of different social groups in Central Asia. They joined hands or acted independently in offerring their services for the cause of the religion of the Tathāgata. Various episodes from the life of the Buddha Śākyamuni and his previous incarnations were depicted on the walls of cave shrines on the Indian models of Ajanta and Bagh as also the Gandhāra pictorial art of Bamian, with the narration following the ancient Buddhist texts. The Chinese influence was equally accepted and the artists from that country were not inactive in their devotion and service in this direction. Other external influences—classical Greek and Roman, Persian and Sassanian—could as well be traced in the pictorial art of Central Asia. While the theme continues to be Buddhist, the actors in the pictorial drama change with the brush of the painter, who fully makes use of his imagination and background, as also his colour scheme. In this context the earliest impact was with the Gandhāra art and its artists, who are supposed to have been inspired by Greek traditions as modified in Rome. These artists carried with them their pictorial and sculptural art to Central Asia. The indigenous talent, however, accepted these artistic influences with discrimination.

While it is difficult to suggest the *terminus a quo* of the wall paintings in Central Asia, fragments of pictorial art still adhering in patches on the walls or fallen and scattered in the accumulated dust and plaster on the floor of ruined shrines, suggest a facile technique of long standing, but equally showing a varying degree of skill in drawing. The decorator's industry seemed to be extensive with a prolonged period of evolution of art. The examples of painting in caves and free-standing shrines suggest that the industry of painters was in a fairly advanced state and equally productive with the cooperative efforts of local talents as also experts, probably foreign ones. The caves afforded greater protection from nature as well as from human aggressive activities. As such, these were best suited for the display of Buddhist pictorial art. With the expansion of Buddhism and the setting up of a large number of stupas and shrines, there was a big demand for sculptors and painters to enrich these monuments with ornamental figures in stone or clay and artistic pictures depicting the life and activities of the Śākyamuni as also those of his previous lives as recorded in the Jātakas. The subject matter provided by the Buddhist legendary accounts was later on enriched with complex Hindu mythological elements, thus expanding the scope and dimension of the artists' plan and pictorial display. The commercial enterprise on the trade routes with the patronage and contribution of the traders and merchants was equally helpful in generating this move with the services of roving artists easily available. It is equally likely that painters sometimes imposed their creations on the earlier ones, serving as palimpsests. The original one might have been better or probably connected with the earlier school of the Hīnayānists, and the second one gratified the donor suiting his personal faith.

Central Asian paintings are rightly grouped under two groups, purely on a geographical basis : those from sites to the south of the great Taklamakan Desert comprise one group; while the other one includes paintings from sites lying on the northern route. Farhad-Beg Yailaki, Balawaste, Dandan-oilik, Khadlik and Miran, on the southern route, and Khara Khoja, Toyuk, Bezeklik, all in the Turfan area on the northern one, represent primarily the centres of art related to the two groups. Tun-Husang, the meeting place of the two routes, is noted for the caves of the Thousand Buddhas. It seems to have adopted Miran's style and iconography as the basis for its own school of art whose artistic expression is in the Chinese manner. The art of Tun-huang[2], however, reflects the constant mixture of

2. For Tun-huang paintings, see 'Essays on the Buddhist Paintings from the caves of the Thousand Buddhas, Tun-huang' by Raphael Petrucci and

influences of diverse origins. According to a seventh century inscription on a stone tablet (beginning of the Tang dynasty), the oldest Chen-Fo-tung monastery was consecrated by an Indian monk in A.D. 366. It is even proposed[3] that China may have acquired her interest in the human figure from Miran, where such renderings are particularly lovely, and that Tun-huang may have owed its delight in landscape and its preoccupation with real and imaginary animals to China. The Tibetan paintings of the Northern Wei and Sui periods, however, reveal the forms and influences received from more western regions.

Well-defined styles of Central Asian paintings no doubt suggest Indian and Chinese inspirations. Indian influence, or rather, qualities dominate in the south with Persian influence intruding, while the Chinese influence is perceptible, in the north of course with modification by Tibetan, Uighur and others. The common factor in all the compositions—both in the North as well as in the South, is the Buddhist legend—variously expressed. Hindu and Tantric importations equally stimulated the imagination of Chinese and Tibetan artists who were more concerned with the stronger attraction of the decorative possibilities than with the spiritual element which inspired the earlier Indian renderings. The paintings are all linked to-gether by a common bond of one basic religion—Buddhism. The manner of expression, however, differs widely in style and treatment. This was due to the changing political situations and the complex social milieu, with the dominant power changing hands from one race to another differing

---

Lawrence Bin Yon—Appendix E; Stein, A : *Serindia*, Vol. III, pp. 1392 ff; Gray, B : *Buddhist* Paintings of Tun-huang, London, 1959; Pelliot, P : *Les Grottes de Touen-houang*, 6 Vols. Paris, 1920-4; Stein, A : *The Thousand Buddhas, Ancient Buddhist Paintings from the Cave Temples of Tun-huang*, London, 1921-22.

3. *Op. cit*, p. 214. Tun-huang is supposed to have adopted Miran's style and iconography as the basis for its own school of art. Miran became the centre for influencing contemporary artists of Niya, Cherchen and Loulan. The reference to an artist Titus working at Miran (Stein : *Serindia*, I. p. 538) is interesting. This Roman Eurasian artist trained in the Hellenistic tradition and impregnated with Buddhism was instrumental in the diffusion of the Central Asian School at Miran. It is suggested by Talbot Rice, that Titus must have been familiar with Byzantine painting and his use of chiaroscuro also reflects Byzantine influence and so too perhaps do the large eyes.

in ideals and traditions in art as also varying in psychological conceptions. That accounts for diversities in design and treatment of the paintings, although identical mannerisms and even use of some compositions in places at considerable distance from each other could be suggestive of the same artist and his troupe of painters moving from one centre to another.

The art of Serindia, as the region came to be called by Aurel Stein, which had developed amidst the political vicissitudes of a number of centuries, roughly from the first of the Christian era until the Muslim invasion, reveals varied influences[4] that had played upon it. In its earliest phase, supposed to be Greco-Buddhist in form, it revealed Indian as also Persian influence depending on the circumstances, and in a way reflected the art of western Asia. Then it followed the Chinese influence, dominating throughout the Tang dynasty. Subsequently, western elements seem to have influenced it. Later on, this art, cut off from its Persian and Indian sources of inspiration consequent to Islamic conquest, absorbed foreign influence only from China. This would be evident from art centres nearer to China proper under the impact and influence of Chinese artists. The southern centres of the silk Route, passing through the Tarim Basin, inhabited over long periods, were later abandoned because of sudden shifts in the course of the rivers. These included Miran, Endere, Niya and those forming the Khotan group : Yotkan, Rawak, Dandan-oilik and Ak-terak. The remnants of art in these centres represent the earlier phases of the Central Asian Art, and, therefore, deserve prior consideration.

4. Numerous artistic currents flowed along the caravan routes leading to and from China. In addition to the Central Asian elements, the influence of the art of the Gupta period also penetrated to the Taklamakan through Central Afghanistan. Hellenism likewise reached the eastern cities both in the form into which it had been fashioned in Gandhāra and also directly from the western world as suggested by Foucher. In the words of Aurel Stein, 'the paintings of Serindia reflect the Mediterranean delight in beauty, youth and life'. Indo-Greek art with its classical elements is traced by Grunwedel both at Kucha and in Khotan, and was even produced in Kashgaria as a centre of Buddhist art and religion. As Buddhism advanced towards the Taklamakan, Kashgaria with Yarkand and Khotan in the west, Tumsuk, Akshu and Kizil in the north; Sorchuk and Karasahr in the east, and Miran and Cherchen in the south became important centres of Buddhist art and thought. These in their turn transmitted their artistic style to religious centres. The Tun-huang

Miran[5] :

The ruins of Miran, located south of Lop Nov in a region probably supplied from Cherchen Darya, comprise a massive building, square in plan. On a circular base in a round room inside stands a stupa invisible from outside. As a result of the protection of the sand, the ruins with wall paintings could be safely preserved through the centuries. These paintings may be dated from the end of the 3rd century or the beginning of the 4th by comparison with other paintings from western Asia. Apart from their artistic and technical interest, the Miran paintings suggest familiarity with the Gandhāra art. In fact, Miran is considered as an outpost of Gandhāra Art. The motive of the festooned garland carried on the shoulders of amorini as also the winged angel busts placed in the upper hollows of the festoon rendered in a more interesting way appear to be in line, or rather an improved version of the same in Gandhāra sculptures. According to Aurel Stein,[6] 'the approach to purely classical design and colouring was closer in these frescoes than in any work of ancient pictorial art'. The painted dado of beautiful winged angels, as 'classical representations of Cherubim, recall cherished scenes of Christian imagery, most surprisingly on the walls of what was beyond all doubt a Buddhist sanctuary'. This might be due to the importation of classical artists. The name of one of the painters Tita—perhaps the equivalent of Titus—very probably a

---

artists encountered in addition styles which, though evolved in the Khotanese area, had undergone alterations in the course of migration. (Talbot Rice : *Op. cit*, p. 180—adaptation)

5. The Miran paintings are first noticed and recorded by Aurel Stein in his *Ruins of Desert Cathay*, Vol. I, pp. 452 ff and later on in his *Serindia*, Vol. I, pp. 497 ff. These are described in detail by F.H. Andrews in his *Catalogue*—1934 as also in detail along with illustrations in his—*Wall Paintings from Ancient Shrines in Central Asia*—1948, XVIII-XX, 2-16; Bussagli has a special chapter on Miran Paintings in his work on *Paintings of Central Asia*—Op. cit, pp. 19 ff. Miran's art is supposed to have stemmed from India and Gandhāra. The reference to the artist Titus and his school envisages closer connection of this art centre with the western art centres of Antioch and Dura Europos. According to Talbot Rice, Miran probably acquired the Greco-Roman elements in its art by direct contacts with the West rather than indirectly (*Op. cit*, p. 214). Its style and iconography was adopted as the basis for its own school of art at Tun-huang.

6. *Ruins of Desert Cathay—Op.cit*, p. 458 ff.

Roman subject of Asian origin but Hellenistic training is recorded in Kharoṣṭhī on the leg of an elephant in the famous Vessantara Jātaka scene. In fact during the third and fourth centuries A.D. the whole of Central Asia formed a peripheral area within the Graeco-Roman sphere of influence. The classical influence emanated from the semi-classical school of Gandhāra art. A single group of itinerant artists comprising the master and his pupils seem to have moved about in these centres of Buddhist monastic establishment, and their services were availed of. While most of the artists remain anonymous, this particular one Tita actually reveals his personality and he also received payment for his services. These artists exhibited classical elements not only in the treatment of drapery, but also made skilful use of chiaroscuro—treatment of light and shade—in their paintings. Further, the wall decorations of Miran are considered as the most extensive group of Gandhāra paintings in view of some highly significant features of their style and iconography. These are linked up with a particular trend of Gandhāra art rich in brilliant elements. These may be recorded with reference to a few specimens of Miran paintings.

The Buddha with six monks[7] is a typical scene of Buddhist iconography. On the left one notices the Master standing, dressed in a simple robe of dark red-brown colour—characteristic of Indian tradition. The halo and the top-knob of hair, partly broken, and the right hand raised in the pose of protection (*abhaya-mudrā*) confirm this figure to be the Buddha. His left hand, held low in front probably supported his drapery (*saṅghātī*). Behind the teacher and to his left are six monks or arhats ranged in two rows and wearing robes in a variety of bright colours. The shaven head of monks is conspicuous. The monk on the left end of the upper row carries a white fan, probably meant for a yaktail or chauri traditionally associated with holy or regal personalities. To the left of the saints, an elliptical mass probably part of a tree, is studded with red and white flowers and poppy-like leaves on dark greyish-green ground. An upraised right hand grasping a handful of white buds or flowers, is shown aga-

7. Andrews : *Opi cit*,, p.3; See also Stein : *Ruins*—Op. cit, p. 470, pl. V.

inst this background suggesting the act of throwing flowers on the distinguished guests. This fresco fragment is considered of great value and interest for the artistic treatment in composition, design and colouring. The details of the subject—no doubt Buddhist—in its presentation point to adaptation from classical models. The head of Buddha is supposed to be of a type unmistakably Hellenistic, in spite of a slight semitic touch in the nose and of compliance with Indian Buddhist convention in regard to the top-knot and long pierced ears. The large straight eyes of the teacher and disciples are equally striking.

Another fragment from Miran (III. 002) depicts a figure seated on a throne. Stein takes[8] it to be that of a teacher meant in all probability for Gautama Bodhisattva. A dark red undergarment reaches from the hips to the ankles, and a buff-coloured cloak is thrown over the left shoulder, leaving most of the upper part of the body bare. The drapery is treated in a fashion, supposed to be unmistakably classical. The same dressing of the folds is noticed in the smaller adoring figure to the right. He appears to be a princely character clearly marked by a curious white conical cap enriched with rings and two lunette-shaped red flaps. This headdress, not traced anywhere in the Buddhist sculpture of Gandhāra or in any later Buddhist shrines of Eastern Turkestan, seems local in character. It recurs in a number of the Miran frescoes. It is, however, proposed that it represents a feature introduced for a time from one of the more western territories like Bactria or Sogdiana. Of a second adoring figure on the left, only parts of the knee and arm are noticed. The big eyes, the drooping ones of the seated figure and the gazing and attentive ones of the adoring one, and the Indian loin-cloth dhotī and the scarf curving are suggestive of Indian influence. The theme is unidentified but appears to be of a religious nature, probably a saintly person or a religious teacher advising the young prince who is fairly attentive with folding hands. The faces are of rather semitic type, with fine straight-set eyes, arched eye-brows,[9] well separated above the nose; small but thick black moustache, carefully pointed and a

8. Stein : *Cathay*, p. 473.

9. Andrews : *Op. cit*, p. 3.

thin wavy lock of hair falling in front of each ear. The hands are strong and broad with the thumb abducted and short finger nails.

Another interesting fresco fragment (M. III. 0019) represents heads of two worshippers—girls with folded hands, as they gaze, with their wide eyes, towards the left. The faces are fair with pink cheeks and are painted with definite chiaroscuro, the shades being pearly-grey. The girl to the left is very young and in an amusing mood, while that to the right appears older and more sophisticated and stern in her look. The smiling lips of the younger one are solid red, while the transverse wrinkle in the necks of both suggest their superior birth. The black hair is long and stylishly dressed, with tresses falling behind the ears to the shoulders and wavy love-locks on the cheeks. The hair on the forehead of the girl on the right, precisely and fancifully arranged, suggest her gentle upbringing. White bands crown the hair of the girls and their eyebrows are delicately arched, distinguishingly separated. The ears are not very much elongated. The dress of the girls is stylish. The robe of the figure to the left is yellow, ontlined with red V-shape opening at the neck; that of the other one is similar in form, but light green outlined with dark grey. Andrew considers them to be the two daughters of Prince Vessantara, ready to participate in the drama of renunciation as narrated in this Jātaka story.

Another interesting feature at Miran is a scheme of a heavy floral garland carried on the shoulders of youthful supporters placed at regular intervals, and undulating completely round the shrine. A typical head and bust of a man or woman rises between supporters from each hollow followed by the downward droop of the festoon. It is a motive widely used in Gandhāra sculpture.[10] The supporters in the example at Miran are reminiscent of Italian *amorini* dipped in Eastern nuances. They are sometimes clothed in Persian garments consisting of a narrow

10. It is suggested by Andrews that this motive does not seem to have survived into later periods in India or Central Asia. Festoons of fruits and flowers, depending from ox-skulls, were used to adorn temples in ancient Rome as offerings; and the motive, in decoration, has persisted widely in the west, but not quite in the form of a continuous garland carried by human supporters. (*Wall Paintings*, p. 10).

sleeved tunic and Phrygian cap, and sometimes only in a scanty loin-cloth. But more remarkable still are the portraits filling in succession the hollows of the undulating festoon. In each rises the head and bust of a man or girl, presented in classical outlines but with a freedom of individual expression. The types of men's head differ, some quite Roman in look, others with their peculiar cut of hair and beard. A graceful girl is shown playing on a four stringed mandoline.[11] A wreath of white flowers is set on her rich black hair, bound by a crimson ribbon and gathered in a bunch behind the neck. A diadem made up of red beads and pendant jewels stretches across the forehead. A crimson flower or ornament of that shape hangs from each ear, before which a curly love-lock descends. The full sensual lips are supposed to harmonize with the elaborate adornment of this mature beauty. Next to her to the right is a Phrygian-capped figure draped in green carrying the festoon, and beyond this facing the girl is a beared male bust, striking in features and dress. His heavy curled hair, the moustache and the long beard clearly distinguish him from other classical male faces seen elsewhere in the dado. Another one[12] shows a young Indian prince, clean shaven, except for a curling moustache and cap similar to the one in the attitude of worshipping the Buddha. The dreamy looking eyes with an expression of softness are supposed to be typically Indian. The characteristic headdress is also Indian, with two red-lined flaps turned upwards over the forehead, and a white pugree-turban wound round it. Its end is gathered behind into a sort of hood, as seen in many Gandhāra sculptures, representing prince Siddhārtha and other royal figures. A large ornament in the ear, a broad jewelled band round the neck, and two heavy armlets over the right wrist suggest his high rank. He holds some object, probably a fruit in his hand. A cloak of light green is thrown over the left shoulder, leaving the rest of the breast bare.

The next pair of busts[13] appear to be strikingly western in look. First the portrait of a young girl carries in graceful pose on her left shoulder a narrow necked jug of transparent ware and in her

11. Stein : *Ruins*, fig. 146.
12. *ibid*, fig. 147, p. 482.
13. *ibid*, fig. 148, p. 483.

right hand a patera. The Greek features, in the words of Stein, 'mingling with Levantine or Circassian type of beauty are gracefully blended with Iranian or Near Eastern dress, the white turban, trimmed with a red bank and held by a large black knot on the rights resting on the rich black hair'. Long ringlets descend in front of the ears while a fringe of hair comes down on the forehead decorated with three bead strings of coral. The ears bear graceful pendants in pink. A close-fitting vest with sleeves in a deep red brown cover breast and shoulders, and from the head dress hangs a veil of a delicate pale green. She is balanced on the opposite side by a male head of a type distinctly Roman, strongly built face, clean shaven, close-cropped black hair covering the head. The dress consists of a dark red coat with a pale green cloak thrown over the right shoulder.

Reference might as well be made to the Vessantara Jātaka scene earlier supposed by Aurel Stein as a princely procession[14] scene. The frieze above the dado at the south-east over a segment more than eighteen feet long illustrates this Jātaka, on the upper part of the wall. There is an appearance of continuity of the several incidents in the painting without any dividing line such as a pilaster—an architectural feature. The incidents seem to be separated from each other by trees. Starting from the left, Stein records a princely figure on horseback riding out of a palace gate, clearly indicated in the picture with the wooden frame work and decorative carving on the gate. The horseman's costume is very much like that of the 'Indian prince' in the dado. A crimson cloak descends across the left shoulder to below the waist while a green garment resembling the Indian loin cloth (dhotī) covers the lower parts of the body. A rich jewelled armlet and a broad necklace painted in red mark the high rank of the rider. The horse, remarkably well-drawn in white, has its head-stall and bridle decorated with red tufts passing across its breast and apparently reaching to the saddle is a broad belt of three straps or strings. The whole suggested saddlery, according to Stein, corresponds with the Roman sculpture of later times.

14. Stein : *Ruins*—Chapter XLIV, pp. 486 ff. This painting on the upper part of the wall in the same shrine (M.V.) was not removed by Aurel Stein and was subsequently destroyed by the clumsy opeations of a Japanese 'archaeologist'.

A chariot in front of the horseman with four white horses abreast bearing harness of the same type as recorded earlier, is being driven by a beautiful woman. Her hair descends in black tresses below the neck, with two love-locks in front of the ears. Her dress consists of a mauve bodice open in front and held together by two head strings across the breast and of a green mantle laid in heavy folds over the left shoulder. The fair lady gives an impression of Iranian influence on some classical model. Behind her are two standing children.

In the next scene is shown a richly caparisoned white elephant, truthfully painted and in a realistic form, as appears from the expression of the animal's eyes and face. The elaborate adornment of the forehead and trunk consists of a diadem of leaves, bands, bosses and rings, with a painted saddle-cloth and carpet-like covering spread over it. A small neatly written inscription of two lines in Kharoṣṭhī, above the right hand of the elephant mentions the name of the painter Tita—Titus and his remuneration of 3000 *Bhammakas* for it. The elephant is being led by a person with the same characteristic dress as in the dado, and the rich jewellery shown on neck, ears, arm and wrist, representing an Indian prince. His left hand supports the elephant's trunk, while the right one carries a peculiarly shaped jug. This procession is met by four plainly dress figures with their bushy hair and beards and their long staffs, symbolising typical Indian anchorites. Comparing the frieze with the dado, Stein finds traces of the Greco-Buddhist style in the former and the contemporary art of the Roman Orient as transmitted through Persia being reflected in the latter.[15] On the basis of the influence exercised by classical art in this remote corner of Central Asia, the frescoed walls of the temples at Miran provide excellent testimony. The inscriptional evidence confirms the classical influence as it also proposes the probable date of these frescoes which might be placed some time about the third century A.D.

There is, however, considerable internal evidence in these paintings to suggest their Indian conception and execution. The men are Indian, some with full moustache and beard, dressed

15. ibid, p. 489.

in Indian garments with bare feet. The hands are also those of Indians. In the destroyed painting of the Vessantara Jātaka, faithfully recorded earlier by Aurel Stein, the elephant shows the accuracy of form and truth of action, as could be faithfully rendered by the Indian artist alone. The girls, although suggestive of the Persian type of beauty, might well have been Indian, as proposed by Andrew,[16] perhaps influenced by contact with Persian fashion. It is further proposed that the use of Kharoṣṭhī and the legend about an Indian colony in Khotan in Aśoka's time strengthen the probability that Indian artists, familiar with Buddhist lore, may have found employment for their skill along the Silk Route between Khotan and China on which Miran stood. The partial shaving of the heads of the garland carrying boys is almost certainly Indian. There is nothing in the Miran paintings, which could be definitely indicative of borrowings from Chinese art, despite trade relations with China.

The technique of the Miran paintings, which are all *in tempera* is in conformity with the well-developed methods. The design is first drawn on paper and then transferred to the whitened wall surface either by pouncing through the pricked drawing or by other familiar means. The transferred outlines are then lightly traced over with a pale colour for fixation. The colour scheme follows next with the use of brush adding shading tints to suggest chiaroscuro. The contours are strengthened with soft brush lines of red or dark grey, blending to some extent with the colours and also providing softness and roundness to the edges. Emphasis is provided with the final touches of black or red, while grey is used for high lights and the eyes. The colours here are few and those locally available from mineral sources, lamp black and indigo and occasionally of other vegetable origins.

It is proposed that the wall decorations of Miran, on the strength of their style and their Buddhist content, symbolic compositions and motifs of the Kushcano-Iranian type form the most extensive group of Gandhāra school's normal area of diffusion. This school is supposed to have been transplanted

16. *Wall Paintings*, p. XXI.

into pictorial terms at Miran or in other words, the art of Miran may be considered as an outpost of Gandhāra art, suggesting contact between the peoples of Central Asia and those of the Kushāṇa empire. In view of their style and iconography they are equally rich in western elements brilliantly recast. The paintings at Miran might appear mediocre to many, but their importance for revealing western impact in the eastern ethos on a Buddhist canvas cannot be lost sight of. As an earlier example of Buddhist pictorial art, the Miran paintings do not appear to be nascent but products of an evolved and fairly matured technique.

The Khotan Complex[17] :

The school of Khotan—as it is called, provides evidence of absorption of Indian, Sassanian, Chinese, Sogdian and perhaps also Chorasmian influences which are all assimilated and recasted here as if in an original form. The imprint of Greco-Buddhist art, however, predominates between the fifth and the eighth centuries. The complex provides examples of the stūpa, of certain Greco-Buddhist elements in the plan of monasteries and in wall paintings, as for instance, in the standing juxtaposed figures of Buddha in Rawak, compared to the decorative arrangements found near Hadda. These elements are also traceable in decorative motifs and elements. Gupta influences are equally noticed in various objects discovered in the Khotan area--fragments of stylized drapery in stucco, oval faces with simplified treatment of the hair and idealized expression, closely clinging drapery, and in particular, flying figures bearing garlands. In several works of art, of a later date, from Dandan Oilik, Hindu influences are traceable. These seem to have come from Kashmir in India, nicely blended

17. For a reference to Khotan and its art, see A. Stein : *Ancient Khotan*, 2 Vols Oxford 1907; *ibid* : *Sand-Buried Ruins of Khotan*, London, 1907; A. Grundwedel : *Alt Buddhisteche Kulofaatten in Chinese Turkistan*, Berlin 1912; P. Pelliot: 'Les influences iraniennes en Asia Centrale et en Extreme Orient' *Reveue d'histoire et de litterature religioues*s III, 1912 pp. 97-119; Stein : *Ruins of Desert Cathay*, 2 Vols. London, 1912; Stein : *Serindia*, 5 Vols. Oxford, 1921; R. Grousset : L' art de l'Asia Centrals et le influences irrainenns, *RAA*. I. 1924. pp. 13-16; A. Stein : *On Ancient Central Asian Treks*, London, 1932; F. Andrews : 'Central Asia Wall Painting', *Indian Art & Letters*. VII, 1934, pp. 1-21; Louis Hambis & M. Hallade : *Sculpture et Peintures de l' Asia Central*, Paris, 1937; also *Encyclopedia of World Art*, Vol. VIII.

in the customary Greco-Buddhist art. Iranian details appear in several examples, like the panels in Dandan-Oiliq No. X concerning the introduction of silk culture into Khotan. With this blending of foreign influences emerged a new style evident from the wall paintings of the shrines and monuments of the Demoko group east of Khotan, and dated about the middle of the sixth century. It is characterised by strictly frontal presentation, highly developed stylization, a flat, almost two-dimensional designs, and a tendency to geometric simplification which also occurs in some votive paintings on wooden tablets from Dandan-Oiliq. Laws of proportion and schematic designs are based on the segment of a circle and the eclipse. Further, the Dandan panels are supposed to represent a peculiar technique of drawing and colour scheme by vague, sporadic reminiscence of Indian art of the Gupta period.

The Khotanese school of painting centred round the monasteries of Rawak, Dandan-Oiliq, Niya and Endere and Balawaste, as also Farhad-Beg Yailaki and Kuduk-Kol, all lying to the north and north-east of Domko on the southern route about four hundred and fifty miles south-west of Miran. This school and its painters were much admired in contemporary China. In late Sui times, about A.D. 620 the work of the Khotanese artists Weich-in the elder, and the younger, were especially in demand in the Chinese capital at Chan-gan. In Tibet, too, the painters of this school were held in great esteem. This impact on Tibet was great in the eighth century in the time of Ral-Pa-Chan when there were Khotanese painters and monk translators there. The prevailing influence exercised by the Khotan art on Tibet at different times, however, varied in subject and type.[18]

18. Talbot Rice : *Op. cit*, p. 208. The Khotanese influence is traced in Chinese Buddhist sculptures as well. According to Bachhofer, it is somewhat surprising to find traces of the Knotanese type in the Chinese Buddha statues, with the narrow face, the slit eyes, the large *uṣṇīśa*, the same mouth and nose, and the leaf-shaped mandorla. The plates of the garment, however, are asymmetrical as they are in the art of north-western India or Gandhāra. The Khotanese type must have reached southern China in the fourth century. It is very likely that a wave of influence from Khotan had reached northern China at the same tine (Bachhofer : *A Short History of Chinese Art*, London, p. 65).

Among the specimens of Khotan school of painting may be noticed the figure of Hāritī from a shrine at Farhad-Beg-Yailaki the surviving bust of a Tantric Buddha in meditation, probably from Balawaste in the Domko region, as also the worshipper from the same region, the Iranian Bodhisattva from Dandan-Oiliq, the silk princess shown on a wooden tablet, the Bodhisattva of the Tantric type from Balawaste and the lovely Nāgini rising from the waters of an artificial fountain in Temple D. 11 at Dandan-Oilik. These might be noticed on a few, representing paintings of the school from different centres. The goddess Hāritī[19] in her regenerate aspect as the protectress and nourisher of children and goddess of fecundity is attended by five children. The two principal figures are shown in front view. In the mingled sadness and sweetness of her expression, with heavy lidded, half-closed, dreamy eyes, could be traced a smouldering survival of the old fives capable of renewed activities as also an introspective mood and nostalgic past. The robe worn by Hāritī has Iranian characteristics, and there is something of the Persian *houri* in her appearance, characterised by the rather insistent love-locks, the bloom on her cheeks (now discoloured) and the voluptuous folds of her plump neck. Large rings are noticed in the ears or the lobes which seem to be pierced with gaping holes. The halo behind the head is turquoise green surrounded with red and buff. In the badly damaged condition of the painting, one could, however, notice Hāritī, sitting cross-legged with her right forearm bent to suppport one of the boys sitting astride her wrist; another embracing her left breast, two astride her shoulders, the one on the left shoulder wearing a terra-cotta clout smock. The other three are nude. The fifth one, badly defaced, on the left of the picture, wears a green smock and seems to be dancing.

The bust of the Buddha from Balawaste,[20] with the symbolic

---

19. Hāritī with Five Children. Wall painting from Shrine XII, Farhad Beg-Yailaki, Mid-Sixth century, 20.c.XII·004, Collection of the National Museum, New Delhi. For a fuller description—see F. Andrews : *Wall Paintings*, p. 17.

20. Buddha in Meditation, Wall Painting, probably from Balawaste, Mid-sixth century. Haray's collection of the National Museum, New Delhi; Bussagli : *Op. cit*, pp. 55, 58.

motifs of the Tāntric type adorning it, symbolises the influence of Mahāyāna Buddhism with local influence accentuating it. Among the Tāntric symbols in this Buddha figure are the sun and the moon, the two flaming jewels on lotus flowers, the two books drawn on the upper arms, also surrounded by flames and standing on lotus flowers, together with the *Vajra* (thunderbolt) on the forearms. Other symbols include a chain ornament, a central motif alluding to life and immortality, a galloping horse and a crown alleged to be of the Sassanian type symbolising royal powers. The base has radiating lines running down from its junction with body to foot. Round the junction is apparently wrapped a snake with a part of its body protecting like a cord on each side and each part terminating in a snake's head. The whole of the device is perhaps a rendering of the churning of the ocean.

Another painted figure from Balawaste,[21] deserving notice is supposed to be that of a worshipper or of Indra. The figure is either kneeling or sitting with his legs crossed. His body leans forward from the hips with the head tilted back. The eyes are downcast and hands folded and uplifted to neck-level. The thumbs, strongly abducted, are upright while the fingers point horizontally. The head is covered with a close-fitting cap with a head band in dark pink colour studded with white dots or pearls. This beautiful picture from Balawaste seems distinctly Indian in structure, colouring, costume and style similar to some of the Ajanta figures datable to the early seventh century. The eyes are heavy-lidded, large and dreamy. The eye-brows are not so arched as in the Bezaklik paintings. In the ear, the ear ring is a quatrefoil, the lowest foil being a green jewel. Round the neck is a plain double band and on breast a massive carcanet. On the upper arms are gold armlets, and there are two bangles on the wrist. On the back of the right hand is drawn an eye in

21. Stein and Andrews : *Catalogue*—Op. cit, p. 13; Bussagli : Op. cit, pp. 55, 57; P. Banerji in his paper on 'Hindu deities in Central Asia' (*Vivekanand Volume*, p. 285) considers this figure to be that of Indra. The presence of the eye on the hand is supposed to be the conclusive proof of this identification. Banerji also refers to the figure of Indra occurring on some other paintings from Central Asia. (See also his paper entitled 'Indra from Balawaste' published in *Indo-Asian Culture*, XVII, no. 4, pp. 14 ff.)

black which makes the figure's identification with Indra certain. Besides various ornaments, the figure is supposed to have a *mukuṭa*, *yajñopavīta* and is endowed with a nimbus.

The Hindu influence on the Buddhist paintings in the context of Tantric symbols is evident from the painting of the Buddhist God of the Tantric type from Balawaste.[22] The fragment shows on lower part a *trimūrti* divinity with a small seated Buddha above to left and the toes of a large figure standing on a lotus to right. The *trimūrti* figure sits full-face with head slightly turned to left, the second and third heads, about two-thirds the size of the central project on either side from behind the ears. The central face has a third eye in the forehead and a long thin moustache. The eyes are heavy-lidded and dreamy. On the head is a skull set against the black top-knob with a pearlshaded taenia. Large plain ear-rings adorn the normal sized ears. Other ornaments include a heavy necklet, bangles and armlets. There are four arms, two upraised holding the sun to the left and the moon to the right. The right lower hand holds a pomegranate against the breast while the left resting on the left thigh, grasps an indistinguishable object. A long yellow stole is thrown round the back of the shoulders while long black hair hangs behind. There is no nimbus and the field of vesica is grey-green, bordered with a red inner band and an outer band of red-brown, with both hands contoured with thin white lines. An example of this figure, with slight variations, is the one painted on an extremely interesting wooden panel, found by Stein at the ancient site of Dandan-Oiliq in 1900[23]. In that panel the figure looks the other way, and holds a white object instead of a pomegranate in the right hand. This could be a drum (*ḍamaru*) or some other fruit. The positions of the two subsidiary heads are also reversed—the smiling (female ?) head to the left and the demon to the right. The positions of the sun and moon emblems (probably wrongly identified as *Cakra* and

22. Andrews : *Wall Paintings*—no Bal 0200 p. 22; Bussagli : Op. cit, p. 60, 63. Of the four arms, the front pair are posed very similarly to those of the Teacher in Miran Painting, III. 002, pl. 1. An example of this painting, with slight variations, is that painted on an extremely wooden panel from the ruined dwelling. D. VII at Dandan-Oiliq (Stein : *Ancient Khotan* Pl. XL).

23. Stein : *Ancient Khotan*, Pl. XL; Talbot Rice : Op. cit, Pl. 1971.

Śaṅkha) are also reversed. In this panel the loins are covered by a tiger skin. It has been suggested that this figure, undoubtedly Śiva, and one of the numberless importations into Mahāyāna Buddhism from Brahmanic Iconography, is adopted as one of the forms of the favourite Bodhisattva Avalokiteśvara.

While the Hindu influences appear to have come through Kashmir, the Khotanese school has example of purely Iranian details and in some cases the Chinese features are also traced. One such example of direct connection between local art and the Sogdian style is corroborated in the Iranian Bodhisattva[24] of Dandan-Oiliq. It is characterised by the elongation of the body and other features. Painted on a wooden tablet, this fine votive image is four-armed, black-bearded, wearing a pale green close-fitting tunic. He sits on a cushion and has nimbus, halo-crown, dagger and other attributes. On the back of the panel is depicted a three-headed goddess of the Tantric type, probably of Śaivite origin but definitely connected with Buddhism.

Another wooden tablet depicts the legend of the famous Silk Princess[25], who secretly introduced the silk worm culture in Khotan. This figure at the top is four-armed and has two of the attributes of the Iranian Bodhisattva, the cup and the knife with a short triangular blade, and both are wearing a crown. Similar images are found, with minor variations, on a number of panels from Dandan-Oiliq, thus testifying to a genuinely Khotanese iconographic type. In the figure of the Silk Princess her oval face, nose, costume and head dress, Chinese influence could be traced. It is, therefore, proposed that various tendencies, Indian, Iranian and Chinese, co-existed in these particular works of Dandan-Oiliq, dating sometime between the sixth and eighth century as the site was finally abandoned in 791. The best known of the Khotan paintings is supposed to be the

24. The 'Iranian Bodhisattva' wooden votive Tablet from Dandan Oiluq (Khotan) Sanctuary D. VII, probably seventh century, now in the British Museum. For a description, see Bussagli : Op. cit, p. 61. It is proposed by Natalia Diakonova that the figure is that of a goddess connected with silk—on the strength of an iconographic analogy with other images, all of them from Dandan Oiluq, which is not convincing.

25. Stein : *Ancient Khotan*. D. X. Pl. LXIII. The Silk Princess wooden votive Tablet from Dandan-Oiliq (Khotan) probably of the seventh century is now in the British Museum, London; See Bussagli : Op. cit, p. 56.

lovely Nāginī[26] rising from the water of an artificial fountain in Temple D. II at Dandan-Oiliq, signifying fusion of Indian and Chinese elements. Unfortunately the painting is lost and the photograph alone displays gesture of maidenly modesty. Fixed symbolism and iconography connected with Buddhist thought conditioned by the display of external factors and forces, enriched Khotanese pictorial art, noted for its vitality and assimilative tendency without sacrificing its originality. Some of the greatest Khotanese painters worked in China in the late Sui and early Tang period and made a deep impression there. Wei-chh Po-Chihna—the elder, and the younger one Wei-Chih (Vijaya), introduced in China a sense of colours and a way of handling it with exceptional power of expression and vigour of style.

The Northern Schools[27]

The art centres on the Northern Route Kizil, Kucha and Turfan with the neighbouring centres. Kumtura (Kucha region) and Bezaklik, Toyuq & Qoco in the Turfan region also provide illustrations of pictorial art which were equally connected or influenced by the artistic developments of the neighbouring centres—eastern and western. Political factors like the exodus of the Sassanians as emigre's at Kucha or the political domination of China over Kucha (which in 658 became the seat of the Chinese Government of the Tarim Basin) were responsible for foreign influence on local art as also on the traditions connected with the art centres. The Kucha school of painting, representing the western aspect of the Northern School, seems

26. Bussagli : Op. cit, p. 66.

27. For a general review of the Central Asian Paintings from centres on the Northern Route, see Bussagli : Op cit, pp. 69 ff; those in the State Museum, Berlin, are catalogued under Central Asian Art—in the work 'Along the Ancient Silk Routes', New York (Op. cit) with a fine introduction by Herbert Hartel, and a description of some of the important pieces, exhibited at the Metropolitan Museum of Art. The finds from these art centres, rich in Buddhist remains, have been studied by several eminent scholars—Russian, German, British and French. Reference to these investigations is given in brief by Andrews in his *Wall Paintings* (Op. cit, pp. xxiv ff). For a fuller bibliography, see note 1 of this Chapter based on the Entry in the Encyclopedia of World Art, Vol. I, pp. 837-38. Individual references would be provided separately. See also Talbot Rice : Op. cit, pp. 180 ff.

to have begun in the 4th century A.D. and continued in a more liberal way till the end of the eighth century A.D. representing broadly its two distinct phases, the first of Indo-Iranian type flourishing around c. 500 A.D. and the second one, strongly Iranian reaching its climax about A.D. 600, 650. The Chinese influence representing the third phase is noticeable in the paintings at Kucha between the seventh and eighth centuries. On the basis of these stylistic differences, two clearly distinguished spheres of artistic influence in the area of the northern Silk Route can be clearly marked out. The western one, fairly older (about A.D. 500-700) centred around Kucha, and an eastern school of the later times (c. A.D. 650-950) in the region of the Turfan Oasis. The styles of the former school are especially illustrated by the numerous wall paintings from the cave monasteries of Kizol, near Kucha. They reveal Indian and Iranian influences. The former is seen in the way of composition of the subjects from the Buddhist texts and in the serene and tranquil way of the Buddha portrayed in the frescoes. The less obvious Iranian influence is traced in the pictorial details, especially of the dress. Crowns and other ornaments are worn by the bodhisattvas and other deities and many decorative ribbons are of Sassanian origin; and numerous decorative features are traced back to patterns from the Sassanian school of silk weaving. On the other hand in the eastern sphere, the Chinese influence is pre-dominant, quite clearly revealed in the facial features as also in the dress of the subjects.

The use of motifs is no doubt helpful in placing any culture in a historical perspective as also in tracing its origin but it could be of little help in defining the style of any work of art. Further, in Central Asian art the absence of the personal data consequent to the anonymity of the artist makes it difficult to ferret out individual art style stamped in the area noted for the evolution of hybrid culture. The artist very often himself a Buddhist monk, had to conform himself to the ideals of the Buddhist faith in stimulating the religious feelings of the votary and motivate him to a higher degree of moral conduct as might help him in coming closer to the goal of his spiritual needs and aspirations. He no doubt fades into the background with his personality submerged in his creations. As such, it is only possible to analyse the pictorial art of different centres with reference to common features, as also distinguishing them on grounds of physiognomy, dress, colour scheme, narration and background and media of light and shade. The eharacters of inscription, if any, could suggest the probable date of the pictorial art, as for instance the earliest paintings in the Painter's Cave at Kizil could be placed in c. A.D. 500. A few caves are painted in the same style as the cave of the Painters, representing the oldest group. One such being the cave of the Statues in Kizil which provide the best specimens of the first Indo-Iranian styles; a cowherd listening to a sermon of the Buddha[28] and of Vajrapāṇi. The paintings show signs of Indian mannerism and style. The vigorous cowherd leans on a knotted stick, watching over his animals as he listens devoutly to the words of the Buddha. So deep is his concentration that he is unmindful of the poor frog being crushed beneath his stick. The two cattles, one dark in colour and the other white, lie on the ground behind the central figure. That of the Buddha shows him seated on the throne with his hand raised in the gesture of teaching.

Vajrapāṇi[29] in the other cave of the Statues, is shown here gracefully seated on a wicker stool, holding in his left hand the vajra, the thunderbolt, resembling the sceptre and with his right hand fans the Buddha of whose figure only parts have been preserved. He is elaborately draped in chains and strings of beads or metal disks. He wears a brown skirt with ruffled green borders and has long green scarves suspended from his head dress with their ends almost touching the ground. On his head is a diadem decorated with beads and discs with a white band hanging from either side. Plumes of feathers at the sides of the head dress are also noticed, with a large ornamented disk in the Centre. Similar diadems appear in the Sassanian art.[30]

28. The Cowherd Nanda. Kizil Cave of the Statues c. 500. MLK. III, 8838; Le Coq & Waldschmidt : *Die buddhistiche Spatantike in Muttelasian* 1928·33.VI. pl. 3 c and p. 66; Bussagli : Op. cit p. 72; Hertel : Central Asian Art no. 9, pp. 66-67.

29. 'Seated Vajrapāṇi'. Kizil Cave of the Statues c.500. MLK 8839. Hertel : Central Asian Art, p. 68-69; Le Coq & Waldschmidt : Op. cit, VI, pl. 36, p. 66.

30. Ghirshman refers for example to a stone relief of the third century A.D. from Sar Meshed depicting king Bahram II as a lion slayer (Ghirshman,

Only the bare knee of the Buddha is visible at the right edge of the fragment, who was seated on a carpeted throne. Below it are two sharp-beaked falcon-like birds, one perched on the ground and the other diving from above. Vajrapāṇi's almond-shaped eyes, his narrow moustache and his cross-shaped navel suggest Indian influence.

Both the paintings provide a very specific choice of colour, with the use of finely distinguished shades of the same basic hue in a variegated scale from whitish yellow through brownish and reddish nuances to deep brown, sometimes merging into black. Contrast is provided by a very bright green colour. Contour to surfaces, objects and persons is rendered by fine strokes of the brush. In the rendering of clothes falling into folds, three-dimensional modelling of the fabric is perceptible, as might be apparent from the cowherd's loin cloth. The semi-circular concentric lines in the area of his right thigh shows the material clinging to the contours of the body. The ground colour, one shade darker determines the colouring of the lines.

Another illustration of the first phase is the picture of a young ascetic[31] in his shells of foliage decorating either a vault or a pendentive in the cave of the Navigator at Kizil. The elongated, dreaming eyes of this figure, of about the same date as the cowherd, show stronger Indian influence. The linear rendering of the hair and the concentric, almost elliptical curves are most conspicuous while the contrasting colours, the handling of the beard and the ornamentation of the scarf over the shoulders provide an interesting study. The image of this young ascetic when compared to that of the mystic one Mahākāśyapa[32] from the so-called Large Cave at Kizil, at least a century later,

---

1962 fig. 215, 216). According to the late professor a royal crown decorated with eagle features was originally the symbol of the Avestian god of victory, Verethragna, who had the same function as Indra, the Vedic god of war, who was included in the Buddhist pantheon (quoted. Hertel : Op. cit, p. 68).

31. 'Young Ascetic'. Wall Painting from the Cave of the Navigator, circa 500, IB 8389. State Museum, Berlin—Bussagli : Op .cit, p. 74; Talbot Rice : Op. cit, p. 192, illus. 181, who traces Indian influence, combined with Graeco-Roman in this head of a young ascetic.

32. 'Head of Mahākāśyapa'—Kizil Cave above the Largest Cave, 7th century, MIK.III. 8373a. Hertel : Op. cit no. 20 pp. 82-83; Bussagli : Op. cit, p. 75.

shows a high degree of stylization with schematized eyebrows, the folds of the mouth and chin and the shape of the eyes. The facial features of Mahākāśyapa are less powerful in expression. The head is inclined before a flowered background, the hair is cut short and shaved back from the temples in two wings. The eyes, eyebrows and nose are strongly accented. Mahākāśyapa's face is framed by a light blue beard of the same colour as his hair. The ear lobes appear stretched with the weight of the ear-rings once worn. The neck, chin and mouth are heavily lined. A fragment of the green patch work robe is preserved on the shoulder. This wall painting seems to form part of the Mahāparinirvāṇa scene.[33]

The group of swimmers from the Cave of the Navigator,[34] Kizil, about 500 A.D., now in the State Museum, Berlin is another example of contemporary painting from that place, supposed to be different in style from the figure of the monk, and representing the personalities of different artists. The scene shows three men swimming among water lilies, the middle one seems hardly able to keep his head above water while the one to the right exhibits his powerful strokes symbolising great determination, which is evident from his expression and gestures. A comparison of his face with those of the cowherd and of Vajrapāṇi reveals stylistic similarity between the paintings of this cave and those of the cave of the Statues. The elongated eyes of the swimmers, the stylized swirls of the water as also line work show Indian influence.

The second phase of Kucha art distinct from the previous one in conception, treatment of space as also devoid of Indian stylistic influence, is revealed from the Goddess and Celestial

33. According to Hertel, this wall painting depicting a Mahāparinirvāṇa scene may be compared with a similar better-preserved painting. It is based on the *Mahāparinirvāṇa Sūtra,* a Sanskrit text found in Central Asia, and its parallels in Pāli, Tibetan and Chinese. Depictions of Mahākāśyapa are very often found in connection with the Parinirvāṇa of the Buddha, while the expression of great grief is noticeable in his face, it is difficult to suggest if Mahākāśyapa was shown kneeling at the head of the Buddha or at his feet (ibid p. 83).

34. Hertel : Op. cit, p. 35 with other references from Grunwedel, Le Coq and Bussagli, p. 73, No. MIK III 8398—State Museum, Berlin.

Musician[35] wall painting from the cave of the Painted Floor at Kizil. Of course, there are Indian elements noticed in both iconography and composition. This work is considered as the most beautiful and best-known of all the Kucha paintings. In a figurative style it is marked by decorative devices. The typical rendering of the space is against the background punctuated by stellar motifs, a rain of falling flowers. The Goddess and musician, the subject of the picture, under a tree in blossom, encircled by a wide double curve with decorative motif of a geometric—abstract order enhance the beauty of the painting as also suggest unity in composition. The style of this painting, supposed to be a little over a century and a half later, is different from the previous one on grounds of colours—the way of their use and space and volume dominating the scene as also suggestive of the movement of Buddhist thought in the direction of mysticism. In the Avadāna of Rūpavatī[36] from the cave of the Frieze of Musicians, Kizil, the figures are much less elongated while the perspective and the figurative elements do not depict any change.

The Kizil art is a composite one with traces of various influences.[37] That of Gupta art on the paintings is obvious, in the rendering of anatonical details. The prevailing colour

35. 'Goddess and Celestial Musician'. Wall Painting from the Cave of the Painted floor. Kizil. 600, 650, IB 84206. State Museum, Berlin; Bussagli : Op. cit, p. 81 and p. 78 for description and comments.

36. 'Avadāna of Rūpavatī' The sacrifice of the Bodhisattva (?) Wall Painting from the Cave of the Frieze of Musicians, Kizil, IB 8390, State Museum, Berlin; Bussagli, Op. cit, p. 84 and for comments p. 83.

37. The Kizil paintings are considered most important amongst the art centres on the northern route, not because of any marked superiority in quality or individuality of style, but because the surviving examples furnish a complete time sequence for dating purposes. The earliest Kizil paintings are assigned to the period A.D. 450-650, and the second phase ending in about 750. As regards foreign influences that of Sogdia and Bactria are reflected in the cut of the clothes, especially of the donors. The tunics often have the characteristically Sogdian single reverse. Hellenistic influence is traced in the pictures of the Buddha· Women are, however, closer in style to Indian than to Iranian or Greek conceptions, while the men are nearer Sassanian models. Even during the last phase while the artists were using highlights of the Chinese type, many of the men still retained a markedly Persian appearance (Talbot Rice : Op. cit, pp. 190-91).

scheme in the earlier style, closely related to that of the frescoes of Bamian, is made up of greens and browns, dulled, soft and without strong contrast. That in the second one consists of malachite green and a shade of blue and shadows rendered exclusively in orange. The frescoes at Kizil as elsewhere served a dual purpose—religious instruction and providing decorative scenes and an overall picture of Buddha's life and activities. The Greco-Buddhist influence is evident in many iconographic details while the undulating elements in the figures along with refinement and lightness characterise Gupta or post-Gupta influence. The Iranian influence is as well traceable in the earlier phase of Kucha art in the form of decorative motifs and certain details of the dress, emphasised rather greatly in the second style. The motif of garland bearers in flight echoes late Hellenistic tradition. This composite nature of art symbolised with traces of influence from different quarters has indigenous base, as is evident from the costume and the racial type of the figure.

Another centre not far from Kizil on the Muzart River is Kumtura[38] where several of the caves are decorated with frescoes in which the styles of Kizil are copied. These also contain frescoes reminding of the second style of Kizil or of a later period influenced by Chinese art. The temples containing these frescoes are hollowed out of the rock except for a small temple built in the open, in which was found the lower portion of a statue of Buddha clad in stylized drapery like the models of the Gupta period. The structural plans of the temples are similar to those of the Kizil sanctuaries—predominantly rectangular with barrel vaults or square with a domed roof. There are a good many examples of the first style in a domed cave with the colour scheme consisting of green, brown and sienna-reddish brown or brownish yellow with the figures like those in the cave of the Peacocks and of the Painter at Kizil. The second style of Kizil is copied at Kumtura in the cave of Nāgarāja with the same stylistic traits and colours. Specimens of the third style in the caves of Nirvāṇa of the Apsarās and of

38. See *Encyclopedia of World Art*, Vol. I, p. 832 for a general description of the site and its monuments. See also Bussagli : Op. cit, pp. 88, 89; Talbot Rice : Op. cit, pp. 188, 190.

the Kinnaras are apparently influenced by the Chinese art of the Tang period. The floral ornament is typical of the art of Chinese derivation in Central Asia, as also of the figures floating in clouds. The figures have round faces and slaunting eyes. A typical Chinese impress is in the rendering of mountains and trees according greater importance to landscape. The colours in the third style are bright and tempered and the composition is subdued, different from that of the Kizil paintings. Kumtura, thus, represents the farthest point of penetration of Chinese influence adding to the confluence brought about by those from India and Iran for the service of the Buddha and his religion. Among the important paintings from this place may be mentioned the Buddha and the Praying Monk[39] (c. 650) and Divinities of the Tushita Heaven[40] from the Cave of the Apsarās (8th century), and the worshipping Bodhisattva[41] (8-9th cent.). In the last one the Mongol features, the head-dress, the drapery, folds of dress and scarves—all traditionally Chinese, are prominent. In this third style, the composition and colouring are also being increasingly dominated by Chinese tastes and tendencies. Besides frescoes, there are sculptures of wood and clay—the latter moulded around a wooden framework, sometimes they formed part of the original decoration of the niche and ledges in the caves. Mostly these were pious donation to the monasteries.

Monastic establishments, systematically arranged around a central court with separate stūpas, were traced eleswhere as well. In the ruins of the buildings, destroyed in fire at Duldur-Akhur[42] not far from Kumtura, were recovered fragments of statues moulded of Stucco with straw or tow, as well as wooden

39. 'Buddha and Praying Monk' from the Cave with a Low Entrance Kumtura. c. 650. I B. 9024, State Museum, Berlin. Bussagli : Op. cit, p. 88.

40. 'Divinities of the Tusita Heaven'. Wall Painting from the Cave of the Apsarās, Kumtura. Eighth century I B 9021, State Museum, Berlin.

41. 'Worshipping Bodhisattva'. Wall Painting from Kumtura, Eighth-Ninth centuries, IB 8377, State Museum, Berlin Bussagli: Op. cit, p. 91; Hertel : Op. cit, p. 126-127. This fragment is one of the finest examples of richly coloured mural paintings.

42. For a general description of the site and its monuments, see *Encyclopedia of World Art*. Op. cit, p. 833.

sculpture and some frescoes. The archaeological finds are reminiscent of classical works, while the Chinese influence is apparent in the wooden sculptures. Fragments of some frescoes show a certain degree of similarity with the first style of Kizil, while others reveal Chinese influences. The same phenomenon of Indian, classical and Chinese influences alternating is also traced at some other places like the ruins of Hinar and Tajzik Karauh-Kosur.

Kara-Shahr[43]

Kara Shahr also offers a complex of many temples and cave temples in which fragments of statuary have been found. These include the remains of a *Parinirvāṇa* there. It is in the round and has Indian influences. Important frescoes have also been found in the cave temples with certain structural variations from the usual rectangular plan of the second Kizil style. In the same sector about 25 Kilometres to the south, south-west from Karashahr extensive collection of Buddhist remains were traced at Shorchuk and at Ming-oi—'the thousand caves to the north of it'. Both the places are of religious and archaeological importance. The buildings are hewn out of rock and also set up in the open air. Excavations at Shorchuk[44] have brought out many fired-clay moulds of not only the head but also the torso and other parts of the body. The reliefs were generally affixed to the wall, given finishing touches with a chisel, and finally gilded, while the elegance of the bodies and the anatomical details visible beneath the drapery betray the influence of Gupta art. The stamp of Indo-Greco-Buddhist art, however, predominates, especially in the smaller statues which appear similar to those found at Hadda in Afghanistan and at Taxila. A seated Buddha in clay from the Kirin Cave in Shorchuk now

43. For a general description of the site and its monuments, see *Encyclopedia of World Art*—Op. cit, pp. 833-34.

44. The geographical position of Shorchuq made it a place of meeting and mutual influence from Kucha and the Chinese one from the east which were absorbed here with the local artists portraying their specific character distinguishing their contribution from others. Narration of Buddha's life activities is replaced by the 'three jewels'. The Chinese elements in the paintings of Shorchuq and of the Karasahr generally differ greatly from those of Kucha. (Bussagli : Op. cit, p. 94).

in the State Museum Berlin[45], is a fine specimen of this art. Seated on a high finely painted pedestal, supported by a rectangular block adorned with a pair of floral medallions, the Buddha is clad in three garments, a transparent under one (*antaravāsa*), a yellowish brown robe (*uttarāsaṅga*) and a reddish upper covering (*sanghātī*). The legs, crossed in the lotus posture, are fully covered; the left hand holds one end of the upper covering, while the right one—broken—was presumably in the protection posture (*abhayamudrā*). The hair is styled in waves, with the hair line marked in red. The *ūrṇa* takes the form of a stylised jewel on the forehead. The painted decoration is unmistakably of Chinese type.

At Ming-oi,[46] the number of grottoes, changing into sanctuaries, was considerably large—may be 'a thousand caves' as the word seems to indicate. These shrines were adorned with sculptures consisting both of large traditional figures of the Buddhas and Bodhisattvas, as well as of numerous smaller ones, depicting with precision and clarity people of every age and walk of life, with a sensitive grasp of pathos and humour. While the geographical position of Shorchuk made it a meeting place of artistic currents from Kucha and China also reflected at Ming-oi, the local artists, assimilating foreign features, equally displayed their ingenuity. Their paintings have a specific character which distinguishes them from many others in Central Asian Art. The subject matter, unlike the narrative tone at Kucha, is taken from the lives of the monks rather than of the Buddha, with deeper interest concentrated in the last of the three jewels—*Saṅgha* or the ecclesiastical community of Buddhism—the 'guardian of the Good Law' or the *Dhamma*. The paintings in general are of exceptionally high quality, with

45. Hertel : Op. cit no. MIK III. 7841 from Shorchuk, Kirin Cave dated 7th-8th century, for description and cross references—Rowland : *The Art of Central Asia* (New York, 1974, pp. 176ff.).

46. The word Ming-oi meaning 'A Thousand Caves' was used to describe the region in the Shorchuq district. It has come to be associated with the sculptures which adorned these shrines. These consist both of large, traditional figures of Buddhas and Bodhisattvas, as well as of numerous smaller ones depicting with vivacity and precision people of every age and walk of life (Talbot Rice : Op. cit, p. 182). See also Andrews : *Wall Paintings* : Op. cit, p. 28.

rich and dark colours, predominantly yellow, brown, rose and green unlike the bright light ones in Kizil art. An extraordinary variety of poses and physical types in the figures is another notable feature of the style of Shorchuk[47]—which is supposed to be a transitional one between the second and the third styles of Kucha.

The Turfan Group[48] :

The Turfan region because of its geographical position was the bone of contention between the nomad empires and China as early as the time of the early Huns, and was exposed to a series of ethnic fluctuations and political changes affecting art development in many ways. The Chinese influence here was strongly felt. Changes in religious thought left their impact on remnants of art. Buddhism, Manichaeism and Nestorianism and subsequent restoration of Buddhism signified changes in iconography and style. The hold of Buddhism was no doubt for a longer period of time. Its influence in the Tarim Basin is supposed to have lingered on even when the forces of Islam had swept over the neighbouring areas. This was due to the interest and power of the Uighurs. Buddhism seems to have survived till the beginning of the 15th century. The Turfan oasis in its complex includes religious and civil monuments, including a great many watch towers, citadels and royal palaces

47. *Encyclopedia of World Art*, Vol. I, Op. cit, p. 834. See also Andrews : Op. cit, pp. 28-39 for reference to fragment of a painting from Ming-oi XIII, now in the British Museum. This and a few others provide a series of scenes in which an elderly teacher lectures to men of various ages dressed as monks and holding a writing tablet and pen or stylus to take notes. Others are seated each in a separate cave cell, apparently studying or writing. Aurel Stein in his *Serindia* provides fuller information on Mingoi and its finds.

48. For detailed references to Turfan and its art, see *Encyclopedia of World Art*, Vol. XIV under Turfan, and also those noticed, mainly duplications under Central Asian Art—ibid, Vol. I, pp. 837-38. Bussagli has a special chapter on the Turfan Group in his work entitled *Paintings of Central Asia*, Op. cit, pp. 95-112. The history of exploration in the Turfan region is recorded by Aurel Stein in his *Serindia*, Vol. III, pp. 1149 ff as also his *Innermost Asia*, Reprint, New Delhi, 1981, pp. 568-89. In the course of his investigations, Stein examined cave and structural shrines at Khara-Khoja, Toyuk, Bezaklik and other sites. See Andrews: *Catalogues of Wall Paintings*, Delhi, 1933 for paintings from Turfan in the National Museum.

connected with the Uighurs. These are traced at Idikut-Shahri, 'the city of Idikut', and Khocho, while Mortuk, Bezaklik and Senghim-aghiz provide best examples of religious art. The degree of Chinese influence varies in these centres, as for instance Murtuq retained many Iranian and Indian characteristics and was directly influenced by Kucha and Shorchuk owing to the monk's adherence to Mahāyānism. At Bezaklik on the other hand, where Tantric influence dominated, the Chinese influence was wide and deep. It constituted an artistic and iconographic phenomena of its own, more complex than at Kumtura. By oscillating between Iranian and Chinese forms, Turfan was in fact a link between the tastes and tendencies of pre-Islamic Iran and aesthetic currents from eastern Asia. The different phases of this complex art are differently rendered from one locality to another.

According to Hackin[49], three phases can be traced in the Bezaklik complex : a first period of Buddhist domination covering the seventh and eighth centuries in which the influence of Kucha was felt. The influence of Tang painting is reflected in a most prevalent manner in this period. The second period covering part of the ninth century is marked by Manichaean domination of the Uighurs with a new influx of Iranian influences. The last period of Buddhist supremacy from the tenth to the eleventh century or perhaps even later, is characterised by the setting in of the process of decadence, and for some time direct representation of some of the Tāntric divinities is traced in certain temples. On the other hand, Murtuk of the same epoch and close to Bezeklik presents a very different style. Here Chinese influence is not predominant, but Indian influence is clearly traced in the figure of the Buddha seated in the European fashion and accompanied by a Bodhisattva of purely Indian type holding a vase. The subject matter is taken from legends connected with Mahāyāna Buddhism. In the flames surrounding Buddha and in the coiffure of one of the donors the influence of the art of Kizil and that of Iranio-Buddhist one is noticed.

49. J. Hackin : *Buddhist Art in Central Asia : Indian, Iranian and Chinese influence from Bamiyan to Turfan*—quoted by L. Hambi in his article 'Asia Central' in the *Encyclopedia of World Art*, Vol. I, p. 835.

This introductory background of the peculiar features of the Central Asian art at Turfan might be helpful in this context noticing a few important specimens of paintings, now in the Berlin Museum, as also in the National Museum, New Delhi.

The best illustration of western influence in Turfan area is provided by a wall painting from Khochu dated between the seventh and eighth centuries and now in the State Museum, Berlin.[50] It depicts the head of a Buddha beneath a canopy. The shape of the eyes, the bold strokes of the eye-brows and the dress resemble the sculptures of Shorchuk. Western figurative tendencies are revealed in other ways as well. This delicate and pensive head of the Buddha from Khocho—called Idigutschai 'the city of Idigut' by the Uighurs in honour of a Turkish hero of that name, is supposed to be an early example of Uighur Buddhist painting. It is classified as one in the second Indo-Iranian style. This beautiful image is inclined slightly towards the left and is surrounded by an oval nimbus and surmounted by an unusual designed canopy.

Another wall painting[51] depicts the 'Great Departure' of Prince Siddhārtha, who is partly visible on the left riding his favourite horse Kanthaka 'away from home to homelessness'. In the mural, the forehead and bristling hair of one demigod can be seen below the horse's head and the fragment of the figure of another one is noticed at the bottom. The partly visible face has the same shape of one of the eye, and an equally bold stroke of the eyebrow, as noticed in the earlier figurehead of the Buddha. It is supposed to be a later execution with realism when the somewhat austere colour scheme of the Uighur art had developed. It is dated in the ninth century.

Central Asia also provides paintings portraying princes and their families meant for hanging at the entrance or in passages in the cave temples. One such fine painting on cloth from Khocho, now in the Berlin Museum, is that of a Uighurian

50. Buddha beneath a canopy. Wall Painting from Khocho—Seventh-Eighth centuries. I.B. 8731. State Museum, Berlin. Bussagli : Op.c it, p. 97; Hertel : Op. cit, No. 90, p. 154; Talbot Rice : Op. cit, p. 196.

51. The Great Departure. Khocho Ruins. 8th century. MIK .III, 4426—Hertel : Op. cit, p. 155 No. 92; Bussagli : Op. cit, p. 26.

prince[52] on both sides. Like all votive banners it consists of three parts : the long, narrow, rectangular banner itself; the triangular segment at the top, which here depicts a seated Buddha; and rectangular strips of material at the bottom with a wooden stick to weigh it down. The aristocratic prince with his long hair and white beard and curved moustache puts on a fine robe, patterned with a large floral design. This long-sleeved, round-necked garment—the typical one of the country, reaches to the feet and a belt fastens it in front with rectangular decorative pieces. A slit in the side of the garment reveals a black knee-length boot. The prince holds a stem in his hand with several blossoms. The small squat body of the prince is in strange contrast with the portraits of Uighurian prince and princess,[53] painted on the walls at Bezaklik, now in the Berlin Museum.

The mourning scene[54] in Shrine IX from Bezeklik, dated in the Eighth century, now in the National Museum, New Delhi, is very realistic. It shows people mourning at the death of the Buddha. These include dignitaries, princes and sovereigns of different nationalities—Arabs, Iranians and Chinese, suggesting popularity of Buddhism and its communion. Another shrine No. XII from the same place also shows musicians and mourners[55] in a grotesque style.

The Turfan area was also a strong centre of Manichaenism as also Nestorian Christianity. Most of the important finds by the four German expeditions to Turfan included thousands of manuscripts with and without illustrations. Most of the Turfan miniatures, richly painted in gold and opaque colours are from Manichaen books.[56] The artists portraying these were probably

52. Hertel : Op. cit, p. 196-7, no. 136. Bussagli : Op. cit, p. 105.

53. Bussagli : Op. cit, pp. 106, 107.

54. Bussagli : Op. cit, p. 110; Andrews: *Wall Paintings* (Bez. XI. A.C. pl. XX, p. xxiv). It depicts a crowd of mourners gathered round the bier of the Buddha, composed of representatives of the many kingdoms present on that mournful occasion, and affords an interesting opportunity of identifying the several types of communities usually at variance, but here united in expressing a common grief.

55. 'Musicians'. Wall Paintings from Bezaklik. Eighth century. Private collection. Tokyo. Bussagli : Op. cit, p. 103.

56. Hertel : Op. cit, p. 174. The most important finds made by the four German expeditions to Turfan were undoubtedly the manuscripts, both with

Sogdian. As Manism was based on Iranian dualism mingled with elements from the Buddhist and Christian creeds, its philosophy found its expression in art as well. The largest fragment of a Manichaean miniature in the Berlin collection,[57] painted on both sides, depicts on one side a Church ceremony. In the background the principal character (his head being destroyed) appears to be a high-ranking Manichaean priest in full vestments with a prince or a king kneeling before him and three of his attendants standing behind him. In the foreground are portrayed Hindu deities : the one with the elephant's head is Gaṇeśa, the boar's head might represent Viṣṇu as Varāha, the third and fourth could be Brahmā and Śiva respectively. Facing them on the left are two Iranian Manichaean gods. The miniature on the other side depicts a religious celebration, the famous feast of Bema, celebrated every year as the martyrdom day of Mani.[58] It is suggested that even when the iconography became Manichean and, by religious affinity, adopted Buddhist or other Indian forms, which it promptly rearranged on new lines and with new values, the encounter of the cultures of India and Iran in the region of Turfan remained abundantly clear. A particular stylistic idiom was born out of this encounter which moved westwards and profoundly reacted on later Islamic art.[59]

---

and without illustrations, on various materials, such as palm leaf, birchbark and paper. These provide significant information on religious, political and philological aspects of eastern Central Asia. Mani's teachings symbolised a syncretism embracing many components in the form of a philosophy of nature. It was based on Iranian dualism mingled with elements from the Buddhist and Christian creeds.

57. 'Leaf from a Manichaean Book'. Khocho Temple, 8th-9th century. Manuscript Paintings, MIK.III.4079. This is the largest fragment of a Manichaean miniature in the Berlin collection and is painted on both sides. Hertel : Op. cit, no. 114, pp. 176-177.

58. It was probably in the spring, for St. Augustine (who was himself at one time a Manichaean) tells us that Mani died in March 276. A podium was erected for the liturgical rites, with five steps leading upto it. It was draped with sumptuous tapestries. The celebration fell into two parts : first, on the eve of the faithful fasted in preparation and kept a vigil during the night in remembrance of Mani's death followed by the feast day itself (Hertel : Op. cit, p. 177).

59. It is suggested by Talbot Rice that Turfan with the Sassanian elements in its sculpture and painting, together with Kucha, Kizil and Pendzikent surely

There are several other sites in the Turfan area including Sengim and Toyuk as also Khocho and Kharakhoja which have been centres of Central Asian Buddhist art. The wall paintings at Sengim reveal a synthesis of different art influences. The figure of nakṣatras, female lunar divinities, with their fluttering scarves illustrate in Grousset's words, 'the most felicitous synthesis of Indian sinuosity, Hellenistic elegance and Chinese grace'.[60] These paintings are found in monasteries, and are well-preserved. At Toyuk, also visited by Klementz and German and French expeditions, Stein discovered[61] fragments of Stucco reliefs there of various types and sizes including a great many small heads and ornaments in the form of necklaces. A painted ceiling in the sixth century portrays a seated Bodhisattva surrounded by rays with floral decorations like those in the Turfan sanctuaries.

Plurality and diversity of artistic life have been the keynotes of Turfan's contribution. Many artistic tendencies converged in this area and had their impact on the Buddhist art. The type of drapery, reduced to concentric folds often used as Pendzikent, seems obviously connected with the art of Sogdiana. The style of this region was to some extent determined by the synthetic religious development, although one could trace differences in Buddhist compositions of Bezaklik and Murtuq[62] and those of the Christian temple at Khocho. Forms of figurative expression far removed from each other because of the different inflections in their religious feelings were adopted. The Buddhist system

---

influenced both the Buddhist art of Tibet and the Islamic art of the Ghaznavids, Samanids and Seljukid Turks. Mongol painters appear, on the other hand, to have been more deeply affected by the Vighurs, for the figural art which the latter created did not die out when Khocho and Tun-huang declined. (Op. cit, p. 203).

60. *Encyclopaedia of World Art*, Vol. I, p. 836. For reference to paintings from these sites, see Hertel : Op. cit, nos. 114-125, 136, 137, 138, 139; (Khocho); 140, 144, 151 (Murtuk); 140, 144 (Tuyok); Andrews : Pl. XI, pp. 64 ff (Khara Khoja).

61. *Innermost Asia*, pp. 616 ff.

62. For Bezeklik and Murtuq finds see Stein : *Innermost Asia*, Op. cit, pp. 633 ff. and also Andrews : *Wall Paintings* Op. cit Introduction pp. 32 ff. and Plate VIII & IX. Those from Bezeklik are also noticed by Andrews : 'Introduction', pp. 51 ff; Plates XII-XXXI. These are also mentioned by Hertel : Op. cit nos. 81-85, 108-110.

no doubt provided a wider canvas for the artists to display their talents and the religious experience of the peoples was a great asset in this direction. The Turfan region on the eastern border of ancient Kashgar was the last province of Central Asia to retain any creative vitality at a time when the artistic activity in the surrounding region had faded or was on the verge of extinction.

Tun-huang[63]

The great monastic agglomeration of Tun-huang further east in Kansu, lying on the last stage of the caravan routes represents a curious blending of Indian imagery and symbolism into the Chinese style of painting. During the third and fourth century A.D. numerous monasteries had come into being there and in these a great many shrines and religious statues were set up. Many of the shrines were located in caves and its walls and ceilings were covered with paintings. Sometimes these also appeared on stūpas. The painters here in Tun-huang adopted Miran's style and iconography as the basis for their own school of art. In fact, Miran was the centre of artistic talents and these influenced as well as helped working in other areas. Tun-huang became a very important centre of Buddhist art. Buddhism reached there by way of both the northern and southern Taklamakan routes. The monastery founded in c. 333 on a site abounding with grottos and caves, gradually expanded in number and space, finally culminating in that of a thousand Buddhas and extended all along with the entire area presenting a vast complex. Most of the buildings have now crumbled with no decorations. The

63. A. Stein : *The Thousand Buddhas:Ancient Buddhist Paintings from the cave Temples of Tun-huang*, London, 1921-22; A. Waley : *A Catalogue of Paintings recovered from Tun-huang by Sir Aurel Stein*, Oxford, 1931; B. Gray : *Buddhist Cave Paintings at Tun-huang*, Faber & Faber, London, 1959; J. Hackin : *Guide Catalogue de Musee Guimet—Les Collections Bouddhique*, Paris, 1923—Chapter II—Touen-Hovang, pp. 33 ff; Mission P. Pelliot : *Le grottes de Tounen-houang*, 6 Vols. of Plates Paris 1920-1924. See also Bibliography under Asia Central—*Encyclopedia of World Art*, Vol. I, p. 837-8 and under Tun-huang (ibid) Vol. XIV pp. Bussagli : Op. cit pp. 115 ff; Stein : *Serindia*, Vol. III. Appendix E entitled 'Essays on the Buddhist Paintings from the Caves of the Thousand Buddhas'. Tun-Huang by Raphael Petrocci and Laurence Binyon pp. 1392 ff. The fourth 'Essay on the Art of the Tun-Huang Paintings' by Laurence Binyon, pp. 1428 ff.

surviving ones, however, contain the statues of Buddha and Bodhisattvas which were set up there many centuries ago. These are mostly made of stucco modelled with great skill, sometimes executed in the Greco-Bactrian style, sometimes in that of Gandhāra. The paintings take the form both of murals and of figural compositions executed on either silk or gauze. In the earlier works the iconography conforms to the pattern of the Chinese artists of the first half of the fifth century, but both the paintings and sculptures range in date from Tang and Sung to Yang times.

The Tun-huang paintings are illuminating documents for the study of Mahāyāna Buddhism, but of yet greater interest for the study of art. They provide an idea of Chinese Buddhist art in concept and design. The paintings, despite a monotony of subject matter exhibit a considerable variety of style. Purely Indian art is represented by a small group of paintings which are probably Nepalese; on the other hand, there are a number of entirely Chinese ones as well. Between these two extremes are pictures of an intermediate style—the productions of the local schools of Turkestan, or in some cases a provincial Chinese school. A few works are Tibetan. These frescoes at Tun-huang belong to a period extending from the 5th to the 8th century and may be divided into two groups : the first one of the Wei period—between the 5th and 6th centuries—was executed in a matured and perfect style, rather unsurpassed thereafter. That of the Tang period, between the 7th and 8th centuries, of the second style, is characterized by heaviness in the contours suggesting emergence of a provincial school of art, no doubt associated with skilled craftsmen. Besides frescoe paintings, those on silk of the Tang period contain some of the masterpieces. Some traces of western influence are noticeable in the rendering of certain figures and the clothes, specially the scarves similarly treated as in the paintings of Kucha or Turfan. While the treatment on the whole remains predominantly Chinese, most clearly apparent in scenes illustrating the lives of monks and in the floral motifs, the draperies, poses and facial expressions, as also linear treatment and grouping suggest the impact of the Graeco-Buddhist school and kinship with India.[64] The colours promi-

64. Talbot Rice : *Op. cit*, p. 219.

nently used are malachite green, pink, pale blue, white and black set with a red ground.

The Tun-huang pictures illustrate the mixed influences prevailing there, of which an interesting example is that large painting[65] showing Avalokiteśvara seated on the lotus, with an infinite number of eyes and hands symbolising the infinite area of his compassion. Above are the sun and the moon; and below are two demon kings wreathed in flame. There is a border around the picture on which blossoms of flowers are painted. Flowers are also shown dropping through the air which is a favourite motive in Buddhist art. The colours are glowing. In another painting of Avalokiteśvara,[66] this time conducting a soul, a difference of mood, style, genius is clearly manifest. In this suavity and flexible movement replaces heavy symmetry in the composition as also 'solid hardiness' in the drawing. Flowers seem floating down in the air. The Chinese genius is traced in the instinct for living movement, and love for sinuous line. Some of the large paintings are seen to be repetitions on silk of the broad style which is seen in the frescoes found at Tun-huang and other sites. The main point to grasp, as pointed out by Laurence Binyon is that the tradition of Buddhist art which we find first formulated in Gandhāra after assimilating certain minor elements (chiefly Iranian) in its passage across Eastern Turkestan, was transformed in China by the genius of that country's art. Indian imagery and symbolism, Indian ideals of form were taken over by the Chinese masters. The examples show that the Indian material was fused in the Chinese style, and a really new phase of Buddhist art was the result. The Buddhist pictorial art is construed by some as merely a continuation of the art of Gandhāra, enriched and shaped by the Chinese master painters according to their formula evolved by the indigenous creative instinct.

Soviet Central Asia[67]

The western part of Central Asia had a cultural ethos of its own and its art forms were handled in an original manner.

65. Stein. *Serindia*. Pl. LXIV

66. *ibid*, pl. LXXI.

67. For the history of the ancient archaeological sites and the material finds in these areas—see Aleksandr Belenistsky : *The Ancient Civilization of*

About the beginning of the Christian era, Buddhism had conquered part of eastern Iran and engendered a Greco-Buddhist art which had originated about the end of 1st century B.C. in the Gandhāra region. It lasted in the same region until the 7th century and to a limited degree in several localities until the 8th century. It gradually spread to Serindia and China, and reached Sogdiana through Bactria. Archaeological explorations and excavations have now brought to light a number of sites in Russian Turkestan, which were centres of urban culture and have also revealed existence of Buddhist monasteries and sanctuaries. The spread of Buddhism in Central Asia was an event of outstanding importance in the Kuṣāṇa period, and the ancient sites testify to this fact. Among the important sites excavated so far may be noticed Termez, Karatepe and Ajina-tepe in the Amu Daryā valley, Kafir-Kala and Kaji-Kala in Tadjikistan, and Afrasayab and Pendjikent near modern Samarkand-Uzbekistan.

Termez (ancient Tarmita), an Uzbek site, situated on the Vakshā river, was an important Buddhist centre in Central Asia where a number of Buddhist monuments were discovered. Fragments of stone statues of the Buddha executed in the Gandhāra style were found at the site. The excavations revealed Buddhist temples with bronze lions. The recent discovery of wall paintings, at Balatik-Tepe, near Airtam Termez, provides interesting study. These are dated in the fifth century and supposed to be contemporary with the earliest of the Tun-huang paintings. Certain features, such as the ornamental motifs on garments, the crowns with veils and bells as well as the small *kusti*, completing the clothing of the figures, are supposed to be of Sassanian inspiration. They confirm close relationship between this peripheral region and the expanding Sassanian

---

Central Asia, London; A.L. Mongait : *Archaeology in the U.S.S.R.* (Pelicans). Bussagli in his work '*Painting of Central Asia*' notices Pjandzikent and the influence of Sogdiana in a single chapter. The comprehensive bibliography provided in Belenitsky's book, includes a few in English language as well, such as L.I. Albaum: *Balalyk-Tepe*, Tashkent, 1960; O.M. Dalton : *The Treasures of the Oxus*, London, 1926; A.V. Gudkova: *Tok-Kala*, Tashkent, 1964; G.A. Pugachenkova : *Khalchayan*, Tashkent, 1965.

world.[68] The spirit and style of the figures, however, are supposed to be original and independent which might have been the result of East Iranian creations carried eastwards with expanding trade and the economic predominance of the western states of Sogdiana, Ferghana and Chorasmia. The Greek influences often prevailed, and very frequently contained the rising tide of Sassanian Persia, as pointed out by Talbot Rice.[69] The earlier Indo-Hellenistic blend is noticed at its best in the fragments of a superb sculptured lime stone frieze of the first century A.D. discovered at Airtam,[70] a fortified Buddhist settlement, located, some 18 Kilometres north-west of Termez in Soviet Central Asia. It is supposed to have adorned a Buddhist monastery. The frieze displays a row of youths and girls shown half-length bearing garlands and musical instruments of local origin. The style is clearly Kushan and the workmanship local. Hellenistic influence is traced in the use of acanthus leaves to separate the youths and girls. The Indian and Hellenistic elements are reflected both in the modelling of the people and in the choice of such decorative motifs as garlands, but their vital rendering points to the hand of a local artist.

The ruins of Khalchayan[71] in Southern Uzbegistan (near the river Surkhan-Darya) to the east of Termez also provide interesting details of archaeological and artistic importance. The finds include some fragments of clay sculpture which had decora-

68. Bussagli : Op. cit, p. 35.

69. Op. cit, p. 131.

70. The first fragment of this frieze was discovered casually by a soldier unconnected with archaeology. In October 1932, at the village of Airtam (Ayrtam) on the right bank of the Amu-Darya, 8 miles above Termez, a carved stone slab lying in the water was noticed by a soldier of the Soviet frontier forces. Masson studied it and published a special monograph on the subject. Later on, in 1936, seven other fragments of the frieze were discovered at Airtam during excavation of the remains of a Buddhist shrine by the Termez Archaeological Expedition led by M.E. Masson. The slab of marble stone is some 20 inches high and has a total length of about 23 feet. On it are carved in high relief high length figures of male and female musicians and bearers of offerings, each figure being framed in acanthus leaves (Belenitsky : Op. cit, pp. 98-99 pl. 49).

71. Belenitsky : Op. cit, pp. 99-102. For a detailed study of the site and excavations, see G.A. Pugachen Kova : *Khalchayan*, Tashkent, 1965.

ted the walls of the *iwan* and the main hall. These included besides gods and goddesses—Athena, Apollo and Satyrs etc.—various personages belonging to the native population of the area. Along the top of the walls ran a frieze of garland carried by boys like Italian *putli* with girls, musicians, dancers, satyrs and other figures connected with the cult of Dionysus. In addition to the sculpture, small fragments were also found at Khalchayan, with remains of human figures and many decorative details. This site and its monuments are supposed to represent an early development of the style which Schlumbergar calls the dynastic style, as opposed to the temple art of Buddhism.

Toprak-Kala[72] is another site of importance which was excavated by Tolstov and his team of archaeologists. Situated near Termez, the town was under occupation from the first century A.D. until the sixth century as the capital of Chorasmia. The town was noted for its large and busy market and contained several hundred rooms, and was defended by three massive towers. Certain sculptural finds including head of alabaster—a stone readily available in Afghanistan—suggest stylistic affinity to the Indo-Hellenic art of the Kuṣāṇas. A clay statue—life size and painted—from Toprak-Kala, found in the 'Hall of Kings' is said to be directly based on Hellenistic example. Stucco and painted decorations, though much deteriorated, seem to have been inspired by Hellenistic works.[73] Both in style and detail the decorations closely resemble those of Pjendzikent. The finest murals appear in the 'Hall of Kings'. Here the walls had pinkish borders with white lilies painted above them on a blue ground. In the 'Alabaster Hall' the walls were decorated with floral motives cut and engraved on alabaster. Next room—the 'Hall of Victories'—was decorated with sculptures

72. The site was discovered by S.P. Tolstov in 1938 and was excavated in 1945 and subsequent years. Summary in Belenitsky's work : Op. cit, pp. 102-03 and also in A.L. Mongait : *Archaeology in the U.S.S.R.*—Op. cit, pp. 239 ff. The excavations at Toprak-kala have shown the high level of individual character of the artistic culture of Chorasmia.

73. See Talbot Rice : Op. cit, pp. 118 ff. The sculptures are so correct anatomically and so naturalistic in conception that they may well have been inspired by Hellenistic works. They are of stucco and form an integral part of the painted decorations.

of seated kings feasting in the company of the goddess of victory. The 'Warriors Hall' contained sculptures of warriors wearing chainmail armour painted black and holding cane shields. Other decorations included a painted frieze of gryphons, dancing couples, vividly rendered musicians and a decorative piece of composition of women gathering pears and grapes. Among the fragments recovered from the filings were paintings of tigers, horses and birds.

Pendzhikent[74]—the Hephthalite capital, some 65 Kilometres south-west of Samarkand in the Zaravashan valley, founded in the fourth and fifth centuries A.D. had a long history of political vicissitudes of fortunes. It was at the height of its prosperity in the seventh century, followed by its destruction at the hands of the Arabs—its subsequent recovery and lingering on until the ninth century, when it finally declined. The wall paintings of Pendzikent adorned the larger buildings, temples and princely dwellings. Their subject matter is often puzzling, with contradictory interpretations provided by scholars of Manichaean or Buddhist interests. The mural decorations include both religious and genre scenes. The former suggest a somewhat different form of Zoroastrianism from the one practised in Persia, with certain local forms of pagan sun and moon worship. The genre scenes—concentrating on ordinary life—provide interesting information. These are supposed to illustrate national epics. Some of the paintings are said to relate some specific passages in Firdausi's *Shāhnāmā*. Talbot Rice notices a wall painting from Pendzikent [75] in which two persons are engaged in a game of chess. He suggests that it has a symbolic meaning and is probably based on an incident in Buddha's early life. Another one, something strangely evocative and appealing[76] shows two riders accompanied by attendants. The marked poetic

---

74. The ruins of Pendzikent form a complex archaeological pattern with the ruler's citadel, the town proper, a sub-urban settlement and the necropolis as four clearly demarcated areas. Systematic excavations were undertaken after the war in 1946 under the leadership of A.Y. Yakubousky.

75. Talbot Rice : Op. cit, illus. 88 p. 105.

76. *ibid.* illus. 90 p. 108.

quality in this painting is equally reflected in another wall painting[77]—of a harpist.

Afghanistan[78]

This land-locked country occupying the central position between the Middle East, the Indian sub-continent, Central Asia and the Far East is described as a typical 'round about' civilization with trade routes and national interests converging and diverging on it. Its importance has been not only in the absorption and transformation of foreign forms but in their dissemination throughout the ancient oriental world. The relation of Afghanistan to Buddhism and Gandhāra art centres round the Kuṣāṇa rulers, especially Kaniṣka, whose empire extended from Khotan in Central Asia to Bihar in Eastern India and comprised men of different nationalities and religions. It is, however, proposed by Talbot Rice that when Buddhism reached Gandhāra, Hellenistic ideals were so firmly entrenched that converts to the new faith must have turned to western artists for the new votive statues they needed. The impact made by the Buddhist sculptures produced by Hellenistic artists was powerfully felt not only in western and eastern Turkestan but in India as well. Buddhist art is supposed to have originated in Gandhāra from where it spread into Central Asia and eastward into China. The Hellenistic influence retained its hold over this art for a number of centuries. Economic prosperity and safe communication consequent to the silk trade, however, led to migration of western sculptors to the East. In the process of rendering the Buddha figure, the Hellenistic element marked by a touch of Parthian vitality underwent a measure of Roman influence, with the cross-legged sitting Indian posture. Western influence is also traced in the use of cointhian columns and acanthus leaves for separating each scene. Broadly speaking it can be said that the setting of Buddhist themes is largely Indian

77. *ibid.* illus. 92 p. 109.

78. For a comprehensive study of 'Art in Afghanistan' see Benjamin Rowland's book on the subject with the same caption, London, 1971, which has also a comprehensive bibliography relating to Afghanistan in general, as well as on individual centres and aspects of art. See also bibliography in the *Encyclopedia of World Art*, Vol. I under Afghanistan.

but the treatment is Greek. The Gandhāra school that originated in the second or the first century B.C. and lasted until the end of the fifth or the sixth century A.D. exercised a profound influence over Buddhist sculptors working in eastern Turkestan.[79]

Central Afghanistan during the Kuṣāṇa period, was dominated by Buddhism and its specific culture. The typical example of this culture is represented by Bamiyan,[80] situated in the valley between the Hindukush and the Kohi-Baba ranges. It occupied in its heyday an important position on the trade route from Bactria to Taxila. The two immense statues of Buddha represented as Lokottara, the Lord of the World, cut in the rock at the eastern and western approaches of the town dominate the Buddhist complex in this region. The cliff between them covering about a Kilometre in circuit is honeycombed with a conglomeration of caves chapels, assembly halls and cells for the Buddhist monks. Some of these grottoes are connected by galleries within and along the front of the precipice for purpose ofcircumambulation. The fifty-three metre Buddha, like the smaller colossus, has provided access to its summit through a system of stairways which was destroyed with the crumbling of a great mass of the face of the cliff. At the time of Hsuan-tsang's visit the great Buddha shone golden in the sun—probably gilt coloured. The Buddhist community at Bamiyam followed the small vehicle or Hīnayāna, but the pilgrim Hu-i-chao who visited that centre in the eighth century describes the monastery as belonging to the Great Vehicle.

79. Op. cit, p. 149. For Buddhism in Gandhāra see Talbot Rice's interpretation. Op. cit. pp. 154-162.

80. Talbot Rice : Op. cit, p. 161. The most creative phase of Gandhāra art probably lasted from the first century B.C. to the second century A.D.—the time of Kaniṣka and his association with Buddhism. Though Shapur I destroyed the Kushan dynasty in c. A.D. 241, the school lingered on after the original impetus had spent itself and probably owed its long survival to Roman conservatism and influence. The Hellenistic tradition continued to hold its own in the east for as long as Roman merchants retained control of the oriental trade. That Romans or Rome's eastern citizen, remained in touch with what are now western India (Pakistan) and Central Afghanistan is proved not only by the presence at Begram of Syrian glass of the fourth century and by the discovery of hoards of Roman coins as far as Saripirl, on the northern slopes of the Hindu Kush, but also by the predominance of Roman influence on the late sculptures discovered at Hadda. (Talbot Rice p. 161)

Bamiyan is also noted for its painting. The surviving examples reveal a synthesis of different styles and trends from Gandhāra, Syria, Sassanian, Iran and Gupta-India. Classical traditions are assimilated by Buddhism. These wall-paintings are divided into cycles of Indian, Sassanian and purely Central Asian styles. The paintings still decorating the top of the niche and the soffit of the vault above the smaller Buddha statue are entirely Sassanian in style. The massive bulk and frozen lifeless dignity characterising the reliefs of the Iranian kings are translated here into painting. Sassanian influence is also traceable in the massive figures of donors alternating with figures of Buddha, as also in the essentially flat, heraldic patterning of forms noticeable in the enormous decoration of the ceiling of the niche. The second one, namely the Indian style of painting, bears resemblence to the surviving examples of wall-paintings in India before the fifth and sixth centuries A.D. The fragments of the decoration one clothing the entire niche and vault of the Colossus Buddha are supposed to belong to this group. The side walls of the niche from top to bottom were painted with row upon row of figures of seated Buddha, each in different and characteristic *mudrā*. Above may be seen medallions with flying divinities and finally, on the vault of the niche, the whole pantheon of Bodhisattvas. The third style of painting bears resemblance to paintings at Kizil and other sites in Turkestan with the combination of line drawing and areas of flat and brilliant colour providing closer resemblances. The decorations surviving on the vault of the bigger Buddha statue and in the adjoining caves belong to a provincial Iranian manner; while the disintegrating fragments in the niche of this Buddha figure are supposed to be local versions of the Indian style of the Gupta period. The blue beautiful Bodhisattva of Group E is considered as a precursor of the decorative heraldic mode of Kizil in Central Asia. Practically all the colours used at Bamian were locally manufactured ones with the exception of indigo which was copiously used in the painting on the niche of the Great Buddha. The procedure adopted here was first the application of a thick layer of mud to the rock wall with large pieces of chopped wood in it to hold it firmly to the surface. This was followed by a thin layer of finely powdered gypsum being spread over it. On this slip the pigments were applied in tempera painting. The same process was employed in Turkestan and at Tunhuang. The dating of the paintings at Bamian is provided by the evidence in the style[81] of the two giant Buddhas. The smaller one with the hair in Apolloman ringlets and the drapery in rather sharply defined classic folds corresponds to the end of the period of greatest Roman influence in Gandhāra proper, supposed by Rowland to be from the early second to the end of the third centuries A.D. The lesser colossus is placed not earlier than the year 200 and the larger one about the fifth and sixth centuries A.D. The small fragments of painting, recovered from Group G at Bamian, to the east of the lesser colossus and actually slightly in front of the main cliff, are supposed to be oldest. The paintings recovered from these ruined vaulted grottoes formed part of an illusionistic scheme of decoration with the combination of sculpture and painting.[82] These may be dated in the seventh century A.D.

81. See Chapter VII of the *Art of Afghanistan* by Benjamin Rowland with the bibliography provided at pp. 65-66 which includes Godard, A and Y; and Hackin, J : *Les Antiquities bouddhiques de Bamiyan*—Memoirs de la Delegation Archaeologique Francaise en Afghanistan, II, 1928; Hackin and Carl, J. : *Nouveilles recherches arch eoloques a Bamiyan*—ibid.III. 1933; Rouland, B. *The Wall Paintings at Bamiyan, Central Asia and Ceylon* (Boston. 1938).

82. Rowland : *Art in Afghanistan*, p. 35 ff. A stylistic analysis of the Wall Paintings of Bamiyan is made by Akira Miyaji in the Report of Japan-Afghanistan Joint Archaeological Survey for 1974—published in 1976, pp. 17 ff. According to the Japanese scholar, there are four syles of Bamian Paintings. The first one confined to the paintings in the inche of the West Grand Buddha received the tradition of Gupta art and digested aspects of far Hellenistic-Roman art. It displays the most classical and naturalistic aspects of all the paintings. The sillful drawings of the Bodhisattvas, sometimes showing the *tribhaṅga* form and in three dimensional representation, are painted in calm colours with red brown outlines on a dark background. The second style shown by the paintings in Caves I, 140, 176, 223 has skilful outlining, detailed depiction, sensualistic shading, bright polychrome and a tendency towards design and deformation. Bright colours such as blue, green and vermillion are used. Lotus becomes a quite schematic pattern. Folds of shawls are schematically depicted. The painting of this style seems to reflect trends seen in Central Asia, Kizil, Khotan etc. The third style seen in the paintings of the niche of the East Grand Buddha. Here the artists abstain from three-dimensional depiction and concentrate mainly on the frontal unity of the

One of the series of caves immediately to the west of the smaller colossus, in the vestibule of Group D, had the room originally painted with a design made up of medallions filled with human heads, boar's heads, birds and floral motifs, all supposed to be devices of a purely Sassanian origin. Every detail represented on this ceiling could be traced to prototypes in Sassanian stucco and textile decoration. This design was also used in weaving and its surviving specimens from Turkestan suggest its popularity. These are assigned to the seventh century A.D.

Another Buddhist centre of pictorial art in Afghanistan was the ravine of Kakrak,[83] several kilometres to the east to the cliff of the Great Buddhas. The painted decoration of these grottoes has been removed in its entirety and shared by the Musié Guimet and the Museum at Darul-Aman. The paintings at Kakrak are the earliest known examples of the mystic diagram of mandalas of esoteric Buddhism, in which the cosmic Buddha Vairocana or his regents, the Buddhas of the Four Quarters, are surrounded by the galaxy of their emanations. Each of the domes at Kakrak was painted with a Buddha image in the centre of the vault, surrounded by a ring of medallions enclosing smaller Buddhas. An outstanding work is the so-called 'Hunter-king' painting,[84] adorning the drum of a dome. It is remarkable not only for the richness and variety of its colours, but also for its lively drawing, intelligent stylization and a definite

---

picture. Dramatically opposed to the classical first style, it seems to be influenced by Sassanian art. Bright flat colours such as blue, yellow, red-brown and white are used. The fourth style has pseudo-naturalistic or ornamentalistic features and is the latest of the group, with the use of rough flat colours—pale blue, light yellow, reddish brown and white. The outlines are considerably thick. Generally the work is gloomy. Lotus figures are depicted in pairs. It is the most retrogressive of those found at Bamiyan.

83. According to Rowland, the style of the heads of Bodhisattvas, Yakshas and arhats from cave G is extremely fresh and cursive in execution, vivid in colour, and the actual types appear like a stylized translation of the familiar forms of Gandhara sculpture into painting. The head of an arhat is similar to many portrayals of holy men in the sculpture of Tumshuk in Central Asia. These fragments appear to be related to a single remnant of Gandhara wall paintings recovered by Tucci in Swab. (*Art in Afghanistan*, p. 39)

84. Talbot Rice. Op. cit, p. 166. no. 151.

touch of refinement. The main figure, a haloed sovereign wearing a crown ornamented with three crescents is seated cross-legged, holding the bow in his hands and the arrows sticking on the ground. The architectural motif of columns and pediments is suggestive of Gandhāran inspiration. The Buddha figures in two different postures with haloes are seated on lotus flowers. The bright cotrasting colours are in harmony with each other. This painting is dated in the sixth century A.D. when the Gupta influence in pictorial art had been completely assimilated. The employment of an Indian type of abstract shading in the painting of the 'hunter-king' and other fragments from Kakrak suggest the fusion of Iranian and Indian elements found at Bamian, a hybrid style that is the direct antecedent of the Buddhist paintings in Central Asia. The varied styles and techniques of the paintings at Bamian and Kakrak closely resemble those of the wall paintings of Kizil and Murtuq. These point to the role of Afghanistan in the diffusion of influences to Central Asia and the Far East.

Fondukistan[85]

The Indian styles of painting and sculpture at Fondukistan in the hidden valley of Ghorband brought to light by the French mission in 1936, provide an interesting study. The chapels in this monastic area, arranged as complete iconographical sculptural ensembles, are packed with figures set off by gaily painted backgrounds. These statues were simply moulded of unbaked clay, mixed with straw and horse hair as a binding medium and built up around a wooden skeleton or armature. The material replaces the use of stone and lime plaster. The statues were made in a technique similar to one used for manufacturing large unbaked bricks in the Ghorband valley even now. The Indian character of the images is reflected by the soft and sensuous opulence of the anatomical form and the

85. Rowland. Op. cit. pp. 43 ff. Chapter 8 entitled *Buddhist Art of the Pilgrimage Roads* : Fondukistan with bibliography at p. 66. See Hackin, J : *Le Monastere bouddhique de Fondukistan* in *Diverse Recherches archaeologiques en Afghanistan—Memoirs*—op. cit (MDAFA). VIII. 1959, published in English in Journal of the Greater India Society. VII. 1940; The description is mostly based on these works.

elegant rhythm of their swaying postures. The seated figure of a Bodhisattva, now in Musié Guimet, in a position of voloptuous ease and soft modelling with the warmth and breathing fullness of the bodily form, is one of the best examples of Indian sculpture from Fondukistan. The exquisite flower-like gestures of the hands and the radiant face suggestive of serenity and spiritual calm appear to be in agreement with the godly concept of the great icons of the Gupta period.

The best specimen of painting is that of Bodhisattva Maitreya —with its thoroughly Indian character. The position of the body suggests its borrowing from movement in the Indian dances with the same elegance of gestures and the same fusion of sensuality and abstraction in the contour of the body as may be seen in the Bodhisattvas and Devatās in Indian caves. The figure is more provocative in its exaggeration of the body. It is proposed by Rowland[86], that stylistically and spiritually the style is strangely parallel to the Tāntric forms of Pāla art in India, and perhaps both are the eventful outgrowth of qualities inherent in the Gupta sculpture and painting of India. The inner stronghold of this late Buddhist style may be placed on an arc running from Kashmir through Central Afghanistan and beyond this in a concentric zone in Central Asia, including Kizil and Tumshuk where it becomes desiccated and patternized.

Begram[87]

The ruins of Begram, ancient Kāpiśa about seventyfive kilometres to the north of Kabul near the banks of the Panjshir River, were discovered by the French mission which carried on excavations from 1937-1940. A vast treasure trove of objects from the Mediterranean and the orient were discovered inside two rooms. The extraordinary collection of wares included glass vessels from Syria or Egypt, bronze vessels of Western

86. Op. cit. p. 48.

87. For a general study of the excavations at Begram, see Ghirshman. R. *Begram, recherches archaeologiques et historiques sur les Koushan's—Memoirs* (Delegation Archaeologique Afghanistan) Op. cit XII. 1946. Hackin, J. *Nouvelles recherches archeologiques in Begram* (1939-1940) ibid. XI. 2 Vols. 1964. See also Rowland : Op. cit, p. 65 for full bibliography.

manufacture, Roman steelyard weights and statuettes, caskets and plaques of carved bone and ivory from India. Lacquer bowls from China were discovered in another room. The Kushān coins of Kaniṣka and Vāsudeva were also found in conjunction with the treasure. The magnificent collection of ivory carvings include those of large figures of dancers or courtesans carved almost in the complete round. These ivory carvings belong to the Indian tradition. One of the most beautiful panels shows ladies at the toilet. The Begram collection contains a number of examples of painted glassware and also bronze statuettes. The Begram art appears to be purely secular and the finds point to active relations between India and the West with the adoption of Western and Indian styles from the first to the third century A.D.

Hadda[88]

The ruined monastic city of Hadda, located some eight kilometres to the south of Jalalabad, with its myriad towers and monasteries, was at its apex in the fifth century A.D. when visited by the Chinese pilgrim Fa-Hsien. In the time of Hsuan-tsang in 632 there were many Saṅghārāmas with few priests and the stūpas ruined and desolate. Here, like the Buddhist structures around Peshawar and at Taxila, the stūpas and vihāras were completely encased with stucco decorations with a school of stucco sculpture flourishing in this ancient site of Nagarahāra between the middle of the third century A.D. and the fifth century. The time of the Hephthalite invasion while preserving the dryly spiritualized Gandhāra art for the Buddha images, the sculptures here portrayed a living and natural array of facial types of such figures. The work at Hadda represents a genuine religious art. The talents of the craftsmen of Hadda are traced not only in these figures but in the numerous fragments of figures and heads of attendant figures in large relief compositions.[89] While the wavy hair and the diademed crown are suggestive of a Greco-Roman prototype, the sensuous fullness of

88. See Barthouk, J.: *Les Fouilles de Hadda, Figures et figurines—Memoirs*. VI. 1930; Rowland : Op. cit, p. 65 for fuller bibliography.

89. Rowland. Op.cit, fig. 109, p. 32 for details.

the face with its sharply modelled brows and eyes point to the Indian ideal of the Gupta period. The extension of the Hadda medium of stucco sculpture throughout ancient Gandhāra as also in Chorasima or Khwarazem in Russian Turkestan is equally interesting. It is not certain that the statuary of Toprak-Kala was a local development of an earlier Bactrian tradition or it was a northerly provincial extension of the figural sculptural art of Hadda and the Kabul valley. The technique of stucco or lime plaster, as used at Hadda and throughout the ancient region of Gandhāra, is supposed to be invented in Alexandria in the late Hellenistic period as an inexpensive substitute for marble.[90]

Gandhāra Region[91] :

The ancient Indian *mahājanapada* or state of Gandhāra, bounded on the west by Lamghan and Jelalabad, on the north by the hills of Swat and Buner, and on the east by the river Indus and on the south by the Kalabagh hill, is closely associated with Buddhist art. It is also described as Graeco-Buddhist art and is closely connected with the Kushan rulers, especially Kaniṣka. Some describe the Gandhāra school as the easternmost appearance of the art of the Roman empire especially in its late and provincial manifestations. The subject matter of the Gandhāra carving is almost entirely Buddhist, but purely classical motifs are used for decorative purposes. Kaniṣka is considered to be the founder of this school, or its great patron. It is assumed that from the days of Kaniṣka until the end of Buddhism in this area, the practice of importing foreign artisans continued, although the contribution of native craftsmen was fairly great. In this school, the first representation of the Buddha in human form is traced. His image is supposed to be 'a compound of iconographical and technical formula adopted by foreign sculptors from the repertory of the classical

90. Rowland. Op. cit, p. 28.

91. A comprehensive bibliography on Gandhāra and its art is provided by H. Deydier in his work entitled : *Contribution al'etude del'art du Gandhāra*, Paris, 1950. Other later contributions include J. Marshall : *The Art of Gandhāra* (Cambridge, 1951); B. Rowland : *Rome and Gandhāra—East and West*, IX, 1958, pp. 199 ff.

world'. So also are the earliest representatives of Bodhisattvas portrayed in all the finery of contemporary nobility of India with western influence traceable in the stiff swallow-tail folds of the *dhoti* or skirt. As such, the Buddhist iconography here is translated into readymade foreign patterns. While the analogy with Roman art and technique are too apparent to dismiss the influence of the Roman West in the development of classical art under the Kushāns, it is suggested by some scholars[92] that Gandhāra art is the final development of a still undiscovered Greco-Bactrian civilization, rather than the result of intercourse with the Roman world. The Kushān's fine temple at Surkh-Kotal with its long inscription in Bactrian Greek is considered by Schlumberger[93] to be a link in this evolution of the art of Gandhāra from the lost culture of Hellenistic Bactria. The Gandhāra art enjoyed a greater period of existence with its monotony of expression, and repetition of type and techniques. Probably the invasion of the white Huns in the fifth century put an end to creative artistic activity in Gandhāra. The final chapters of Gandhāra art are said to have their setting not in Gandhāra but in Kashmir and such remote centres as Fondukistan in Afghanistan where artistic activity lasted till the seventh century A.D. The examples of Gandhāra stone sculptures in Afghanistan are extremely limited, being fragments from Paitava and Shotorak, near Begram, now in the Kabul Museum. A seated image from the former place shows the Buddha in *dhyānamudrā* with figures of Indra and Brahmā in his halo.[94] This image like others from Shotorak belongs to a late phase of the Gandhāra style more in keeping with Indian ideals and form. The original classical drapery is reduced to a convention

92. This view of Roman Ghirshman and Daniel Schlumberger is quoted by Rowland. Ghirshman points to the extraordinary finds of Hellenistic, perhaps Bactrian art at the Parthian capital of Nisa near Akshabad in Soviet Turkmenistan as an ultimate source for the influence of Greek art in Asia. Schlumberger proposes that the Kushan fire temple at Surkh-Kotal with its long inscription in Bactrian Greek is a link in this evolution of the art of Gandhāra from the lost culture of Hellenistic Bactria. (*Art in Afghanistan*, p. 24); Schlumberger, 'Le Temple de Surkh-Kotal en Bactriane', *Journal Asiatique*, J.A. CCXC. 1952 pp. 433-53).

93. *Journal Asiatique*. CCXC. 1952 pp. 433-53.

94. Rowland : Op. cit. p. 26.

of string-like ridges attached to the surface of the body. This formalism of the late Gandhāra Buddhas provided the models for repetitions of the type in Central Asia and China as late as the eighth century.

Tibetan Art[95]

A switch over from the south-western to the south-eastern sector of Central Asia concentrating on the countries lying at the periphery no doubt means change in the art technique as also in the form, but the matter substantially remains the same. It is in the context of Buddhism in Tibet that the art of this region need be considered. Its source of inspiration was no doubt India. The contribution of Indian Buddhist scholars in the propagation of the ideals of Buddhism in the local ethos was fully advanced by the local artists who assimilated the art traditions of the Pālas, as also those of Kashmir. The Khotanese artists who trekked into Tibet are said to have brought with them their own styles, and iconographic traditions, imposing these on the Tibetans. Further, with the inclusion of numerous deities in the decoration of their temples, with their personal colours,[96] banners—painted and embroidered—were used for embellishment and decorative purposes. Painted Replicas of these banners were portrayed on the walls of the temples and

95. A comprehensive bibliography on Tibetan Art is provided in *Encyclopedia of World Art*, Vol. XIV, pp. 61 ff. as also in Coomaraswamy: *History of Indian and Indonesian Art*, New York, 1965, pp. 148n. Some important ones include Hackin, J. : *Illustrations tibetanies d'une ligende du Divyāvadāna*, Musié Guimet, Paris, 1914; *ibid* : Guide—*Catalogue Du Musié Guimet*, Paris, 1923; 'Notes on Tibetan Paintings'—Rupan, 7, 1921; Getty.A. : *The Gods of Northern Buddhism*, Oxford, 1914; Francke, A.H. : *Antiquities of* Indian Tibet, A.S.I. Calcutta, 1914; Roerich, G.N. : *Tibetan Paintings*, Paris, 1928; Gordon, A.K. : *Tibetan Religious Art*, New York, 1952; Tucci, G. : *Indo-Tibetica*, 4 Vols., Rome, 1932. A special number of the *MARG* Vol. XVI, September-November 4, contains rich material on Tibetan Painting, bronzes, calligraphy and ritual objects—with numerous illustrations. As regards Tibetan Paintings at Tun-huang, see Aurel Stein : *Serindia*, Vol. II, pp. 836 ff.

96. Each Buddha in the Tibetan hierarchy was invested with a personal symbol and a colour appertaining to his rank, as for example, Vairochana was awarded dragon white, Ratna Sambhava lion yellow, Akṣobhya elephant blue and so on. (Talbot Rice. Op. cit, p. 210).

shrines. These depicted religious ceremonies and divinities. Some of the banners were painted on canvas, some on paper and occasionally some on silk. The native style is prominently displayed in these banners than on the wall paintings. Here the subjects chosen are mystical in content and include ritual dances as well. These banners with their pictorial art demand special attention.

It is considered likely that painting in Tibet developed mostly under Indian influence. The wall-paintings in Tasparang, Western Tibet, reveal the influence of Ajanta. Chinese and Persian influences, however, mingled with this basic Indian ore in Tangut area in the north-west. Later, the influences were mainly Indian and Chinese with the colour symbolism and fine brush work of the former and the line drawing of the latter along with the fanciful projections of feeling for landscape, cloud effects and dramatised imagery. The paintings mostly represent the divinities of the pantheon or saints, as the principal figure with scenes from his life as well as minor divinities figuring in on a smaller scale. There are paintings which show the *maṇḍala* or the domain of the saint, and also important monasteries. Some of the prominent pictures show the wheel of life in this transitory world (*saṁsāra*). In these a big dragon projects a disc formed of three concentric circles. The smallest of these, in the centre, encloses three animals, the snake, the pig and the chicken, symbolising anger, ignorance, and voluptuousness. The larger surrounding circle is divided into six segments showing the life of the six categories of living beings.[97] The third circle contains twelve images representing more or less vaguely the connection between twelve causes and effects.

An important class of painting[98] known as Tsog-shin represents the total Pantheon of the Lamaite divinities. The

97. These include two kinds of beings living upon earth : men and beasts. Those living beneath the earth are condemned to an eternal hunger and thirst drink by reason of their narrow throats, which shook forth fire when they desire to drink. The inhabitants of hill are divided into twenty classes according to their torments. And then there are those living in heaven, the *asmas*, who always struggle against the gods. And above them are the various divinities themselves. All these beings are seen in movement in symbolic colours. (Marg. *Op. cit*, p. 19).

98. ibid, p. 20.

Buddhas (48), the Bodhisattvas (12), the feminine divinities (9), the protectors or tutelary gods (42), the defenders of the faith and the eight terrible ones (27), and the minor divinities and the guardians of the four cardinal points. The whole painting of this class is concentric. The main divinities are nearest to the central point of the pyramid occupied by Avalokiteśvara. Above the chief divinities are the three ranks of Bodhisattvas, and on his right are the three Buddhas. Thus, the central group includes the main divinities surrounded on the right and the left by the goddesses. Above the principal group is the double rank of the protectors with feminine divinities of the second order on the right and the left. Under Avalokiteśvara are the Buddhas overflowing on the sides of the pyramids while different Bodhisattvas appear below. Further down are others connected with Tibetan Lamaism with the bottom rung occupied by the defenders.

The subject matter of all Tibetan art is purely religious, providing as elsewhere in Central Asia and here in India too, the outward form and expression of the inner ideals of Buddhism. Incidents from the life of the Buddha, portraits of the great Indian scholars and teachers of Buddhism in Tibet who founded philosophic school and propagated Buddhism there, as also portraits of their disciples, illustrations of the Jātaka tales, the Buddhist hierarchy of gods and goddesses and Buddhas and Bodhisattvas, including the future ones—often in series—are all included in the theme of Tibetan paintings. Frescoes and illuminated manuscripts also engaged the attention of Tibetan artists in the first centuries after the introduction of Buddhism into Tibet. Despite Indian or Chinese influence on Tibetan paintings, there is a blending of one with the other in the Tibetan ethos. As pointed out earlier, the Chinese influence is apparent in the treatment of landscape—with the clouds, rivers, mountains, flowers and vegetation, all finely depicted.

The Indian influence is traced to the time of the Pālas of Bengal. The monastery of Nālandā not only gave form to the religion but also inspired the art of Tibet under king Dharmapāla. Two artists from Northern India—Dhiman and Bitpāla are supposed to have helped in the task of executing paintings and modelling statues at the same time. The former was influenced by the Eastern school while the latter was indebted to the art of Madhya Pradesh. Besides these two Indian master minds in the realm of art, there were others who came to Tibet from Central Asia, Swat, Kashmir, Nepal and from China.[99] Some inscriptions do mention the school of the artist as for instance the style of *Lilugs* suggest that the painters came from *Li viz* Khotan. Some paintings discovered by G. Tucci in the small temple at Mangnang in Western Tibet are accurate imitation of the style of painting that probably existed in Kashmir in the 12th century. So also the paintings of *lha Khan* of Alchi in Ladakh can also be attributed to the Kashmir school of a much later period.

The Chinese influence is mostly confined to the monastery of Shalu—the residence of Bu-stan (1290-1361). Artists here were called from China and Mongolia. This style assumes prominence in the 17th and 18th centuries. These paintings conform to fixed norms, precisely defined in literature. They are rich compositions in which Buddhas, Bodhisattvas and other divinities are always depicted with inferior retinues of acolytes. Deities also dominate the composition amid a choir of elect in their own paradise of which the sceneries are also portrayed according to set norms. The colours vary according to the nature of the principal subject: white is used for god in his calm aspect; red or dark blue is used for the terrifying one or in combat. Aspects of Tibetan life and landscape are depicted with lively colours and great animation and landscape is just an echo of the Chinese one. In ancient paintings no part of the surface is left free. It is completely covered with images, figures, symbols etc. The illustrated manuscripts have images of divinities and the Buddhist masters painted on the first and last page, and sometimes miniature paintings decorate the inner pages as well.

Besides paintings, reference might as well be made to Tibetan architecture and sculpture[100]—especially the bronze. Not much can be said on the subject of Tibetan architecture from the Indian point of view except that the Tibetan stūpa or Chorten—

99. *Encyclopedia of World Art*, Vol. XIV, Op. cit.

100. See—*Encyclopedia*—Op. cit and *Marg*—Op. cit, pp. 14 ff.

a bulbous dome set on one or more square bases was dedicated to great events from the Buddha's life, such as his Nativity and Nirvāṇa. It is like the Nepalese type surmounted by a square *hārmikā* and a mast upholding a teer of 'telescoped umbrella' with a flame finial at the top. A large monument at Gyantse has an unusual plan and elevation. It is erected in fine stepped terraces on a polygonal plan with multiple recensions or step-backs. The actual dome built on this *prāsāda* or pyramid was circumambulated at each successive level. In plan it resembles the great Mahāyāna monument of Borabudur in Java. The sky-scraper structures like the Potala at Lhasa, built of stone and sun-dried bricks with the white-washed walls thicker at the bottom, provide the contours of the surrounding mountain peaks. This palace-monastery at Lhasa is a noble pile of successive stages.

The sculptural art is confined to bronzes. There is a legend that the first images were brought into Tibet by the Chinese and the Nepalese wives of king Srong-san-gaupo in the seventh century. And they went on being imported from India and Nepal for a long time afterwards. The talent of the Tibetan craftsmen introduced a great dynamism into the imagery. These craftsmen took the dimensions, the number of heads, arms and legs and other symbols from the canon but displayed their freedom and technical virtuosity in their creation. Metal sculpture of the various divinities, big and small, multiplied and the Tibetan bronze, brass and copper image makers flourished in their art. The images are made by cire-perdu or lost wax method. The figure is modelled in wax and covered with sand, fixed by silicate and plaster or some other substance. Then it is baked. The wax melts leaving the mould free. Metal is then poured into the cavities. After the metal cools down the mould is destroyed. The figure is then finished by hand with the chisel and tools. A cavity in the image is always left to insert the magic formula printed on rolls of paper. After the insertion the hole is sealed and the image becomes sacred.

The Buddhas—past, present and future are shown in contemplation, with their hands shown in different mudrās. The Bodhisattvas wear rich garments and jewellery, unlike the unadorned and uncovered Buddhas except the robe covering the left shoulder. There are tutelary divinities called *yei-dam* taken mostly from the Tantra. The Dhyānī Buddhas are shown with their consorts in the image called *yab-yum*[101]—the honourable father and mother. The Dharmapālas or the guardians of the law are shown in a furious mood with numerous heads, arms and leg. The Kālachakra or the lord of time has four faces and twenty-four arms with his consort having only eight arms. The former tramples on demons. Jambala or the god of wealth is a fat Kubera-like figure holding a bowl of jewels in one hand, a mongoose vomitting jewels in the other. Vajrapāṇi with many forms and Avalokiteśvara symbolising wisdom are also included among the bronze icons. Reference might as well be made here to a beautiful bronze image of the Buddha in the *Bhūmisparśa-mudrā.*[102] The elegance and grace of this image with its delicate and sensitive handling of the whole body in repose is an example of the highest workmanship in Tibetan bronze making. The Pāla workmanship may have contributed to its elegance. Another bronze[103]—representing a yab-yum image—is equally interesting with the melodramatic expression equally graceful. The male figure inclining backwards with his tender eyes and open mouth is inter-locked with his Śakti in a close embrace. The lines of the arms and the torso are drawn with a delicate pliant touch. The collections at the Music Guimet are fairly rich in Tibetan bronzes and paintings.[104]

101. Zimmer : *The Art of India Asia*, p. 195. This posture is a common one in Tibetan Buddhist images, and was derived from the earlier archetype of Śiva and the Goddess. The example of Vajrasabha, the president of the group of Dhyānī-Buddhas—the five others being Vairochana, Akṣobhya, Ratna-Sambhava, Amitābha and Amoghasiddhi, is shown with his Śakti (Zimmer pl. 610). The male and female principles in eternal embrace, represent, as in Śivaitup iconography, the coincidence or union of opposites. The divine couple are both the goal and the way; fulfilment and the means or process of attaining it; enlightenment or way to enlightenment. (ibid, p. 196).

102. Marg. Op. cit, p. 44.

103. ibid. no. 2, p. 45.

104. For a fuller and detailed reference, see J. Hackin : Op. cit, part IV, Le Tibet, pp. 63ff. Chapter II, pp. 70 ff entitled' Les peintures et les bronzes' notices the biographical scenes with general characteristics, scenes from the life of the Buddha, the Dhyānī-Buddhas and Bodhisattvas, female divinities, Mahāsiddhas and saints, grand Lamas and ritualistic objects. It might be out of context to make a detailed study of Tibetan paintings and

Central Asia with its eclectic outlook took over and recasted with considerable success the art forms of the great sedentary civilizations, those of the semi-classical of the East, of Iran, of Indo-Greek and Indo-Scythian art, of China and of Gupta India. The borrowing results are traceable in the cultural evolution of different zones, no doubt varying in their extent and intensity and extending from minute details to essential concepts of art style and iconography. The Iranian elements, however, predominate in the western zone, while south of the desert the Indian influence or traits have an upper hand along with the intruding Persian influence. The eastern zone has certainly close Chinese impact. Despite these diversities, the Central Asian peoples were close to each other in their spiritual outlook and artistic expression, with extraordinary analogies of style and iconography. The inexhaustible subject matter was provided by the Buddhist legends—the Jātakas—for the artists to display their talents. When elements from the Indian complex mythology, with the rich possibilities offered by Hindu and Tantric importations, were added, the scope of the artist was immensely extended. The vast material collected by the explorers and excavators from different nationalities no doubt reveals a bewildering diversity of style and treatment. This was due to the complex social and political conditions prevailing in the zones of artistic activities. The change of political powers during the long course of Central Asian history, passing on from one race to another differing in ideals and traditions in art and varying in psychological conception, was responsible for this lack of uniformity except on a religious plane.

In the light of the above observations the Buddhist artistic contributions in different areas have been recorded in sequence of time and space. The earliest ones were, of course, Miran and the sites lying on the old silk route. The paintings here suggest familiarity with the Gandhāra art. Besides classical elements like the motive of the festooned garland carried on the shoulders of *amoriṇī*, as also the wringed angel busts, there is continued

---

bronzes from this Museum from the iconographic or artistic point of view. A general observation of Tibetan Art in the context of Central Asian Art alone is provided here.

narration as provided in the Vessantara Jātaka scene. Indian conception and execution could be noticed in the type of persons putting on Indian dress, but the Persian type of beauty suggests Iranian contacts. The reference to Titus and the fees paid to him—as recorded in a Kharoṣṭi inscription—confirms the role of the Indo-Greek artists in this area. The Gandhāra school is supposed to have been transplanted into pictorial lines at Miran where Roman-Hellenistic influences are quite apparent. In the Khotan complex the imprint of Greco-Buddhist art predominates between the fifth and eighth centuries. Indian, Sassanian, Chinese, Sogdian and even perhaps Chorasmian influences are no doubt assimilated here. Out of the blending of foreign influences emerged a new style characterised by strictly frontal presentation, highly developed stylization, flat almost two-dimensional designs and a tendency towards geometric simplification. The elongated matching eyes are drawn in Indian fashion and the beautiful figure of a worshipper kneeling in prayer from Balawaste in structure, costume, colouring and style reminds one of the Ajanta figures. The direct connection between the local art and the Sogdian influence is evinced from the painting of the Iranian Bodhisattva of Dandan-Oiliq. The figure of the Silk Princess as also other ones suggest Chinese influence co-existing with Indian and Iranian art tendencies and style. The Khotan School had its impact on Tibet and references to Khotanese painters are traced in Tibetan records.

The Buddhist art centres on the Northern Routes—Kizil, Kucha and Turfan—were equally connected with or influenced by the artistic developments of the neighbouring ones. The Kucha centre beginning about the fourth century A.D. continued till the end of the eighth century with its two distinct phases: the first of the Indo-Iranian type (c. 500 A.D.) and the second strongly Iranian, reaching its climax about 600-650 A.D. The Chinese influence is noticeable here in the paintings between the seventh and eighth centuries. The vigorous cowherd leaning on a knotted stick is a good illustration of the first type. Indian influence is more prominent in the group of swimmers scene at Kizil. The paintings at Kumtura form a third phase marked by Chinese influence with more attention to line and the colours. Iranian types and motifs are virtually eliminated or absorbed in the Chinese element. The Mongolian features, head dress, drapery and folds of dress and scarves are traditionally Chinese. The local painters at Shorchuk, a meeting place of figurative currents from Kucha and China, concentrate on the lives of the monks and the other two of the Three Jewels—the Dharma and the Saṅgha.

The Turfan group of Central Asian paintings, covering a period of three hundred years, exhibit mannerism in physiognomy, pose and costume of the figures. The different phases of the complex art in the Turfan region vary from one locality to another with varying degrees of Chinese influence and dominance of Tāntric features, associated with Mahāyānism. At Khocho, the Turkish name for the ancient capital Kao-Chang, Manichaean and Nestorian influences dominate, and so also different phases of interaction of Chinese and Iranian cultures are traced. Marked differences could be seen in the figures of Buddha at Khocho and at Bezaklik. The mourning scene at the latter place in shrine IX shows people of different nationalities distinguished by their faces and dress demonstrating the universal aspect of the Buddha religion.

Reference has also been made to paintings from Tun-huang—the meeting place of the two routes as also noted for the caves of the Thousand Buddhas. They provide an idea of Chinese Buddhist art in concept and design. Purely Indian art is represented by a small group of paintings. A few works are Tibetan. These frescoes at Tun-huang belong to a period between the fifth and the eighth centuries A.D. Those on silk used as banners contain some masterpieces. While the treatment on the whole remains predominantly Chinese, traces of impact of the Graeco-Buddhist school and kinship with Indian art could be traced.

The western part of Central Asia—now comprising part of Soviet Central Asian Republics, had its own cultural ethos as also its art forms. A number of sites in this region were ancient Buddhist centres. The recent discovery of wall paintings at Balalik-Tepe near Airtam Termez are supposed to be of Sassanian inspiration with the Greek influences often prevailing, and occasionally containing the rising tide of Sassanian Persia. The earliest Indo-Hellenistic blend is noticed at its best in the fragments of a superb sculptured limestone frieze of the first century A.D. The ruins of Khalchayan, Toprak-kala and Pendzhikentthe Hephthalite capital, have provided stucco figures, and wall paintings adorning the larger buildings. Their subject matter is rather puzzling.

Both Afghanistan and Tibet at the periphery of Central Asia are notable for Buddhist art. The former was connected with Gandhāra art and provides examples of rock-cut statues, sculptures and paintings as well as stucco figures. The pictorial art here is remarkable for richness and variety of colours and a definite touch of refinement. The fusion of Iranian and Indian elements produced a hybrid style, the direct antecedent of the Buddhist paintings in Central Asia, especially at Kizil and Murtuq. The paintings in Tibet are supposed to have developed mostly under Indian influence, with the Chinese and Persian influence mingling with it at the western and eastern parts of Tibet respectively. The subject of all Tibetan art is purely religious providing as elsewhere, the outward form and expression of the inner ideals of Buddhism. Here artists from Northern India as well as from Khotan participated in the realm of pictorial art. The art of Central Asia—eclectic in character—assimilated the forms of great sedentary peoples around them. At an early stage it came to be known, according to the French archaeologist. Schlumberger, as the non-Mediterranean descendant of Graeco-Roman art. It subsequently gave birth to a series of independent movements which influenced and were influenced by the major civilization of Asia. Despite the multiplicity of ways of rendering space and perspective as also providing colour scheme, the theme—the all-pervasive Buddhism, was the religious force unifying a large part of Asia in the spirit of humanism and universalism. Art only catered to the projection of this concept.

CHAPTER VII

THE SUMMING-UP

Central Asia is supposed to have been the cradle of human civilization. Its geographical position, however, accords it a receiving as well as a transmitting centre. In metaphorical language it has not been so much a basin as a pool in a tidal river, flowing alternately to and from the sea. In such a pool could be found creatures of different provenance. Currents—cultural and political—passed through it from east to west and in the reverse direction leaving some remnants over there. Being in touch with Bactria and the regions conquered by Alexander and through them with the western world in its art and thought, the Tarim sampled the stream fragments that had drifted from Asia Minor and Byzantium through the Iranians. Chinese civilization and administration were imported from the east while the south provided other currents connected with Buddhism. From the dawn of history down to the middle ages warlike nomads continually passed through this region picking up and transporting the ideas and institutions of others. This factor necessarily involved simultaneous use of a number of tongues for popular as well as for learned purposes. This is evident from the recovery of great polyglot libraries at Tun-huang, and manuscripts in several languages at other places including Indian Buddhist, Manichaean, Syriac, Sogdian, Uighur and Chinese ones. Written on palm leaves, birchbark, plates of wood or bamboo, leather and paper from the first century A.D. onwards, these manuscripts convey the story and doctrine of the religious cults with which they were associated.

A fuller account of the religions of which these codifications are a part, no doubt, demands a detailed study of the available source material. This material is ample, confined to art and literature as also to epigraphic records which shed light on the material culture as well. Explorations and excavations have revealed numerous sites connected with Buddhism. The religious monuments of Central Asia comprise stūpas, caves and covered buildings which were used as temples or vihāras. The caves were decorated for Buddhist worship with frescoes as well as figures executed in stucco. Many stūpas have also been found. The ideas and designs of Indian Buddhism dominate in these monuments except in regions nearer to China. Information relating to Central Asian relations with China is provided rather in detail by the Chinese annals. These relations were often interrupted and the data available from the Chinese accounts have occasional missing links, particularly in relation to the history of Buddhism in Central Asia and its transmission to China. This study of Buddhism in Central Asia, based on these varied sources of information is, therefore, projected within the framework of geographical information, particularly, the land routes passing through the important political and trade centres, kingdoms and their rulers who patronised Buddhism, the role of the Buddhist missionaries and savants and their contributions—religious and secular.

Detailed information about the routes passing through Central Asia is provided by the Chinese accounts including those of the pilgrims who passed through these on way to India. These are also known as the silk-routes during the first few centuries of the Christian era. Two routes passed through the Tarim basin from the frontiers of China upto Balkh. These were used by the Buddhist monks and savants as well for the dissemination of Buddhist thought and culture in the States of Eastern Turkestan and finally in China. The ancient route, from the capital of China, Chang-an (present Sian) in the province of Shansi, after crossing the Gobi desert reached the oasis of Tun-huang from where, approaching the Taklamakan desert, it bifurcated in two directions. The northern one passed through Hami, Turfan, Karasahr, Kucha, Aksu, Tumshuk and Kashgar to Samarkand. The southern route traversed via Miran, Cherchen, Keriya, Khotan and Yarkand to Herat and Kabul. It was in the first century A.D. that Buddhism was taken to the states lying on the routes. Peoples from Kashmir and North-west India proceeded to Khotan and Kashgar and set up small colonies with kings claiming descent from Indian regal families. The routes starting from north-west India in those days passed by Hadda and Nagarahara (Jalalabad) and reached Bamiyan before crossing the Hindukush. Bamiyan was thus a halting place for the Indian monks and grew into an important centre of Buddhism. Further to the north, Bactriana (modern Balka)known as Nava-Saṅghārāma, was a great centre of Buddhist learning. It was also the meeting place of two different roads leading to Central Asia and China.

The importance of Kashgar both from the point of view of commercial activity as well as of expansion of Buddhism was equally great. Its location provided relief and hospitality to the travellers and the pilgrims alike and numerous monasteries had come up here. From this place again there were two routes extending up to the borders of China. The southern one running along the fringes of the Tarim basin passed through Yarkand, Khotan, Niya and also a number of other sites like Dandan-Oiliq, Endere and Miran. These places were notable for Buddhist monasteries and as centres of learning. According to the accounts of the Chinese pilgrims, Fa-hien and Hsuan-Chuang they were associated with the Mahāyāna school of Buddhism. The centres on the northern route Kashgar, Kucha and Turfan were, however, Hīnayānist. The inhabitants of Kashgar were sincere Buddhists and there were more than a thousand monks of the Sarvāstivādin school, but their knowledge was not in proportion to their zeal. This school flourished at Osh and Kucha and also at Balkh and at Bamiyan. The Great vehicle was predominant at Yarkand and Khotan as also in Kāpiśa. The people and language of the countries or centres on the northern route were different from those of the south, but both had common affinities in the form of Buddhist religion and culture.

Kucha or Kuchi, like its counterpart Khotan on the southern route, was the most important centre of Buddhism with Indian names of rulers like Suvarṇapuṣpa, Haradeva, Suvarṇadeva etc. The Buddhist monks of this place were well conversant with Sanskrit, as is confirmed by the finds of manuscripts in Sanskrit and bilingual documents in Kuchean Sanskrit. In the words of the Chinese pilgrim Hsuan-Chuang, it was not only a centre of Buddhist studies but it also provided famous scholars and savants who translated Buddhist texts and also gave discourses. The noted Buddhist scholar Kumārajīva was one such scholar who shone as a luminary radiating his lustre throughout Central Asia and China. He was connected with the Kuchean regal family. The grottos in the hills in the neighbourhood of Kucha provided a safe and solitary retreat for the monks.

Agnideśa in the region of Karasahr—the next place on the northern route was linked with Kucha in culture and language as also in ethnical affinity and common religion—Buddhism. The finds of literary texts and art objects in this region testify to its importance as a Buddhist centre. Turfan, the next stage on the northern route further east was equally connected with Buddhism with strong Chinese cultural impacts. Extensive literary remains include words in Sanskrit, Chinese and various Iranian and Turkish idioms in two dialects.

The Northern as well as the Southern routes met on the Chinese frontier at a place called Yu-men-Khan or the 'Jade Gate', close to the famous Tun-huang which was noted for its thousand grottos. These were carved out between the fifth and the eighth centuries A.D. for the Buddhist monks proceeding to China as also for holding discussions between groups of Buddhist scholars from various countries. Some Indian families had settled down at Tun-huang in the third century A.D. promoting activities both secular and religious. The finds of a large number of manuscripts suggest its importance as an active centre of Buddhist learning. Twenty-thousand manuscripts were discovered from the walled up chamber at the Tun-huang. These are in Brāhmī, Kharoṣṭhī, Tibetan, Turki, Uighur and Tokharian, and point to the cosmopolitan character of the monks and others frequenting or living in this area of Central Asia. A study of the geographical factors as also the nature of the peoples of different regions—nomadic as well as pastoral, receptive to external influences but equally independent, has, no doubt, been necessary in this context. The process of the introduction of Buddhism in Central Asia and through it into China was gradual and steady. It was the work of missionaries, political exiles, savants and scholars rather than of zealots. The Chinese sources point to royal invitations extended to Indian Buddhist scholars to visit their country and propagate the message of the Tathāgata. These were mostly from the Buddhist religious establishments in Central Asia itself. Tradition connects Buddhism in Khotan with Kuṇāla, the destitute Mauryan prince from Taxila. A number of Indian colonies had come up in Central Asia as recorded by the Chinese pilgrims. While the earlier picture of Buddhism and expansion of Indian culture in Central Asia might not be distinct and vivid, that of the later period is more pronounced and specific as might be evident from the finds of Buddhist manuscripts, monuments, sculptures and paintings. Patronage to the Buddhist scholars was extended by local rulers whose historical account no doubt demands some study.

The study of political history of Central Asia in relation to Buddhism and its expansion in this vast area as also in China involves reference to those rulers who patronised Buddhism in their kingdoms. While the date of introduction of Buddhism through Kashmir or Afghanistan is uncertain, it is clear from the accounts of the Chinese pilgrims that both the schools of Buddhism were flourishing in different centres. That suggests not one but at least two or may be even more currents of Buddhist religion which swept over this vast expanse. The earliest account of Buddhist activity could be traced to the first century A.D. with the despatch of Kāśyapa Mātaṅga and Dharmaratna proceeding to China in A.D. 65. The arrival of the first Buddhist missionaries is no doubt mixed up with the legend of the Emperor Ming of the Han dynasty seeing a golden man in a dream—apparently the Buddha—who asked him to invite the two Buddhist monks. Emissaries were for inviting these two savants and they did go to China with sacred texts and relics. The first Buddhist monastery was built for them in the capital. These monks spent the rest of their lives translating Buddhist texts into Chinese and doing evangelical work. They are mentioned as natives of the country of the Yue-che i.e. Tokharistan, since the word Che (from Yue-Che) is prefixed to their names. This country provided other monks as well for academic and missionary purposes. Lokakṣema of Tukhāra origin, and a man of exceptional learning went to Loyang in A.D. 147 and translated there some of the important Buddhist texts into Chinese. He stayed there till 188 and was followed by one of his young disciples, Che-Kien, who left towards the end of the second century and was in China for nearly three decades. Dharmarakṣa—another Buddhist monk, called Fa-hu in China, belonged to a Tukhāra family. He settled down in Tun-huang towards the middle of the 3rd century. A.D. A master of thirty-six languages he was widely travelled in Central Asia before leaving for China in A.D. 284 and worked there till A.D. 313 translating nearly 90 Buddhist texts. He was followed by another Tukhāra monk named She-lun who came to China in 373, and eleven years later by Dharmanandi from the same kingdom. Both the monks translated Buddhist texts into Chinese. Intellectual scholarship and religious zeal accounting for the migration of Buddhist scholars to China on invitation could be possible only in an age of awakening and maturity as also in the area of Buddhist learning. Tokharistan—the land of the Tukhāras—Tuṣāras must be crowded with Buddhist savants. It was during the Kuṣāṇa period that Buddhism was taken to Central Asia where the people from Kashmir and North-Western India (now Pakistan) had set up small colonies with kings claiming descent from Indian regal families. Bamiyan in Afghanistan had risen to be a great centre of Buddhism in the early centuries of the Christian era, and it continued to retain that position for a number of centuries. Bactriana (modern Balkh)—Chinese Fo-ho and Indian Bahlika, further north, was another Buddhist centre. Here the religion of the Tathāgata was introduced in the first century B.C. or even a little earlier. Its political history slides from the Greeks to the Sakas, followed in turn by the political ascendancy of the Yue-ches and the Huns.

The establishment of Buddhism in Tokharestan under the Kuṣāṇas stimulated its process of expansion. The Parthians to the south-west took active interest in this region, and equally participated in the emigration programme of their Buddhist savants to China. According to the Chinese Annals a number of such scholars distinguished by the prefix An (Ngan) went to propagate and translate the gospel of the Buddha. A Parthian prince, known to the Chinese as Ngan-She-Kao or Lokottama, visited the western frontier country of China with a load of

Buddhist texts. He was a prince of the ruling family who waived his claim for the throne in favour of his uncle and took up the robes of the Buddhist order at a young age. He settled down at the White Monastery in A.D. 144—which was earlier built for the two pioneer Indian monks Kāśyapa Mātaṅga and Dharmatrāta. He founded a school for translating Buddhist texts and personally contributed more than a hundred items in this programme. Other Parthian scholars who were associated with the school of translators of Buddhist texts were Ngan-Hivan, originally a merchant, and Ngan-She-Kao and the Indo-Scythian monk Lokakṣema. Ngan-She-Kao madethe first organised effort to translate the Buddhist canon into Chinese. This academic exercise of translating Buddhist texts was later undertaken by some Parthian monks who, though not very celebrated, went to China during the third and fourth centuries A.D. Besides doing the translation work, they also contributed towards the propagation of Buddhism. Some Sogdian monks also collaborated with Ngan-She-Kao, including the illustrious Seng-hui (Saṅghamati ?). The names of the Sogdian monks are distinguished by the prefix Kang, a short form of the Chinese Kang-Kiu, the name given to Sogdiana. He was the first to introduce Buddhism in Southern China in the third century A.D.

The contribution of these Buddhist scholars from Tokharestan, Parthia and Sogdiana is suggestive of the prevailing prosperous condition of Buddhism in their homelands, enabling them to move out for evangelical work in distant China after transgressing natural barriers in the way. The credit for Buddhist activity and expansion should go to Kaniṣka, the patron of the fourth Buddhist Council and himself an ardent Buddhist. Buddhism seems to have made considerable progress not only in India but also in Central Asia during this period, as seems evident from Buddhist monuments at Bamiyan of Surkh-Kotal in Afghanistan and Adjina-Tepe in Tadjistan (now in Soviet Central Asia). The knowledge of Indian Kharoṣṭhī script is revealed from the documents found at Niya, not very far from Khotan, and such Buddhist scriptures as the Gandhārī Dharmapada. Further, it is proposed that the interference of the Yueh-chih in the political affairs of Kashgar accounted for the introduction of Buddhism in that kingdom. This assumption seems to be in agreement with the tradition recorded by Hsuan-tsang about the princely hostages from Sha-la or Kashgar residing in a Buddhist convent as a result of Kaniṣka's conquest of that region. It is further presumed that the Buddhist Church and its establishment, whatever be its period, was the result of impact from Baktra and not Khotan, as Mahāyānism was the prevailing form of Buddhism in Khotan, while Hīnayānism was popular in Kashgar.

The information relating to Buddhism in Kashgar is no doubt given by the Chinese pilgrims who visited this place on their way to or from China. To the early Chinese geographers the country was known as Shu-le, and later on it was called Kie-Sha. Its general description, including that of the people, is substantially the same as given by Hsuan-Chwang. Chih-mong (A.D. 404) saw at Chih-sha (Kashgar) Buddha's alms bowl as also his spittoon made of a variegated colour stone. The famous savant of Kucha, Kumārajīva also visited this place about A.D. 400 and he records the miraculous quality of this bowl changing its weight according to the merit of the person carrying it. Fa-hien also describes his stay at Chich-Cha (Kashgar) enjoying royal hospitality and participating in the great quinquennial assembly of monks. It was a Hīnayānist centre of Buddhism with a thousand monks residing here. The place also boasted of a tooth of the Buddha for which the people had set up a stūpa. In Hsuan-Chuang's time, Buddhism was in a flourishing condition. He records several hundreds of Saṅghārāmas with some ten thousand followers, studying the Little Vehicle and belonging to the Sarvāstivādin school. Several stūpas were explored close to Kashgar. Two other pilgrims, Dharmacandra of India and Wu-kong of China passed through Kashgar, the former on his way back from China and the latter on his way to Gandhāra.

Indian scholars frequently visited Kashgar. Kumārajīva, son of Kumārāyaṇa and Jīvā of the Kucha royal family, on his return journey from Kashmir, where he had gone for his education, stayed at Kashgar for nearly a year and studied Abhidharma of the Sarvāstivāda school with its six divisions under able teachers. It is reported that Hi-Kien, a master of Tripiṭaka requested the ruler to retain Kumārajīva permanently in Kashgar. Before leaving for home, Kumārajīva also studied the four Vedas, the five sciences, the Brāhmaṇical Śāstras and also astronomy at Kashgar· During the period of his stay (last decade of the 4th century), two other important personalities—Sūryabhadra and Sūryasoma, the two sons of the King of So-Kiu (Karghalik-Yarkand) were also ordained here and Kumārajīva taught them *Śataśāstra* and Mādhyamika-Śāstra before leaving for Kucha. He in his turn was assisted in his studies by Buddhayaśas of Kashmir who had earlier come here and stayed here as an adviser to the ruler. He later on joined Kumārajīva in China where he was taken by the Chinese General Lu-Kuang. Another Buddhist scholar at Kashgar was Dharmacandra who was originally from Magadha and had gone to China in 730 from Kucha at the invitation of the Chinese ambassador. On his way back in 741 he stayed for some time at Kashgar. Political unrest in the way finally landed him in Khotan where he died two years later.

On the southern route from Kashgar to Khotan across the Sitā (Yarkand Daryā) river was Che-Kiu-Kia or Tsen-ho according to the Chinese sources and Cu-gu-pan of the Tibetan texts, corresponding to Cokkuka of the Central Asian documents. It has been identified with Karghahalik-Yarkand. According to Hsuan-Tsang, the people were sincere Buddhists and the country had some tens of monasteries with more than a hundred monks who were all followers of Mahāyānism. The two princes of this place Sūryabhadra and Sūryasoma had gone to Kashgar and received initiation from Kumārajīva and studied Mahāyāna texts with him. The ruling family seems to be of Indian origin.

Further south was the kingdom of Khotan which in the time of Hsuan-tsang had a hundred monasteries with five thousand monks who were all followers of Mahāyānism. Buddhism was supposed to be introduced here in the time of Vijayasambhava, the grandson of Kutsana, its founder. The monk Vairocana, supposed to be an incarnation of Maitreya, had come here from Kashmir bringing with him the relics of the Buddha. The earliest monastery was built for this monk by the ruler, followed by the setting up of several other such establishments by the Khotanese rulers including the one built by the Chinese princess Puṇeśvara (Pu-nye-shar), queen of king Vijayadeva in honour of Kalyāṇamitra. The ruler's eldest son Dharmānanda who had joined the Buddhist order also established several monasteries. The school of the Greater Vehicle (Mahāyāna) was prospering in Fa-hien's time as well with three thousand monks in the famous Gośṛiṅga monastery there. Its greatness as a centre of Mahāyāna Buddhistic studies in the third century A.D. is evident from the visit of the Chinese monk Chu-She-hing who came here in A.D. 290 for the study of Buddhism under eminent teachers and sent through his disciple 9000 bundles of original Buddhist texts to China for translation. The noted Buddhist scholar Buddhasena was a famous savant, known as 'the lion of learning'. There are references to visits of Buddhist scholars from China and carrying with them texts from Khotan. The quinquennial assembly no doubt was a great attraction for such inquisitive visitors on a religious mission.

Besides Khotan, there were several other Buddhist centres on the southern route. Fragments with inscriptions in Brāhmi, manuscripts and other records, as also Kharoṣṭhī documents of the 3rd century A.D. were found in excavation. Both the schools of Buddhism prospered in this part of Central Asia around the fourth century A.D. Lou-lan, the Na-fo-po also called Shan-Shan in the Han Annals, was another important centre—a stronghold of Buddhism as also of Indian culture. According to Fa-hien there were 4000 monks here, all followers of Hīnayānism. The original name of this place was Kroraina or Kroranjina of the Kharoṣṭhī documents. These records from the Central Asian sites on the southern route at Lou-lan, Niya and Endere shed considerable light on the material culture of the people in this area. The names of donors in these inscriptions appear to be of Indian origin. Frescoe paintings from Miran with the Buddhist subject matter and linked with Gandhāra art bring out the importance of this place in the history of Buddhism and its expansion in Central Asia.

The famous Buddhist centres on the Northern route—Aksu, Kucha, Agnidesa or Karasahr and Kao-Chang-Turfan with a common racial heritage and language, of course with minor dialectical differences of a local nature, had a uniform cultural background. They were linked with each other in the sphere of Hīnayāna Buddhist school. Among these States, Kucha was the most important politically as well as for its eminent Buddhist savants. The date of the introduction of Buddhism here is uncertain. It was no doubt in a flourishing state in the third century A.D. According to the Annals of the Tsin dynasty (265-316), at that time there were nearly one thousand Buddhist stūpas and temples in Kucha and it also sent Buddhist monks to China for translating sacred texts into Chinese. In the fourth century A.D., the capital was virtually changed into a Buddhist city with numerous monasteries controlled by the Abbot Buddhasvāmin—a great scholar, a follower of the Āgamas. Among his disciples was the famous Kumārajīva. Nunneries for the Bhikṣuṇīs included those from royal and noble families, observing a strict disciplined life. The role of Kumārajīva and his disciples in the dissemination and expansion of Buddhism in Central Asia and in China is a well-known fact, and his life history is a saga of service to the religion of the Lord. Kumārajīva was well-versed in all branches of Buddhist learning as also in languages—oriental and Chinese. He could remove doubts and dispel erroneous interpretations of scholars from all quarters. He was joined at Chang-ngan by his Sarvāstivādin guru Vimalākṣa who was staying all along in Kucha after Kumārajīva's departure. Another scholar Dharmamitra from Kucha also joined him in his new sojourn, followed by the Kashmirian scholar Buddhayaśa under whom Kumārajīva had studied in Kashgar, and Buddhabhadra from the same place.

The Kuchean savant was responsible for introducing Mahāyānism in the countries of the Tarim basin and also in China in a more responsible and authoritative manner. He was one of the greatest exponents of the school of Buddhism and also of the Mādhyamika philosophy. As an institution in the true sense, he drew votaries to his shrine of learning both in Kucha as also in the Chinese capital where he stayed till the end of his life. Many other scholars joined Kumārajīva in China after spending quite some time in Central Asia. These included Saṅghabhūti, Gautama Saṅghadeva and Puṇyatrāta—all from Kashmir—who went to China by the end of the fourth century A.D. Dharmayaśa, pupil of Puṇyatrāta, was also associated with the translation of a number of important texts of the Buddhist Sarvāstivādin school. He stayed there till 453 and then returned to Central Asia and was finally back home in Kashmir.

Among the Buddhist savants of the first quarter of the fifth century A.D. were Buddhajīva also from Kashmir who collaborated with Fa-hien in translating a couple of manuscripts brought from India. A great teacher of Vinaya and a follower of the Mahiśāsaka school, he translated three important works of this school. Guṇavarman, a prince of the royal family of Kashmir, another erudite scholar from Kashmir, was invited by the Chinese emperor, and during his short one year's stay at the Jetavana monastery he translated eleven works into Chinese. Another inmate of the same monastery was Dharmamitra from Kashmir.

The Buddhist savants from Central Asia who contributed to its thought and literature in later times can be assessed on the basis of their translation of Buddhist texts into Chinese as also their frequent visits to Central Asia for the collection of textual material. Dharmakṣema, originally from Central India and a follower of Mahāyānism translated 25 texts into Chinese. He wished to return to Khotan in A.D. 433 but was killed in the way. This was in connection with the incomplete text of the *Mahāparinirvāṇa-Sūtra* of which the other part was probably in Khotan. His pupil Tsiu-Kiu-Kingsheng, a nobleman, later went to this great Mahāyānist centre and studied the texts of this school with Buddhasena, a great scholar. This centre of Buddhist learning with its famous savants continued to attract many Chinese monks, and equally played an important role in the transmission of Buddhism to China in the Tang period (A.D. 618-907). One of its greatest scholars in this period was Śikṣānanda who went to China and stayed there till his death in A.D. 710. Another scholar from this place was Devaprajña or Devendrajñāna, who stayed in the Chinese capital till A.D. 689. Shih-Kiyen of the royal house of Kustana (Khotan) was another emigrant to China. All these scholars translated a number of Buddhist texts which are fully recorded. Many such scholars from other parts of Central Asia, who went to China and translated Buddhist texts include Mitrasanta, Ratnacinta, Thien-si-tsai (-deva), Prajña, and Danapāla from Tukhāra, Kashmir and Kabul respectively. Tibet also contributed in this matter.

Pa-ho-sz-pa—Bashpa—a śramaṇa of Tu-po (Tibet) was the confidential adviser of Kublai-Khan as also his *altar-ego*. He translated one work and in A.D. 1269, devised an alphabetical system of the Mongol language which was utilised for writing.

While the Chinese source material provides information about the life and activities of Central Asian savants as also their contributions, archaeological finds of stūpas, sculptures and paintings equally testify to the flourishing state of Buddhism in Central Asia with its two prominent schools—Hīnayāna and Mahāyāna and their offshoots. The available artistic material warrants a detailed study of Central Asian Buddhist art in all its phases and facets. The finds of Kharoṣṭhī records, numbering nearly eight hundred in a language which might be termed Prākrit with various Iranian idioms and vocabulary introduced into it, provide sufficient information for a detailed study of material culture as also of its impact on the life of Buddhist monks. This aspect is taken as a separate area of study. The religion of the Tathāgata in its relation with Brahmanism as also other religions has also been brought out. The Tarim basin and the lands of the Oxus afforded the necessary base for the mingling of different religions and cultures; and it is quite likely that besides Hinduism, Zoroastrianism and Christianity as also Manichaeism had their impacts on Buddhism. In fact, Central Asia appears as an area representing exchange of religions, ideas and art from India as also from Iran, as is evident from the finds of a number of manuscripts in different Iranian idioms. So also is its debt to India unquestionable. But equally important is the assessment of Central Asian contribution to Buddhism particularly in respect of Buddhist literature and art. The relationship with Tibet was, of course, on a mutual basis. The Tibetans occupied the Tarim basin for nearly a century, and the Buddhist scholars and artists from Khotan made their contribution in the 'land of the snow'.

The Buddhist literature as also its art from Central Asia represent several periods and strata. The older one is revealed from the fragments of Sanskrit Āgamas, found at Turfan, Tunhuang, and in the Khotan district, fragments of dramas and poems of Aśvaghoṣa from Turfan; the Prātimokṣa of the Sarvāstivādins from Kucha and numerous versions of the anthology called Dharmapada or Udāna. These along with the Prākrit version found in the neighbourhood of Khotan, as also fragments in Tokharian and Sanskrit—all those representing the Buddhist canon as it existed during the time of Kaniṣka coinciding with the efflorescence period of Gandhāra art—are supposed to represent the older stratum. The latter one is symbolised by the abundant discovery of the Mahāyāna sūtras.

The new stratum is said to comprise Mahāyānist sūtras, found in abundance, particularly the *Prajñā-Pāramitā*, the *Saddharma-puṇḍarīka* and the *Suvarṇa-prabhāsa*. The last one was translated from Chinese into Uighur, and into 'Iranian Oriental'. The 'Dhāraṇīs' or magical formulae discovered in large numbers belong to a later period. It is proposed by Sylvain Levi that some Mahāyāna-Sūtras were written or re-edited in Central Asia, since they contain references to Central Asian place names, which could be the result of local patriotic instinct. This is evident from the praises showered on the mountain Gośṛiṅga, near Khotan in the *Sūryagarbha-Sūtra* or from the list of holy places in the *Chandragarbha-Sūtra*. Manifestations of Buddha through his ray of light in Central Asia also outnumber those mentioned in Indian texts. Further, one of the Turkish Sūtras discovered at Turfan contains a discourse of the Buddha to the merchants Trapusha and Bhallika who are described as Turks, and Indra is called Kormusta, that is Hormuzd. In another Sūtra, Brahmā is called Asura, identified with the Iranian deity Zervan. All these facts point to the local colouring of the Buddhist doctrine; and might as well imply amendations made in the Buddhist texts here.

There are also traces of interaction of Chinese ideas—Confucian and Taoist—on Buddhism, as also the admixture of Buddhism in Manichaeism. The dated inscription of the temple erected in Turfan in A.D. 469 is suggestive of the former influence. This record in honour of Maitreya, regarded here as the future Buddha and an active and benevolent deity manifesting himself in many forms, also speaks of heaven (tien) as appointing princes, and of the universal law (tao) and it contains several references to Chinese literature. The Chinese edict of 739 confirms the second hypothesis by accusing the Manichaeans of falsely taking the name of Buddhism and deceiving the people. This is not surprising as Mani mentions that Zoroaster, Buddha and Christ had preceded him as apostles. His followers in Buddhist countries naturally adopted familiar words and symbols to propagate the message of the Prophet. Manichaean deities are represented like Bodhisattvas sitting cross-legged on a lotus, and Mani is called Ju-lai or Tathāgata. Besides reference to Amida's Paradise with holy trees bearing flowers which enclose beings styled Buddhas, the construction and phraseology of Manichaean books resemble those of a Buddhist Sūtra.

The co-existence of different religions in the Tarim basin, with their impact on each other, did not exclude Nestorian Christianity, introduced into China by A-lo-pen in A.D. 635, almost simultaneously with Zoroastrianism. While the Nestorian monument at Si-ngan-fu, commonly called the Nestorian stone, and the finds of the fragments of the New Testament at Turfan mostly of the ninth century could be definite proofs of this new creed and its propagation in Central Asia, the reference to many Buddhist phrases, such as Seng and Ssu for Christian priests and monasteries, and the deliberate omission of the crucifixion suggest adaptation of the Christian doctrine to suit the native sentiments. It is thus possible that in western China and Central Asia Buddhism, Taoism, Manichaeism, Nestorianism and Zoroastrianism made mutual impacts on each other. There is of course not much evidence of the modification of Buddhism except in local colouring, as proposed earlier. Buddhism in strength and in numbers was the most important of all the religions and equally the earliest to reach Central Asia.

From the point of view of material culture, Central Asia presents a picture of rich and assimilative cultural pattern. Physical configuration, with vast areas covered by the deserts, and mountainous and hilly tracts, accounting for difficult communication tracts, had no doubt, contributed to the development of local cultures particularly nomadic and pastoral. Historical factors, however, helped in establishing some form of cultural integration. This was symbolised by Buddhism and a common way of life, at least in those areas where it was dominant. The finds of inscriptions at Lou-lan, Endere and Niya no doubt present a picture of material culture in its multifacet forms. The plantation of Indian colonies and that of others on the trade routes had set the process of cultural fusion into operation. The Chinese pilgrims passing through Central Asia between the fourth and the seventh centuries have recorded this fact with reference to Buddhist thought and way of life. There are references to rulers bearing Indian names in both the sectors, such as the Vijaya rulers in the south at Khotan and Puṣpa and Deva ending rulers at Kucha, and those with Arjuna suffix at Karasahr (Agnideśa) on the Northern route. Other Indian names appearing in records are Ānanda and Buddhamitra, Dharmapāla, Puṇyadeva and Vāsudeva, as also Epic names like Arjuna, Bhīmasena, etc. The titles taken by the rulers are also Indian, like *mahārāja rājātirāja* and *avijitasiṃha*—'unconquered lion'. Sometimes there are mixed names like Vasu Mogiya, Vasukekeya etc. suggesting understanding and assimilation in the cultural ethos. The impact of Buddhism seems to have eliminated caste consciousness, but there were several classes of people, ones including chiefs, feudal lords (cozbo), affluent householders and administrative officers, forming the upper crust of society, while the lower one included slaves, workers and artisans. Inter-class or caste marriages as also between the Indians and the natives—apparently as their names suggest—were equally known. A priest Sāriputra receives an adopted child Dewga Amto—naming her Siratoyae and finally marries her to another priest Buddhavarma in a lawful manner. Their daughter later marries the priest Jivalo Athane. Three generations of cross relationship through marriage is significant. The family continues to be a well-knit joint unit consisting of the father, mother, brother and younger sisters, as also grand-father. Indian terms are used, such as *kula* and *parivāra* for the family. The head of the unit exercised control over other members and also looked after their welfare. Adopted children and even slaves formed part of the family. Ladies of the upper stratum were commonly educated and could communicate in writing with friends and relations. Slaves constituted the property of the master who generally utilised their services in farming. They could be immune from bondage after payment of the money invested on them. Even Buddhist monks kept slaves to look after their farms and property interests and there could be change of masters as well. Food, dress and ornamentation as well as pastime and items of recreation appear to be more in tune with the Indian pattern of social life. It appears that along with Buddhism, Indian music was taken to Central Asia—an inference based on the depiction of such musical instruments in paintings from Khotan and Kucha regions. Actors, musicians and dancers were actually taken by the Chinese General Lu-Kuang to China in A.D. 382 when the kingdom was conquered.

The economy of Central Asia was confined to agriculture, cattle rearing and trade as well as some avocations. Irrigation had its importance which was well-realized in the absence of rainfall and that too when the land was barren or not so fertile and productive. There are references to several types of land—arable, *mishi* and barren—*akri*. The ploughing and sowing operations are also recorded as also the amount of seed required for a measured plot of land which equally determined its market value. Slaves and women could own as well as alienate their lands. The Khotan area was noted for cotton and hemp production. Animal husbandry, connected with pasture lands equally engaged Central Asian peoples in their economic activity. Camels and horses were used for transport purposes and the former also catered to exchange deals. Sheep provided wool, while rams carried light goods. Cows yielded milk from which ghee was produced. *Ghrita*– or *ghee*,—a purely Indian product—was made on a big scale, as might be inferred from the reference to a hundred ghee jars. Industries, especially related to carpet and silk, leather, cotton and utensils are also mentioned in records. Vineyards provided grapes for processing and the distilleries had the support of the government. There was a special department for the collection of taxes on old and new wines. There were also state dairy farms, like the state distilleries. An officer called *Satavida* looked after the State enterprises.

There appears to be a mixed economy with the participation of different interests, not excluding the Buddhist monks who were well-off and not much different from other householders. They could marry and also own property, including slaves. The sale of yellow metal—gold is recorded in several records. There are also references to different types of coins—*sadera-stater*, *trachma* –drachm, *muli* and *ghare*. These suggest trade dealings in cash as well. Weights and measures are also mentioned such as *khi*, and *milima* etc. Labour and transport facilities were equally available to prevent the economic stagnation. Administra.i.n too had close links with the rural economy as also with industries and avocations, and the despatch of taxes was not delayed. The material finds in excavations reveal a fairly good standard of socio-economic life, closely associated with native traditions and equally receptive to foreign impacts and influences. It is no doubt difficult to sift or apportion the contributions—Indian, Iranian and Chinese—to the composite culture of the Central Asian peoples in different sectors. There was not much change till the tenth century A.D. when Islam had spread its influences and gradually changed the tenor and temper of the converted population.

Buddhism and its expansion from India to Central Asia and thence to the Far East, no doubt, provided the base for the artistic activities in both the areas. Buddhist art centred round the life activities of the Buddha and his previous births based on the narrations in Buddhist texts. In this enterprise all the Buddhists joined hands or acted independently in offering their services. That accounts for the impacts or influences from different quarters—classical Greek and Roman, Persian and Sassanian—in the pictorial and sculptural art of Central Asia. While the theme continues to be Buddhist, the actors in the pictorial drama change with the painter who makes full use of his imagination and background and evolves his own colour scheme. In this context the earliest impact was with Gāndhāra and its artists who are supposed to have been inspired by Greek traditions as modified in Rome. These artists carried with them their pictorial and sculptural art to Central Asia. The native talent accepted these artistic influences with discrimination. A facile technique is, thus, traced in Central Asian art. The examples of painting in caves and free-standing shrines suggest an advanced state and productive capacity with the expansion of Buddhism and the setting up of a large number of stūpas and shrines, the demand for artists and sculptors considerably increased. The commercial enterprise on the trade routes with the patronage and contribution of traders and merchants provided incentives for artists—experienced and young, who were roving from one centre to another. They received handsome payments for their services.

The paintings rightly grouped into two—on a geographical basis—reflect, as proposed earlier, the impacts and influences of diverse origins. Well-defined styles of Central Asian paintings, no doubt, suggest Indian and Chinese inspirations in their respective areas. Indian qualities dominate in the south with Persian influence intruding, while the Chinese features are perceptible, of course, with modification by Tibetan, Uighur and others in the north. The common factor in both is the Buddha and his legend—variously expressed. Hindu and Tantric importations as well stimulated the imagination of Chinese and Tibetan artists who were more interested in the decorative part than the spiritual element which inspired the earlier Indian renderings. The manner of expression in art renderings differs widely in style and treatment. This could be due to the changing political situations through the centuries and the complex social milieu. Diversities in design and treatment did not completely rule out identical mannerism in some compositions at places which might be at considerable distance from each other. This might be due to some artist and his troupe of painters moving from one centre to another.

The earliest Buddhist paintings are from Miran and the sites lying on the old silk route. Indian conception and execution are noticed in the type of persons in Indian dress; the Persian type of beauty no doubt suggests Iranian contacts. The reference to Titus and the fees paid to him, as recorded in a Kharoṣṭhī inscription confirms the role of the Indo-Greek artists in this region. The Gandhāra school is supposed to be transplanted into pictorial lines at Miran where Roman-Hellenistic influences are evident. This influence from Gandhāra predominates in the Khotan complex between the fifth and eighth centuries with the assimilation of other foreign characteristics. The Centres on the Northern routes—Kizil, Kucha and Turfan—were equally connected with or influenced by others. At Kucha—the Indo-Iranian (c. 500 A.D.) and strongly Iranian (c. 600-650 A.D.) phases are noticed. Indian influence is prominent in several paintings like the one depicting the cowherd listening to the sermon of the Buddha or in the group of swimmers at Kizil. The paintings from Kumtura suggest a third phase characterised by Chinese influence eliminating or absorbing the Iranian motifs and types. The Mongolian features, head dress, drapery and folds of dress and scarves are traditionally Chinese. The Turfan group covering a period of three hundred years is noted for mannerism is physiognomy, pose and costume of the figures. Its different phases vary from one region to another with changing degrees of Chinese influence and dominance of Tantric features. At Khocho, Manichaean and Nestorian influences are conspicuous with interaction of Chinese and Iranian cultures on local art.

The paintings at Tun-huang, the meeting place of the two routes is noted for the caves of the thousand Buddhas, providing an idea of Chinese Buddhist art in concept and design. A small group is supposed to represent Indian art, and a few are Tibetan. These paintings are placed between the fifth and eighth centuries A.D. At the other end the western part of Central Asia now in Soviet Central Republics had its own art forms as revealed from a number of sites representing old Buddhist centres. The recent discovery of wall paintings at Balatik-Tepe near Airtan Termez, are supposed to be Sassanian inspiration. The earliest Indo-Hellenistic blend is noticed in the first century A.D. superb sculptured lime-stone frieze.

The two countries at the periphery of Central Asia—namely Afghanistan and Tibet--are also significant for their contribution to Buddhist art. The former was connected with the Gandhāra art, and provides examples of rock-cut statues, sculptures and paintings. Here the fusion of Iranian and Indian elements produced a hybrid style, the direct antecedent of the Buddhist paintings in Central Asia, especially at Kizil and Murtuq. The paintings in Tibet are supposed to have developed mostly under Indian influence with the participation of artists from Northern India as also from Khotan. The Art of Central Asia was Buddhist in character, assimilating the forms of great sedentary peoples around them. At an early stage it depended on the Greco-Roman art of Gandhāra, but subsequently gave birth to a series of independent movements which influenced and were influenced by the major civilizations of Asia.

The Central Asian Buddhist art and religion exhibit certain traits like deification, pantheism, creation of radiant or terrible deities, extreme form of idealism or nihilism. Buddhism lately borrowed many personalities from the Hindu pantheon, and one finds Buddhas and Bodhisattvas such as Amitābha Avalokita or Avalokiteśvara, Mañjuśrī and Kṣitigarbha which might not be having antecedents in India. It is suggested that they were borrowed from some other mythology. Amitābha, a benevolent deity with his paradise of light is compared to Ahuramazda. All the features of his paradise are said to be Persian, though the concept of Tuṣita heaven is Indian Buddhist and fairly old. Avalokita is also connected with Amitābha's paradise. There is no reason for his special association with Central Asia, since he assumes distinctness and importance much earlier in India. Later works describe him as the spiritual son or reflex of Amitābha. The Zoroastrian doctrine of the Fravashi—the spiritual being conceived as a part of a man's personality but existing before he is born and independent of him—seems to be more appropriate in defining the relationship between a Dhyānī Buddha and his Bodhisattva.

Further, Bodhisattva Mañjuśrī according to Sylvain Levi is supposed to be of Tokharian origin being worshipped at Wo-tai-Shan in Shan-si. He is connected with China according to the Indian tradition, while local ones associate him with Nepal, Tibet and Khotan. There is no clear proof of his Central Asian origin. The same might be true about the Bodhisattva Kṣitigarbha as well. While he was known in India in the fourth century A.D. his cult was not prominent here; it flourished in China, finally making him a popular deity in the Far East, second only to Kuan-Yin. He was gradually transformed into a god of the dead.

Central Asia seems to have played a very active role as a transit centre, sending ideas, icons and merchandise from one end to the other. It further provided its Buddhist savants and scholars to propagate Buddhist doctrines and canons in the Far East, especially in China, translating these in the language of the country. From the beginning of the Christian era onwards monks went eastwards from Central Asia to preach and translate the scriptures and it was through this country that Chinese pilgrims came to India 'in search of truth'. A long history of Central Asian Buddhism is a saga of creative religious and artistic activities displayed on a wide horizon, in which peoples of all shades and ethnic origin seem to have taken a fairly active part.

SELECT BIBLIOGRAPHY

BOOKS

Andrews, F.H. : Descriptive catalogue of Antiquities recovered by Sir Aurel Stein during his explorations in Central Asia, Kansu and Eastern Iran, London, 1936.

———Wall Paintings from Ancient Shrines in Central Asia, London, 1948.

Anand, Mulk Raj : Tibetan Art. Marg Special Number, Vol. XVI, No. 4, 1963.

Bachofer : History of Chinese Art.

Bagchi, P.C.: India and Central Asia, Calcutta, 1955.

Le Canon Bouddhique en Chine, Tome I, Paris 1927; tome II, Cal. 1938.

———India and China, Calcutta, 1944.

Banerji, J.N. : Development of Hindu Iconography, Calcutta, 1956.

Banerji, P. : Hindu Trinity from Central Asia, Bulletin, New Delhi, 1970.

Beal, Samuel: Buddhist Records of the Western World, Vols. I & II, London, 1906.

Benjamin, R.: The Wall Paintings of India, Central Asia and Ceylon—a comparative study, Boston, 1938.

Belenitsky, A. : Central Asia, London, 1969.

Bhattacharya, Chaya: Art of Central Asia, Delhi, 1969.

Boyer, A.M., Rapson, E.J. & Senart, E.: Kharoṣṭhī Inscriptions discovered by Sir Aurel Stein in Chinese Turkestan, I-III, Oxford, 1921-29.

Brough, J.: The Gandhārī Dharmapada, London, 1962.

Burrow, T.: The Language of the Kharoṣṭhī Documents from Chinese Turkestan, Cambridge, 1937.

———A Translation of the Kharoṣṭhī Documents from Chinese Turkestan, London, 1940.

Bussagli, M.: Paintings of Central Asia, Geneva. 1963.

Chattopadhyaya, A : Atiśa and Tibet, Calcutta, 1967.
Coomaraswamy, A. : History of Indian and Indonesian Art, London 1927, 1965.
Dabbs, J.A. : History of the Discovery and Exploration of Chinese Turkestan, The Hague, 1963.
Eitel: Handbook of Chinese Buddhism.
Eliot, Charles : Hinduism and Buddhism, Vols. I-III, London, 1921.
Emmerick, R.E. : Tibetan Texts concerning Khotan, London, 1967.
Foucher, A. : L'art greco-bouddhique du Gandhara, Vols. I. III. Paris, 1905, 1918, 1933.
Thomas, L. A : Beginnings of Buddhist Art, London, 1917.
Gaulier, S. et others : Buddhism in Afghanistan & Central Asia, 2 Vols. Leiden, 1976.
Giles, H.A. : The Travels of Fa-hien, Delhi, 1972.
Grey, B. : Buddhist Cave Paintings at Tun-huang, London, 1959.
Grunwedel, A. : Buddhist Art in India, London, 1901.
———Alt buddhistiche Kultstattin in Chinese Turkestan, Berlin, 1917.
Hackin, J. : Buddhist Art in Central Asia etc. London, 1937.
Hambly, G. : Central Asia, New York, 1969.
Hambis, L.: L'Asie Histoire et Civilisation, Paris, 1977.
Hedin, S.: Central Asia and Tibet Towards the Holy City of Lassa, 2 Vols. London, 1903.
———Scientific results of a journey in Central Asia, 1899-1902, Stockholm, 1904-7.
———Through Asia, London, 1898.
Hopkirk, P. : Foreign Devils on the Silk Road, London, 1980.
Huloewe, A.F.P. : China in Central Asia—The Early Age, Leiden, 1979.
Ingholt, H. : Gandhāra art in Pakistan, New York, 1937.
Kumagai, N. : Central Asian Painting.
Legge, J.: Fa-hien's Travels, Oxford, 1886, Tokyo.
Le Coq, A. Von. : Buried Treasures of Chinese Turkestan, London, 1928.
Mac-Govern, W. M : The Early Empire of Central Asia, University of North Carolina Press, 1939.

Majumdar, R.C. : The Age of Imperial Unity, Bombay, 1960.
———Classical Age, Bombay, 1964.
———The Age of Imperial Kanauj, Bombay, 1964.
Marshall, J. : Gandhāra Art, Cambridge, 1968.
Pelliot, P. : Les grottes de Touen-houang, 6 Vols. Paris, 1920-24.
Petech, L. : Northern India according to Shui-Ching-Chu, Rome 1950.
Petrucci : Les peintures bouddhique de Touen-houang, Paris, 1916.
Puri, B.N. : India under the Kushāṇas, Bombay, 1950.
Remusat, Abel. : Histoire de la ville de Khotan, Paris, 1820.
Rice Talbot, T. : Ancient Arts of Central Asia, London, 1965.
Rapson, E.J. : See under Boyer.
Rockhill, W.W. : The Life of the Buddha, London, 1884.
Rowland, Benjamin : The Art and Architecture of India, London, 1969.
———The Art of Central Asia, New York, 1974.
———Art in Afghanistan, London, 1971.
Rudolf Hoernle, A.F. : Ms. Remains of Buddhist Literature found in Eastern Turkestan, Oxford.
Stein, A. : Sand Buried Ruins of Khotan, London, 1904.
———Ancient Khotan, 2 Vols. Oxford, 1907.
———Ruins of Desert Cathay, 2 Vols. London, 1912.
———Serindia, 5 Vols., Oxford, 1921.
———Innermost Asia, 5 Vols., Oxford, 1929.
———On Ancient Central Asian Tracks. London. 1920.
———Ancient Buddhist Paintings from the Cave Temples of Tun-huang, London, 1921-22.
Walters, T. : On Yuan-Chwang's Travels in India, London, 1905.

PAPERS

Aalto, P.: On the Role of Central Asia in the spread of Indian Cultural Influence. (Vivekanand Commemoration Volume, Madras 1970, pp. 249-62).
Agrawala, R.C. : Some Aspects of Indian Culture in the Kharoṣṭhī Documents from Chinese Turkestan (Vivekanand Volume, pp. 275-81).
———Position of Women and dependents in the Kharoṣṭhī

documents from Chinese Turkestan (Indian Historical Quarterly—IHQ—1952).

———Position of slaves and Serfs in the Kharoṣṭhī documents—IHQ 1953, pp. 97-110.

———Numismatic data from Kharoṣṭhī documents—Journal of the Numismatic Society—JNSI—1953, pp. 103-06.

———Numismatic data in Niya Kharoṣṭhī documents—JNSI—1954, pp. 219-30.

———A study of weights and measurements in the Kharoṣṭhī documents—Journal of the Bihar Research Society—JBS—pp. 365 ff.

———Form of Taxation in the Kharoṣṭhī Documents, IHQ. 1953, pp. 340-53.

———Some family letters in the Kharoṣṭhī documents. IHQ. 1954, pp. 50-67.

———A study of textiles and garments in the Kharoṣṭhī documents. (Bharatiya Vidya) Bombay, 1953, p. 75-94

———Life of monks and serfs in the Kharoṣṭhī documents. (Swaroop Bharati) 1954, pp. 173-81.

Bagchi, P.C.—Indian Culture in Central Asia, JBORS, 1946, pp. 9-20.

Banerji, P. : Indra from Balawaste. Journal of Indo-Iranian Culture, 1968, Vol. XVII.

———Hindu deities in Central Asia. (Vivekanand Volume) pp. 281-88.

Bhattacharya. C. : India—a major source of Central Asian Art (ibid, pp. 289-298).

Bailey, H.W. : Indo-Iranian—Bulletin of the School of Oriental and African Studies. BSOAS. 1949-50. pp. 121-39; 920-938.

———Gandhārī, ibid. 1943-46. pp. 764-97.

———The Khotan Dhammapada—ibid. pp. 43-56; 488-512.

———The Rāma story in Khotanese (Journal of the American Oriental Society) JAOS, Vol. LIX, pp. 460-8; See also in BSOAS.

Binyon, L. : Essay on the art of Tun-huang Paintings. Serindia, Vol. III, pp. 1428-31.

Brough, J. : Legends of Khotan and Nepal, BSOAS, 1947-48, pp. 333-39.

Burrow, T. : Iranian words in the Kharoṣṭhī documents from Chinese Turkestan, BSOAS, 1934, pp. 509-16; 779-90.

——— Tokharian elements in the Kharoṣṭhī documents from Chinese Turkestan, JRAS, 1935, pp. 667-79.

——— Further Kharoṣṭhī documents from Niya, BSOAS, 1937, pp. 111-123.

Bushell, S.W. : Early History of Tibet, JRAS, 1888.

Bussagli, M. : Indian Influence in Central Asia (5000 years of the Art of India).

Das, S. C. : Contributions on the Religion, History etc. of Tibet. (JASB, 1881, pp. 187 ff; 1882, pp. 1ff and 87 ff.)

——— Indian Pandits in Tibet—Journal of the Buddhist Society of India, I 1893.

Diakonova, N.: A Document of Khotanese Buddhist Iconography, Artibus Asie, Vol. XXIII, 1960, pp. 229-30.

Dikshit, K.N. : Buddhist Centres in Afghanistan (Vivekanand Volume, pp. 229-238).

Filliotzat, J. : The expansion of Indian Medicine abroad (ibid. pp. 239-248).

Giles, H.A. : Tun-huang, JRAS, 1914, pp. 703 ff; JRAS 1915, pp. 41 ff.

Gupta, S.P. : Pre-historic Indian Cultures in Soviet Central Asia (Vivekanand Volume, pp. 239-248).

——— Some Aspects of Buddhist Art in Central Asia (A.N. Jha Volume-I, pp. 43-60).

Hackin, J. : Buddhist Art in Central Asia Indian, Iranian and Chinese influences from Bamiyan to Turfan (Studies in Chinese Art and some Indian influences, 1937, pp. 14.)

——— The work of the French Archaeological mission in Afghanistan.—Indian Arts and Letters—IA & L, Vol. XVV, pp. 41-9.

——— The Buddhist Monastery of Fondukistan (Journal of the Greater India Society—JGIS—1940, pp. 1-14; 85-81).

Hambis, L. : Asia-Central (Encyclopedia of World Art, See also articles on Khotan, Tibetan Art, Tun-huang and other centres by the same author in this work. Vols. I-XIV).

——— Sculpture et peintures de Haute Asie—Inedits de la collection Pelliot La Revue des Arts. III, 1956, pp. 3-8.

Hirth, Friedrich: Story of Chang Kien—China's Pioneer in Western Asia. Text and translations of Chapters 123 of Ssi-ma-Tsien Shiki, JAOS, XXXVII, pp. 89-152.

Kingsmill, T.W. : The intercourse of China with Eastern Turkestan, JRAS, 1882, pp. 74 ff.

——— The Migration and Early History of the White Huns, JRAS, 1878.

Konow, Sten: Documents relating to the ancient history of the Indo-Scythians.

——— Strater and Drachin in old Kharoṣṭhī Inscriptions (Acta Orientalia—AO, 1928, pp. 255-56).

——— Some Notes on Central Asian Kharoṣṭhī documents (BSOAS, 1943-46, pp. 513-540).

Litvinsky, B.A. : India and Soviet Central Asia (Vivekanand Volume, pp. 263-274).

——— Buddhism in Central Asia (Diushanbe Conference papers, 1968).

Le Coq, A. Von : The Fourth Turfan expedition (JRAS, 1928, pp. 227-30).

Pelliot, P. : Indian Influences in early Chinese Art in Tun-huang (IAL, 1926).

Puri, B.N.: Geographical Information from Rājaśekhara's works (Journal of Indian History—JIH 1962, pp. 412ff.)

Rowland, B. : Studies in Buddhist Art of Bamiyan—Art & Thought, 1947, pp. 46-50.

Stein, Aurel. : Archaeological Discovery in the neighbourhood of Niya (JRAS, 1901, pp. 569-72).

——— Archaeological work about Khotan (JRAS, 1901, pp. 295-300).

——— Ancient Manuscripts from Khotan (JRAS, 1906, pp. 695 ff).

Rudolf Hoernle, A.F.: Ms. Remains of Buddhist Literature (JRAS 1910, pp. 834-8; 1283-1300; 1911, 447-77).

Ross : The caves of the Thousand Buddhas (JRAS, 1913 pp. 434 ff).

Siren, O. : Central Asian Influences in Chinese Paintings of the Tang Period, Arts Asiatique III, 1956, pp. 3-4

Silva, A : The spices and Silk Road (Vivekanand Volume, pp. 299-304).

Thomas, F.W. : Buddhism in Khotan & its deciine (Asutosh Mookerji Volume III, pp. 30-52).

——— Glimpses of Life under Tibetan Rule in Chinese Turkestan Man. Vol. XXXIII, pp. 101 ff.

——— Some Notes on the Kharoṣṭhī documents from Chinese Turkestan (AAO, XII, 1934, pp. 39-90).

——— ibid. XIII, pp. 45-80.

——— Some Notes on Central Asian Kharoṣṭhī Documents (BSOAS, 1943, pp. 513-40).

——— The terms employed in Central Asian documents (BSOAS, 1935-37, pp. 789-94).

Williams, J. : The Iconography of Khotanese Paintings (East & West, Vol. 23, 1973, pp. 109-154).

INDEX

Plate I. Buddha with Six Monks—from Miran (p. 261)
(Courtesy, National Museum, New Delhi)

Plate II. Bodhisattva Seated on a Throne with a Devotee—from Miran (p. 262)
(Courtesy, National Museum, New Delhi)

Plate III. Two Girl Worshippers—from Miran (p. 263)
(Courtesy, National Museum, New Delhi)

Plate IV. Hariti—from Farhad-Beg-Yailaki (p. 270)
(Courtesy, National Museum, New Delhi)

Plate V. Bust of Buddha—from Balawaste (Courtesy, National Museum, New Delhi) (p. 271)

Plate VI. Worshipper or Indra—from Balawaste (p. 271)
(Courtesy, National Museum, New Delhi)

Plate VII. The Trimurti Divinity with a Small Seated Buddha—from Balawaste
(Courtesy, National Museum, New Delhi) (p. 272)

Plate VIII. Cowherd Listening to the Sermon—from Kizil (p. 276)
(Courtesy, Berlin Museum, West Germany)

Plate IX. Head of Mahākāśyapa—from Kizil (p. 277)
(Courtesy, Berlin Museum, West Germany)

Plate X. Group of Swimmers—from Kizil (p 278)
(Courtesy, Berlin Museum, West Germany)

Plate XI. Goddess and Celestial Musicians—from Kizil (p. 279)
(Courtesy, Berlin Museum, West Germany)

Plate XII. Buddha and Praying Monk—from Kumtira (p. 281)
(Courtesy, Berlin Museum, West Germany)

Plate XIII. Worshipping Bodhisattva—from Kumtira (p. 281)
(Courtesy, Berlin Museum, W. Germany)

Plate XIV. Buddha under a Canopy—from Turfan (p. 286)
(Courtesy, Berlin Museum, W. Germany)

Plate XV. An Uighurian Prince—from Bezeklik (p. 287)
(Courtesy, Berlin Museum, W. Germany)

Plate XVI. Bodhisattva—from Hadda (p. 304)
(Courtesy, late V. P. Trivedi)